MOUNTED RAIDS
OF THE
CIVIL WAR

ALSO BY EDWARD G. LONGACRE:

*From Union Stars to Top Hat: A Biography of
the Extraordinary General James Harrison Wilson*

MOUNTED RAIDS
OF THE
CIVIL WAR

Edward G. Longacre

South Brunswick and New York: A. S. Barnes and Company

London: Thomas Yoseloff Ltd

A. S. Barnes and Co., Inc.
Cranbury, New Jersey 08512

Thomas Yoseloff Ltd
108 New Bond Street
London W1Y OQX, England

Library of Congress Cataloging in Publication Data

Longacre, Edward G.   1946-
    Mounted raids of the Civil War.

    Bibliography: p.
    Includes index.
    1. United States—History—Civil War, 1861-1865—Cavalry
operations.   I.   Title.
E470.L82   973.7'3   73-151
ISBN 0-498-01171-2

PRINTED IN THE UNITED STATES OF AMERICA

for
Kathy

CONTENTS

7

ACKNOWLEDGMENTS

I wish to express my gratitude to the staffs of the following institutions, who assisted in the preparation of this book: The Library of Congress, Washington, D. C.; The War Library and Museum of the Pennsylvania Commandery, Military Order of the Loyal Legion of the United States; The Nebraska State Historical Society; and the University of Nebraska's Don L. Love Library (particularly the staff at the Interlibrary Loan Desk, who furnished me with several rare books borrowed from institutions across the country). A note of thanks is due Mr. Julien Yoseloff, president of A. S. Barnes & Co., who made available pertinent illustrations from the reprinted edition of *The Photographic History of the Civil War*. For various editorial assistance I should also like to thank Mr. Thomas Doering of Lexington, Kentucky; Mr. Gary K. Leak of Seattle, Washington; my brother, Lawrence T. Longacre; and my father, Edgar Thorp Longacre.

INTRODUCTION

Because our era has witnessed the passing of the mounted soldier, memories have grown dim: today's students of history tend to believe that the nineteenth-century cavalryman was a privileged and exalted individual. After all, he rode to war while his comrade in the infantry pounded rough roads and sloshed through muddy ones afoot. A soldier in the saddle seems to conjure up a vision of an aristocrat fighting a conflict in sublime fashion. By and large, such a man must have led a rather easy life, free of the mundane annoyances and hardships that fell to the lot of the infantryman. In fact, this same image of the horse soldier was prevalent in America when the Civil War began.

Four years of bitter, prolonged strife effectively destroyed the myth, though it has been resurrected in our time. The unvarnished fact was that the Civil War cavalryman, precisely because of the speed and mobility given him by his horse, was compelled to render service more frequent and more arduous than that asked of most infantrymen. While foot soldiers remained in camp for extended periods of time, such as during lulls between campaigns and when active operations were suspended due to bad weather, most troopers saw daily activity. When not engaged in battles or skirmishes, they rode in all directions, scouting, reconnoitering, demonstrating against enemy forces, carrying messages to headquarters, escorting field commanders, and clearing paths for movements by the main army. On the whole, they also saw more active fighting, in the form of minor engagements, outpost skirmishes, and patrol encounters, than the foot soldiers, who only occasionally took part in pitched battles.

One of the most important and most taxing assignments that devolved upon Civil War troopers was raiding. Quite often horse soldiers were ordered out in mass either to drive deep into enemy territory on a long, sustained march, or to make a quick stab in the rear of the opponents' lines.

Basically, the objectives of cavalry raiders, whether on full- or limited-scale, long- or short-range expeditions, were to strike unexpectedly and decisively at assigned targets, to avoid battle with enemy forces of equal or larger size when at all possible, to gather intelligence about opponents' positions or campaign plans, to create maximum damage to enemy resources in minimal time, and to return to home base while suffering as few casualties as possible.

Favorite targets of Civil War raiders included enemy communication lines (particularly railroads), supply bases, garrisons, wagon trains, and loosely defended cities of military value. Raids were conducted either as ends in themselves or as diversionary maneuvers designed to distract the enemy's attention from larger movements by the main army.

Several conditions had to exist if a mounted raid were to be conducted successfully. First of all, the officer in charge had to be bold and aggressive but also prudent, capable of exercising strict authority when necessary and allowing subordinates the discretion to launch secondary operations when desirable. He had to be adept at meeting unexpected turns of events, at implementing contingency tactics, and at fighting on the defensive as well as on the offensive, as conditions warranted. Likewise, his subordinate officers had to be enterprising and imaginative, as well as deeply committed to serving their commander faithfully in moments calling for unity of purpose and action. Then, too, the common soldiers had to be adaptable and resourceful, willing to endure the hardships of a long march in any sort of weather, capable of acting with individual initiative but also as members as a unified team, and able to wield axes and crowbars with vigorous precision. Finally, the scouts and guides needed a full, accurate comprehension of the country to be traversed, a knowledge of nearby enemy troops and hostile citizens, and a wealth of detail about back trails and blind roads to be used in event of emergency.

Military strategists have drawn up some informal rules

that, if followed, would have led to a successful raid. One of the most important of these concerns the degree of value a raid might reach. To be considered a complete and enduring success, a raid had to be linked in some way with a larger operation. Damage to enemy property, however extensive, was not deemed a sufficient feat unless it materially aided the greater designs of the general-in-chief of the army. In other words, a raid could be pronounced a full success only when it made strategic as well as tactical contributions to the fortunes of the army.

Another informal rule stated that a raiding force had to be small enough to facilitate speed and mobility (the key features of mounted campaigning) but at the same time sufficiently large to handle all of its assigned duties and, if necessary, follow contingency planning. Hence, the amount of work to be done in large part dictated the size of the force sent to accomplish it.

In raiding, the horse was used primarily as a means of transporting the soldier to the scene of duty. After reaching the target, troopers completed their work afoot and, except in rare cases when conditions favored a mounted charge, would battle pursuers or attack garrison troops in infantry style. In this sense, most raiders could be considered dragoons or mounted infantry rather than saddle-bound cavalry.

As mentioned above, members of raiding forces had to be quite familiar with the lay of land along their proposed route of march, knowing at the outset the location of hostile units as well as all communication and transportation lines of consequence. Since the greater part of the Civil War was fought in Southern territory, Confederate horsemen enjoyed a solid advantage in being familiar with matters of terrain and population.

It was also deemed desirable that raiding commanders be guided by detailed instructions, that they might achieve everything expected of them. On the other hand, high-eschelon generals who authorized raids had to entrust their leaders with sufficient latitude and discretion in handling unexpected difficulties, rearranging priorities to conform to fluctuating conditions, and redirecting their routes of march in the event of heavy pursuit or the blocking of an assigned avenue of retreat.

Usually it was considered necessary that the command

march in the lightest possible order, to increase speed and maneuverability when moving through hostile territory. Often this meant stripping the raiding column of supply and forage wagons—which necessitated living off the land—and carrying ammunition aboard swift-footed pack animals. A trooper was encouraged to pack a saddle load so light that he himself was the heaviest burden his horse had to carry.

It was thought best to vary the rate of march during a raid, whenever possible, to relieve the tedium occasioned by a sustained gait. Often the canter was temporarily substituted for the predominating gait, the trot, and sometimes a limited gallop would be employed for short periods. The minimal rate of travel over most terrain was slightly less than three miles per hour; any slower speed, except when riding over rough and broken land, was considered undesirable. Usually the raiding column would halt for a ten-minute rest period every hour or two, with stops coming more frequently in unfavorable weather (unless, of course, the raiders were being closely pursued by enemy forces). Longer halts for midday and late afternoon meals were dictated by circumstances. The horsemen encamped for at least a portion of the night, for it was difficult if not impossible to sustain a cohesive movement in total darkness.

Infrequently, and usually only for emergency reasons, would a raiding force countermarch over the same road or roads it had previously taken. Such a tactic invited local defenders and mounted pursuers to close off retreat routes or ambush the raiders.

Finally, a certain amount of secrecy during the preparatory stage of a raid was required to make such a project successful. Disaster cold result if specific information regarding objectives was leaked to the enemy before the march commenced. Though this precaution might seem a blatantly obvious necessity, more than a few Civil War raids came to ruin precisely because intemperate conversation in camp or in the high circles of authority quickly came to the ears of opponents.

A cavalry raid was more of a grueling test of endurance and skill than a highly dangerous undertaking—although some degree of danger was present during every raid. Often, troopers spent twenty hours a day in the saddle, seeking rest as best they could, especially when being tracked by hard-riding pursuers. If wagon trains did not accompany the mounted column, the soldiers sometimes went hungry for long periods; this was particularly true when marching through a region that had been laid bare during previous months of campaigning. Since most of the raiders would be given little or no advance information about the objectives of their operation, they were constantly plagued, to some degree, by uncertainty and doubt. Although extreme danger seldom materialized, cavalrymen in unfriendly territory could never be certain that a bushwhacker was not hiding behind the nearest tree, with his rifle cocked and aimed. To combat all of these hardships, a raider needed an enduring spirit, a high degree of adaptability, implicit faith in his commander's judgment, and, ideally, a professional soldier's stoicism.

A raiding force usually consisted of several cavalry regiments, whether parts of a single larger unit such as a brigade or a division, or individual detachments culled from an entire field army. Since the command had to close up when marching through an enemy's country, the column or columns traveled on a single road or a limited number of roads that ran closely parallel to one another, to facilitate mutual support among the various units. As a rule, the column marched in a particular order. Scouts, who knew the territory well, rode far in advance of the main body—usually several miles ahead—on the "point" of the column. Quite often these men were disguised as civilians or enemy soldiers, which made them liable to execution as spies if unmasked and captured, but usually enabled them to travel in relative safety. Some cavalry leaders preferred to send their scouts into a designated territory a week or more in advance of the raiding force, if such time was available. Confederate commanders such as John Hunt Morgan often employed this tactic, with gratifying results. These "advance men" would ascertain the state of affairs along the route to be traveled and would report to the main force at prearranged locations, to guide the raiders, at regular intervals, along their way.

Behind the scouts on point came the advance guard of the raiding column, which ordinarily consisted of a small band of soldiers, usually one or two companies from a single regiment. The size of the advance guard, which rode perhaps a half mile in front of the main column, would vary according to the extent of the enemy forces liable to be encountered along the way. As with the scouts, the advance guard had to consist of men who knew the lay of the land, who were capable of thinking and acting quickly under pressure, and who could speedily warn the raiding force if any trouble developed at the point. An especially observant officer was needed to take charge of the advance guard.

Following the advance guard came the main body of the raiding force. Usually several regiments followed one after another with narrow gaps among them. The commander of the raiding column rode in the midst or to the rear of this body, escorted by aides and couriers. Any artillery and supply wagons present also traveled in the middle of the column; such a position made them readily available to the commander and also afforded protection to the teamsters and train guards, as well as to the gunners who rode mounted alongside their cannon.

On either side of the main body, usually a mile or less away, rode several companies of flankers. These soldiers were directed to alert the main force to enemy units moving along perpendicular roads and to curtail stragglers from the main body; they presented the raiding leader with a wide front along which to engage any opponents who might appear ahead.

The rear guard—usually several companies from the last regiment in the line of march—covered the route of the entire force. Here, again, an able officer was required to oversee the fulfillment of a number of demanding duties. These included rounding up stragglers, fending off pursuers, and putting finishing touches to the destruction of bridges, rail lines and supply depots that the main column had seized. The rear guard had to be able to move in any and all directions to handle its assigned tasks. Like the point, advance guard, and flankers, the rear guard was changed often to keep such a heavy burden of responsibility from resting too long on the same shoulders.

Raiding was one of the most frequent duties required of Union and Confederate cavalry during the war. Only during the first two years of the conflict did one army have the advantage at raiding. Southerners—many of them aristocrats bred in the gentlemanly tradition of horsemanship—adapted to the duties of mounted warfare more readily than the laborers and storekeepers who predominated in the Federal ranks. Then, too, the bulk of purebred stock came from the Southland, affording Confederates an early advantage in quality horseflesh. Furthermore, as noted above, the Southerners fought the war almost wholly in their native region. For these and other reasons, Confederates under such renowned leaders as J. E. B. Stuart, Nathan Bedford Forrest, John Morgan, and Turner Ashby took the early initiative at mounted raiding. Being more daring and innovative than their counterparts in the Federal cavalry, they constantly outwitted enemy garrisons and supply-base defenders, many times infiltrating the blue ranks and after inflicting great damage while suffering few losses, quickly slipping away to safety. It took considerable time for the Federals to develop cavalrymen of comparable enterprise.

Nevertheless, the Federals progressed in this gradually but surely. By the early months of 1863 the Northern armies had developed experienced cavalrymen capable of standing toe-to-toe with the men of Stuart and Morgan. Later that year, improved methods of cavalry administration accelerated the progress of Federal mounted training. Finally the two-year period that many authorities believed necessary to transform a civilian into an accomplished cavalryman had passed. At the same time, the army infused new blood into the mounted ranks by discarding conservative cavalry leaders and promoting young and resourceful officers such as Philip Sheridan, James Harrison Wilson, George Armstrong Custer, and Wesley Merritt. By the midpoint of the war Federal cavalrymen were raiding through hostile territory with skill comparable to that which their foe had previously displayed on a grand scale. A gradual decline in the availability and quality of Southern horseflesh, the result of a costly war of attrition; a corresponding increase in Federal cavalry resources, owing to the solicitude of the U. S. Cavalry Bureau; and the deaths of such Southern heroes as Stuart, Morgan, and Ashby, accentuated the improvement of the fortunes of the Federal horse soldiers. By mid-1864 Federals had at last excelled their enemy at long-distance raiding, and at war's end were striking wildly and almost at will through the heart of the faltering Confederacy.

* * * * *

This book attempts to give an objective, balanced picture of cavalry raiding by presenting (roughly in chronological order, although some raids overlap) a cross-section of the more important expeditions, Federal and Confederate, in

various theaters of action. These were among the most con-
sequential raids of the war; yet, a number of them were not
wholly successful. While some achieved notable short- and
even long-range contributions to the war effort, others failed
miserably and disasterously. Some of the raids—such as Colonel Abel Streight's, in which infantrymen took to Alabama
roads aboard mules—were innovative, while others proceeded more or less along established lines of mounted
cavalry warfare. Some of the expeditions demonstrated bold
planning, some were well-launched but timidly executed,
some—notably the Kilpatrick-Dahlgren raid—stirred national
controversies and inflamed the bitter feelings that stemmed
from sectional rivalries. Some exhibited more than a few
moments of comedy—as did Streight's, as well as Bedford
Forrest's "naval" assault against Union steamboats in the
Tennessee River. And some were of great strategic value and
made true contributions to significant military victories—such
as General Benjamin H. Grierson's raid during the Vicksburg
campaign.

A few of these expeditions have been deemed so interesting that entire books have been written about them. However, never before have twelve of the most noteworthy been
linked together and discussed, both tactically and strategically, as parts of an overview of Civil War mounted warfare.

In effect, this book attempts to enlarge upon a statement
made after the war by a young Federal trooper who served
with Grierson during his 1863 expedition through Mississippi. Summing up his impressions of such an operation, the
trooper opined:

"A cavalry raid at its best is essentially a *game* of strategy
and speed, with personal violence as an incidental complica-
tion. It is played according to more or less definite rules, not
inconsistent, indeed, with the players' killing each other if the
game cannot be won in any other way; but it is commonly a
strenuous game, rather than a bloody one, intensely
exciting. . . ."

MOUNTED RAIDS
OF THE
CIVIL WAR

.

1
SECOND TIME AROUND
Stuart's Chambersburg Raid
(October 9-13, 1862)

1

Oftentimes, the Bower seemed more like a pleasure resort than a military headquarters. A sumptuous plantation near Charlestown, Virginia, abounding in wide, neat lawns and spacious fields, it had been taken over in the early autumn of 1862 by Major General James Ewell Brown Stuart's cavalry division of the Army of Northern Virginia. Stuart was not one to neglect the creature comforts whenever he could indulge himself and his men, and the elegance of the surroundings well satisfied his tastes. Forever after, his staff officers considered the plantation the ideal haven for a cavalryman. Stuart's engineer chief, Captain William W. Blackford, fondly recalled that the inhabitants, who had invited the troopers to use their estate, consisted of "Mr. Stephen Dandridge, his wife and a house full of daughters and nieces, all grown and all attractive—some very handsome. . . . The host and hostess were fine specimens of Virginia country gentry under the old regime, hospitable, cultivated, and kind hearted. Every afternoon, after the staff duties of the day were performed, we all assembled at the house for riding, walking or fishing parties, and after tea, to which we had a standing invitation which was generally accepted, came music, singing, dancing and games of every description mingled with moonlight strolls along the banks of the beautiful Opequan or boating upon its crystal surface. The very elements seemed to conspire to make our stay delightful, for never was there a more beautiful moon or more exquisite weather than during that month we spent there."[1] Other staff officers expressed similar sentiments; the massive German, Major Heros von Borcke, who served as Stuart's chief of staff, was particularly impressed by the abundance of game that made the Bower a fine hunting range.[2] In such an idyllic setting, it was almost possible for the Confederate horsemen to ignore the bitter warfare that went on, unabated, in nearby sections of Virginia.

However, J. E. B. Stuart was not using the Bower as a sanctuary. He had gone there late in September to direct the operations of his troopers, now screening the front of the army along the Charlestown-Darkesville line, as well as to rest and refit the body of his command.[3] Stuart had no desire to remain behind the fighting front for a period longer than was absolutely necessary. At twenty-nine, he had been a professional soldier for the past eight years; not once during that time had he sought to absent himself from the theater of action when his services were deemed crucial. Darkly complexioned, he wore long, silken hair upon a high forehead; and a luxurious cinnamon-colored beard gave added strength to an already rugged face. His eyes were clear and their gaze sharp and direct. He was broad shouldered, with a powerful physique and especially long legs that made him look more imposing on horseback than when strolling along a street. His compelling appearance had prompted his old classmates at West Point to dub him, rather sarcastically, "Beauty"—a nickname that had lingered.[4]

Stuart was a kindly and, essentially, an uncomplicated man.

★★★★★★★★★★★★★★★★★★★★★★

1. Douglas Southall Freeman, *Lee's Lieutenants: A Study in Command*, 2: 284-85. For another Confederate's opinion of this country retreat see Edward A. Moore, *The Story of a Cannoneer Under Stonewall Jackson*, pp. 208-9.

2. Heros Von Borcke, *Memoirs of the Confederate War for Independence*, 1: 291.

3. Channing Price, "Stuart's Chambersburg Raid: An Eyewitness Account," *Civil War Times Illustrated* 4 (January 1966): 9.

4. Curt Anders, *Fighting Confederates*, p. 151.

J. E. B. Stuart. COURTESY LIBRARY OF CONGRESS.

He was fond of music and gaiety—so much so that he sometimes acted like an overgrown child who delighted in the
pageantry of warfare. He rarely missed the opportunity to
don gaudy trappings, often wearing the scarlet cloak and the
plumed hat that were his hallmarks in the Confederate service. Flamboyant cavalry reviews and genteel camp life, such
as he enjoyed in his present surroundings, invariably warmed

his heart. He loved the company of pretty women (though in an innocent way, for he remained thoroughly true to his wife, Flora) and they, in turn, delighted in his boyish attentions. It was a rule that wherever and whenever Stuart made his headquarters, there would soon be dancing and music—much of it provided by his own banjoist, a mustachioed Virginian named Sam Sweeney—plus the gentle undercurrent of feminine laughter.[5]

But Stuart was just as much at home on the battlefield as on the dance floor. He rode prominently at the head of his troopers when ordered out on long marches and sustained reconnaissances, and fought side by side with his men. By this autumn of '62 he had acquired, as well, a solid reputation as one of the most skillful collectors and evaluators of enemy intelligence.[6] Rarely did the drudgery of life in the field or the bloody madness of battle lower his spirits, for he was incurably romantic, with the ability to see glory and grandeur in combat.

The opportunities for drama and excitement afforded by long-distance cavalry raiding very much appealed to his nature. He had had his first taste of such raiding the previous June, two weeks before General Robert E. Lee's forces clashed with Federal Major General George B. McClellan's Army of the Potomac during the first of the so-called Seven Days Battles along the upper Virginia peninsula. Preparing for the campaign, Lee had ordered "Beauty" to reconnoiter the right flank and rear of McClellan's position astride the Chickahominy River. Stuart started off with only one thousand troopers, but soon reasoned that he had enough men to enlarge upon Lee's plan. Expanding his instructions, he led his riders in a full circle around his befuddled enemy, marching nearly 150 miles. Along the way he destroyed a substantial amount of enemy materiél, captured several prisoners, and returned to his own lines after losing only one soldier.[7] The operation had flabbergasted General Lee almost as much as it had McClellan.

Perhaps deciding that a repeat performance would yield an

★★★★★★★★★★★★★★★★★★★★★★★

5. John Esten Cooke, *Wearing of the Gray*, pp. 8-9.

6. Ezra J. Warner, *Generals in Gray: Lives of the Confederate Commanders*, p. 296.

7. Mark M. Boatner III, *The Civil War Dictionary*, p. 816.

especially powerful return at the present time, General Lee was now mapping plans for another extended cavalry reconnaissance—one that might be extended into a raid behind Federal lines. In so doing he set in motion the chain of events that eventually pulled Stuart out of his plantation camp.

Almost four months of maneuvering and fighting by both armies had occurred since Stuart's previous raid. General McClellan's attempt to seize Richmond by moving up the peninsula had long ago failed, resulting ultimately in the relief of "Little Mac" from army command. Major General John Pope had later taken over most of the Federal forces in Virginia and had sacrificed them at the disastrous battle of Second Bull Run, during the last days in August. After Pope's inept performance, President Abraham Lincoln had reinstated McClellan, but the most that Little Mac had since achieved was a strategic draw in the bloodiest single day's fighting of the war, along the banks of Antietam Creek, in Maryland, on September 17. McClellan's showing at Antietam had been far short of brilliant, but as autumn made its appearance he was still in field command, still trying to rationalize past failures and to overcome an inherent fear that his seventy-five thousand-man army was somehow numerically inferior to his opponents' force (Lee had approximately forty-thousand effectives).[8]

At the present time, the Army of the Potomac was encamped in the areas around Sharpsburg, Maryland and Harpers Ferry, Virginia, several miles northeast of the main Confederate force, which was near Winchester, Virginia. The Federals showed little desire to again come to grips with their enemy, but their very presence in and above Virginia was a matter of much concern to General Lee, who, despite a wide-ranging intelligence network, lacked information about the dispositions of the main Federal army as well as its probable intentions.[9]

To learn where Little Mac was encamped and what he might have in mind, Lee conferred at length with his chief subordinate, Lieutenant General Stonewall Jackson. In the course of their conversation Stuart's name was raised often.

★★★★★★★★★★★★★★★★★★★★★★★

8. Ibid., p. 21.

9. Price, "Stuart's Chambersburg Raid," p. 9.

On Monday, October 6, they put out a call for the cavalry commander, and with only slight reluctance, Stuart detached himself from the merriment at the Bower and rode seven miles south to army headquarters.

What Lee had in mind was a deep penetration of enemy territory to study Union communication lines. In addition, if conditions allowed, a raiding force might move as far north as lower Pennsylvania. North of the sizeable Keystone State village of Chambersburg, which nestled in the Cumberland Valley, a strategic railroad crossed a branch of the Conococheague Creek. The road was valuable to the North as a route of supply to McClellan's railhead at Hagerstown, Maryland. Destruction of the railroad bridge over the creek would force the Federals to rely exclusively on the overburdened Baltimore & Ohio for rail communication, and would be a serious blow, perhaps a crippling one, to the Union war effort in the East.[10]

Stuart was at once responsive to the idea. By this time his command had been refreshed and overhauled and was in sufficient shape to resume arduous campaigning. An expedition of the sort Lee and Jackson favored seemed to offer all the excitement and martial grandeur that Stuart could possibly desire.

Stuart was called to army headquarters several times in the course of a week, to finalize details of the operation. His comings and goings could hardly escape the notice of his officers, and though no official word of the raid would leak through for some time, Stuart's staff put their gear in order, saw to the grooming of their horses, and prepared to draw rations and forage for the trip that they sensed was upcoming.[11]

Even the rumors of forthcoming campaigning, however, could not disrupt the gaiety of life at the Bower. On Tuesday evening a bevy of civilians—many of them attractive young girls—attended a ball given by Stuart's officers. Banjo and violin music filled the Dandridge house, accompanying the movements of hoop-skirted women and elegantly uniformed staff members. There were rounds of chorusing and the continual tinkle of glasses as the guests drank round after round

★★★★★★★★★★★★★★★★★★★★★★★★

10. Freeman, *Lee's Lieutenants*, 2: 284.

11. Burke Davis, *Jeb Stuart, The Last Cavalier*, p. 213.

of toasts. In the midst of the partying, J. E. B. Stuart danced and flirted and contributed solos in his deep, smooth voice —then collapsed in laughter upon the entrance of a "Pennsylvania bride"—none other than the fun-loving Von Borcke, all six-feet-250 pounds of him, dressed in a long white gown and spurred cavalry boots.[12]

By the next morning the Bower was rife with speculation of a raid across the Mason-Dixon Line. Toward the close of the day Stuart gave the word to his closest aides: Lee had instructed him to choose between one thousand two hundred and one thousand five hundred of his best-mounted men and strike for the bridge above Chambersburg, provided such a movement could be properly concealed at the outset. The troopers would be authorized to inflict on enemy property any damage that would legitimately contribute to Confederate military fortunes. Horses were to be gathered from the countryside to replenish the Southern supply, and Northern hostages of prestige and position were to be collected for use in bartering for the exchange of loyal Confederates imprisoned by Federal commanders. Possibly Stuart also informed his officers of a stern stricture that General Lee had imposed on him: "Reliance is placed upon your skill and judgment in the successful execution of this plan, and it is not intended or desired that you should jeapordize the safety of your command, or go farther than your good judgment and prudence may dictate."[13] In substance the warning duplicated the caution that Lee had given Stuart before his first ride around McClellan's army. On that occasion, however, Stuart had not paid such close heed as Lee might have wished.

From the outset, Stuart indicated that even now he had listened to only that part of his instructions which interested him. Rather than mount only one thousand five hundred men, he told off one thousand eight hundred for the expedition, apparently unconcerned about the limitation thus imposed upon the mobility of his force. The men did represent, however, the cream of Stuart's crop, and the subordinate commanders chosen to lead them—Brigadier General Wade Hampton and Colonels W. H. F. "Rooney" Lee (the army

★★★★★★★★★★★★★★★★★★★★★★★★

12. Von Borcke, *Memoirs*, 1: 293-94.

13. Freeman, *Lee's Lieutenants*, 2: 285.

commander's son), William E. Jones, Williams C. Wickham, and M. Calbraith Butler—were Stuart's most reliable lieutenants.[14] With the exception of the quarrelsome and stern-minded Jones (whose fitting nickname was "Grumble"), Stuart was on excellent terms with each of these men. He knew that he could count on all of them, Jones included, to provide as much support as he might desire during the expedition.

October 8 was a day of bustle and commotion at the Bower. Cavalrymen raced in every direction, stocking rations and weapons and outfitting their mounts. Stuart met at length with his subordinates, carefully explained what was expected of them, and infected them with the excitement of again carrying the war into the enemy's country. One of the general's aides, twenty-one-year-old Lieutenant R. Channing Price, a kinsman of Stuart, later wrote his mother about the activity at headquarters: "On Wednesday night I felt sure that the next day would see the beginning of the movement whatever it might be, as the General directed me (at that time discharging the duties of Adjt. Genl.) to get all the papers requiring his attention ready for his action that night. We had a pleasant time, music and dancing, until 11 o'clock, then returned to our tents, the General finished up all his business, and about one o'clock we got the music (violin, banjo, and bones) and gave a farewell serenade to the ladies of the Bower."[15] Young Price omitted one interesting fact: once again Stuart regaled the ladies with song, contributing four solos to the evening's entertainment.[16] Afterward, when the impromptu party broke up, staff members retired, lower eschelon commanders went back to the fields where their troopers were sleeping under the autumn moonlight, and Beauty Stuart turned in, leaving word that he be awakened at an early hour. After saying his evening prayers, he fell quickly to sleep.

2

The sun had not yet scrubbed the darkness from the sky

★★★★★★★★★★★★★★★★★★★★★★★

14. W. W. Blackford, *War Years with Jeb Stuart*, p. 164.

15. Price, "Stuart's Chambersburg Raid," p. 9.

16. Davis, *The Last Cavalier*, p. 214.

when Stuart's three brigades marched the next morning toward the nearby village of Darkesville, the point of rendezvous for the expedition. With them rode mounted gunners escorting four light cannon, under the command of Stuart's boyish artillerist, Major John Pelham.[17] They assembled at the town during the forenoon and, despite the unavoidable realization that a great deal of hard marching and some danger lay before them, formed their ranks casually and with an air of merriment, as though embarking on a holiday jaunt. In the evening Stuart led his legions to Hedgesville, several miles up the Potomac River from Williamsport, Maryland, and bivouacked them for the night.[18] As the horsemen prepared to bed down, staff officers read them copies of an address that Stuart had written to prepare them for the expedition. The document could hardly have better revealed the romantic spirit of its author:

"Soldiers: You are about to engage in an enterprise which, to insure success imperatively demands at your hands coolness, decision and bravery; implicit obedience to orders without question or cavil, and the strictest order and sobriety on the march and in bivouac. The destination and extent of this expedition had better be kept to myself than known to you. Suffice it to say, that with the hearty cooperation of officers and men, I have not a doubt of its success—a success which will reflect credit in the highest degree upon your arms. The orders which are herewith published for your government are absolutely necessary, and must be rigidly enforced."[19] The accompanying documents, also read to the men, related to the march and the necessity of respecting all public and personal property not marked for destruction.

Therefore, Stuart's troopers were still in darkness about the objectives of the operation. However, the address probably bolstered their determination to do everything asked of them during the trip.[20] The cavalrymen of the Army of Northern Virginia were intensely loyal to their commander;

★★★★★★★★★★★★★★★★★★★★★★★

17. Charles G. Milham, *Gallant Pelham: American Extraordinary,* p. 176.

18. Davis, *The Last Cavalier,* p. 216; Freeman, *Lee's Lieutenants,* 2: 286.

19. *War of the Rebellion: A Compilation of the Official Records of the Union and Confederate Armies,* series I, vol. 19, pt. 2, pp. 55-56.

20. H. B. McClellan, *I Rode with Jeb Stuart: The Life and Campaigns of Major General J. E. B. Stuart,* p. 138.

only brief words from him were needed to spur them into doing his bidding.

Stuart and his staff spent part of the evening in a straw rick amid a vacant field, grasping at a few hours' sleep. By four o'clock in the morning on October 10 they were up and about, and the entire camp began to stir. Without waiting to cook breakfast, the troopers swung into the saddles and marched through a heavy fog toward the great river, only a handful of miles to the north.[21] Even as they moved, the advance guard, under command of the towering patrician, Wade Hampton, was already splashing across the Potomac in the vicinity of McCoy's Ferry, to engage a Federal cavalry picket post on the upper shore.[22] They routed the enemy with ease, for the pickets, a party from the 12th Illinois, could pit only a handful of men against Stuart's thousands. A small detachment from the advance guard held the Illinoisians at bay while the rest of the division sloshed through the cold waters, bypassing the enemy position. Because of his limited strength, the Federal captain in charge of the post could not send a force to pursue them; but he did take note of the extent of the Rebel force crossing in his front. His estimate ran to two thousand five hundred horsemen and eight artillery pieces (he exaggerated the size of Pelham's battery in the fog). He also noted that Stuart's men were taking the road that led northward to Mercersburg, Pennsylvania. Soon the captain was rushing the news to the several Federal outposts that dotted the Maryland shore. Thus, word of Stuart's movement had reached the enemy, and General Lee's hope that the raid might be concealed had already faded out.[23] Yet Stuart betrayed no overt sign of concern as he led the remainder of his command across the river. Perhaps he could already sense the clicking of telegraph keys as the news of his coming rushed along the Federal military telegraph network. But there was little help for it; he knew that sooner or later the movements of one thousand eight hundred riders in enemy territory would have been reported.

At eight A.M., between the Maryland cities of Hagerstown

★★★★★★★★★★★★★★★★★★★★★★

21. John W. Thomason, Jr., *Jeb Stuart*, p. 300.

22. *Official Records*, series, I, vol. 19, pt. 2, p. 57.

23. Ibid., p. 38; McClellan, *I Rode with Jeb Stuart*, p. 139.

and Hancock, the advance guard crossed the old National Road, which ran diagonally through the state, and struck directly north. Part of the force tarried long enough to surround a Federal signal station and capture a dozen soldiers, their flags, and lanterns. From the captives, as well as local citizens, Stuart learned that six regiments of blue-clad infantry and two batteries of artillery had passed that region only an hour before, heading westward.[24] He was glad that the Yankees had not been delayed, for although his force could have handled the foot soldiers quite easily, Stuart did not relish losing valuable time fighting a pitched battle. Speed was of the essence if he were to reach and strike his target before the rest of McClellan's forces could initiate a cohesive pursuit.

At ten o'clock the riders reached the Pennsylvania line,[25] and a great deal of shouting and cheering broke out. Once again Stuart's men had violated Union territory—and Union territory would provide them with much needed rations and forage as well as a lift to their morale.

Stuart bolstered morale further by riding down the fog-shrouded column and halting at the head of each brigade as staff officers read aloud additional orders, concluding with: "We are now in enemy country. Hold yourselves ready for attack or defense, and behave with no other thought than victory. If any man cannot abide cheerfully by the order and spirit of these instructions, he will be returned to Virginia with a guard of honor."[26] In other words, refrain from plundering and unauthorized violence; conduct yourselves as gentlemen of the South and as soldiers doing a soldier's job.

The first large Pennsylvania town reached by the column was Mercersburg. About noon the advance riders pounded through the village streets, scaring the citizenry out of their wits but doing no damage to the place beyond commandeering some horses and a great quantity of footwear from local stores. Some of the Confederates robbed an elderly gentleman of the sorrel mare that had pulled his carriage, and were highly amused when the man shrilly protested that the

★★★★★★★★★★★★★★★★★★★★★★

24. *Official Records,* series I, vol. 19, pt. 2, p. 52.

25. Davis, *The Last Cavalier,* p. 218.

26. Ibid.

Federal government had given them no authority to impress animals: no amount of explaining could convince him that his antagonists were not Union soldiers.[27]

Stuart's adjutant, Major Henry B. McClellan, recalled that "once the Pennsylvania line was crossed, the seizure of horses was prosecuted with system and diligence. Six hundred men scoured the country on either side of the line of march, and as far as scouts could extend the country was denuded of its horses." But McClellan added that "With his usual courtesy toward ladies, Stuart gave orders that, whenever they might meet his column, they should be allowed to pass in their conveyances without molestation."[28]

At Mercersburg Stuart gave some thought to turning southward again, before driving onward to Chambersburg, and striking the bulging Federal storehouses at Hagerstown, where Little Mac's advance base was located. Supplies confiscated there would outfit Confederate soldiers for months. But he decided that news of his coming had by now alerted many troops, who might halt him short of that goal.[29] Giving up his idea, he pushed his column along the roads leading toward Chambersburg, while his outriders continued to round up herds of serviceable animals from the countryside. Their job was made particularly easy because heavy rains had recently fallen and the ground was still wet. Therefore, nearly all the farmers in the region were busily working in their barns, some of them threshing wheat. Following the sounds of this activity, Stuart's men went directly to the large stone-and-wood barns that dotted the nearby fields and found scores of powerful draft horses penned inside. They led the giant beasts away from their enraged owners, and throughout the afternoon the size of Stuart's column continued to swell.[30]

The riders reached Chambersburg between seven and eight o'clock in the evening. Rain had again begun to fall as the advance guard came up to the town, and by the time the main body arrived it was, according to Lieutenant Price,

★★★★★★★★★★★★★★★★★★★★★★

27. McClellan, *I Rode with Jeb Stuart*, p. 140.

28. Ibid.

29. Thomason, *Jeb Stuart*, p. 305.

30. Blackford, *War Years with Jeb Stuart*, p. 166.

Wade Hampton. COURTESY LIBRARY OF CONGRESS.

"pitchy dark" as well as wet.[31] Wade Hampton, commanding the vanguard, worried that because of the darkness a reconnaissance of any local defenses might not be possible. There seemed no way to ascertain if the people of Chambersburg

★★★★★★★★★★★★★★★★★★★★★★★

31. Price, "Stuart's Chambersburg Raid," 10.

had heard of the Rebels' approach and, reinforced by Federal troops, were ready to fight.

Not wishing to ride into a trap, Hampton sent a lieutenant and twenty-five men from the 2nd South Carolina Cavalry to demand the town's surrender. What followed assuaged the general's anxiety: "In reply to this summons three citizens, on the part of the citizens at large, came forward to ask the terms proposed. I demanded the unconditional surrender of the town, assuring them at the same time that private persons should be protected and private property unmolested, except such as should be needed for the use of our army. These terms being agreed on, I moved the brigade into the city about 8 P.M., and immediately made dispositions to establish a rigid provost guard."[32]

However, before Chambersburg was given up, the local provost marshal wired a message to Governor Andrew G. Curtin in Harrisburg, the state capital. Curtin, who had known of Stuart's invasion since early in the day, had been feverishly trying to construct a network of defense and to initiate a statewide pursuit. Now, after hearing the news from the provost marshal, and soon afterward finding that telegraph wires to the town had been cut, Curtin telegraphed Secretary of War Edwin McMasters Stanton in Washington: THE PEOPLE HAVE SURRENDERED CHAMBERSBURG.[33]

Meanwhile, Stuart prepared to take full possession of the town. He designated Hampton "Military Governor" for the length of time the column would remain, sent Colonel Calbraith Butler and part of his command to relieve the local bank of scrip and currency, and directed Grumble Jones to burn the important railroad bridge over Conococheague Creek. Then Stuart set up temporary headquarters in a public building, mounted a strong guard in the village square to prevent indiscriminate looting, and searched about for prominent citizens to hold for hostage. At first, he was frustrated in the latter effort, for he found that "The officials all fled the town on our approach, and no one could be found who would admit that he held office in the place."[34]

★★★★★★★★★★★★★★★★★★★★★★★

32. *Official Records,* series, I, vol. 19, pt. 2, p. 57.

33. Davis, *The Last Cavalier,* pp. 220-21.

34. *Official Records,* series, I, vol. 19, pt. 2, p. 52.

Two of his other plans also failed. Colonel Butler entered the Bank of Chambersburg with an armed guard, but was informed by the cashier that all funds had been spirited away earlier in the day. To offer proof, the employee opened the vault and cash drawers for Butler's inspection: they were indeed empty. Butler, a philosophical man, did not threaten recriminations, and his gentlemanly deportment favorably impressed the officials of the bank. Major McClellan later remarked that the cashier went so far as to summon his wife and daughters from their home, and told them to prepare food for the cold, wet, and hungry cavalrymen. Butler and his armed guard ate well that night.[35]

Grumble Jones was also stymied. When his troopers, carrying combustible materials and axes, reached the railroad bridge, they found it built almost wholly of iron. For a short time Jones's men chopped fruitlessly at the superstructure, then gave up the impossible chore and returned to the town.[36] The Confederate high command who had planned the raid evidently had relied upon faulty intelligence. A major objective of the expedition could not be achieved.

Stuart tried to make the best of his situation. He personally directed his men in their continuing search for horses and did manage to round up a few local officials who might be used during a future exchange of prisoners. He sent other soldiers to the government supply depot in the town; they came away with welcome quantities of army overcoats, jackets, breeches, underwear, socks, and boots, plus five thousand brand-new rifles, and numerous sabers and pistols.[37] The night was wet and raw and the troopers bundled up in their new-found clothing before falling off to sleep in their bivouac. Stuart himself settled for the night in a small tollhouse at the edge of the town, where he stretched out on the kitchen floor in the midst of his staff members.[38] Outside the house their horses were tethered, still saddled and ready to be ridden at a minute's notice. Stuart was fully aware that Federal pursuers might not be at all far from the Chambersburg limits.

★★★★★★★★★★★★★★★★★★★★★★★

35. McClellan, *I Rode with Jeb Stuart*, p. 141.

36. *Official Records*, series I, vol. 19, pt. 2, p. 52.

37. Freeman, *Lee's Lieutenants*, 2: 288.

38. McClellan, *I Rode with Jeb Stuart*, p. 147.

3

Had he known the caliber of the officers directing the pursuit of his column, J. E. B. Stuart might have slept much more comfortably than he did. He did know that General McClellan was an indecisive, timid commander, given to overestimating the strength of opposing forces and acting too slowly in combating them. But he did not know just how ineptly McClellan's subordinates might act in trying to track down a raiding force that had invaded Northern territory.

Little Mac had got word of Stuart's movements shortly after the Confederate horsemen had splashed over the foggy Potomac early that morning. But even after further reports verified Stuart's movement and course, the army leader remained largely idle for perhaps fourteen hours before mobilizing any large body of pursuers.[39] And when he did act, he entrusted the pursuit to officers who were just as dilatory, just as reticent and indecisive (if not more so) than he.

One of these subordinates was Brigadier General William W. Averell, who was stationed along the Baltimore & Ohio line at the mouth of the Potomac's south branch. By two P.M. on October 10 Averell, commanding six regiments of cavalrymen, knew that the Rebels were running loose above the river. By seven that evening army headquarters finally directed him to come down the Potomac and pick up Stuart's trail. Averell could rarely resist the urge to improve on given orders, and the urge came upon him this day. Instead of starting off at once, he remained on the B & O for eight hours, then moved northward instead of marching down the river, and rode fifty-five miles into the mountains of Pennsylvania—which took him out of the pursuit picture for good. For some strange reason, he hid in the mountains for two days, returning to the Hagerstown vicinity long after Stuart had gone.[40]

Another slow mover was Brigadier General Alfred Pleasonton, who commanded a full cavalry division near the centrally located town of Berlin, Maryland and thus was in a posi-

★★★★★★★★★★★★★★★★★★★★★★★

39. Price, "Stuart's Chambersburg Raid," p. 43. The editorial commentary is by Wilbur S. Nye.

40. Ibid.

tion to move either east or west of the mountains to intercept Stuart on his return trip from Chambersburg. Pleasonton was destined to remain at his field headquarters until the morning of the 11th,[41] almost twenty-four hours after Stuart had crossed into Maryland. Then he would move northward toward Chambersburg—but by that time the Confederates would be involved in departure preparations.

A third subordinate, Brigadier General George Stoneman, was told off for the pursuit. He was stationed with a small unit of troopers and a much larger force of foot soldiers at Poolesville, Maryland, only a few miles southeast of the point at which Stuart was fated to cross the Potomac on his return trip into Virginia. Stoneman sensed that Stuart's men, if they eluded other pursuers, might try to force a crossing somewhere in the vicinity of White's Ford. But Stoneman was nagged by uncertainty and could rarely muster the nerve to take decisive action. Afraid to commit his total force to a central position in case his initial hunch proved wrong, he spread his troops over a wide area north and south of the probable crossing site.[42] In so doing he assured that the Confederates would not have to face a strong enemy force at any point along the river.

General McClellan—still feeling residual embarrassment from Stuart's June raid—did not stop his pursuit efforts at that point. In a final attempt to ensure the Rebels' capture, he ordered one of his ranking infantry commanders, Major General Ambrose E. Burnside, to dispatch two brigades by rail from Berlin to a point on the river far upstream from Stoneman's position. Burnside, another free-thinker with a penchant for making a botch of things, proved his worth by sending his soldiers instead to Frederick, Maryland. There, like General Averell and his cavalry, they found themselves effectively out of the game.[43]

While all of these frantic and ill-starred attempts at pursuit were proceeding, Beauty Stuart and his troopers awoke, and prepared to take leave of Chambersburg and return to Virginia.

★★★★★★★★★★★★★★★★★★★★★★★

41. *Official Records,* series, I, vol. 19, pt. 2, p. 38.

42. Ibid., p. 43.

43. Price, "Stuart's Chambersburg Raid," p. 43. Commentary by Nye.

4

"I got up early," reported Lieutenant Channing Price, "found it still raining, and went into the town to get some plunder . . . and supplied myself with a nice black overcoat, a pair of blue pants, one dozen pr. of woolen socks, pr. of boots, and various other little things as much as I could carry." Loading his saddlebags, he mounted and rode off with the General and his entourage to the head of the mounted line.[44]

The officers at the point of the column had already turned their men to face the logical direction for a return trip —westward, eventually to head south, completing the circuit around McClellan. All stared in surprise when Stuart directed them to wheel about and start toward the east. The new course would lead the raiders toward a small college and seminary town in Adams County of which few of them at that time had ever heard—Gettysburg.[45] After a few minutes of confusion, Stuart had his men moving over the muddy road, their colors encased under the steel-gray sky, trumpets squalling in the morning gloom.

Some hours later, as the last of the raiders prepared to ride out of Chambersburg, the rear guard put final touches to their campaign in lower Pennsylvania. Lieutenant Price noted that the small unit put to the torch "all the public property left (machine shops, depots, 5 or 6,000 stand of arms, etc.). . . ."[46] He later calculated that one million dollars worth of army supplies went up in the flames. By nine A.M. on that Saturday, October 11, the rear guard had packed its gear and was following the tag end of the main body out of the town.[47] At last the harassed citizens of Chambersburg could come forth to express relief, to study the extent of their losses, and to begin repairs.

Riding with the main body of the column, Stuart meanwhile came abreast of Captain Blackford, his engineer and personal friend, and indicated to him a desire to talk pri-

★★★★★★★★★★★★★★★★★★★★★★★

44. Ibid., p. 11.

45. Freeman, *Lee's Lieutenants*, 2: 288.

46. Price, "Stuart's Chambersburg Raid," p. 11.

47. McClellan, *I Rode with Jeb Stuart*, p. 149.

vately. The two men pulled out of formation and rode a short distance ahead of the van. Stuart, it seemed, wished to make himself understood as to why he had chosen an eastward return route. He told Blackford that "if I should fall before reaching Virginia, I want you to vindicate my memory."[48] The engineer officer, impressed by the tone of earnestness in his commander's voice, waited quietly for him to continue.

Stuart took out a topographical map, spread it atop his saddle, and jabbed his finger along the route that his soldiers had expected to take back to Virginia. He pointed out that the one large Federal contingent known to be in the general vicinity—the six-regiment infantry force they had avoided meeting the day before—had doubtless heard of the raiders' presence in Pennsylvania. By now it had probably halted along the National Road to await their return, deploying in a hilly region that would make a Confederate passage difficult. On the other hand, the eastward route would carry the mounted column into an area where its presence would be entirely unexpected and in which the Potomac fords would be harder for the Federals to defend from the rear.

Blackford mulled over Stuart's reasoning and his additional remark that the new route posed only two problems, the much greater marching distance called for, and the inevitability of the column's passing close to the Federal stronghold at Harpers Ferry. As soon as Stuart added that these obstacles could be surmounted by an especially quick march, Blackford nodded in approval of the plan. The captain felt a close, almost kinship tie with his commanding officer, and was especially touched by the way Stuart had chosen him as the recipient of his personal revelation. As the two men returned to the column, chatting in the manner of intimate friends, Blackford noted that Stuart's eyes glistened with tears; his own had misted over, too.[49]

The raiding force marched as far eastward as Cashtown, only a few miles short of Gettysburg, and soon afterward Stuart swung it abruptly south.[50] From there it was a short

★★★★★★★★★★★★★★★★★★★★★★★

48. Blackford, *War Years with Jeb Stuart*, p. 169.

49. Ibid., pp. 169-70.

50. Frederic Ray, "Chambersburg, Pa.—War Came Three Times to This Northern Town," *Civil War Times* 2 (May 1960): 12.

jaunt to the Maryland line. As soon as the latter point had been reached, the wide-scale collection of animals was halted. But from that time onward the troopers took into temporary custody all travelers they encountered, so that none could sound an alarm.

At Emmitsburg, Maryland, which the column reached at nightfall, Stuart rounded up some enemy stragglers and continued directly south, as though heading for Frederick, where General Burnside's infantry had massed. However, six miles south of Emmitsburg, Stuart's outriders captured an enemy courier who bore dispatches revealing Burnside's wide-ranging dispositions. Vowing to steer clear of Frederick, Stuart veered eastward across the Monocacy River onto a thoroughfare that bypassed the city.[51]

Stuart's good fortune in intercepting the messenger indicated that his advance guard, composed of alert and resourceful troopers, was handling its duties with skill. Equally vigilant where the flanking units thrown out on either side of the main body, as well as the scouts and guides who led the march—men who had been raised in this very region. Escorted by so many well-trained specialists, Stuart's raiding force proceeded rapidly and confidently along its return route.

As the march continued, however, fatigue began to overtake the riders. Tired muscles and dulled minds caused some of Stuart's officers to beg their commander to call a short rest halt. Stuart, himself apparently tireless, refused. To allow a respite for men and horses was to invite disaster.[52]

Potentially bad news spurred him on. Southern sympathizers living in this stretch of upper Maryland informed the cavalry leader that General Stoneman, who commanded along the nearest portion of the Potomac, had stationed almost five thousand men at the river fords near Poolesville.[53] But Stuart did not allow the report to unnerve him. Near the town of New Market, more than two-thirds of the way through his return trip, he accompanied Captain Blackford and other staff officers on a courtesy call at the nearby home

★★★★★★★★★★★★★★★★★★★★★★★

51. Thomason, *Jeb Stuart*, p. 309.

52. Ibid., p. 292.

53. *Official Records*, series I, vol. 19, pt. 2, p. 53.

of a charming lady friend. After a short jaunt cross-country, the small group reached the woman's residence, where she and several friends threw an impromptu party for their unexpected but entirely welcome guests. Nearly half an hour passed before Stuart and his men said their good-nights and remounted for the ride back to the column, which had continued to move eastward and southward.[54] Once again Stuart had done his duty as the Confederacy's gift to Southern womanhood.

When Beauty rejoined the main body, twelve treacherous miles still stretched between the column and the safety of the Potomac. Somewhere in the near distance were several Federal outposts, including those manned by the large forces under Stoneman and Pleasonton. Stuart sent out word that if the advance guard encountered any Union patrols in the darkness, they must be captured after a brief, quiet struggle; heavy gunfire might alert still other bands of enemy soldiers.[55]

Nearing the river, Stuart questioned the captain in charge of his scouts as to the probable condition of the nearest fords. There were at least four such crossing sites along that part of the river toward which the Confederates were marching. The nearest one, close to the mouth of the Monocacy, might seem to the Federals along the river to be Stuart's probable crossing point. On the other hand, the enemy might believe that Stuart would wish to give a wide berth to any Union troops descending the river and so would detour farther south, to Edwards's Ferry. Stuart knew that General Stoneman was waiting for him, and he tried to imagine himself in Stoneman's position. At last he decided to go to neither ford, taking no chances. He would pretend to move to Edwards's Ferry, but hoped to make a crossing at another site that would enable him to circumvent the enemy defenses.[56]

The scout captain, who was traveling through country in which he had spent his boyhood, came immediately to Stuart's assistance. He led his commander along an old,

★★★★★★★★★★★★★★★★★★★★★★★★

54. Davis, *The Last Cavalier,* pp. 229-30.

55. Freeman, *Lee's Lieutenants,* 2: 293-94.

56. Ibid., pp. 294-95.

weed-grown cart track which he himself had taken as a youth. The road took the column on a mile-and-a-half cross-country jaunt. Eventually the raiders found another road that would bring them to little-used White's Ford. The ford was precisely what Stuart had been looking for—it lay slightly more than three miles below the mouth of the Monocacy and nine miles above Edwards's Ferry. The road would also carry the Rebels above Stoneman's outpost at Poolesville. By taking it, Stuart could slip neatly past several groups of Federals, who were looking for his approach elsewhere.[57]

Still, crossing at any point along the Potomac was risky. Cautiously feeling his way in morning blackness, Stuart followed his scout's lead, turning at last onto the final trail, which led westward to the Potomac.

But about eight A.M., just as the advance guard moved ahead on this last leg of their homeward march, they saw a unit of Federal cavalry bearing down on them from the north.

These were troopers from Pleasonton's command, who the day before had pounded northward toward Chambersburg in a futile attempt to catch Stuart in the town. Eight hours ago, General Pleasonton had heard from local Unionists that the Rebels were on their return march, already far below him. Accordingly he had turned his column around and by hard travel had moved through Frederick and then past the mouth of the Monocacy, hoping to trap the Rebels between his own force and Stoneman's. A mile and a half below the Monocacy his outriders had spotted the Confederate vanguard.[58]

Pleasonton might have played hob with Stuart's plans, had the Confederates not been favored by good fortune. The Federal advance unit moved down at a canter, then suddenly halted after coming close enough to spy riders wearing caped greatcoats of dark blue. These were the coats which Stuart's men had appropriated from the Chambersburg depot to keep them warm amid chilly October weather. But the Union troopers were uncertain whether they had met disguised Rebels or cavalry from Stoneman's command.[59] While they

★★★★★★★★★★★★★★★★★★★★★★★★★

57. Davis, *The Last Cavalier*, pp. 230-31.

58. Price, "Stuart's Chambersburg Raid," p. 43. Commentary by Nye.

59. McClellan, *I Rode with Jeb Stuart*, p. 155; Thomason, *Jeb Stuart*, p. 313.

paused in a spell of uncertainty, Stuart rode to the head of his advance guard and led it in a charge, with pistols cracking and sabers swinging.

Completely stunned, the Federals turned northward and fell back to the protection of two infantry regiments that were temporarily serving under Pleasonton. While the Federals regrouped, Stuart unlimbered Pelham's artillery, then dismounted a squadron of sharpshooters and directed them to keep the enemy at arm's length while the rest of the column crossed the river. High ground on the shore line concealed the body of Stuart's command as it neared the Potomac, now swollen from the recent rains. Meanwhile, the Rebel artillery and its cavalry support performed brilliantly, keeping Pleasonton's bemused soldiers at bay. Eventually the Federals brought up a few pieces of light artillery but their guns blasted ineffectual volleys at the well-positioned Confederates.[60]

While the stand-off ensued, the officer now leading Stuart's advance, Colonel Rooney Lee, went to the river's edge and found that several Federal infantry pickets were stationed along the Chesapeake & Ohio Canal, which ran down the Maryland shore, above and below White's Ford. Hastily forming plans to encircle the picket force, Lee had already divided his brigade for the task when he learned that the Federals had abandoned their positions in the face of so many enemy cavalrymen. Aided by one of Pelham's cannons, which secured the far shore, Lee began to cross his horsemen at about nine-thirty A.M.[61]

Stuart held his ground on the near bank as long as he could. When the enemy began to press forward in heavy force, and upon receiving word that some of Stoneman's men were heading toward the scene from the Poolesville area, he gradually withdrew Pelham's gunners and the dismounted sharpshooters. The artillery commander covered the final stage of the withdrawal by increasing his rate of fire to create the impression that his position was continuously held in strength.[62]

★★★★★★★★★★★★★★★★★★★★★★★

60. Wilbur S. Nye, "How Stuart Recrossed the Potomac," *Civil War Times Illustrated* 4 (January 1966): 46.

61. Ibid., 46-47.

62. Milham, *Gallant Pelham*, pp. 188-89.

The crossing was made with much difficulty. Exhausted men and animals foundered in the high water. Some of the animals, weakened by thirst, fought to stop and drink as their riders spurred them through the water. But Stuart's subordinates brought order out of chaos, landing their men and mounts, captured animals, plunder, and Pennsylvania hostages safely on Virginia soil.[63]

At the last, Lieutenant Channing Price was sent to order Pelham's artillerymen to disengage. "The enemy were closing in rapidly," the lieutenant later recalled, "no doubt thinking they had cut us off. We all got safely across, and going 3 or 4 miles, halted to feed."[64] Captain Blackford was sent on an even more dangerous errand, galloping into the rear-guard melee to extricate the sharpshooters, under Colonel Butler, before the Federals could encircle them and cut them off from the river. Butler's men broke free at the last minute and escaped by a razor-thin margin.[65]

As the last of the Confederate troopers reached dry land on the Virginia side, their weary and enraged pursuers gathered on the far shore and fired a parting fusillade. But this effort came too late and proved too little; Stuart and his raiders had escaped with their hides intact.

5

By the morning of the 13th, Stuart's jubilant troopers returned to the Bower to start a new series of balls and parties.[66] By that time, accolades had already been bestowed upon the Confederate leader by his commanders and the citizens of Virginia. By all accounts his raid had been a smashing success, even though it had failed to destroy the Chambersburg railroad bridge, an original primary objective. The raiders had located McClellan's outposts and communication lines, had wrecked almost a million dollars worth of property above the Mason-Dixon Line, had captured valuable hostages and no fewer than one thousand two hundred ser-

★★★★★★★★★★★★★★★★★★★★★★★

63. Freeman, *Lee's Lieutenants*, 2: 300-302.

64. Price, "Stuart's Chambersburg Raid," p. 13.

65. Blackford, *War Years with Jeb Stuart*, pp. 176-78.

66. Von Borcke, *Memoirs*, 1: 300.

viceable horses, had eluded at least four large Yankee units dispatched for the express purpose of chasing them down, and by marching 126 miles round-trip, the last eighty of which were covered in twenty-seven hours, had demonstrated the endurance and intrepidity of the Cavalry Division, A. N. V. and the skillful daring of its young commander. The moral effects of the raid were especially significant. They included, according to Lieutenant Price, "teaching Pennsylvanians something of war, and showing how J. E. B. Stuart can make McClellan's circuit a pleasure."[67]

The latter fact concerned not only Southerners. President Lincoln himself soon gave an indication of official Northern reaction to the news of Stuart's slashing raid. While aboard a ship in the Potomac one afternoon late that month, Lincoln was asked about General McClellan's future. Without looking at the politician who had inquired, the President drew a ring on the deck with his shoe and said, sternly: "When I was a boy we used to play a game—three times round, and out. Stuart has been round him twice; if he goes round him once more . . . McClellan will be out!"[68]

It was not to be. A few weeks later, without waiting for Stuart to act again, the government relieved the slow and uncertain McClellan from command of the Army of the Potomac. He never again led field troops. Perhaps Lincoln simply had reconsidered, and had decided that in war, the rules had to be changed. Perhaps two times round ought to be enough.

★★★★★★★★★★★★★★★★★★★★★★

67. Boatner, *The Civil War Dictionary*, p. 814; Price, "Stuart's Chambersburg Raid," pp. 15, 42.

68. Davis, *The Last Cavalier*, p. 235.

2
ACT OF REDEMPTION
Van Dorn's Holly Springs Raid (December 16-28, 1862)

1

In the military, as in all walks of life, appearances often deceive. As a case in point, consider the background of Major General Earl Van Dorn. Few contemporaries, noting his martial bearing and the caliber of his wartime efforts prior to the outbreak of the secession crisis, would have believed him destined to fail as a Confederate general. But fail he did —frequently, sometimes disastrously, often because of flaws in personality and judgment and almost as often, it would seem, through simple bad fortune. Luck rarely sided with Earl Van Dorn, and in fact, only once gave him the sort of untarnished success that many thought to be his due.

From earliest days he seemed endowed with credentials that guaranteed glory. His birthplace was a plantation near Port Gibson, Mississippi and his family was one of the best known in that community. Family ties extended even to the White House; it was a distant cousin, President Andrew Jackson, who fulfilled Van Dorn's youthful ambition to become a soldier by helping him obtain appointment to the United

States Military Academy.[1] Van Dorn graduated in the Class of 1842, ranking fifty-second among fifty-six cadets, but soon bettered his military standing by embarking on a series of duty tours that offered him the opportunity to gain a solid reputation. He first served in the campaigns against the Plains Indians, and when the Mexican War broke out in 1846 was a twenty-seven-year-old lieutenant.[2] In the Mexican conflict he won fame, distinguishing himself by raising the American flag under heavy fire during one battle, by being the first soldier to scale enemy walls in another fight, and by charging in the forefront of a force that stormed the Belen Gate during action at Mexico City. The war below the Rio Grande fully confirmed his desire to follow a military career: "I never could be happy out of the Army," he declared, "I have no other home. . . ." He won new honors after the war by serving as captain, then major, in the prestigeous 2nd United States Dragoons, whose field officers included two future Confederate greats, Albert Sidney Johnston and Robert E. Lee. The framework of success around which Van Dorn's life seemed to be built was almost complete by the time Confederate guns bombarded Fort Sumter in April 1861.

At the outbreak of war, Van Dorn appeared the archetypal Southern officer and gentleman. He was slim waisted and broad shouldered, with a handsome face adorned by chestnut-colored hair, an elegant imperial mustache, and a goatee. Although only five feet, six inches tall, he was rugged and strong, an accomplished horseman, and something of an esthete as well, dabbling in poetry and art.[3] Women invariably found him attractive—some irresistible, despite the fact that he had married Caroline Godbold in 1843 and, though no longer close to his wife, had never been legally separated from her. Van Dorn seemed to go out of his way to live up to his reputation as a ladies' man, an effort which in time would result in his death.[4]

★★★★★★★★★★★★★★★★★★★★★★

1. Robert G. Hartje, *Van Dorn: The Life and Times of a Confederate General*, pp. 6-8.

2. Warner, *Generals in Gray*, pp. 314-15.

3. Albert Castel, "Earl Van Dorn—A Personality Profile," *Civil War Times Illustrated* 6 (April 1967): 38; Dabney H. Maury, "Recollections of General Earl Van Dorn," *Southern Historical Society Papers* 19 (1891): 191.

4. Hartje, *Van Dorn*, pp. 16-17.

Earl Van Dorn. FROM *Photographic History of the Civil War.*

This rakish side of his personality notwithstanding, Van Dorn was the epitome of the dashing fire-eater, a man cut from much the same cloth as other Confederate cavalrymen such as J. E. B. Stuart and John Hunt Morgan. He once expressed his fascination with soldiering in a letter to one of his sisters: "What does the gambler know of excitement who has millions staked on a card? He can lose but millions, he can win but millions. But here *life* is to lose—glory to win."[5]

High rank, but no glory, came his way in the early months of his service with the Confederacy. In June 1861 he received an appointment as a brigadier in the Southern ranks. Already stationed in Texas, he garnered some headlines by capturing several Yankee troop ships in the Gulf of Mexico. That September he earned a second star and soon afterward found himself in Virginia, where a period of inactivity intensified his desire to win renown in battle.[6]

★★★★★★★★★★★★★★★★★★★★★★★

5. Castel, "Earl Van Dorn," p. 38.

6. Warner, *Generals in Gray*, p. 315.

The next January he was placed in command of the Trans-Mississippi District—Missouri, Arkansas, part of Louisiana, and what is today the state of Oklahoma—and at last received his chance to grasp glory. In a maneuver calculated to eventually seize Federal-held St. Louis, he divided his sixteen thousand-man army for a two-pronged strike at Yankee forces invading Arkansas. Unforeseen delays in marching orders prohibited Van Dorn's forces from cooperating, and other instances of bad fortune, including an errant ammunition train, compounded numerous tactical mistakes and resulted in Union victory at the battle of Pea Ridge.

Van Dorn was subsequently transferred to the Army of Mississippi, headquartered at the river stronghold of Vicksburg, where he repulsed a Union amphibious attack that summer. Sent to invade West Tennessee in September, he began his task in fine style, then suddenly returned to Mississippi, hoping instead to seize the strategic rail center of Corinth from Federal Major General William S. Rosecrans, his West Point classmate. Van Dorn's men suffered severe repulses after a series of bloody attacks and were forced to retreat. Afterward Van Dorn remained in command of Confederate forces in northern Mississippi but came under the strict supervision of the new departmental chief, Lieutenant General John C. Pemberton, and was assailed by widespread criticism of his military abilities. By late summer of '62 his once-intact pattern of success had unraveled. Not even a court of inquiry, which cleared him of official allegations of gross neglect of duty at Corinth, could stop the downward arc of his career.[7]

However, even as Van Dorn's military fortunes neared rock bottom, a good many of his soldiers could not account for his disgrace. They considered him a gallant and gifted general, one in whom they had much faith. One officer who knew him well declared that his appearance and demeanor "gave assurance of a man whom men could trust and follow."[8] And Van Dorn himself could hardly believe the sorry times upon which he had fallen. He keenly felt his double humiliation at Pea Ridge and Corinth, and fervently

★★★★★★★★★★★★★★★★★★★★★★★

7. Castel, "Earl Van Dorn," pp. 39-41; *Official Records*, series, I, vol. 17, pt. 1, pp. 415-16, 459.

8. Maury "Recollections," 191-92.

hoped that another opportunity to restore luster to his reputation might soon materialize.

Finally, in December of 1862, by a stroke of that same
good fortune which had eluded him for so long, Van Dorn
got his chance.

2

In that chilly and blustery autumn—a season of despair for
the Confederate armies in the West—Major General Ulysses
S. Grant advanced relentlessly down the corridor of land in
central Mississippi, angling toward Vicksburg. Riding a wave
of victory that had carried him through battles at Forts
Henry and Donelson, Grant hoped to take that vital river
fortress and so control the Father of Waters. To rule the
Mississippi was to cut the Confederacy in half—doubtless a
mortal blow. As Grant came on, Pemberton's outnumbered
army fell back ever deeper into the state, searching desperately for a way to curtail the invaders' advance.

Pemberton put his subordinate officers to work studying
the situation, probing for weak points in Grant's strategy. It
was a lieutenant colonel of Texas cavalry who came up with
an idea that the Confederate high command finally adopted.
The Texan was convinced that the only way to stop Grant's
thrust along the axis of the Mississippi Central Railroad was
to strike at that rail line as well as at a parallel road, the
Mobile & Ohio. By these lines, Grant drew his supplies from
the great depot at Columbus, Kentucky. A cavalry expedition, the lieutenant colonel felt, would so disrupt Federal
communications as to cause Grant to fall back north into
Tennessee, abandoning his overland campaign against Vicksburg.

Looking more closely at the project he had suggested, the
Texas officer focused his attention on yet another great supply depot that the Yankess had recently established on the
Mississippi Central, at a town named Holly Springs, in the
northern portion of the state. The base was not so formidable as that at Columbus, but it too was a vital link in Grant's
supply network and damage there might accomplish much
the same result as a strike at the Kentucky depot. Moreover,
as Pemberton himself learned when he gave the officer's plan
close scrutiny, Holly Springs reportedly was held by only two
thousand five hundred Federals. The present situation was

considered so critical that the plan was quickly accepted, and Pemberton allowed Earl Van Dorn, whom the Texas officer had recommended, to command the raiding force.[9]

It seemed apparent that no other tactic was capable of stopping the Federal movement. Yet this vital task now rested on the shoulders of a man whom destiny had frustrated time and again. Quite possibly Pemberton, in choosing him for the assignment, felt that Van Dorn was due for a drastic change of luck.

Three brigades of cavalry, comprising troopers from Texas, Tennessee, Missouri, and Mississippi, assembled in the village of Grenada, on December 12. When Van Dorn ceremoniously arrived to take command of the force, his dramatic appearance caused many of the cavalrymen to break into loud cheering. At once Van Dorn turned happy; he had been given a command that he felt ably suited to lead and whose personnel obviously appreciated his talents.[10]

By the 16th, when the column started its northeastward march toward its unpublicized objective, the riders had sized up their diminutive but impressive-looking leader. Many had not previously served under him, but irrespective of the bad publicity he lately had received, decided they liked him. One of them described him as "a man apparently about forty years of age, small of stature, dark skinned, dark haired, bright, keen black eyes, clear cut and well defined features, straight as an Indian, sitting [on] his horse like a knight, and looking every inch a soldier."[11]

The three thousand five hundred troopers marched through a rainstorm toward the town of Houston, which they reached about noon the next day. On the 18th they rode over muddy trails until they struck Pontotoc, whose citizens, awed by the sight of rank upon rank of gray-clad cavalrymen, offered them king-size portions of meat, fowl, fruit, milk, and other edibles.[12]

Some miles east of Pontotoc the raiders first encountered the enemy, to the rear. These were cavalrymen led by one of

★★★★★★★★★★★★★★★★★★★★★★★★

9. Edwin C. Bearss, *Decision in Mississippi: Mississippi's Important Role in the War Between the States*, pp. 84-88.

10. Hartje, *Van Dorn*, p. 255.

11. Ibid., p. 256.

12. Bearss, *Decision in Mississippi*, pp. 89-90.

Grant's mounted commanders, Colonel T. Lyle Dickey, returning westward after carrying out an assignment to cut those parts of the Mobile & Ohio line that lay in Rebel hands. Van Dorn's scouts reported the whereabouts of Dickey's small force early that afternoon. Refusing any combat that would slow his march and divert his attention from Holly Springs, Van Dorn largely ignored Dickey's presence and continued to ride northward.[13]

Marching away from an enemy force—especially one that would have been easy pickings in a fight—was not something that came easy to Van Dorn. Essentially, he was a man of action and daring, preferring to enter any fight in which he stood a reasonable chance to win. But by now, perhaps, he had grown leery of trusting fate in that manner, and did not wish to make any mistake that might destroy this latest opportunity to recoup lost prestige. When a courier sent by the commander of the rear guard pounded up to the head of the column with an urgent message, Van Dorn exhibited commendable coolness and restraint. The soldier shouted that his superior "sent me to inform you that the Yankees have fired on his rear!"

"Are they still in the rear?" asked the general.

"Yes, sir," replied the courier.

"Well," Van Dorn said, "you go back and tell your Colonel that the Yanks are just where I want them."[14]

Seeing that the Confederates were not going to stop and accept battle, Colonel Dickey hurried toward Grant's headquarters at Oxford, more than twenty miles below Holly Springs and far to the west of Van Dorn's raiders. Ahead of him rode couriers with the news of the Confederates' advance toward the supply base, but that evening the messengers went astray, and so Grant did not learn the facts until the morning of December 20.[15] By then it was too late to send a cavalry force to intercept Van Dorn short of his objective—and barely in time to warn the garrison at Holly Springs that thousands of Rebels were heading their way.

On the night of the 18th the raiders camped on the west

★★★★★★★★★★★★★★★★★★★★★★★★

13. *Official Records,* series I, vol. 17, pt. 1, pp. 498-99.

14. Hartje, *Van Dorn,* p. 258.

15. *Official Records,* series, I, vol. 17, pt. 1, p. 499.

bank of the Tallahatchie River, seeking sleep in the middle of a chilling, drenching rainstorm. The next day they continued northward for a short distance, then turned west toward the line of the Mississippi Central. They were now only a few miles from their destination. The day was miserably cold; the horses' hooves kicked up clods of frosty earth as the long, winding column made its way through the countryside. The riders—some of whom wore six or more shirts beneath their coats to ward off the cold—were hungry as well as chilly and weary.[16] Yet their officers noted that their spirits were remarkably high; they had confidence in Van Dorn and were looking forward to surprising their enemy.

To avoid a skirmish with Yankee outposts, Van Dorn halted his command some miles from Holly Springs, separated it into two large contingents for a concerted attack,[17] then sent a scout familiar with the local geography, to study the enemy defenses. After a tense waiting period, Van Dorn welcomed back the scout, who brought the happy news that the Yankees suspected nothing; so blissfully unaware of danger were they that they were planning a gala Christmas ball.[18] Before dusk, Van Dorn's two forces moved out, their carbines, pistols, and swords ready—they would do some celebrating of their own.

In the darkness the raiding units slipped inside the local picket lines, then halted for another short rest. Soldiers were dismoutned and posted along all roads leading into the town as a security measure,[19] while the rest of the raiding command was allowed to rest so long as the men remained standing in readiness beside their still-saddled horses. At dawn Van Dorn would charge his units through the town, hoping to scatter all enemy soldiers and make a dash for the depot buildings where supplies and rations were stored.

The troops garrisoned at Holly Springs consisted of detachments from three infantry regiments, the 20th, 62nd, and 101st Illinois, plus six companies of the 2nd Illinois

★★★★★★★★★★★★★★★★★★★★★★★

16. Bearss, *Decision in Mississippi,* pp. 91-93.

17. J. G. Deupree, "The Capture of Holly Springs, Mississippi, Dec. 20, 1862," *Publications of the Mississippi Historical Society* 4 (1901): 54.

18. Bearss, *Decision in Mississippi,* p. 92.

19. Deupree, "The Capture of Holly Springs," 54.

Cavalry, under overall leadership of Colonel Robert C. Murphy. They totalled approximately one thousand five hundred effectives—much fewer than Pemberton had supposed—and were concentrated in three major areas. Some of the infantrymen—only about five hundred of them—were stationed in the town proper; other foot soldiers were encamped near the railroad station; and the cavalry companies were deployed on the fairgrounds just beyond the town limits.[20]

Despite the scattered nature of these troops, and contrary to the report of Van Dorn's scout, Colonel Murphy had received sufficient warning that Confederates were sweeping down upon him. Shortly before dawn he wired Grant at Oxford that "Contraband [Negro] just in reports Van Dorn only 14 miles from here with 5,000 cavalry, intending to destroy stores here. . . ."[21] Van Dorn had been diligent in stopping potential messengers from reaching the town; still, a black man had managed to evade the cordon of raiders. Had another officer commanded the garrison, Van Dorn's attack plan might have been in jeopardy.

But Colonel Murphy was no Napoleon. Though forewarned of the danger, he failed to alert the infantry camp at the depot or the cavalry billet on the fairgrounds. Apparently several of Murphy's officers had already begun celebrating Yuletide in disorderly fashion; some were reported drunk at the time Van Dorn's people came calling.[22] All in all, affairs at the depot garrison were very much at loose ends at a critical juncture.

Murphy belatedly made an effort to remedy the situation. Before the Rebels could attack, he raced to the rail depot to dispatch two locomotives to alert other garrisons along the railroad, above and below Holly Springs. At each station, officers aboard the trains were to sound an alarm and muster reinforcements, who were to head straight for the supply base town. Construction crews working for the military railroad were also supposed to hasten to the town's defense,

★★★★★★★★★★★★★★★★★★★★★★★

20. Bearss, *Decision in Mississippi*, pp. 99, 103; A. F. Brown, "Van Dorn's Operations in Northern Mississippi,—Recollections of a Cavalryman," *S. H. S. P.* 6 (1878): 156; Hartje, *Van Dorn*, p. 260.

21. *Official Records*, series I, vol. 17, pt. 2, p. 444.

22. Hartje, *Van Dorn*, p. 261.

erecting cotton bale barricades around the depot and public buildings.[23]

But time quickly ran out on Colonel Murphy. Before his orders could be carried out, Van Dorn's raiders came charging into Holly Springs from three directions, shouting the Rebel yell at the top of their voices.

The Mississippians entered the town from the northeast, charging through blue-clad infantry and then piling into the cavalry camp; behind them came the Missouri troops in support. East of the village, the Texas riders cut off routes by which Federal supports might rush to the scene of fighting; and north of Holly Springs, the Tennesseans massed to counter any Federal attempt to send troops down from the direction of Bolivar, Tennessee, where part of Grant's army was encamped.[24]

One cavalryman, who rode into a Yankee infantry billet alongside Van Dorn himself, heard his comrades give the general a wild cheer. The shout awoke some of the unsuspecting garrison troops, he later remembered, "but before its echoes ceased to reverberate, we had literally ridden over them. . . . When the alarm was given, they rushed out of their tents, and taking in the situation at a glance, promptly commenced a series of maneuvers, not laid down in tactics, to avoid being run over."[25]

To the Federals, stumbling out into the frigid dawn wearing sleepwear and various vestiges of outer clothing, a nightmare had come true. All around them, fierce-looking cavalrymen were charging through the streets, blasting away with rifles and revolvers, shrieking like banshees, singling out foot soldiers and methodically running them down. Scores of wide-eyed infantrymen threw down their guns, raised their hands high, and shouted their willingness to surrender.

A journalist accompanying the raiders offered a graphic picture of the fracas: "The scene was wild, exciting, tumultuous. Yankees running, tents burning, torches flaming, Confederates shouting, guns popping, sabres clanking; Abolitionists begging for mercy, 'rebels' shouting exultingly, women *en dishabille* clapping their hands, frantic with joy, cry-

****

23. Bearss, *Decision in Mississippi,* p. 103.

24. Hartje, *Van Dorn,* p. 261.

25. Brown, "Van Dorn's Operations," p. 157.

ing 'kill them, kill them'—a heterogeneous mass of excited, frantic, frightened human beings presenting an indescribable picture, more adapted for the pencil of Hogarth than the pen of a newspaper correspondent."

The soldiers in the infantry camp capitulated after only a brief struggle, but their cavalry comrades at the fairgrounds put up stiffer resistance. Realizing that the depot would be captured unless they stood firm, the troopers formed a hollow square surrounding their camp, drew sabers, and met the onrush of Van Dorn's Mississippians. While his men were gradually forced backward, the Federal cavalry commander was captured, and thereafter the troopers' strength faded rapidly. The Confederates managed to encircle the camp and break through the eastern side of the square, menacing all other angles of the formation. Only a swift and desperate charge by 130 of the Illinoisians, who fought their way to safety by slashing wildly with their swords, prevented the garrison cavalry from being captured en masse. By eight A.M. Holly Springs was securely in Confederate hands.[26]

Van Dorn could rejoice that he had finally achieved unalloyed success. Within his reach was a vast conglomeration of warehouses and shops that housed everything necessary to supply a large field army during a lengthy campaign. The material to be found there would immeasurably benefit his soldiers, some of whom wore clothing so ragged as to appear mendicants. And, of course, destruction of those supplies which could not be carried off could spell disaster to General Grant.

The extent of Van Dorn's spoils startled many a Rebel cavalryman. One of them noted that "Every available building at and near the depot, including the machine shops, round house and large armory and foundry buildings, and many houses on the public square, were filled with commissary, quartermaster and ordnance stores. In addition to these were numerous sutlers' shops, stocked with articles so well suited to the wants of Confederate soldiers, that they seemed to have been provided for their especial use."[27] Appropriately, it was the Christmas season: here were gifts galore for the Rebel cavalry.

★★★★★★★★★★★★★★★★★★★★★★

26. Hartje, *Van Dorn*, pp. 262-63.

27. Brown, "Van Dorn's Operations," p. 158.

But Van Dorn did not allow himself to rejoice for long. He was well aware that General Grant would not let the attack go unavenged. In quick time trains would come chugging from north and south, carrying reinforcements from other garrisons. Time was a crucial concern, what with the amount of work still to be done. Therefore he headquartered himself in a centrally located building and doled out assignments to his subordinates. Soon the lower echelon commanders were hustling about, directing the enlisted men to remove Federal prisoners and townspeople from the projected path of destruction, then to ignite hundreds of torches.

The raiders worked furiously, with a passion that consumed the full extent of their energy and made them forget the rawness of the weather. Details of soldiers removed all useable quantities of arms, ammunition, medicine, clothing, blankets, and horse equipments from the government storehouses. Afterward the torches were applied, and within minutes sheets of flame rolled above the plundered buildings and a dense black cloud curled atop the fire to mingle with the sullen grayness of the winter sky. All warehouses, cotton stores, machine shops, and sutlers' shacks were fired, one after another, with almost patterned thoroughness. Soldiers, Confederates and Federals alike, stood in the rutted streets, watching the conflagration and warming themselves by the flames. Whiskey, salvaged from medical supply houses, began to trickle over the curbs from smashed kegs. More than a few observers sampled the brew as the fires raged,[28] some of them drinking so avidly that they began to reel about in a ludicrous frenzy. Finally officers put an end to the strange orgy by leveling pistols at their own men.

Deafening explosions ripped through the town as some store houses filled with powder blew sky-high. Some of the flames fell onto houses not designated for ruin, spreading destruction even further.

One of Van Dorn's men watched as several of his comrades, their faces reflecting the glow of the fires, scurried to their horses with plunder. It was curious to note their preferences for loot: "Boots and hats seemed to be the most popular articles in the way of clothing, but it was amusing to see how tastes differed. Some men would pass by a dozen

★★★★★★★★★★★★★★★★★★★★★★

28. Bearss, *Decision in Mississippi*, pp. 107-9.

things which they really needed, and shouldering a bolt of calico, walk off apparently perfectly satisfied with their selection. Sugar, coffee, crackers, cheese, sardines, canned oysters, &c., were not neglected. . . ."[29] Indeed they were not, for the ride to Holly Springs had been an especially hard one, and little time had been set aside for partaking of food.

By sundown the sacking of Holly Springs had been completed, and the Federals had been paroled as prisoners of war. More than one million dollars worth of rations and matériel had gone up in flames or had been removed from the warehouses, and a vast amount of physical damage had been rendered other military resources, including trackage on the Mississippi Central and the rail depot buildings in Holly Springs.

Despite the extent of the damage they had inflicted, Van Dorn's soldiers had injured neither the local citizenry nor the hordes of freed Negroes who in previous months had flocked to the town to receive Federal protection. The troops also treated with respect Mrs. Grant, whom they found temporarily residing in a Holly Springs home while her husband campaigned in the field.[30] And only buildings deemed of military value were destroyed by flames, with the exception of a hospital and a few situated alongside those fired and which could not be protected from flying sparks.

With the principal warehouses in the process of being reduced to ashes, Van Dorn had no reason to linger any longer in Holly Springs; his work here was done, and additional chores that he had planned for his men still lay ahead, farther to the north. About four P. M. he remounted his command and led it through the maze of smoldering ruins.

The general seemed euphoric. Some of his critics later alleged that he was drunk at the time of his departure from the town.[31] They failed to note that Van Dorn's condition came naturally to a man who, after years of failure, had at last won redemption.

★★★★★★★★★★★★★★★★★★★★★★★

29. Brown, "Van Dorn's Operations," p. 158.

30. Deupree, "The Capture of Holly Springs," p. 58; *Official Records*, series I, vol. 17, pt. 1, p. 503.

31. Hartje, *Van Dorn*, pp. 264-65.

3

When Ulysses Grant, at Oxford, heard from Colonel Murphy about the Rebels' proximity to Holly Springs, he grew highly concerned for the safety of the depot (as, of course, for the safety of his wife). Some time after Van Dorn's men entered the town, Colonel C. Carroll Marsh, commander of the Union District of the Tallahatchie, headquartered about fifteen miles south of Holly Springs, sent official word of the town's impending capture, which he had received from a Federal officer who had deserted Holly Springs shortly before the raiders arrived. Grant soon had infantry regiments moving northeast by rail from his headquarters to Colonel Marsh's station at Abbeville, on the Mississippi Central, and also ordered one thousand two hundred cavalrymen under Colonel John K. Mizner, posted even farther to the south, to join Marsh before daybreak on the 21st and cooperate with him in nabbing the Confederates. A detached cavalry regiment, the 6th Illinois, commanded by an officer himself soon to become famous as a raider, Colonel Benjamin H. Grierson, joined Mizner before the latter could overtake Colonel Marsh's infantry.

However, Marsh's men moved so quickly toward Holly Springs that the two cavalry colonels despaired of ever catching them. Sensing a hopeless task ahead, Mizner went into camp several miles below the captured town instead of pushing onward, as Grant wished. Learning this fact, the general-in-chief lost his temper and tersely ordered Mizner to resume his advance or be placed under arrest.

Mizner sought to make amends by again hurrying after Marsh's infantry. Yet it was two A. M. on December 21 before the cavalry got under way once again.[32] Grant must have groaned with frustration as he watched the pursuit get off to such a sorry start.

Earl Van Dorn was of course unaware of his opponents' movements. He took his cavalrymen into camp north of Holly Springs early that morning, allowed them some cherished rest, and had them back in their saddles a few

★★★★★★★★★★★★★★★★★★★★★★★

32. *Official Records*, series I, vol. 17, pt. 2, pp. 439-43.

hours later. A short march on the La Grange Road brought his column to the village of Davis's Mill, eighteen miles above Holly Springs and just below the Tennessee line, where it encountered another Federal garrison.[33] Here he had visions of repeating his smashing success of the day before, with particular reference to destroying the trestle that carried the trackage of the Mississippi Central across nearby Wolf River. Van Dorn waxed confident when he learned that barely 250 Yankees defended the post—especially since he had easily defeated more than five times as many at Holly Springs.

His assurance was misplaced. Unlike Holly Springs, Davis's Mill was commanded by a resourceful, determined officer —Colonel William E. Morgan of the 25th Indiana Infantry. Morgan had learned of the Rebels' approach well in advance of their arrival and had arranged the best possible defensive positions, utilizing every resource at his disposal to make maximum resistance possible. He had built block houses, had manned them with sharpshooters to protect the approaches to the rail trestle, and had dug rifle pits to accommodate dozens of other marksmen.[34]

Wasting no time, Van Dorn ordered an attack on foot, hoping to smash the enemy works by sheer force of numbers. Just before noon his assault commenced, spearheaded by four Texas regiments that rushed forward with impressive speed. But the soldiers in the block houses stood firm, pouring volleys of rifle fire into the oncoming ranks. The Texans recoiled, came on again, were ripped apart by another fusillade, charged a third time, and were beaten back once more. A fourth attack enabled the Texans to reach the trestle, the floor of which they discovered to have been unplanked by the garrison troops. The surviving attackers scrambled behind a levee that adjoined the bridge, to avoid suffering further casualties, and huddled there for safety, wondering why these Yankees did not react as Colonel Murphy's soldiers had.

Van Dorn pondered the situation and finally decided to withdraw. Without artillery, he had no hope of driving the enemy from their strategically located fortifications. But even as he recalled the remnants of his attacking force, some of

★★★★★★★★★★★★★★★★★★★★★★

33. Hartje, *Van Dorn*, p. 265.

34. *Official Records*, series I, vol. 17, pt. 1, p. 521.

the Texans nearest the trestle tried to set it afire by peppering it with balls of cotton, soaked in turpentine. The tactic might have been successful had not Colonel Morgan ordered his men to increase their rate of fire so greatly as to compel the Confederates to abandon the contest for good. Embattled cavalrymen raced from behind the levee toward the main body of the raiding column, many of them dropping in their tracks from sharpshooters' bullets.[35] When Van Dorn calculated the arithmetic, he found that twenty-two of his men had been killed and thirty others so badly wounded that they could travel no farther. Several other troopers, pinned down at the bridge, had already surrendered to Morgan's riflemen.

After an unsuccessful attempt at convincing Morgan he must surrender his outnumbered garrison, Van Dorn rode away from the scene of this minor defeat, crossing into Tennessee and heading farther north, then eastward.

For the next couple of days, his column plodded on its way over rocky ground and frozen mud, the soldiers huddling inside their captured clothes. As they rode, they rendered damage to Federal-held sections of lower Tennessee by cutting rail lines and downing telegraph wires. The men continually cast glances over their shoulders, looking for signs indicating a large enemy pursuit force was after them.

Despite the element of real danger in this march, Van Dorn played the part of a confident, even cocky, warrior. He took his men toward the Union base at Bolivar and feigned an attack on the garrison. But he struck only the pickets below the village, captured many of them, and finally turned south for the long ride home.[36]

Meanwhile, Grant's pursuit continued to move sluggishly. Colonel Mizner, despite his apparent desire to make amends for past slowness, had pushed northward with less than desirable speed. Without waiting for Mizner to join him, Colonel Marsh and his foot soldiers had reached Holly Springs at ten A. M. on the 21st, to find the base a shambles and the Rebels long gone. For his continuing lethargy, Mizner again incurred Grant's wrath, and this time the commanding general relieved him of his command. Colonel Grierson, an abler officer, succeeded to leadership of the cavalry command that

★★★★★★★★★★★★★★★★★★★★★★★

35. Ibid., pp. 522-23.

36. Hartje, *Van Dorn,* pp. 266-67.

hereafter would take on most of the responsibility for chasing the Confederates.[37]

Grierson moved north through Holly Springs at a speed that should have warmed Grant's soul. Below Bolivar, he finally picked up Van Dorn's trail and determined to turn the contest into a simple, old-fashioned race. Though outnumbered by the Rebel raiders, Grierson was akin to Colonel Morgan—he was unafraid to challenge heavy odds.

Still a comfortable distance ahead of his followers, Van Dorn stopped once again during his march, to call for the surrender of another Union garrison. However, at Middleburg, Tennessee, seven miles below Bolivar, he was again repulsed by entrenched Federals, this time after a two-hour struggle.[38] Nursing his latest wounds, Van Dorn decided to play it safe; from now on, he would concentrate his energy in getting his column home freely instead of trying to reap further glory by thrashing enemy outposts into submission. It was well that he determined thus, for along the Tennessee-Mississippi border thousands of Yankee troops of all arms, activated by Grant, were awaiting marching orders should Van Dorn tarry too long in one locale and place himself in position to be overtaken.

Christmas Day, 1862 was a day of almost continuous marching for Van Dorn's troopers. Arriving at Ripley, due east of Holly Springs, a town he had ridden through several days before en route to his primary objective, Van Dorn left a small rear guard behind, to fend off Grierson's fast-riding soldiers, then pushed on via a road that led southwestward. Some hours later the Federal pursuers came up to Ripley, encountered the guard, and spent precious time sparring with it at long range. The Confederates would fire at Grierson's troopers, keeping them back, and then skillfully withdraw from harm's reach, repeating the procedure when the Federals followed. In this manner Van Dorn effectively delayed the enemy while pushing his main force ever closer to safety.[39] The general's confidence in his ability to escape would have been bolstered had he known that Girerson's sol-

★★★★★★★★★★★★★★★★★★★★★★★

37. *Official Records,* series I, vol. 17, pt. 1, p. 518.

38. Ibid., pp. 523-24.

39. Hartje, *Van Dorn,* pp. 266-67.

diers had been overtaken by the cavalry officer whose dilatory habits had become so conspicuous. Now the entire pursuit force was again under the leadership of Colonel Mizner,
whom Grant, for some unknown reason, had forgiven and
placed in field command once again.[40]

Mizner exhibited his timidity anew by vetoing Grierson's
suggestion that at nightfall on the 25th they attack Van
Dorn's rear guard below Ripley, then smash straight toward
his main force. Too risky, thought Mizner, and he may have
been correct.[41] But in so deciding he wasted his final chance
to carry out Grant's orders.

Thanks to his rear guard's delaying action, Van Dorn outdistanced his pursuers during the morning of the
26th—rather, outdistanced all but one unit. This was yet
another cavalry force dispatched from army headquarters
—an understrength brigade under Colonel Edward Hatch of
the 2nd Iowa. For the past several days, after receiving his
instructions, Hatch had been roaming in many directions
near Oxford, responding to a series of conflicting reports
about the Rebels' whereabouts. At dawn on Christmas Day,
Hatch finally took his eight hundred riders along an eastward road that he hoped would enable him to intercept his
quarry short of its home base. The next morning he neared
the town of Pontotoc; at this juncture Van Dorn's men were
still near Ripley, many miles to the north, but coming on
with a full head of steam. Hatch thought of erecting barricades across roads the Rebels might take, barely noting that
the raiders, though tired and riding upon jaded horses, far
outnumbered his own force on hand.

At a point near New Albany, Hatch rounded up some Rebels who were straggling far afield of Van Dorn's column.
Questioning them, he learned that the main body of the
Confederate command was still farther north, and at Ripley
had fought a skirmish with Federals to their rear. Hatch, a
conscientious officer, felt that he should place himself where
the action was: he pushed his eight hundred men directly
toward Ripley. But his choice of roads was unfortunate, for
as he rode on, Van Dorn's column passed him farther to the
west, riding in the opposite direction. Hatch's scouts were too

★★★★★★★★★★★★★★★★★★★★★★

40. *Official Records*, series I, vol. 17, pt. 1, p. 519.

41. Ibid., p. 520.

thinly deployed to ascertain this fact, and Hatch did not learn of it till it was too late. By then he was entirely willing to call it quits, for during the previous thirty-two hours he had marched sixty grueling miles. Later he communicated with Mizner and Grierson, learned that the former had ordered the chase discontinued since it was now obviously a futile effort, and made plans to rejoin the main army as soon as possible.[42]

The great pursuit was over. Once he realized he was beyond the threat of capture, Van Dorn led his men at a leisurely pace, to conserve horseflesh, and by nightfall on December 28 had returned to the camps he had left twelve days earlier.[43] He rejoined Pemberton's army amid circumstances unusual to him: he was welcomed back with much pomp and was bestowed with a flurry of congratulations by his commanding officer. At long last, Earl Van Dorn seemed to have found his place in the hallowed Confederate hierarchy.[44]

4

The raid on Holly Springs—coupled with a simultaneous and highly successful expedition by Brigadier General Nathan Bedford Forrest against the Mobile & Ohio line in Union-held portions of Tennessee—[45] had a decisive effect on the Civil War in the West. Deprived of the sinews of war, Grant's army could not continue its overland campaign toward Vicksburg,[46] and had to retrace its steps to the Mississippi-Tennessee border, where it sat out the winter, seething with frustration and anger. Van Dorn's depot attack was a major factor in prolonging the struggle in that sector of combat, keeping the Mississippi River in Rebel hands until July 1863, when Grant finally succeeded in taking the river stronghold by siege.

In respect to Earl Van Dorn's memory, it would be pleas-

★★★★★★★★★★★★★★★★★★★★★★★★

42. Bearss, *Decision in Mississippi*, pp. 137-39.

43. Hartje, *Van Dorn*, p. 267.

44. Shelby Foote, *The Civil War: A Narrative*, 2: 72.

45. Deupree, "The Capture of Holly Springs," p. 60.

46. *Official Records*, series I, vol. 17, pt. 2, p. 463; Maury, "Recollections," p. 197.

ant to record that he went on to win even greater renown or at least stabilized his reputation as a gentleman and soldier. But history was not kind to him. The Holly Springs expedition marked the apogee of his career, and even his success in that operation was overshadowed by the circumstances of his death, only five months later.

His character traits rather than his actions in battle brought about his untimely end. Van Dorn's avowed fondness for the company of lovely women led him, in the spring of 1863, into an affair with a married woman. The lady's outraged husband sought revenge one day by firing a pistol ball into Van Dorn's skull as the general lolled in his headquarters at Spring Hill, Tennessee.[47]

It was certainly not the most elegant way for a Confederate commander to depart his army's service. And yet, considering the controversial circumstances that attended many of Van Dorn's endeavors, his demise may have been fitting, after all.

★★★★★★★★★★★★★★★★★★★★★★

47. Warner, *Generals in Gray,* p. 315. Van Dorn's allies forever contended that he had been assassinated for political gain.

3

IN PURSUIT OF
THE MULE BRIGADE
Streight's Raid through Alabama
(April 11-May 3, 1863)

1

Early in 1863, General Braxton Bragg's Army of Tennessee held a fairly comfortable position among the rich farming lands of Middle Tennessee. For his supplies Bragg nevertheless placed reliance on the Western & Atlantic Railroad, which connected his field headquarters with large bases in the Deep South.[1] Since Bragg's opponent, Federal Major General William S. Rosecrans, was committed to the task of destroying the Army of Tennessee by any means practicable, he inevitably concentrated on this long and efficient line of communications. Rosecrans believed that if the Western & Atlantic could be extensively damaged, Bragg would be forced out of his sanctuary and would perhaps retreat eastward into mountainous regions where food and forage were not so easy to obtain. If, instead, Bragg fell back into Georgia, Rosecrans's Army of the Cumberland would be able to

★★★★★★★★★★★★★★★★★★★★★★★★

1. Foote, *The Civil War,* 2: 179.

66

occupy the strategic city of Chattanooga. That would mean that Rosecrans had deprived his enemy of their interior communication network, quite possibly a fatal loss.[2]

One previous attempt had been made to wreck the Western & Atlantic. In April 1862 twenty-two Union spies, disguised as Southern civilians, had infiltrated Confederate lines in northern Georgia, finally capturing an engine on the W & A. The spies hoped to render great damage to trackage and rolling stock, but were captured after a swift and massive pursuit by Confederate railroad officials and soldiers aboard other trains. The adventure, which in time became known as the Great Locomotive Chase, resulted in only minimal destruction to the line.[3]

In this April of '63, however, General Rosecrans gave new thought to cutting the rail route, if only because it seemed the simplest way to deal with Bragg's elusive army, which thus far had proved difficult to outmaneuver. A detailed plan for the project had been submitted by one of Rosecrans's infantry officers, Colonel Abel D. Streight of the 51st Indiana, who projected a mounted strike at the W & A in the vicinity of Rome, Georgia. Although he did not have experience in mounted campaigning, Colonel Streight believed himself fully capable of leading such a force on an expedition southward from Rosecrans's headquarters at Nashville, then across the northern portion of Alabama on a one thousand-mile journey to Rome. The colonel had in mind a quick stab into a portion of the Confederacy in which few people, mostly Union sympathizers, resided.[4] If aided by properly conducted diversionary movements, he believed his force could so effectively mangle the line in Georgia that Bragg would have to abandon his present position posthaste. Returning from such an undertaking would be chancy, of course, but Streight indicated that he was not particularly worried about the matter.

Beyond coolness and courage, Colonel Streight possessed many qualities that made him an ideal choice to lead this mission. He was a steady and dependable officer who could

★★★★★★★★★★★★★★★★★★★★★★★

2. Andrew N. Lytle, *Bedford Forrest and His Critter Company*, p. 150.

3. Boatner, *The Civil War Dictionary*, pp. 16-17.

4. John Allan Wyeth, *Life of General Nathan Bedford Forrest*, pp. 186-87; Robert Selph Henry, *"First With the Most" Forrest*, p. 139.

Abel D. Streight. COURTESY LIBRARY OF CONGRESS.

be counted on to carry out his orders precisely. He was also blessed with enough initiative and resourcefulness to improvise tactics when needed. He was considerate of the well-being of his soldiers and enjoyed their fullest cooperation, trust, and respect. Even his external appearance hinted at inner strength: stocky and tall, he stood always erect, his face characterized by a square jaw, hooded eyes, thinning dark hair, and an impressive-looking growth of beard.

The colonel's abilities were well known to General Rosecrans; for that reason the army leader was at once responsive to his plan. Rosecrans was enthusiastic not only because of what might be accomplished but also because such a raid would demonstrate that his opponents had not monopolized that field.[5] In past months, Rosecrans's army had been the target of numerous raiding forces, led by such renowned generals as Bedford Forrest and "Fightin' Joe" Wheeler. They had made the Army of the Cumberland look helplessly vulnerable, and its own cavalry had not been able to even the score.

Early in the month Streight met with Rosecrans and several of the general's subordinates to discuss strategy. The army leader gave him command of a "provisional brigade" of mounted infantry, including, in addition to Streight's own regiment, the 3rd Ohio, 18th Illinois, and 73rd Indiana regiments. Also assigned him were two small mountain howitzers, plus two companies of so-called Middle Tennessee Cavalry.[6] The latter were actually composed of "homemade Yankees" from the same Unionist-predominant counties of northern Alabama as Streight would traverse on his expedition.

Streight was primarily concerned with breaking the W & A, but he took on a secondary objective. On April 9 he informed Rosecrans's chief of staff that he considered the destruction of Confederate factories and warehouses along his route "a duty which I have no right to leave undone, when in my power, even in the absence of any instructions."[7]

In finalizing Streight's plans, Rosecrans also got up a large diversionary mission. A seven thousand five hundred-man

★★★★★★★★★★★★★★★★★★★★★★★★

5. Foote, *The Civil War,* 2: 179.

6. Wyeth, *Life of Forrest,* p. 187.

7. *Official Records,* series, I, vol. 23, pt. 2, p. 224.

infantry force, under Brigadier General Grenville Dodge, would be sent into western Alabama from Corinth, Mississippi along the line of the Memphis & Charleston Railroad. Dodge's movements were calculated to draw off those Confederates in position to offer resistance to Streight's raiders. That done, Streight's path should lay clear, for Bragg's main army would remain in position far to the north of the Federal route of march. It was decided that Streight should meet Dodge's command at Eastport, Mississippi on April 16, shortly before Streight cast loose from his supports and moved out on his own.[8]

At the outset of the expedition, Streight would place his command aboard transports at Nashville, then sail down the Cumberland River to Palmyra, Tennessee. From Palmyra the raiders would trek overland to Union-held Fort Henry, at which point the transports, after gathering rations on the Ohio River, would carry the troops up the Tennessee River to Eastport.[9]

With these details pinned down, only one matter needed to be resolved. Streight wished his operation to be conducted in the accepted style, aboard horseback. But Rosecrans balked, insisting that Streight should mount his men on mules. He explained that mules were more enduring than horses and surer of foot in rugged, broken land such as that the raiders would encounter in northern Alabama. In truth, however, Rosecrans was concerned about what he supposed to be the numerical inferiority of his cavalry corps. He believed that it could scarcely hold its own against Bragg's horsemen; thus he could not afford to deplete its supply of animals to outfit Streight's two thousand-man command. Rosecrans was agreeable to furnishing enough horses to outfit only a small portion of the colonel's raiders, including the Alabama-born troopers. As it turned out, Rosecrans was needlessly worried, for he had almost twenty thousand cavalry jumpers on hand—more than enough to supply Streight and still operate against Bragg's supply routes in Middle Tennessee.[10] Because of this unwillingness to accede to Streight's request, he in-

★★★★★★★★★★★★★★★★★★★★★★★

8. Henry, *"First With the Most" Forrest*, pp. 141-42.

9. Lytle, *Bedford Forrest and His Critter Company*, p. 151.

10. James F. Cook, "The 1863 Raid of Abel D. Streight: Why It Failed," *The Alabama Review* 22 (October 1969): 258-59.

sured that the "Mule Brigade" would conduct one of the most unusual mounted operations of the war.

Thus, when Streight's soldiers finally crowded aboard twenty transports on the evening of April 10, they found themselves sharing ship space with eight hundred quarter-master mules. This meant that one thousand two hundred men would be forced to travel afoot during the first leg of the mission, but Rosecrans was certain they would soon be able to procure mounts in Tennessee and Alabama.[11]

The raiders were quite put out by the mules' hideous bray-ing and skittish movements, and they had to endure other discomforts as well. A sergeant in the 3rd Ohio remarked that "the lower deck [was] crowded with mules—the odor of which was not agreeable . . . but as we were much fatigued we made our beds side by side with our long-eared friends, and soon were in the realm of Morpheus."[12]

When the sergeant awoke the next morning, the fleet was under way.

2

Late on the 11th, the transports arrived at Palmyra, on the left bank of the Cumberland around the bend from the vil-lage of Clarksville, and began to unload their human and equine cargo. Once a thriving little community, Palmyra had been thoroughly ravaged by two years of war and now, ac-cording to one of Colonel Streight's aides, was "only a heap of black and charred ruins."[13]

Even more depressing was the sight of the mules when un-loaded. Some logistician had erred, for many of the animals were obviously unfit for riding, sick with distemper; and a few had died en route from Nashville. At once Streight or-dered his subordinates to cull the unhealthy animals from the herd. When the process had been completed, more than fifty mules had been lost to the command. A dozen others

★★★★★★★★★★★★★★★★★★★★★★

11. Henry, *"First With the Most" Forrest*, p. 141.

12. "Colonel Streight's Expedition: Journal of H. Breidenthal, Sergeant Co. A, Third Ohio Vol. Infantry," *The Rebellion Record*, Supplementary Volume 1, p. 337.

13. Alva C. Roach, *The Prisoner of War and How Treated, Etc.*, p. 12.

died before the journey to Fort Henry could get under way.[14]

Streight's troubles multiplied when he formally introduced his soldiers to their means of conveyance. The mules proved a mean and highly active lot, for their heels, as a lieutenant reported, "were most of the time performing evolutions in the air something after the style of the wild Highland Fling." The raiders approached them warily and strove to climb aboard only when sternly commanded to do so. Most were quickly tossed off and had to muster the courage to remount. Others had to run through Palmyra, chasing animals who had no intention of standing still long enough to accommodate a rider. Watching all of this, Colonel Streight wondered why he had complied so graciously with Rosecrans's desire that he use animals supposedly more intelligent and gentler than horses.

The colonel spent more than a full day preparing his riders for mounted duty. But this crash course produced only mixed results. Realizing that he could no longer prolong his stay in Palmyra, Streight reluctantly directed his soldiers to march toward Fort Henry.

He could have taken his good time, for when he reached the garrison on the 15th he found that the transports and their four-gunboat escort had not yet appeared. The delay gave him time to scour the vicinity for more mounts, and by the time the navy finally arrived, late the next day, Streight had secured enough mules and horses to mount perhaps one thousand two hundred soldiers.[15] Still, the question of how long the infantrymen could be expected to remain aboard the temperamental critters could not be answered.

As if Streight had not already encountered enough troubles, low stages of water compelled the transports and gunboats to remain at the fort until April 17. Only then did the command reembark for its trip up the Tennessee to Eastport.[16]

While the raiders dawdled along the Tennessee, General Dodge had experienced some annoying problems of his own.

★★★★★★★★★★★★★★★★★★★★★★

14. *Official Records,* series I, vol. 23, pt. 1, p. 286.

15. Roach, *The Prisoner of War,* pp. 14-15.

16. Henry, *"First With the Most" Forrest,* p. 142.

With his large command he had moved out of Mississippi at the designated time and reached the rendezvous point, Eastport, well in advance of Streight's arrival. But along the way he was slowed and harassed by a Confederate cavalry brigade led by Colonel Philip D. Roddey. After Dodge decided to push beyond Eastport, Roddey struck him so viciously near Tuscumbia, Alabama, that Dodge was propelled into a twenty-three-mile retreat. At Bear Creek, about twelve miles from Eastport, he halted to recover his composure and to wire for reinforcements.[17] Therefore, when Streight landed at Eastport on the 19th (three days behind schedule), he found that he had to travel to Bear Creek to confer with Dodge.

The expansiveness of Streight's convoy—which included a shipboard contingent from Brigadier General Alfred W. Ellet's Marine Brigade—attracted widespread attention at Eastport.[18] Streight was not certain that the enemy had detected his arrival, but he must have suspected so. As it happened, observant Confederate scouts notified Colonel Roddey that "transports were landing an army at Eastport" that day.[19] This ought to have boded ill for the expedition. Nonetheless, four days would pass before Rebel cavalrymen were dispatched to run Streight down.

On Sunday evening, the 19th, Streight rode to Bear Creek to meet Dodge, leaving Colonel Orris Lawson of the 3rd Ohio to herd and corral the disembarked animals. New troubles developed as soon as the herd set foot on solid ground. The mules threw back their heads and let loose with a fearsome braying, celebrating, as one Confederate supposed, "their deliverance from their natural dread of a watery grave."

The racket alerted some of Roddey's troopers, who carefully had worked their way into Streight's encampment to estimate the size of the Federal force. Some of them saw an opportunity to spread confusion and destruction along the riverbank. That night, under cover of darkness, several scouts crept inside the corrals and began shouting and firing

★★★★★★★★★★★★★★★★★★★★★★★

17. Wyeth, *Life of Forrest,* pp. 188-89.

18. Lytle, *Bedford Forrest and His Critter Company,* p. 151.

19. Henry, *"First With the Most" Forrest,* p. 142.

their pistols. The herd panicked and ran, smashing through makeshift barriers. Most broke for the timberline along the bank, while some stumbled into the Tennessee, meeting the same fate they had been so relieved to escape earlier. During the fracas, Roddey's men slipped away and returned to their main force.[20]

When Streight returned from Bear Creek after midnight, he found that four hundred mules had scampered to freedom or had been drowned. The loss was quite serious; another commander might have considered it the final straw. But Streight spent the next day and a half patiently rounding up the scattered herd, finally recovering about half.[21] Then he moved out on his expedition.

On the 21st the raiders moved eastward, marching slowly behind Dodge's screening advance. Three days later both Union commands reached Tuscumbia, now devoid of Roddey's men. At Tuscumbia Streight made a short layover, waiting for final authorization to move out on his own. During the interval, General Dodge made the raiding leader a present of a few hundred mules, which he had gathered from the Tennessee Valley, and on April 25 and part of the 26th Streight's brigade surgeons examined the entire force. Five hundred soldiers were found to be in no condition to withstand the rigors of a long forced march and were dropped from the active duty rosters, leaving the colonel approximately one thousand five hundred picked men for the mission.[22]

While at Tuscumbia, Streight learned that the gravest of his difficulties was only now materializing. On the 26th, Dodge told him that cavalry under Nathan Bedford Forrest was reportedly heading toward Tuscumbia, spoiling for a fight.

For almost a full year, Forrest had been a holy terror to the Federal forces in the West. He was tirelessly combative in a fight, relentless in pursuit, dangerous in any situation no matter the odds he faced. An ex-slave dealer and cotton planter from Tennessee, he was hulking and hard-eyed; his

★★★★★★★★★★★★★★★★★★★★★★★★

20. *Official Records*, series I, vol. 23, pt. 1, p. 286; Wyeth, *Life of Forrest*, p. 189.

21. *Official Records*, series I, vol. 23, pt. 1, p. 286.

22. Henry, *"First With the Most" Forrest*, p. 144.

appearance was usually stern enough to convince others not to antagonize him in any manner. He had never perused a book on military tactics—his education had been rudimentary in most areas—but he was a natural, instinctive soldier and had risen from the enlisted ranks to become perhaps the greatest cavalry commander in the Confederate army. The soldiers he led were as rough, as hard-bitten, as he; they wore faded uniforms, fought with miscellaneous weapons, and rode unprepossessing horses, but they seldom failed in a pitched battle, and no other cavalrymen, in either army, could ride as hard as they.

Prior to Streight's movement south from Nashville, Forrest had been stationed at Spring Hill, Tennessee, informing Bragg of the activities of Union troops in and near Franklin. On the evening of April 23 Bragg notified him of Dodge's movements in the Tennessee Valley and ordered him to march his brigade to the Tennessee River, there to unite with Roddey's force and assume overall command. Bragg had failed to heed the reports of Streight's arrival at Eastport; he did not even mention the Yankee raiding force in his dispatch to Forrest.[23]

Forrest responded at once. Upon receiving his instructions, he sent his 11th Tennessee Cavalry, under Colonel James S. Edmondson, to join Roddey in advance of the rest of his brigade. A couple of hours after Edmondson had moved off, Forrest marched south with the body of his command, the 4th, 8th, 9th, and 10th Tennessee regiments, plus Captain John Morton's veteran eight-gun battery of horse artillery.[24] Throughout that day and the next two as well, the Confederate column pushed on; Forrest allowed his troopers only short rest halts along the way. The speed with which he moved enabled his troops to come up to the Tennessee in the afternoon of Monday, April 27.[25]

By the time the main force drew up on the north shore, Edmondson's regiment had crossed and joined Colonel Roddey near the village of Leighton. Now Forrest divided the rest of his command, leaving the 8th and 10th Tennessee, as

★★★★★★★★★★★★★★★★★★★★★★★

23. Ibid., pp. 143-44.

24. Rucker Agee, "Forrest-Streight Campaign of 1863," p. 15.

25. Lytle, *Bedford Forrest and His Critter Company,* p. 153.

well as two of Morton's guns, on the north side. They were ordered to move westward toward the city of Florence, threatening Dodge's rear. In the meantime the two other regiments, plus the major portion of Morton's battery, crossed the river aboard two steam ferries, then hurried twelve miles southwestward to meet Roddey.[26]

Even before Forrest arrived there, Dodge had again been harassed by Roddey's small but scrappy command. On the 27th, however, Dodge began to use his great numerical advantage to telling effect, flanking Roddey's brigade and forcing it backward. That afternoon he drove Roddey to the east bank of Town Creek and camped on the opposite shore, intending to force his way across the next day.

But at dawn on the 28th Dodge saw that he was no longer facing a single Confederate brigade. Now strengthened by Forrest's cavalry and artillery, Roddey resisted Dodge's efforts to cross the creek, whose water level had risen due to late rains. For five hours Dodge hammered away at the Rebels' positions with eighteen cannon, but succeeded in crossing only a handful of infantrymen, who eventually were forced back to the west bank. Later in the day, the two regiments Forrest had left north of the Tennessee began to demonstrate against the Federals' rear, whereupon Dodge, fearful of being caught amid pincers, pulled back from the creek. On the 29th one of the Tennessee units above the river blasted the Federals' rear so severely that Dodge retreated to Tuscumbia, then to Bear Creek. In moving back through the Tennessee Valley, the Union commander laid waste to the region, burning all produce, provisions, and forage of use to the Confederate forces. By the 30th he was back in his old bailiwick around Corinth.[27]

Although he had allowed Rebel forces whose combined strength was less than half his own to fight him to a standstill, Dodge had fulfilled the requirements of his diversionary operation. By facing Forrest and Roddey across Town Creek, he had diverted their attention from Streight. Late in the evening on the 26th, Streight's men had finally slipped out of

★★★★★★★★★★★★★★★★★★★★★★★

26. Agee, "Forrest-Streight Campaign," p. 15.

27. Ibid., pp. 16-17.

Tuscumbia, commencing their thrust toward the Georgia railroads.[28]

3

As the expedition got under way, the rains that swelled Town Creek came down upon Streight's soldiers in driving sheets. They turned the roads to deep pools of gumbo in which mules and horses sank to their knees. The raiders donned rubber ponchos to protect themselves from the elements, but about one hundred and fifty of their number still lacked transportation[29] and had to slog through the mud as best they could. By now the soldiers had been told a little about the objectives of the mission, but any enthusiasm they brought to the task had been already worn thin by the weather, the ornery animals, and the various other difficulties they had been forced to bear during their journey from Rosecrans's headquarters.

Streight's soldiers plodded through the hill country of Alabama, moving as far south as Russellville, which one of the Ohio soldiers found to be "a small, mean-looking Secesh hole." In Russellville the Federal advance was fired upon by bushwhackers, who fled before the vanguard of the column came up.[30] After an hour's halt in the village, the Mule Brigade turned directly east, heading for its first important objective, Moulton, the seat of Lawrence County. The night of the 27th, the riders bivouacked in the rain at Mount Hope, three dozen miles southeast of Tuscumbia. During that stopover Streight collected numerous stragglers who had finally caught up with the main column, and received a report from General Dodge, then driving Roddey's men across Town Creek. Dodge reported having the situation firmly in hand and suggested that Streight push onward with dispatch.[31]

★★★★★★★★★★★★★★★★★★★★★★

28. Roach, *The Prisoner of War*, p. 18.

29. Henry, *"First With the Most" Forrest*, p. 144.

30. "Colonel Streight's Expedition: Journal of H. Breidenthal," p. 340.

31. Wyeth, *Life of Forrest*, p. 192.

The colonel required little persuading; with Forrest coming on, it was necessary that the raiders get as far as possible from the Tuscumbia-Town Creek area in the shortest possible time. Leaving Mount Hope at ten o'clock the next morning, the Federals forged ahead through more rain, scouring the countryside for remounts and reaching Moulton at sunset.[32] By now only fifty of Streight's soldiers lacked animals.

On the day the Federals marched from Mount Hope to Moulton, however, Bedford Forrest got wind of their doings and set out after them. That evening he learned from one of his scouts, who had circumvented Dodge's flank on an extended reconnaissance, that a force of about two thousand mounted men had cut southward from Tuscumbia and thence eastward from Mount Hope.[33] By this time, the newly discovered force was more than twenty miles from Forrest's position.

Forrest tried to make sense of the developing situation. The nature of Dodge's operations along Town Creek suggested that he was trying to divert his enemy's attention from the movements of the new force. Perhaps the latter was moving to strike the Confederate left flank. On the other hand, it had already marched so far south as to indicate that it was pursuing an independent mission. The nature of such a mission remained a mystery to Forrest.

Still, the newly discovered column posed a sublime threat to Confederate security in Alabama, and only Forrest was in a position to remove that threat. To meet all contingencies, he divided his forces once again. He deployed about five hundred of Roddey's men, with two guns, to keep pressure on Dodge, then sent the remainder of Roddey's command, some 450 men, with another two-gun section of artillery and Edmondson's 11th Tennessee, to interpose between Dodge and the assumed location of Streight's force. This, hopefully, would prevent either Federal column from supporting the other. The two Tennessee regiments above the river would be held in readiness to strike Dodge in flank and rear if the opportunity arose.[34]

★★★★★★★★★★★★★★★★★★★★★★★

32. Roach, *The Prisoner of War*, p. 19.

33. Thomas Jordan and J. P. Pryor, *The Campaigns of Lieut.-Gen. N. B. Forrest and of Forrest's Cavalry*, p. 253.

34. Ibid., p. 255; Agee, "Forrest-Streight Campaign," p. 16.

Forrest then turned to his other two regiments, Colonel Jacob Biffle's 9th Tennessee and Major W. S. McLemore's 4th Tennessee Cavalry. Although all of these troopers were saddle-weary from several days of almost constant travel and had skirmished with Dodge for many hours, they would have to chase down the Federals marching eastward from Mount Hope. Forrest explained the critical situation to his officers and stressed that during the long ride that lay ahead all would have to display the fullest measure of endurance and determination. That done, he set to other important tasks. In early evening darkness he organized his command for the pursuit, issuing ammunition to his troopers and artillerymen, inspecting their horses, doling out rations and forage, double-teaming his guns and caissons, and shouting out advice and encouragement as well as orders.

By one A. M. his command was ready to move.[35] Through heavy rain his men trotted onto the road that led southward from the village of Courtland, and started off in column. Forrest rode at the head of the force, his face grim and taut, his eyes steel-cold, his jaw set. His appearance was that of a hunter, and although Colonel Streight did not yet know it, he himself had become, in this early hour on April 29, the hunted.

Before Forrest marched, Streight's soldiers had left Moulton behind, striking for the tall mountains farther eastward. On the 29th they progressed thirty-five miles through the rain and at night camped at the foot of Day's Gap, a narrow defile through which an ancient Indian trail wound to the uppermost plateau of Sand Mountain. Although Streight's men were learning the fine points of mounted duty very slowly, few stragglers turned up this day. By evening the colonel had rounded up enough horses and mules to mount his entire brigade.[36] These facts, plus the amount of ground covered thus far, restored the confidence that earlier mishaps had drained from Streight.

Such confidence would not remain in full strength very long, for Forrest's people were pushing on at an increasingly swift rate. At eleven A. M. on the 29th, the Confederate troopers reached Moulton after a furious ride, and were re-

★★★★★★★★★★★★★★★★★★★★★★

35. Henry, *"First With the Most" Forrest*, pp. 145-46.

36. *Official Records*, series I, vol. 23, pt. 1, p. 287.

warded by a brief respite. In that village Forrest ascertained the identity of the force he was chasing and realized that it was aiming to break Bragg's communications, possibly those in Georgia. He considered that unpleasant idea for only a brief time before remounting his command and pushing it onward. Riding out of Moulton, sunlight brightened the sky, and Forrest's men cheered the cessation of the pursuit-slowing rain; it seemed a happy omen.

Streight's trail toward the mountains was clear, and Forrest followed it with little difficulty. That afternoon he overtook the force he had dispatched on the 28th to move between Dodge and Streight—Roddey's four hundred troopers and Edmondson's six hundred Tennesseans.[37] At this point, Forrest had more than two thousand soldiers under his authority, a greater number than Streight led.

By two A. M. on April 30, Forrest was within four miles of the raiders' encampment at the base of Sand Mountain. Now he could permit his command a sustained period of rest. His exhausted troopers dropped from their saddles and sank to the ground, many of them falling immediately to sleep. But the general ordered his younger brother, Captain William Forrest, to immediately lead a company of scouts to the fringes of the Yankee camp. With stoical endurance Bill Forrest and his men made the four-mile journey and managed to slip around Streight's rear, capturing his pickets without waking the main force.[38]

Next morning, Streight's mules unleashed another unearthly braying, which echoed through the valley and the mountain passes and awoke a good many of the raiders before dawn. Streight shrugged off the disturbance, for he was in good spirits today. He had reached an area populated by pro-Unionists and in their presence felt assured of success. To date he had detected no signs of an enemy pursuit and believed himself so distant from organized Confederates as to be home free.[39] Therefore, when he led his brigade up the mountain road to the summit, he moved without undue haste.

★★★★★★★★★★★★★★★★★★★★★★

37. Agee, "Forrest-Streight Campaign," p. 17.

38. Wyeth, *Life of Forrest,* p. 196.

39. Henry, *"First With the Most" Forrest,* p. 146.

However, when his vanguard reached the top, more than a mile from the base of Sand Mountain, Streight was shocked to hear the sounds of battle from down below. Captain Forrest's scouts had struck the Federal rear guard; now they were capturing stragglers and wagons and were chasing other soldiers up the winding mountain road.[40]

While the fighting raged, Bedford Forrest rushed up to the scene with Roddey, Edmondson, and Morton's battery. He had already sent the 4th and 9th Tennessee through an eastward pass to head off Streight in the direction of De-catur. With a little more than one thousand men Forrest skirmished with Streight's rear eschelon for a distance of two miles up Day's Gap, then charged toward the summit to bat-tle the main portion of the raiding force.

Most of Streight's soldiers had never campaigned in this section of Alabama, but his two companies of "Middle Ten-nessee" Cavalry knew the surrounding territory quite well. They helped the colonel recover his composure by guiding the command across Sand Mountain via little-known trails. Meanwhile, Streight's rear guard fought a delaying action within the gap, buying time in which the colonel might plan further strategy.[41]

Streight's dream of reaching Georgia without opposition had disintegrated. His only hope lay in outfoxing and out-maneuvering his enemy. Fortunately he could think quickly under pressure; atop the mountain he sent horses and mules forward, then placed his soldiers and two howitzers in am-bush along a wooded ridge. Acting on Streight's orders, the officer in charge of the Alabama-born cavalrymen, most of whom were bringing up the rear, dashed up the side of the mountain. Bill Forrest's scouts, in close pursuit, rode directly into the trap. Several Rebels toppled from their saddles, in-cluding the captain, who was severely wounded.[42]

Bedford Forrest soon reached the summit with reinforce-ments, and formed line of battle preparatory to charging Streight's position. He dismounted Edmondson's regiment and sent its men forward, side-by-side with Roddey's

★★★★★★★★★★★★★★★★★★★★★★

40. *Official Records*, series I, vol. 23, pt. 1, p. 288.

41. Wyeth, *Life of Forrest*, pp. 197-98; Jordan and Pryor, *Campaigns of Forrest*, p. 257.

42. Henry, *"First With the Most" Forrest*, p. 147.

mounted troopers. Simultaneously, he ran two of Captain Morton's guns within three hundred yards of the Federal lines. The charge proceeded effectively until Roddey's troopers suddenly surged ahead of their comrades, throwing the Confederate line into disorder. Seizing the opportunity, Streight directed one of his ablest subordinates, Colonel Gilbert Hathaway, to charge the Rebel battery with his 73rd Indiana Infantry, plus Streight's own regiment, the 51st Indiana, now under Lieutenant Colonel James W. Sheets. Meanwhile, Streight's two other infantry regiments attacked the enemy troopers. The weight of the Federal counterattack shattered Forrest's line, sending his main force into retreat and causing two caissons, forty prisoners, and both cannon to fall into the hands of the enemy. However, Streight paid dearly for his success, suffering thirty casualties, including Colonel Sheets, who had been mortally wounded.[43]

The loss of his cannon drove Bedford Forrest into a fearsome rage. Determined to recover them, he reorganized his force, adding to it stragglers who had recently come up from the gap below. He formed another assault column with every man on hand, permitting none to go to the rear as horseholders.

However, Colonel Streight had no intention of waiting to receive a new charge. The battle at Day's Gap, plus intermittent skirmishing that followed the repulse of Forrest's attack, had consumed five hours. The raiding leader could not afford another such delay. He gathered up his men and mules and galloped eastward across the plateau.[44]

At noon Forrest went forward, only to find that his enemy had withdrawn, dragging off the guns they had captured. His anger was not in the least assuaged when a short time later he was rejoined by the 4th and 9th Tennessee, which had failed to encounter the Federals on their flank detour.

Before resuming his pursuit, Forrest made new strategic dispositions. He sent Roddey's soldiers back toward the Tennessee Valley to keep an eye on Dodge's men, who were devasting the region as they fell back into Mississippi. Next, Forrest sent Edmondson's unit eastward toward Somerville,

★★★★★★★★★★★★★★★★★★★★★★

43. Agee, "Forrest-Streight Campaign," pp. 18, 32; *Official Records*, series I, vol. 23, pt. 1, pp. 288-89.

44. Henry, *"First With the Most" Forrest*, p. 147.

to get between the raiders and the Tennessee, thus prevent-
ing Streight from escaping across the river and rejoining
Dodge. By two P. M. the general was able to pick up
Streight's trail once again, and set out with Biffle's and
McLemore's regiments, plus Morton's battery. Forrest
realized that now he had less than nine hundred soldiers
with whom to bring his more numerous adversaries to bay.[45]
But he felt that in the rocky, tree-fringed passes of Sand
Mountain a heavier force would prove a hindrance by hand-
icapping the pursuit.

An hour after resuming the march, Forrest overtook
Streight's rear guard and skirmished briskly with it, but could
not halt the raiding column. The Confederate outriders kept
up their harassment for a few miles, fulfilling their leader's
wish that they "shoot everything blue."

Late that afternoon Streight was compelled to halt and
make a stand on a ridge known as Hog Mountain, six miles
beyond the Day's Gap battleground. The fight that broke out
lasted until evening and was sharp and vicious, but proved
inconclusive. During it Forrest had three horses shot from
beneath him, although he escaped without serious injury and
succeeded in retrieving his captured cannon after Streight
abandoned them. When a Confederate movement threatened
his rear, where his mounts were tethered, Colonel Streight
elected to resume his march southeastward.[46] In the bright
moonlight, the Rebels followed with intimidating speed.

Shortly before midnight, the Yankee leader set another
ambush, placing Colonel Hathaway's regiment in a roadside
thicket. Streight later reported that when the Rebel advance
came up, "the whole regiment opened a most destructive
fire, causing a complete stampede of the enemy." However,
Confederate accounts state that some gray-clad scouts detected Hathaway's ambushers and that Forrest chased them
away with a few well-placed cannon shots.[47] In either event,
Streight moved on, marching well into the next morning.

Near the ford over Big Creek at one A. M. on May 1,
Streight's rear guard was again struck. This convinced the

★★★★★★★★★★★★★★★★★★★★★★★★

45. Agee, "Forrest-Streight Campaign," p. 18; Lytle, *Bedford Forrest and His Critter
Company,* p. 160.

46. Henry *"First With the Most" Forrest,* p. 148.

47. *Official Records,* series I, vol. 23, pt. 1, p. 289; Wyeth, *Life of Forrest,* pp. 203-4.

colonel that yet another delaying action was needed. By now he was fully aware that it was the redoubtable Bedford Forrest who was in his rear—information that might have filled another Union commander with fear. But Streight carefully deployed several sharpshooters, who held off the Confederates until the main body of his force could ford the creek. After the crossing had been completed, the colonel led his fatigued men and animals eastward, while Forrest allowed his men a needed rest.[48]

Streight's constant marching and fighting began to take a heavy toll among men and riders. He himself admitted that by ten o'clock that morning, when the brigade reached Blountsville, forty-odd miles from Day's Gap, "many of our mules had given out, leaving their riders on foot." But he added that "there was very little straggling behind the rear guard."

At Blountsville, in answer to petitions from his officers, Streight called a halt. He found a great quantity of corn in the village, which was given to the ravenous animals.[49] After a two-hour stopover, he abandoned and torched a train of supply wagons that he had captured shortly before reaching Sand Mountain, then forced his sore-footed animals to plod onward. But before the rear echelon could depart Bountsville, Forrest struck again, inflicting several casualties and scattering the survivors. The Confederates then extinguished the fires and saved many of Streight's wagons, salvaging a cache of badly needed supplies.[50]

Skirmishing continued beyond Bountsville after Forrest's main column resumed the chase. By mid-afternoon the Rebels were pressing Streight's rear so closely that he had to halt on the shoreline at the east branch of the Black Warrior River, to cover the fording operation of his column. Once on the far shore, Streight moved on through falling darkness, "though the command was in no condition to do so."[51]

Shortly after sunrise on May 2, the Federals forded Will's

★★★★★★★★★★★★★★★★★★★★★★★

48. Agee, "Forrest-Streight Campaign," p. 20.

49. *Official Records,* series I, vol. 23, pt. 1, p. 290.

50. "Colonel Streight's Expedition: Journal of H. Breidenthal," p. 342; Agee, "Forrest-Streight Campaign," p. 20.

51. *Official Records,* series I, vol. 23, pt. 1, p. 290.

Creek, in the valley below the southern point of Lookout Mountain, and moved east toward the city of Gadsden. As ever, Forrest was hard on his quarry's heels, and Streight's concern began to build. But soon afterward the colonel executed a maneuver that offered new hope that he might outlast his pursuers and reach Georgia. Four miles beyond Will's Creek he crossed his men over a bridge spanning Black Creek, then burned the bridge and mounted a strong rear guard to keep Forrest's people on the far side of the deep stream. It appeared that the Rebels would find it impossible to continue the chase. Much relieved, Streight led the Mule Brigade toward Gadsden.[52]

But Forrest was stymied only temporarily. In his moment of travail, he was aided by a sixteen-year-old girl who lived with her mother on a nearby farm. Under fire from the Federal rear guard, the girl directed Forrest to a blind ford some distance from the burned bridge, where the pursuers could cross in safety and with ease. In a matter of minutes, the cavalrymen were splashing through the water and Forrest was penning an autographed note of thanks:

> Hed Quaters in Sadle
> May 2 1863
> My highest regardes to miss Ema Sanson for hir Gallant conduct while my posse was skirmishing with the Federals across Black Creek near Gadesden Allabama.
> N. B. Forrest
> Brig Genl Comding N. Ala—[53]

Unexpectedly, Streight found Forrest directly behind him once more. For this reason he halted in Gadsden only long enough to destroy stores of flour, stands of arms, and a ferryboat. When that was done, Streight, himself groggy with fatigue, ordered the journey resumed.

By this time the colonel seemed to sense coming doom. In a desperate attempt to reach the Georgia line ahead of his pursuers, he sent two hundred of the most alert raiders, aboard the freshest mounts, to seize and secure the Oostanaula River Bridge at Rome. He entrusted command of this flying detachment to Captain Milton Russell of his old

★★★★★★★★★★★★★★★★★★★★★★★

52. Henry, *"First With the Most" Forrest*, p. 150.

53. Foote, *The Civil War*, 2: 183.

regiment, sending him forth from a point eight miles past Gadsden.[54]

After Russell's unit moved off, Streight's main column marched four miles farther, halting at Blount's Plantation at four P. M. to dismount and feed. When Forrest reappeared, the colonel again deployed Hathaway's 73rd Indiana to delay him. However, the Confederates attacked with great fury, killing the regimental leader and scattering his soldiers. For Streight, the colonel's loss was "irreparable. His men had almost worshipped him, and when he fell it cast a deep gloom of despondency over his regiment. . . ."

Another blow to Streight's morale was his discovery that most of his soldiers' ammunition was worthless. From rough travel aboard pack mules, most of the vital percussion caps had become so frayed as to be rendered useless; and hundreds of cartridges had been ruined by water during recent fording operations.[55]

The colonel refused to give up. As he marched, he continued to contrive new ambushes and delaying maneuvers —but they failed to materially hinder Forrest. At eleven P. M., after a particularly arduous march, the Mule Brigade reached the important ferry crossing of the Chattooga River, a short distance above its confluence with the Coosa. Streight was bitterly disappointed to find that Captain Russell, who had passed that way, had neglected to guard the ferry boats, which had since been removed by local residents.[56]

Knowing no other route to follow, Streight wearily turned northward toward a bridge reportedly standing eight miles upstream, near Gaylesville. Temporarily the pressure on his rear had abated, for Forrest, confident that he had his prey in a corner, had decided to give his Tennesseans an eleven-hour rest near Blount's Plantation.[57]

On their way upstream, the Federals took time to complete their only extensive chore of destruction. Men of the 3rd Ohio filed off the main road and came up to the Round Mountain Iron Furnace, which they quickly set afire as well

★★★★★★★★★★★★★★★★★★★★★★★★

54. "Colonel Streight's Expedition: Journal of H. Breidenthal," p. 343.

55. *Official Records*, series I, vol. 23, pt. 1, pp. 290-91.

56. Henry, *"First With the Most" Forrest*, p. 152.

57. Agee, "Forrest-Streight Campaign," p. 22.

as mangled in various other ways.[58] A bit later, however, the entire brigade stumbled upon a treacherous parcel of land marked by "coal choppings," where timber had been cut and burned to charcoal to feed machine shops in Rome. During the night the raiders became lost and scattered as they wandered over the choppings area, across a confusion of wagon ruts and through a tangled maze of timber. Daylight found Streight frantically regrouping his command and leading it across the Chattooga via Dyke's Bridge. On the other shore, the soldiers turned south for the last leg of their trip to Rome.

Russell's detachment reached the city first, on the morning of Sunday, May 3. Unhappily, the captain learned that couriers from Forrest as well as a Gadsden citizen had preceded him to warn the city, Paul Revere fashion, of the enemy's approach. Armed inhabitants and two pieces of artillery now confronted Russell beyond cottonbale barriers. Duped by captured residents, who greatly exaggerated the size of the forces defending the place, Russell erroneously decided that Rome was impregnable. After some hesitation he turned back to rejoin Streight, ensuring that the expedition would result in utter failure.[59]

4

In the meantime, Forrest had closed in for the kill. After fording the Chattooga River, his refresned troopers had cornered Streight's main force in Lawrence, Alabama, where the colonel had halted for essential rest.

When the Confederates arrived, Streight had to wake his men to put them into lines of battle—where they quickly fell to sleep again, with bullets whistling overhead. The colonel tried to rally them into action, but finally concluded that "nature was exhausted."[60]

Despite apparently holding the upper hand, Forrest had only about six hundred troopers on the scene—the others had failed to keep up with the main force—while the Federal

★★★★★★★★★★★★★★★★★★★★★★★★

58. "Colonel Streight's Expedition: Journal of H. Breidenthal," p. 343; Roach, *The Prisoner of War*, p. 37.

59. Henry, *"First With the Most" Forrest*, pp. 152-55.

60. Foote, *The Civil War*, 2: 185; *Official Records*, series I, vol. 23, pt. 1, p. 292.

brigade numbered approximately one thousand three hundred. Perceiving that only a crafty man could succeed in this situation, the Rebel leader determined to make the widest possible display of his troops, so that his adversary might think himself outnumbered. Boldly he called on Streight to surrender, and a truce was called while the latter considered Forrest's terms.

Streight conferred with his subordinate commanders, who advised him to capitulate. He agreed with them that the men were worn out, their animals all but unmanageable, and most of his ammunition valueless. The colonel had formed the notion that Forrest had three times as many soldiers as he; and recently he had learned of Russell's failure at Rome. Yet, after deep thought and second guessing, he could not bring himself to surrender. He informed Forrest that he would continue to fight unless it could be proved to his satisfaction that he was indeed outnumbered.

Meeting with Streight in a woodlot, Forrest answered this strange request by a covert nod to one of his staff officers. The aide hurried back to the only artillery that had closed up—a two-gun section of Morton's battery—and ordered it to move back and forth along a ridge that Streight was facing. In addition Biffle and McLemore, on the flanks, marched portions of their regiments in and out of sight beyond the hills, in Streight's view. These movements made the colonel believe that a continuous stream of cavalry and cannon was swirling around him. Forrest aided the effectiveness of the ruse by interrupting his conference with Streight to issue frequent orders for the deployment of imaginary units.[61]

Streight stared over Forrest's shoulder for a long time, his eyes widening. Finally he could stand the sight no longer, and blurted out: "Name of God! How many guns have you got? There's fifteen I've counted already!"

Forrest turned in the direction the colonel faced and with a poker face replied, "I reckon that's all that has kept up."

"I won't surrender till you tell me how many men you've got!" cried Streight.

Forrest said cooly, "I've got enough to whip you out of your boots!"

★★★★★★★★★★★★★★★★★★★★★★

61. Henry, *"First With the Most" Forrest*, pp. 155-57.

The colonel thought things over once again, his frustration getting the better of his temper. Finally he repeated: "I won't surrender!"

At once Forrest turned to a bugler and ordered him to signal the main force to attack. But he had hardly spoken when Colonel Streight hollered: "I'll surrender!"

Forrest may have permitted himself the briefest of smiles. He told Streight to stack his arms and to march his men into a neighboring hollow, where the Confederate troopers would herd them into line as prisoners.[62]

And so the drama had come to an end at last. The number of Union soldiers who lay down their weapons, including Captain Russell's contingent, which Forrest later bagged when he moved on toward Rome, outweighed Forrest's force on hand nearly three to one.[63]

It was a humiliating end for Colonel Abel Streight, who during his journey across Alabama had shown more daring and initiative than a dozen or so of those comrades who had faced Bedford Forrest in earlier combat. Bad luck, harsh weather, ill-timed delays, and other difficulties beyond the accepted margin of error for such an operation had combined to make his expedition a debacle. All he had to show for his efforts were some minor acts of destruction to Confederate factories, supply bases, and wagon trains—as well as some bad moments that he had given the man who eventually had tricked him into surrendering.

For Nathan Bedford Forrest, the fruits of accomplishment were more numerous and much sweeter. By driving his troopers relentlessly, he had inflicted dozens of casualties upon the Federal raiders and had saved Bragg's communication lines. This, his most extraordinary victory to date, would help bolster Southern morale, still sagging after the bitter defeat at Murfreesboro, four months earlier. In the near future, news of Forrest's triumph would spread throughout the Confederacy and the cavalry chief would receive the thanks and acclaim of such officials as General Bragg and the Congress of the Confederate States of America.[64] In the mean-

★★★★★★★★★★★★★★★★★★★★★★

62. Lytle, *Bedford Forrest and His Critter Company,* p. 173.

63. Henry, *"First With the Most" Forrest,* p. 157.

64. *Official Records,* series I, vol. 23, pt. 1, p. 295.

time, the Yankee raiders would languish in various prison camps.

Perhaps a premonition that all of this would come to pass nagged Colonel Streight from the moment he agreed to surrender. Certainly he was painfully embarrassed after he handed over his men's weapons, for as soon as Forrest's units came forward out of the hills Streight saw that he had been hoodwinked. Pointing at the thin Confederate lines, he turned his apopleptic anger on Forrest, demanding that his men be given back their rifles, that they might continue to fight to the finish.

Bedford Forrest responded by throwing back his head and laughing loudly. Then, stifling his merriment, he patted Streight on the shoulder and said: "Ah, Colonel, all is fair in love and war, you know!"[65]

★★★★★★★★★★★★★★★★★★★★★★★

65. Lytle, *Bedford Forrest and His Critter Company*, p. 173.

4

THE BOLDEST THING EVER DONE

Grierson's Mississippi Raid (April 17-May 2, 1863)

1

When eight years old, Benjamin Henry Grierson was kicked in the face by a pony. The force of the blow split his forehead, badly sliced one of his cheeks, and left him blind for two months. The incident scarred him figuratively as well as literally: afterward, not unnaturally, he deeply distrusted all horses and did his utmost to avoid their company.[1]

In a stroke of irony perhaps unparalleled in American history, Grierson grew up to become one of the greatest leaders of volunteer cavalry during the Civil War, achieving one of the conflict's most spectacular feats of mounted campaigning. Seldom has a man overcome a childhood phobia with such a degree of success.

Even if the accident with the pony had never occurred,

★★★★★★★★★★★★★★★★★★★★★★★★

1. D. Alexander Brown, *Grierson's Raid: A Cavalry Adventure of the Civil War*, p. 25.

there was little in Grierson's civilian background to indicate that he was to become a renowned cavalryman—or, for that matter, a soldier at all. Born in Pittsburgh in 1826, he moved to Ohio with his family early in life and as a young man settled down to a profession as a produce merchant and part-time music teacher in the Youngstown area, and later in western Illinois. The life of an esthete suited his mild-mannered personality; he enjoyed composing music and organizing concert bands in his off hours.[2]

The approach of war led him into less gentle pursuits. By 1858 Grierson, now a solid citizen of Jacksonville, Illinois, was stumping the local community as a partisan of Abraham Lincoln. Lincoln's election as president in 1860 and the resulting intensification of national discord made Grierson realize that soon he would have to take an even more active part in the secession crisis. Early in '61 he answered Lincoln's first call for volunteers by marching to Cairo, Illinois to enlist in a state infantry unit.

Grierson would have preferred to remain in infantry service even if forced to serve as a private soldier, rather than accept a commission in the cavalry. But as luck had it, the state authorities decided that Ben Grierson was cavalry officer material. When the ranking commander in the western theater, Major General Henry Halleck, had a chance to size him up, he proclaimed him to be "active and wiry enough to make a good cavalryman." In time Grierson was given a major's commission in a mounted regiment, much to his dismay. He tried to avoid serving, asked for a transfer back to infantry service, but saw such attempts foiled time after time by the generals in command. Thus it was that Grierson, an avid hater of all horses, went off to war as a field officer in the 6th Illinois Volunteer Cavalry.[3]

Despite his misgivings, he proved the state authorities shrewd judges of military talent. He was by nature an intelligent and resourceful leader and was qualified to command in any branch of the service. He learned the subtleties of mounted warfare so quickly and so well as to become one of the best volunteer horse soldiers in the West. In large part,

★★★★★★★★★★★★★★★★★★★★★★★

2. Ezra J. Warner, *Generals in Blue: Lives of the Union Commanders,* p. 189; Earl Schenck Miers, *The Web of Victory: Grant at Vicksburg,* p. 148.

3. Brown, *Grierson's Raid,* p. 25.

Grierson and staff. FROM *Photographic History of the Civil War.*

too, his military prowess was aided by the fact that his soldiers were among the finest Illinois had to offer.[4]

By early 1862 Grierson had attained the colonelcy of his regiment, and in subsequent months command of a full brigade of cavalry devolved upon him. He demonstrated his competency in brigade leadership on many occasions, leading his men in scouting and reconnaissance duties, facing enemy guerrillas, and protecting the flanks of Major General William T. Sherman's infantry in lower Tennessee and upper Mississippi. His record did not show unbroken success—he had, for example, been unable to overtake Van Dorn's raiders during their retreat from Holly Springs, although a plethora of obstacles, including inept superior officers, had slowed his pursuit. Still, by the spring of '63 his reputation as an excellent regimental and brigade leader was well established.

It was this reputation that brought him to the attention of Ulysses Grant. And it was Grant who, in April of 1863, gave him the opportunity to lead a cavalry raid that was destined to become a model of its kind.

2

In that season Grant was ready to make his fifth attempt to capture the river stronghold of Vicksburg, a step that President Lincoln considered crucial to decisive strategic Federal victory.[5] Thus for Grant had been hamstrung by many factors, embracing a variety of logistical problems, dissension among his officer corps, and the alertness and tenacity of the Confederate forces under John Pemberton. Grant's inability to take the "Gibraltar of the West" had infected the entire North with symptoms of frustration and unrest. As a result, his position as ranking field general in the West had become precarious. During the previous winter, he had received unfavorable publicity when his projected overland campaign to Vicksburg had been cut short by Van Dorn's raiders. His troubles multiplied when a second disaster—Pemberton's

★★★★★★★★★★★★★★★★★★★★★★★

4. An infantryman commented on Grierson's soldiers: "I don't believe that Napoleon had any better cavalry than this brigade here for fighting. Second Iowa, 6th and 7th Illinois are the regiments, and well handled they'd whip the devil." Charles W. Wills, *Army Life of an Illinois Soldier,* p. 168.

5. Boatner, *The Civil War Dictionary,* pp. 871-73.

bloody repulse of Sherman at Chickasaw Bluffs—followed Van Dorn's strike by only a few days.

In short, Grant's new plan—which included an amphibious movement down the Mississippi and then an overland attack against Vicksburg from the east—had to succeed, or his personal fortunes might suffer disaster. Therefore he took all precautions to ensure that the spring campaign gained the maximum possible momentum. To divert Rebel attention from the movement and relieve some of the pressure Pemberton might bring to bear on the invaders of Mississippi, Grant proposed several cavalry raids, including a major one through the eastern portion of the state. Such expeditions might result in the destruction of railroad lines that carried badly needed supplies into the Confederate fort as well as divert reinforcements earmarked for Pemberton's army.[6]

The most important expedition had to be made by a force of seasoned, rugged cavalrymen guided by a leader of expertise. Grant at once made Grierson his favorite candidate for the position. As early as February the commanding general envisioned the nature of the cavalry strike. He wrote one of his chief subordinates, Major General Stephen A. Hurlbut, commanding the XVI Army Corps at Memphis: "It seems to me that Grierson, with about five hundred picked men, might succeed in making his way south, and cut the railroad east of Jackson, Miss. The undertaking would be a hazardous one, but it would pay well if carried out. . . ."

General Hurlbut then thrashed out the details of the project with the commander of his La Grange, Tennessee base, Brigadier General William Sooy Smith, Grierson's immediate superior. During their planning sessions, other experienced cavalry leaders were considered for the command. But Grant emphasized his preference when he wired Hurlbut again on March 9: "I look upon Grierson as being much better qualified to command this expedition than either [Colonel Albert] Lee or [Colonel John] Mizner. . . . The date when the expedition should start will depend upon movements here. You will be informed of the exact time for them to start." Thereafter Grierson was the only commander seriously considered for the task.

By April 10 the Tennessee and Mississippi roads had

★★★★★★★★★★★★★★★★★★★★★★★

6. Ulysses S. Grant, *Personal Memoirs*, 1: 460-61, 488-89.

thawed sufficiently to permit the movement Grant had in mind, and he all but completed preparations for his large amphibious campaign against Vicksburg. More specific instructions for conducting the raid were formulated on that date. By now the size of the raiding force had been enlarged to include three regiments—Grierson's 6th Illinois, plus the 7th Illinois and the 2nd Iowa Cavalry, and a mounted six-gun detachment from Battery K, 1st Illinois Artillery—in all, one thousand seven hundred men. The projected route lay southward through eastern Mississippi. On the first leg of the journey Grierson was supposed to send various detachments to destroy Confederate supply depots as well as the Mobile & Ohio Railroad, which ran parallel to the path of the main column. Then, after "destroying the wires, burning provisions, and doing all the mischief they can," the troopers were to pounce on the Vicksburg Railroad, which ran horizontally through the center of the state directly to Pemberton's army. The Vicksburg line was the major target of the raid; the cavalrymen were to thoroughly damage as much of it as possible. Finally, taking steps to elude any regular or local forces who gathered to stop them, Grierson's people should swing eastward into Alabama and make their way homeward through that state.[7]

The aims of the expedition seemed neat and simple on paper, but as Grant had so vividly predicted, the project would be both complicated and dangerous. The extent of the resistance that Grierson would encounter in Mississippi was a matter for conjecture. The Federal high command had received no detailed reports of large enemy forces stationed along the raiders' proposed route. Yet Pemberton, when he learned of the expedition, would certainly mobilize pursuit forces in many quarters. Then, too, there were garrison and outpost troops, plus many thousands of home guards, throughout the eastern half of the state. In fact, each sizable town that Grierson entered might be a Confederate stronghold. If the Federals did manage to evade such forces, their southward march would eventually bring them within range of the large Confederate army under Major General Franklin Gardner at Port Hudson, Louisiana. Lastly, when the raiders veered into Alabama on their homeward ride, they would

★★★★★★★★★★★★★★★★★★★★★★

7. Brown, *Grierson's Raid*, pp. 6-9.

enter the bailiwick of Bedford Forrest, who would eagerly put his command on their trail. (As it turned out, Forrest would find his time wholly occupied by the pursuit of Abel Streight's cavalrymen, but the Union high command had no sure foreknowledge of that situation.)

Most certainly, the conditions of the journey called for a commander with the ability to outsmart his opponents, to divert and confuse them, and to move his own soldiers swiftly and nimbly through enemy territory. Grierson filled this bill, and he did not fear matching wits with Pemberton. In truth, he hoped that he would encounter large-scale resistance. The very nature of the expedition meant that the number of Confederates dispatched to head off the raiders —Confederates thereby prevented from combating Grant's main army—would be an indication of the degree of success Grierson achieved.

3

April 17 brought excellent weather for the commencement of the raid. Under a polished blue sky, Grierson's troopers and artillerymen started south from General Smith's headquarters at La Grange, and wound through the pine forests of lower Tennessee.[8] Most of the one thousand seven hundred soldiers were eager to be off on what they supposed was merely a long reconnaissance that promised some excitement and diversion but a minimum of danger. The blue-coated cavalrymen were rugged and experienced—many were completing the two-year training period that was needed to create effective troopers—and they respected the commander who marched at the head of the column. They would follow Ben Grierson wherever he led them.

Moving at the normal three-miles-per-hour rate, the troopers soon crossed Wolf River and adjacent mountains, into Mississippi. Even as they marched, General Grant was leading thousands of infantrymen and cannon down the shore of the Mississippi River and was readying his fleet of thirty transports to make the run past the fort's heavy guns. Only passing time would indicate whether the simultaneous

★★★★★★★★★★★★★★★★★★★★★★

8. *Official Records,* series I, vol. 24, pt. 3, p. 202.

Grierson's raiding column. FROM *Photographic History of the Civil War.*

movements of Grant and Grierson accomplished desired results.

On the first day out, little occurred to disturb the regularity of the march. Few Confederates appeared, other than stragglers encountered near the town of Ripley.[9] The second day of the journey found Grierson's men crossing the Tallahatchie River at New Albany. The line of that stream marked the farthest penetration by an aborted amphibious expedition launched against Vicksburg earlier in the year. The crossing was made in leisurely fashion, with the horses being permitted to drink and rest once they had reached the far shore. However, a battalion of Colonel Edward Prince's 7th Illinois discovered that a neighboring bridge was held by some Confederates who had already partially dismantled the span to prevent the Yankees' crossing. Colonel Prince sent the battalion into the muzzles of the Rebels' rifles and watched his men chase off the guards. The cavalrymen repaired the bridge and crossed without further resistance. They then joined the balance of the command, which had forded the stream at a shallow crossing-point, and pushed on toward the village of Pontotoc.[10]

On the night of the 18th the raiders bivouacked on the estate of a planter named Sloan. Mr. Sloan had received no advance warning of the Yankees' approach and was flabbergasted as well as enraged when he saw troopers grazing their horses on his lawn, exchanging worn-out plugs for his best-blooded stock, and pilfering foodstuffs from his barn and smokehouse. When Grierson himself rode up, Sloan pleaded his case before him, but without result. Then both he and his wife began to moan piteously over their fate, the planter several times proclaiming that Grierson might as well take him out and cut his throat and be done with it.

Colonel Grierson, in addition to being fond of music, loved dramatics. Irritated by his host's incessant whining, he turned to one of his orderlies and said, after a concealed wink: "Mr. Sloan is very desirous of having his throat cut. Take him out in the field and *cut his throat, and be done with it!*" Carrying out his part in the little tableau, the orderly drew a huge hunting

★★★★★★★★★★★★★★★★★★★★★★★★

9. Brown, *Grierson's Raid*, pp. 7, 20.

10. Albert G. Brackett, *History of the United States Cavalry, From the Formation of the Federal Government to the 1st of June, 1863*, p. 290.

knife and waved it below the planter's chin, then grabbed the man and began to drag him toward the doorway.

Mrs. Sloan, entirely convinced that Grierson meant business, began to plead for her husband's release. Grierson allowed her to wring her hands for a few minutes before ordering Sloan freed. In the end, the colonel agreed to leave behind more than enough cavalry horses to compensate for the mounts carried off by his soldiers.[11]

Despite taking some pleasure from the little drama, Grierson could not afford to let his thoughts stray too long from the objectives of the raid. Neither could he shut his mind to the realization that by this time his advent must have been detected by enemy forces. The troops he had routed at the Tallahatchie bridge near New Albany would have brought warning of his approach to local commanders by now.

Unknown to him, Rebel home guardsmen near the town of Molino, several miles east of the main column, had alerted that part of the countryside to the movements of one of the Union regiments. Earlier that day Grierson had detached the 2nd Iowa, under Colonel Edward Hatch (another of those able but luckless cavalrymen who had pursued Van Dorn's raiders the previous December), and had sent it on a four-mile feint eastward toward the Mobile & Ohio line. The home guards at Molino had skirmished with Hatch's larger force, continually dogging the cavalry's heels and spreading word that at least six hundred of the enemy were running loose in east Mississippi.[12]

On the third day of the journey, the command plodded through a steady rain from the Sloan plantation to a point some miles south of Pontotoc. During this morning of the 19th Grierson also sent a number of small units to operate in various areas north, east, and west of the line of march, to divert attention from the movements of the main body. One such detachment made contact with Colonel Hatch, who was still moving southward along the line of the railroad, parallel to Grierson's path. Another unit moved northwestward to disperse Rebels reportedly organizing to form a local cavalry regiment. A third detachment galloped back to New Albany,

★★★★★★★★★★★★★★★★★★★★★★

11. E. L. Wolcott, comp., *Record of Services Rendered the Government by Gen. B. H. Grierson During the War*, p. 102.

12. *Official Records,* series I, vol. 24, pt. 1, pp. 529-30.

where it ran into a force of two hundred Confederates, skirmished fiercely with them, inflicting several casualties, then returned southward. When all three forces rejoined the main body, Grierson resumed his march toward Pontotoc. En route, he was also met by the 2nd Iowa; Hatch reported having captured a large number of those home guards who had harassed him the day before.

Early that evening, at Pontotoc, the main force encountered a band of guerrilla fighters, dispersed them after a short struggle, and seized, among other spoils, a great amount of mail and about four hundred bushels of salt. Wet and uncomfortable, the raiders spent that night at another plantation, this one five miles farther south, on the road toward Houston.[13]

Before he permitted himself some needed rest, Colonel Grierson sat down to write his wife, Alice, a letter—the only communication he found time to send home during the expedition. In it he expressed confidence that his operation would end in success and tried to assuage any fears his wife might have about the dangers he would yet have to face:

> . . . We have had considerable skirmishing with the rebels; killed and wounded a number, and captured about 25. No loss on our side, and no one injured. May have an opportunity of writing again in a week or two; if not, do not be uneasy. I have still faith and hope that all will be well. The column will move at 3 o'clock; want to march over 40 miles before night. This will be mailed to you at La Grange. I want to get one hours sleep, if possible, before starting. Love to all. Hastily, but truly and affectionately,
>
> B. H. G.[14]

4

Even though Grierson spent the early part of the 19th dispatching several diversionary forces, his efforts did not fool every Rebel commander in the eastern half of the state. Several of them began to suspect that the colonel was leading a dangerously large force and was sweeping south to strike at supply lines along the direct route into Vicksburg. Far from being an extended reconnaissance, as early appearances had

★★★★★★★★★★★★★★★★★★★★★★★

13. Ibid, pp. 522-23.

14. Wolcott, *Record of Services*, p. 95.

seemed to indicate, the Yankee movement posed a real threat to the security of communication lines, and thus had to be curtailed forthwith.

Lieutenant Colonel Clark R. Barteau, commander of the 2nd Tennessee (Confederate) Cavalry, was one of these discerning observers. When on the evening of the 19th he was apprised that a heavy Union mounted force was stationed at Pontotoc, he too at first thought it to be a scouting command. But as he studied the reports more closely, he began to realize the magnitude of the danger at hand. Quickly the lieutenant colonel put his men on the road and marched them toward Pontotoc throughout the evening. By dawn on the 20th he was slowly but steadily closing in on his quarry. By this time his own unit had been reinforced by another cavalry regiment and a mounted battalion of Mississippi state troops, with himself in overall command.[15]

That morning Barteau's troopers, many of them clad in butternut-colored uniforms rather than the usual gray, approached the environs of Pontotoc. There they found, to their surprise, a myriad of hoof prints that indicated that a large body of horsemen had recently gone northward toward the Tennessee border. Much time passed before the Confederates discovered that this was the result of another ruse that Grierson had played on his opponents.[16] Before dawn on that same morning the colonel had directed a "Quinine Brigade," composed of every ill soldier and jaded horse in his command, under Major Hiram Love of the 2nd Iowa, to leave the main column and return to La Grange. In addition to relieving the main force of all troopers who could not be expected to keep up a rapid marching pace, Love's operation would create the impression that a great many Yankees —perhaps, in Rebel minds, the entire force—had turned back.[17] (Love's was the force that would carry Grierson's reassuring letter to his wife.)

By the time Barteau discovered the true nature of the prints, he realized that Grierson's column was several hours

★★★★★★★★★★★★★★★★★★★★★★★

15. R. R. Hancock, *Hancock's Diary, or a History of the Second Tennessee Confederate Cavalry*, pp. 238-39.

16. Brown, *Grierson's Raid*, pp. 50, 53-54.

17. Brackett, *History of the United States Cavalry*, p. 293.

in advance of his pursuers, and still moving southward.[18] Raging, the lieutenant colonel ordered his march to resume at an even faster pace. He determined to catch Grierson even if that meant exhausting his horses and their riders.

Meanwhile, the Yankee invaders rode on, passing the village of Houston late in the afternoon and proceeding a dozen miles below the town before encamping for the night on the road to Starkville. That afternoon's march had gone very smoothly; the only Confederates the riders had encountered were civilians who stared in amazement at the long line of riders, inquiring, "Where are you'ns all going to?"[19]

Increasing numbers of Confederates in Mississippi were beginning to ask that question. That afternoon General Pemberton, who soon would have his hands full with Grant's army of invasion, had taken official note of Grierson's expedition. However, the tone of the message he wired to the departmental commander at Columbus, Mississippi, Brigadier General Daniel Ruggles, indicated that he was not vastly concerned with Grierson's advance: "This is a mere raid, but should not be unmolested by you."[20]

On the morning of April 21, Grierson planned still another diversionary effort. To again create the impression that the whole of his force had turned back, he directed Colonel Hatch and his Iowans, plus one of the artillery pieces in the column, to head back toward the Mobile & Ohio near West Point, destroy trackage and telegraph wires for a long distance, if feasible attack General Ruggles's headquarters at Columbus, and at last return to Tennessee by the safest route.[21] The remaining one thousand-odd cavalrymen of the 6th and 7th Illinois would continue south with Grierson.

Hatch's duties were many and difficult, but the Iowa officer was willing to carry them out to the ulmost of his abilities. His regiment filed out of the wooded bivouac in sodden darkness, trundling the single cannon behind. With much concern, Grierson watched the troopers ride off, realiz-

★★★★★★★★★★★★★★★★★★★★★★

18. Hancock, *Hancock's Diary*, p. 239.

19. R. W. Surby, *Grierson Raids . . . Also the Life and Adventures of Chickasaw, the Scout*, p. 28.

20. *Official Records*, series I, vol. 24, pt. 3, p. 770.

21. Wolcott, *Record of Services*, p. 97; Lyman B. Pierce, *History of the Second Iowa Cavalry*, p. 49.

ing that he would not hear how well they fared until after the close of the expedition.

In point of fact, they would fare very well. Hatch would find himself unable to carry out some of Grierson's instructions, such as inflicting further damage on the Mobile & Ohio, or attacking Columbus, but he would discharge the most important task required of him—drawing enemy pursuers from Grierson's trail.

Hatch got off to a late start on the morning he left camp. He had been unable to march until the Illinois regiments had hit the roads leading south, and the Illinoisians had been very leisurely in breaking camp. But once he moved off in the rainy dawn, Hatch headed quickly crosscountry toward the railroad.[22] In the vicinity of Palo Alto, several miles east of Grierson's latest bivouac, the Iowans collided with Lieutenant Colonel Barteau's command. Earlier, Barteau had detected Hatch's movements by following his horses' hoof marks on the trail; once again he believed that the newly discovered enemy unit constituted the whole of the Yankee raiding force. Now Barteau was ready to smash both Hatch's front and rear.

Barteau's force was larger than his opponent's, but the Federals had field experience whereas many of the Confederate state troops were pea green. Then, too, Colonel Hatch knew how to use his two-pounder cannon to great effect. Soon after the Tennesseans and Mississippians attacked him, Hatch broke up their charge with well-directed cannon fire. Some of the state troops panicked and broke in wild disorder. The other Confederates were held back by Company H of the 2nd Iowa until the remainder of Hatch's command could counterattack on horseback, their Colt's revolving rifles spattering furiously.[23] Eventually, the state troops were pushed rearward a distance of three miles, losing twenty-five of their number and inflicting no severe casualties upon Hatch's force. Some of Barteau's more experienced regulars skirted Hatch's flank, however, and at nightfall dug in between the Federals and the Mobile & Ohio line. Barteau knew that other Rebel forces had gotten word of Hatch's move-

★★★★★★★★★★★★★★★★★★★★★★★

22. *Official Records*, series I, vol. 24, pt. 1, p. 530.

23. Pierce, *Second Iowa Cavalry*, p. 50.

ments and by morning would be on the scene.[24] He had no knowledge of Grierson's operations farther south. Even had he spotted the hoof marks made by the main raiding column, he would have found it difficult, if not impossible, to believe that the Yankees would be so foolhardy as to march so deep into the Confederacy.

Hatch had no idea of remaining near Palo Alto until dawn. During the night he pulled his men out of the vicinity, crossed the Houlka River, and pounded off toward Okolona and points westward.[25] Finally he turned his men toward the north and started back for Tennessee, leaving his antagonists far behind. Next morning, Barteau was joined by an Alabama cavalry regiment and again started off in pursuit of Hatch, woefully unaware that he was rapidly moving in the opposite direction from that which Grierson had taken.

Colonel Hatch had little trouble reaching safety. His followers were delayed by all sorts of obstacles, including a deep and treacherous swamp, into which they stumbled; they had to countermarch, wasting valuable time, to continue their ride. Two days later Barteau managed to close the gap by furious riding and skirmished with Hatch's rear guard till the latter crossed and then burned a vital river bridge, ending the pursuit. Hatch traveled on without further molestation and returned to La Grange on the 26th. He had effectively misled Grierson's opponents as well as destroyed a great quantity of public property, gathered up some six hundred horses from the countryside, and liberated two hundred slaves.

There was nothing left for the frustrated Barteau, whose soldiers had spent six days covering 240 miles during a fruitless march, but to return to the Okolona vicinity and await further orders.[26]

5

On the 21st, the day he sent Hatch toward Palo Alto, Grierson rode slowly through the town of Starkville and to-

★★★★★★★★★★★★★★★★★★★★★★★

24. Hancock, *Hancock's Diary*, pp. 239-40.

25. *Official Records*, series I, vol. 24, pt. 1, p. 530.

26. Hancock, *Hancock's Diary*, pp. 240-41; Pierce, *Second Iowa Cavalry*, p. 52.

ward Louisville. The next day he sent two battalions, one from the 6th and the other from the 7th Illinois, to seize the latter village and destroy a nearby tannery and leather-goods factory. In due course the column trotted through the streets of Louisville, arousing the fears of the townspeople. But as Grierson later reported: "Those who remained at home acknowledged that they were surprised. They had expected to be robbed, outraged, and have their houses burned. On the contrary, they were protected in their persons and property."[27]

On this sixth day of the expedition, Colonel Grierson grew acutely aware that Rebel troops must be surrounding him. By now Hatch's movement would have been discovered to be of a diversionary nature. By now, also, enemy telegraphers must be sitting by their instruments, ready to transmit orders for the massing of pursuit columns as soon as they received timely word of the Yankees' appearance in a specific area. Clearly, still another detached operation was called for. Even before reaching Louisville, Grierson had discussed that matter with Colonel Prince and with his aid had selected B Company of the 7th Illinois, under Captain Henry Forbes, and ordered it to dash eastward to the town of Macon. At that depot on the Mobile & Ohio, Forbes was supposed to attract widespread notice, and, if possible, destroy a railroad bridge in the vicinity. That done, he had the option of attempting to rejoin the main column or following Colonel Hatch's trail to La Grange.

Once again Grierson's choice as leader of a diversionary movement reflected astute judgment. Henry Forbes was one of the finest volunteer army officers Illinois had bred —intelligent, sensitive, and brave. He wasted no time before riding off with the thirty-four men under him—one of them his younger brother, Sergeant Stephen Forbes—and made a conspicuous showing of his presence in the area marked out for his journey.[28]

Forbes's company reached the Macon vicinity after a twenty-four-hour jaunt, but found it too well guarded to be captured by so small a force. Yet he did set townspeople to

****

27. Wolcott, *Record of Services*, p. 97.

28. Brown, *Grierson's Raid*, pp. 78-79.

babbling about the Yankee invaders, then headed southwestward to rejoin Grierson—if he could.

At several other stopovers, including the small village of
Philadelphia, Forbes ran into home guardsmen who dog-
gedly attempted to fight off the raiders. The captain made
short work of such fighting, capturing and paroling the inexperienced troops and damaging their weapons beyond repair. As the Yankees continued farther, however, guerrillas
and bushwhackers took pot-shots at them from both sides of
the road.[29]

On April 25, the third day of his side operation, Forbes
decided to return to the Mobile & Ohio, to do further damage to its right-of-way. He found the depot at Enterprise
garrisoned by a great many Rebels, but by some bold-faced
lying convinced the enemy commander that his thirty-four
men were the advance contingent of a force many times that
number only a short distance away. Forbes went so far as to
call for the garrison's surrender, giving his opposite number
in gray "One hour only for consideration, after which
further delay will be at your peril."

While the Confederates deliberated, Forbes and his soldiers remounted and put spurs to their horses. In minutes,
they were beyond the reach of the troops in Enterprise and
were hurrying again after Grierson's column. It was well that
they rode off so quickly, for by that evening more than two
thousand train-bound Rebels were scouring the countryside
above and below Enterprise, ready to battle what they supposed to be a Federal cavalry force of comparable size.

Forbes's return trip was less hazardous than his journey
toward the railroad, for only home guards and guerrillas
were spied along the last leg of the march. Some of his advance riders, disguised as Alabama cavalrymen, learned from
local citizens of the approximate route taken by Grierson's
men. On the 26th, after five days of riding, Company B
overtook the column as it was about to cross the Strong River
near the town of Westville and then burn the bridge.
Nineteen-year-old Stephen Forbes, sent ahead to bring advance word of the company's return, rode up to Colonel
Grierson, saluted, and stated proudly: "Captain Forbes pre-
sents his compliments, and begs to be allowed to burn his

★★★★★★★★★★★★★★★★★★★★★★★

29. Ibid., pp. 81-85, 98-99, 116-17.

bridges for himself!" Grierson—who for several days had feared for the safety of the prodigal unit—grinned at the young sergeant. Congratulating him for his enterprise, the colonel assured him that the span would not be fired till his brother and the rest of the company had crossed.[30]

While Forbes and his men were making such a success of their operation, the main column had been handling the most vital work to be done during the expedition.

Marching south from Louisville on the 22nd, Grierson's men had come upon a succession of deep, dangerous swamplands near the Noxubee River, in which many horses had foundered and drowned and riders had been forced to splash through the stagnant water to reach safety. After nightfall the command moved over roads that seemed no less hazardous. One cavalry historian noted: "This deary night-march was made along dark roads, rendered doubly black by the overhanging branches of the great trees which loomed up on each side of the way in the swamp."[31]

Daylight on April 23 brought some relief from this ordeal. Struggling out of the river bottoms, the column took a muddy road toward Philadelphia and the flooded Pearl River, which flowed six miles above the village. The bridge there was especially important because high water precluded a fording operation.[32] To secure the structure, Grierson decided to send Lieutenant Colonel William Blackburn of the 7th Illinois to reach the river and challenge any Rebel soldiers or citizens who might be guarding the span. With Blackburn would go the half-dozen cavalrymen who comprised the so-called Butternut Guerrillas.

The Guerrillas were a hand-picked force of young and enterprising scouts whom Grierson had collected during the first days of the raid. They rode at the point of the column, some miles in advance of the main body, to inspect the countryside through which the entire command would eventually march. The scouts moved about inconspicuously because they had procured either citizens' clothes or butternut-colored uniforms such as many of the Mississippi state troops wore.

★★★★★★★★★★★★★★★★★★★★★★★★

30. Ibid., pp. 128-32, 140-42.

31. Brackett, *History of the United States Cavalry,* p. 294.

32. Wolcott, *Record of Services,* p. 98.

Two of the Guerrillas were particularly notable. In many ways, the leader, Colonel Blackburn, rivaled J. E. B. Stuart as an extravagant, daring warrior. A man of action, he could be counted on to commit himself to any charge or pitched battle, no matter the size of the opposition—a quality that more than a few times had led him into dangerous situations. Sergeant Richard Surby, one of his most experienced noncommissioned officers, was almost as energetic and pugnacious as he, although more prudent and less dramatic. A thirty-two-year-old Canadian who had moved to Illinois some years ago, Surby had a keen eye and cool nerves, and was, as he himself later phrased it, "possessed of a venturesome disposition." In after years he would pen one of the most vivid accounts of the Grierson expedition.

Early on the 23rd the Butternut Guerrillas rode forward to the Pearl River bridge, carrying explicit instructions from Grierson to secure the span immediately if unguarded, but to use extra caution in approaching it if held by a sizable group of Confederates. After a gallop down a narrow country road, Sergeant Surby and a few comrades, riding ahead of the other scouts, came within sight of the bridge and met an old gentleman approaching on a mule. In civilian attire, Surby did not arouse suspicion, and the old man stopped to chat with him. The conversation revealed that five citizens were guarding the bridge; one was the man's son. They had piled cumbustibles upon the partially dismantled bridge floor and were ready to light the materials should Yankees appear on the road.

A minute later Surby and his companions dropped their disguises and closed in on the man. The sergeant, pistol in hand, began to growl in his most menacing voice: "It lies in your power to save your buildings from the torch, to save your own life, and probably that of your son, by saving the bridge!"

While the old man trembled with fear, Surby directed him to go to the bridge and advise the guards to surrender and accept paroles. Otherwise the raiders would burn his nearby home and ruin all his property and possessions.

When the man started off, Surby and a few of his companions followed to within three hundred yards of the bridge, where they halted to watch him approach the guards. As the old man talked, the Federal sergeant examined the span, which stood on a solid trestlework across the muddy, churning river. Many of the wooden side-rails on both edges of the bridge were no longer intact. Should the guards dismantle the span further, there would be no way the raiders could hope to cross the stream safely.[33]

Surby and friends did not have to linger in concealment for long. The story that the old man had relayed brought action almost instantly: the guards jumped upon waiting horses even before he had finished talking, and pounded off into the distance. Looking back upon the tense situation in later years, Surby wrote: "This incident is mentioned as one of the many in which the *Power above* seemed [to be] shielding us from harm. . . ."[34]

After the Butternut Guerrillas had repaired the captured bridge, Grierson's soldiers rode up and crossed upon it. The colonel was supremely relieved to find that his good luck still held. He praised the scouts for their intrepidity, but left them little time to savor the compliments. Toward the close of the day, after his regiments had passed through Philadelphia, Grierson mapped another mission for the point riders. The new assignment concerned Newton Station, a depot on the Vicksburg Railroad that was the primary objective of the expedition.

Below Philadelphia the raiders were only a few miles from the strategic railroad line. To make certain that he would not ride into a trap when he entered the town, Grierson sent Colonel Blackburn, Surby and his crew, plus two battalions of the 7th Illinois, to reach the depot ahead of the main force and evaluate its defenses.

The two hundred men sent out under Blackburn's leadership reached the town of Decatur, just above the railroad, early on the morning of the 24th.[35] At six A. M. they crossed the Vicksburg line and found they could enter Newton Station without fear; few uniformed Confederates were stationed there. Surby and his men went among the townspeople, creating little suspicion and garnering information concerning the arrival times of incoming trains. In short order the rest of Blackburn's detachment trooped into the

★★★★★★★★★★★★★★★★★★★★★★

33. Brown, *Grierson's Raid,* pp. 72-74, 94-95.

34. Surby, *Grierson Raids,* p. 38.

35. Brackett, *History of the United States Cavalry,* p. 294.

depot, causing the citizens to stand about, gawking at the invading horde.

Although the town seemed all but devoid of Rebel soldiers, Blackburn and his soldiers experienced some tense minutes upon hearing the whistle of a locomotive, which was approaching the station from the east. The train might be carrying armed men, sent to run down the Yankees. At once the lieutenant colonel deployed pickets throughout the town, afterward concealing dozens of soldiers behind buildings and foliage along the right-of-way.

Shortly after the cavalrymen had taken up their posts, the train chugged onto the depot siding and squealed to a halt with a blast of steam. At a given signal, the Federals nearest the train rushed on foot from their hiding places, their pistols and carbines at the ready. Only after the crew of the train surrendered did the soldiers find that it contained no enemy troops, but did hold valuable supplies for the Rebel forces in Vicksburg, chiefly ordnance and commissary stores.[36]

An hour later, when Grierson and the main force galloped up to the depot, they found that Blackburn had also captured a second train, a passenger express that had been heading eastward. The Federals emptied both trains, which, as Grierson later wrote, were then "exploded and otherwise rendered completely unserviceable." In addition, the soldiers tore up a long stretch of track, destroyed a bridge half a mile west of the station, and captured seventy-five prisoners, comprising the train crews and a few local warriors. Leaving no avenue unexplored, Grierson sent a detachment to rip down telegraph wires and smash other nearby bridges. Finally, after his cavalrymen had thoroughly destroyed the military utility of Newton Station, Grierson ordered them to hurry back to their horses and fall into line. After company officers smoothed the marching formation, the long ride resumed.

The march continued southward to Montrose, several miles below the depot, where Grierson bivouacked his soldiers, who had ridden hard for the past forty hours. Whether or not the majority of the command slept soundly, the commanding officer was bothered that night by the

★★★★★★★★★★★★★★★★★★★★★★

36. Wolcott, *Record of Services*, p. 98; Brown, *Grierson's Raid*, pp. 107-10.

knowledge that on either side of the column, as well as to its rear, the hounds were closing in. By intercepting telegraph messages and questioning Mississippians, Grierson had learned that General Pemberton had set in motion a wide-scale plan to bag the raiders. With the countryside beginning to swarm with local defenders, there was no way to gauge how much longer the invaders' luck could survive.[37]

However, the next day revealed that Grierson was still on top of the situation. One of the Butternut Guerrillas, roving far from the main force, met a large command of Confederate cavalry that was unwittingly following a path that would lead it across the Federals' line of march. The scout, who had been raised just above the Kentucky line and possessed a passable Southern accent, convinced the Rebels that he was a local citizen who had been forced to serve as a guide to the Yankee column, and had recently been paroled as a prisoner. When cross-examined by his captors, he exaggerated the size of Grierson's force and stated that it was moving eastward toward the Mobile & Ohio. Entirely deceived, the Rebels marched in that direction and so did not meet the Federals in battle.[38]

Despite Grierson's continuing good fortune, it was true that many other pursuit forces had taken up the hue and cry. Pemberton was compelled to concentrate on many important matters other than the Yankee force that had recently cut his eastward line of supply. By this time Grant's flotilla had made its run down the river past Vicksburg, and the situation demanded Pemberton's immediate attention. Nevertheless, the Confederate commander found the time to wire several local leaders in east Mississippi to track down the raiders.

Already, for example, he had sent Major General W. W. Loring to Meridian, Mississippi, a short distance east of Grierson's route, to take command of an infantry force that had assembled there, and to lead it in pursuit of the Yankees.[39] And on April 24, when he got word of Grierson's presence at Newton Station, Pemberton dispatched several

★★★★★★★★★★★★★★★★★★★★★★

37. Wolcott, *Record of Services,* p. 98.

38. Brown, *Grierson's Raid,* pp. 124-26.

39. John C. Pemberton, *Pemberton: Defender of Vicksburg,* p. 102.

other pursuit troops. He sent Colonel John Adams and three infantry regiments to Morton, about twelve miles west of the depot, to prevent Grierson from riding toward Jackson, the state capital. To cut off a northward Federal retreat, Brigadier General James R. Chalmers, with an infantry brigade, was ordered to Okolona. In an attempt to block a retreat toward the northwest, Pemberton even instructed Brigadier General Lloyd Tilghman to deploy forces in and near Carthage, Mississippi. Finally, cavalry belonging to General Gardner's army in upper Louisiana were told to block southward routes along the Jackson-New Orleans Railroad, east of Baton Rouge.[40] If Pemberton's plans were carried out to the letter, a multijawed trap would soon close on the Federal raiders.

6

The day after the quick-thinking scout deceived the large Rebel contingent tracking Grierson, Captain Forbes returned to the column at the Strong River bridge, amid comrades' shouts that "Company B has come back!" When Forbes was reunited with his commander, he learned that Grierson was now trudging southwestward to elude his followers. Striking out from Newton Station during Forbes's absence, the raiding leader had made a fateful decision. Although his orders called for him to retreat into Alabama after hitting the Vicksburg line, he had opted to march some miles farther through Confederate-held Mississippi. He realized the move might prove suicidal; yet he believed it no more hazardous than an attempt to fight his way again northward through country now rife with mounted Rebels.

Early on the 27th Grierson sent Colonel Prince and his regiment to seize ferry boats on the lower portion of the Pearl River, the shallower upper reaches of which the column had crossed four days before. A martinet, Prince was popular neither with his soldiers nor with Grierson, who felt that he possessed several military failings; however, on this occasion the Illinois officer turned in a creditable performance. At the crossing site he impersonated a Confederate officer so well

★★★★★★★★★★★★★★★★★★★★★★

40. Boatner, *The Civil War Dictionary*, p. 360.

that the local ferry operator hustled to make several vessels available.

Even after transporting the Illinois soldiers over the river, the ferryman, deceived by their dust- and mud-covered uniforms, believed them to be Confederates. Supposing that Grierson was the Rebel officer in command, he treated the colonel and his staff to a lavish breakfast at his nearby home. Grierson sat down at table with the man, his wife, and daughters, and later recollected: "The breakfast was well served, the ladies were all smiles, when up came some blunderhead and blurted out something to me about the 'Sixth Illinois Cavalry,' and what they were doing. The countenances of the hosts changed and some persons immediately left the room."[41]

After the meal, Grierson decided to pull another bold stunt to confound his enemy. Noting that his brigade now stood only twenty-five miles below Jackson, temporary headquarters of General Pemberton, he sent some of his men into a nearby telegraph shack and had them send a carefully worded message to Pemberton himself. "The Yankees have advanced to Pearl River," the telegram read, "but finding the ferry destroyed they could not cross, and have left, taking a northeasterly direction." Grierson must have chuckled at this latest ruse, realizing that the already harassed Pemberton would soon visualize Federal troopers sweeping toward his command post.[42]

Perhaps the deception was unnecessary. Although he continued to barrage departmental commanders with orders to overtake the raiders, General Pemberton was now flailing about almost blindly. He was so thoroughly confused by the movements of Grierson's diversionary forces that the day before he had commanded one general to concentrate his men in an area some two hundred miles north of Grierson's true position.[43]

In his desperate search for the Yankees, Pemberton dislocated a crucial portion of his Mississippi River defense line, exactly the sort of mistake Grant and Grierson had hoped he

★★★★★★★★★★★★★★★★★★★★★★

41. Wolcott, *Record of Services*, p. 104.

42. Brown, *Grierson's Raid*, pp. 148-49.

43. D. Alexander Brown, "Grierson's Raid," *Civil War Times Illustrated* 3 (January 1965): 11.

would make.[44] On the 27th he ordered Colonel Wirt Adams's cavalry out of western Mississippi, the area in which Grant was about to push his boatloads of soldiers ashore, and sent the troopers eastward after Grierson. Adams's orders were terse: "Annoy and ambush them if possible. Move rapidly." But by leaving the Rebel infantry stationed on that stretch of the Mississippi without mobile support, Pemberton ensured that Grant's landing near Grand Gulf would go largely unopposed.[45]

Although Grierson's bogus telegram stated that he was moving northeastward, he turned his column to the southwest on April 26 and headed toward the very region that Wirt Adams's cavalry was evacuating. Before leaving Tennessee, Grierson had been apprised of Grant's timetable for landing his army below Vicksburg; now he considered linking up with the landing forces near Grand Gulf or Port Gibson. While riding steadily westward, various segments of the raiding column again filed off to right and left for the purpose of destroying Rebel supply depots, telegraph lines, and trackage along the third railroad they had encountered, the New Orleans & Jackson, which they crossed at Hazlehurst.[46]

On the afternoon of the 28th, the twelfth day of the expedition, the Federals in the main portion of the command were set upon by the first large pursuit force to catch them. Near Union Church Grierson halted his column to allow his weary troopers to rest and his hungry animals to feed. During the interval, Wirt Adams's cavalrymen, having ably fulfilled their orders, came up and showered minié balls upon the Yankee pickets, wounding one of them. At first startled, Colonel Grierson formed his men and charged into the leading element of the enemy force, sending its men whirling through the country town. The Rebels reorganized north of Union Church and set up an artillery battery, but after being threatened by a detachment of the 7th Illinois, which formed in their rear, decided to turn right and ride back toward the Mississippi shore.

Grierson made a demonstration in that same direction, to

★★★★★★★★★★★★★★★★★★★★★

44. Pemberton, *Pemberton*, p. 102.

45. Brown, *Grierson's Raid*, p. 157.

46. *Official Records*, series I, vol. 24, pt. 1, pp. 525–26.

give the impression that he too intended to continue toward the river. But now he once again changed his course. The encounter with Adams's troopers had increased his concern about the dangers confronting his command. So he collected his men, headed eastward and finally turned south, this time with the intention of riding through to Louisiana.[47] Baton Rouge was the nearest city known to be in Federal hands, but it lay more than one hundred miles away. For at least a few days more, Grierson's good fortune would have to hold.

The tired march resumed, with the cavalrymen plodding through small villages in lower Mississippi, including Brookhaven (in which Grierson's advance troops routed a poorly armed force of five hundred citizens and conscripts), Bogue Chitto, and Summit. In and near these places the raiders destroyed public property of import to the enemy, especially railroad track, trestle work, and telegraph cable. At Bogue Chitto the Federals also wrecked a fifteen-car freight train, but in his official report Grierson sounded more pleased that he had captured "a very large secession flag."[48] An even longer train was found on the siding at Summit and it too was smashed and ruined, along with a large cache of government sugar and thirty barrels of rum. The liquor was destroyed primarily because Grierson's own troopers began casting fond glances at it: the colonel did not wish his men to complete the final leg of the expedition while reeling in their saddles from the effects of inebriation. The detail he assigned to destroy the rum "with great reluctance stove in the head of each barrel," according to Sergeant Surby, "and thus did waste the balm of a thousand flowers."[49]

In an attempt to make it appear as if he planned to continue along the New Orleans & Jackson, Grierson marched southward out of Summit, certain that the residents would misdirect pursuers. After the rear guard had cleared the village, however, the column angled off to the southwest, to put itself on a direct course for Baton Rouge.

That evening the raiders bivouacked on a plantation fifteen miles below Summit. Unknown to them, two enemy

★★★★★★★★★★★★★★★★★★★★★★★

47. Ibid., p. 527.

48. Wolcott, *Record of Services*, p. 99.

49. Brown, *Grierson's Raid*, p. 184.

units were only a short distance behind them, one being the force that had surprised them at Union Church. Wirt Adams had retraced his steps in a second trial at nabbing the invaders, and had placed his men in camp just five miles from them. However, Adams had no idea that he was so close to his adversaries. Additionally, three companies of mounted infantry under Tennessee Colonel Robert V. Richardson, which had personally been dispatched by Pemberton, were this night surrounding Summit, in which they believed the Federals to be lingering, ready to pounce on them when dawn came. Richardson had previously tried to contact Adams's unit and form a junction with it. But he had been unable to locate it, and in turn, Adams knew nothing of Richardson's presence in the vicinity.

By dawn on May 1 Grierson's soldiers were moving through the timberlands between the Amite and Tickfaw Rivers, coming ever nearer to their ultimate destination. The soldiers in the column were nearly exhausted from two weeks of continual travel. Their uniforms were sweat-stained and begrimed beyond recognition, and their mounts were dropping by the wayside in droves. Fortunately, few men had to march afoot, for local plantations furnished Grierson with enough animals—but barely enough—to keep the march going. The soldiers had not been told the location to which they were moving, and unanswered questions were roving up and down the column. Some of Surby's comrades on the point calculated that they were now less than one hundred miles from New Orleans. "Were we going there?" the sergeant wondered. The idea seemed farfetched, but no one other than Grierson's highest-ranking subordinates knew that he had opted for Baton Rouge.[50]

Late in the morning of the 1st, Surby's unit discovered the tracks of an enemy force that had moved in the direction the raiders themselves must take to cross Wall's Bridge over the Tickfaw. When he learned the news, Grierson sent Lieutenant Colonel Blackburn and the Butternut Guerrillas ahead to reconnoiter the bridge.

Riding in front of his comrades once again, the resourceful Surby came upon two small groups of Confederates deployed near the span; the sergeant captured them with ease. But as

★★★★★★★★★★★★★★★★★★★★★★★

50. Ibid., pp. 186-88.

he herded his prisoners toward the rear, Colonel Blackburn came up with the rest of the scouts and ordered them to follow him across a cotton field that led toward the bridge. Suspecting that a Rebel force was waiting in ambush within a woodlot beyond the river, Surby was surprised to see Blackburn press onward without waiting for the advance guard of the main column to close up with him. Yet the sergeant followed his commander, pistol in hand, his eyes nervously scanning the far shore.

Surby's foresight was keen, for even before Blackburn had reached the bridge a barrage of shots came from the foliage on the other side. But the lieutenant colonel dearly loved action, and did not slacken his pace. He charged across the span, Surby and the scouts close behind, waving their swords and firing their revolvers.

"It seemed as though a flame of fire burst forth from every tree," Surby later recalled. Before they could gain the far bank, Blackburn's horse went down with a bullet wound, and the colonel, himself shot, toppled onto the bridge floor, blood trickling down his forehead and into his dark beard. Surby, struck by a minié ball in the right thigh, painfully dismounted from his horse.[51]

Soon afterward the Federal advance guard, riding some distance ahead of the balance of the command, appeared on the scene and made an ill-advised charge over the bridge in Blackburn's wake. However, the Confederates—a cavalry pursuit contingent dispatched from Port Hudson by General Gardner—wounded three of the troopers and captured five others, forcing their comrades to retreat in haste across the span.

Finally Grierson and the main column came up to the Tickfaw. The colonel at once emplaced his cannon and blasted the Rebels's hidingplaces, then charged a battalion of troopers across the span, while other units forded the river in flanking movements. Outgunned, the enemy took to their heels, and were pursued across the Louisiana line by part of the 6th Illinois. In the skirmish at Wall's Bridge, several raiders had been so badly injured that they were able to travel no farther, and had to be left behind, where they would soon fall into Confederate hands. Those later captured included

★★★★★★★★★★★★★★★★★★★★★★★

51. Surby, *Grierson Raids*, p. 110.

Blackburn and Surby. The sergeant survived and eventually was paroled and exchanged, but the fire-eating Blackburn died of his head and chest wounds while a prisoner.[52]

The fighting at the bridge had been the bloodiest encounter of the expedition, but was the last Grierson would have to endure. From this point on, he and his men were home free. After tending to the injured soldiers, the raiders proceeded into Louisiana, with less than sixty miles left to travel.

7

It was fortunate that the ordeal was almost over. The men of the 6th and 7th Illinois were in no shape to fight another delaying action, let alone a sustained skirmish. Nor could they be counted on to perform a routine diversionary movement, had there been time to launch one. For almost fifty miles Grierson kept them moving only in one direction, southwestward, across the Amite and Comite Rivers—barely avoiding several pursuers near Williams's Bridge—and into middle Louisiana. He himself was so weary from fifteen days of nerve-wracking and bone-numbing travel that he had all he could do to keep himself alert in the saddle.

Early on May 2, three miles west of the Comite, the column stopped for another rest period on an extensive Southern estate. Most of the soldiers did not even bother to draw rations before falling into a sound slumber beside their equally tired animals. To keep himself awake, Grierson entered the plantation house, found a piano in the parlor, and did what came naturally to him—pounded out a rousing tune. The occupants of the house stood about, staring at him in wonderment.[53]

While the colonel was fortifying himself with music, two troops of Federal cavalry, sent out from Baton Rouge by Major General C. C. Augur, cautiously approached the raiders' resting place.[54] Learning of their advent, Grierson tore himself away from the piano and rode down the trail to meet

★★★★★★★★★★★★★★★★★★★★★★★★

52. Brown, *Grierson's Raid*, pp. 199-203.

53. Ibid., pp. 203-15.

54. S. L. Woodward, "Grierson's Raid, April 17th to May 2d, 1863," *Journal of the U. S. Cavalry Association* 15 (1904-5): 110.

them. The newcomers were suspicious of Grierson's mud-spattered troopers, thinking they might be Confederate irregulars. They had heard no rumors of a Union raiding force ranging through the state.

Grierson dismounted and walked toward them, waving a handkerchief and calling out his name. When he reached them, the Baton Rouge soldiers ascertained his identity and gave him a rousing shout of welcome. A short time afterward Grierson rounded up his men for the last trek, and led them along the road into the Louisiana capital, six miles away, escorted by Augur's patrol.

The citizens of Baton Rouge, though loyal Confederates, turned out in mass to witness Grierson's triumphal entry. They sensed that these tattered, dirty-looking troopers—who had marched the final eighty miles of their statewide journey in twenty-eight hellish hours—were brave men.[55] In fact, one Southerner who had met the Yankees in the course of their travels through Mississippi had admitted, with unconcealed admiration: "You are doing the boldest thing ever done."[56]

The man had hardly exaggerated. These soldiers had ridden through an entire state, eluding all manner of pursuers, had wrecked more than fifty miles' worth of rail lines, had devastated numerous supply bases, had distracted Pemberton's attention from many of Grant's operations, and in the process had lost only three men killed and seven wounded—incredible feats as well as bold.

It is likely that neither Grierson nor his soldiers realized the truly continental significance of the six hundred-mile, sixteen-day campaign just completed. The annals of American military history had not recorded an operation of comparable scope, and never would again.

The deeds accomplished by the former Illinois music teacher and the one thousand troopers who had followed him from La Grange to Baton Rouge would garner widespread and unqualified praise for a very long time. Signifying as it did the first wholly successful large-scale Union cavalry raid of the conflict, a raid outdoing anything previ-

★★★★★★★★★★★★★★★★★★★★★★★

55. Boatner, *The Civil War Dictionary*, p. 360; *Official Records*, series I, vol. 15, p. 1075.

56. Wolcott, *Record of Services*, p. 109.

ously attempted by the most daring Confederate riders, an expedition whose results had not been anticipated by even the high command who had authorized its launching, Grierson's operation fully measured up to the description later given it by General Sherman. "The most brilliant expedition of the war," Sherman called it with terseness, insight, and ample justification.[57]

★★★★★★★★★★★★★★★★★★★★★★

57. Brown, "Grierson's Raid," 32.

5

RIVER ON FIRE

*The Jones-Imboden West Virginia Raid
(April 20-May 22, 1863)*

1

Late in 1862, Governor John Letcher warned the Virginia Legislature: "The Baltimore and Ohio rail road has been a positive nuisance to this state, from the opening of this war to the present time; and unless its management shall hereafter be in friendly hands, and the government under which it exists be a part of our Confederacy, it must be abated. . . ."

Letcher was entirely correct to focus his concern on the Baltimore & Ohio system, one of the greatest communications resources available to the Union armies. Yet he understated his case; the term *nuisance* was hardly powerful enough to convey an impression of the menace that the road posed to the Confederacy, for it was a primary base for Federal military operations in both the Trans-Allegheny and lower Shenandoah Valley theaters of combat. As the shortest route between the Potomac and Ohio Rivers, its trains transported a vast amount of troops, matériel, and rations to Yankee garrisons and outposts in several states. Then, too, timber and coal cars that traveled its route brought fuel to thousands of homes throughout the North as well as to the

Federal navy, whose blockading ships were slowly strangling the Southern coast.[1]

By every standard of judgment, the B & O was one of the South's most vexing problems. Because it stretched for five hundred miles through portions of three states,[2] it seemed vulnerable to hit-and-run raiding. Yet, most of its trackage ran through areas in which loyal Confederates were in short supply. Maryland was a border neutral, Ohio was strong for the Union, and even that section of Virginia through which the road crawled—the mountainous and thickly forested northwestern corner of the state—was a sanctuary for Unionist settlers. Much of the road lay near the southern border of Pennsylvania and its easternmost section connected Washington, D. C. to Baltimore: Confederates bent on damaging the line could operate neither freely nor comfortably in such areas. Nevertheless, the great amount of traffic that the road made available to the Union made inevitable Confederate attempts at sabotage.

The most ambitious project aimed at cutting the road was launched in the spring of '63, a time in which such an expedition ought to have appeared impractical from the standpoint of weather conditions. In that season, most of western Virginia was colored white and brown—white from late and heavy snow, and brown from mud-coated roads produced by intermittent rain. The fortunes of the Confederate forces had turned as bitter as the climate, for part of Lee's Army in Virginia was starving, ill-clothed, and cold. As it happened, a major factor contributing to the organizing of the project was Lee's hope that forces sent into the well-stocked counties in the northwest could confiscate enough beef cattle to alleviate his soldiers' hunger.[3]

There were other objectives to the plan, most of them directly concerning the B & O. In addition to gathering cattle, horses, and grain, the raiders who would handle the job were to destroy all bridges, depot property, and rolling stock along the line between Oakland, Maryland, and Grafton, Virginia,

★★★★★★★★★★★★★★★★★★★★★★

1. Festus P. Summers, *The Baltimore And Ohio in the Civil War*, p. 118.

2. Festus P. Summers, "The Baltimore and Ohio—First in War," *Civil War History* 7 (September 1961): 239.

3. Robert B. Boehm, "The Jones-Imboden Raid Through West Virginia," *Civil War Times Illustrated* 3 (May 1964): 15.

a distance of about thirty-five miles. Along that route they should also attack enemy forces gathered at the Virginia outposts of Beverly, Philippi, and Buckhannon, as well as overthrow the recently organized Unionist government at Wheeling. The Confederate authorities who authorized the mission hoped that the raiders could hold the northwestern portion of the state until they mangled the greater part of the B & O west of the Alleghenies. They also hoped that the operation would draw Federal troops out of the lower Shenandoah Valley, thus opening that area to their own recruiting and quartermaster officers.[4]

Obviously, a sizable force had to be selected for the task, since raiders would be required to hold ground along the rail system for an indefinite period, that the greatest possible extent of damage might be rendered. Hence the expedition was not to be a cavalry raid in the strictest sense. A cohesive, fast-moving force would be sent not merely to snipe at many different sections of track, doing limited damage and sneaking back to base after suffering a minimal amount of casualties. Rather, a self-sufficient force of cavalry, with infantry and artillery attached, would be dispatched to seriously cripple the rail network along a wide front. It would be expected to assume the offensive by assaulting enemy garrisons and even capturing a provisional state capital as well as diverting, if necessary, enemy forces sent to break up the raid.

Commanders of true mettle had to be assigned to the project. The Confederate high command started off in proper style by authorizing two resourceful and intelligent generals to oversee the mission. One was Brigadier General John D. Imboden, who had originated the project. He was a forty-year-old Virginian, a former state politician of some renown who in war had already proven himself an able artillery and mounted infantry commander.[5] He was stocky and swarthy, with a patrician face adorned by a neat mustache and dark, bushy hair.

Early in March, Imboden had submitted a proposal of his project to General Lee, who had approved it swiftly. In its original form, the plan called for a two-pronged strike at the

★★★★★★★★★★★★★★★★★★★★★★

4. Summers, *The B & O in the Civil War*, pp. 125-26.

5. Haviland H. Abbot, "General John D. Imboden," *West Virginia History* 21 (January 1960): 88-89.

John D. Imboden. COURTESY LIBRARY OF CONGRESS.

B & O, one to be delivered by two thousand five hundred mounted men under Imboden's command, marching north-westward from Staunton, Virginia, and the other to be made by a covering force of mixed arms. The secondary movement was designed to occupy the attention of enemy troops in the towns of Romney, New Creek, and Cumberland, while Imboden's men moved in two columns to wreck strategic depots and spans, as well as to capture various Union garrisons near the rail line.[6]

The commander of the diversionary force was to be Brigadier General William Edmondson Jones, one of the most gifted cavalry leaders in Virginia but perhaps the most cantankerous as well. He had performed notable service in the field on numerous occasions, including Stuart's Chambersburg expedition, and was an excellent administrator and outpost commander. By the spring of 1863, however, Jones had more than proven himself worthy of his nickname, "Grumble." A Virginian like Imboden, he was thirty-eight, a West Point graduate and former Indian fighter with a nearly bald head, a luxurious black beard, and a perpetual scowl. He commanded respect from almost every soldier he led, but won affection from few. Stuart considered him an excellent officer, but although the Confederate cavalry leader was a gregarious sort who won many friends, he could not get along at all with the irascible Jones and had constantly sought to transfer him from his division. Only after Jones was assigned a cavalry brigade in the Department of the Shenandoah in December '62 had Stuart been able to breathe easily.[7]

One of Grumble's most noteworthy traits was a desire to advance his military standing by any means practicable. Conversely, he was ever alert to any situation that might diminish his authority. Therefore he was unresponsive to Imboden's plan for the expedition because it would not provide him with an opportunity to render bold service to the Confederacy. During late March and early April, while the chosen raiding forces waited in the Valley for roads to dry sufficiently to permit the commencement of the movement, Jones sent a series of messages to Lee and Imboden that revealed his lack of enthusiasm for the original project. At his urging, General Lee finally amended Imboden's plan to accommodate the unhappy subordinate, proving that upon occasion Grumble's grumbling did get results.

Lee decided that Imboden should move a force of cavalry, mounted infantry, foot soldiers, and horse artillery in a single column against the towns of Beverly, Philippi, and

★★★★★★★★★★★★★★★★★★★★★★★

6. Ibid., p. 100; Summers, *The B & O in the Civil War*, p. 126.

7. Warner, *Generals in Gray*, pp. 166-67.

"Grumble" Jones. COURTESY LIBRARY OF CONGRESS.

Grafton, while Jones's cavalry pressed forward to Moorefield, Virginia, reached the Northwestern Turnpike, and ruined the B & O bridges at Oakland and Rowlesburg—the latter objectives being those which the original scheme had assigned Imboden's men. The revised plan called for the two forces to start out independently but to link up at an early stage of the mission and launch joint attacks against Oakland and Grafton.[8] The majority of the work—and presumably the glory—now seemed to have devolved upon Jones instead of his comrade. Certainly Jones would cover the greater amount of territory and would strike the greater number of targets. Imboden—whose bands of regulars and partisans had been raiding western Virginia for many months already but who was junior to Jones according to the dates of their commissions—may have been disappointed about the new shape of the project but, unlike Grumble, he kept silent.[9]

2

Toward the close of April, the sloppy weather moderated a bit, and on the 20th Imboden started toward the B & O. On that day he moved his three regiments of Virginia infantry, one regiment of Virginia cavalry, and a six-gun battery out of Staunton and into the far reaches of the state. A day later, his force was augmented by another Virginia cavalry regiment and two other state units that marched afoot—an infantry regiment and a dismounted cavalry battalion.[10] The reinforcements had been supplied by Major General Samuel Jones (no kin to Grumble), who commanded the Confederate Department of Western Virginia and who obviously hoped to share in the spoils of the expedition.[11] In all, Imboden had more than three thousand three hundred men—many of them partisan rangers, including some who had won fame under the "Gray Ghost," John Singleton Mosby—but less than one quarter of the command was mounted. Still, all the soldiers were experienced in spreading destruction along the

★★★★★★★★★★★★★★★★★★★★★★

8. Summers, *The B & O in the Civil War*, pp. 126-27.

9. Abbot, "General John D. Imboden," 100.

10. *Official Records*, series I, vol. 25, pt. 1, pp. 98-99.

11. Warner, *Generals in Gray*, p. 166.

Baltimore and Ohio and relished the opportunity to do it permanent damage.

The march began auspiciously; however, it did not proceed smoothly for very long. Imboden's men had to cross the Shenandoah and Allegheny Mountains to reach Beverly, their initial destination, and the mountains were snow-covered, rugged, steep, and treacherous. The bad weather quickly returned in full fury, showering rain upon the marching column and swelling streams over which the raiders must cross. Four long days were spent crossing the Appalachians; encountering so many delays and difficulties lowered the soldiers' morale. Mud-spattered cavalrymen noted that the mountain roads were among the most wretched they had ever taken, and Imboden himself called the weather that they encountered "the most gloomy and inclement I ever saw." On Cheat Mountain he reported seeing snow piled as high as eighteen to twenty inches and having to face a pelting storm of sleet.

By the evening of the 23rd, the column had reached Huttonsville, Virginia, having come seventy miles in four days. There they heard rumors that a party of Union scouts were carrying news of their coming to the garrison at Beverly. Imboden began to fret, for the town was heavily defended; he had counted on employing surprise to great advantage. Now he sent a group of twenty guerrillas in pursuit of the enemy couriers—but soon learned that they had failed to overtake their quarry. Imboden assumed that the scouts got through with their warning, for as he moved closer to Beverly he found that the Federal pickets usually posted in the vicinity had disappeared, as though withdrawn by the commander at the Federal stronghold.[12]

But Imboden had guessed incorrectly, for when his men approached Beverly on the morning of April 24, the Federals remained wholly unaware of their coming, and were ripe for capture. The town was well guarded by some infantry regiments and cavalry companies, but the aggregate force of one thousand five hundred was too small to handle the Rebel column. The garrison troops, under Colonel George Latham, were unable to offer effective resistance until Imboden's advance guard was nearly upon them. Imboden sent various

★★★★★★★★★★★★★★★★★★★★★★

12. *Official Records*, series I, vol. 25, pt. 1, p. 99.

portions of his command to surround the garrison, then raked it with skirmish fire and pounded away with his artillery. But the Federals proved tenacious far out of proportion to their strength, and managed to hold on for over two hours, foiling Imboden's attempt to cut off retreat routes above and below the town. Finally Colonel Latham ordered his troops to withdraw from the besieged stronghold, and marched them northward toward Philippi.[13] Imboden pursued with part of his column, but thick woods and growing darkness prevented him from overtaking the remnants of Latham's force. Some one hundred thousand dollars worth of supplies—including vast amounts of ammunition, rations, and forage—came into the raiders' possession. For Imboden's cold and famished soldiers, the expedition suddenly seemed worth all the effort.[14]

The capture of Beverly had an immediate and powerful impact on other Federal outposts in western Virginia. The Union commander in the northwestern region, Brigadier General Benjamin Roberts, was numbed by the news. That officer, whose headquarters were in Buckhannon, several miles above the captured town, had been in independent field command for only a few weeks, having recently come to his post after a stint on frontier duty.[15]

Roberts was one of two Federal leaders principally concerned with protecting the Baltimore and Ohio system and adjacent territory, but he panicked at the thought of having to lead troops against the raiders, whose numbers had been greatly exaggerated by wild rumor. Quickly he wired General-in-Chief Halleck in Washington that he could not be expected to cover the B & O at the present time because the roads in that region were impassable. General Halleck was a paper-shuffler but, curiously enough, had little patience with subordinates as inactive as he. Promptly he told Roberts to assemble his men and protect the railroad, adding that "I do not understand how the roads there are impassable to you, when, by your own account, they are passable enough to the enemy." Halleck's question was a logical one, but Roberts

★★★★★★★★★★★★★★★★★★★★★★

13. Boehm, "The Jones-Imboden Raid," 17; John A. McNeil, "The Imboden Raid and Its Effects," *Southern Historical Society Papers* 34 (1906): 307-8.

14. *Official Records*, series I, vol. 25, pt. 1, p. 100.

15. Warner, *Generals in Blue*, p. 406.

dismissed it, preferring to let the other Federal commander in the region, Brigadier General Benjamin F. Kelley, deal with the enemy. Roberts gathered up his soldiers, led them out of Buckhannon, and via a circuitous route headed northwestward to Clarksburg—a shameful retreat.[16]

Not realizing that his enemy was fleeing, Imboden believed that he must neutralize the threat to his flank posed by Roberts before he could pursue the troops who had fled Beverly. So, on the 26th, he led his mounted and dismounted force northwest to a point between Buckhannon and Philippi, a dozen miles from either town, intending to attack one or the other, as circumstances dictated. He also sent couriers pounding off to find Grumble Jones's column, which by now had set off but had not established contact with Imboden.[17]

Then, hearing that a large enemy force had recently moved west of the Alleghenies to occupy Philippi, Imboden engaged in some panicky self-doubt all his own. The force reported to be at Philippi could have arrived only if Jones had failed to do a proper job of cutting the B & O. As a result, Imboden began to entertain the dark suspicion that his comrade had failed entirely in his mission.[18] Feeling isolated and unprotected, Imboden agreed with his regimental commanders that "the safety of the command required that we should fall back to a position where escape would be possible if we were overpowered." Accordingly, he countermarched his column toward Beverly.

He was near the latter on the 28th, when he finally received word that the report of enemy forces at Philippi was in error. Rather sheepishly, one imagines, Imboden went forward again, and the next day took possession of recently abandoned Buckhannon. Warehouses in the village were still smoldering; Roberts had set them afire before fleeing to Clarksburg. Imboden salvaged what he could in the way of supplies, and afterward dispatched units to scout the country for cattle, which were to be sent to the rear of the column.[19]

★★★★★★★★★★★★★★★★★★★★★★★

16. Boehm, "The Jones-Imboden Raid," p. 17.

17. *Official Records,* series I, vol. 25, pt. 1, p. 100.

18. Summers, *The B & O in the Civil War,* p. 136.

19. *Official Records,* series I, vol. 25, pt. 1, pp. 101-2.

Meanwhile, he settled his men comfortably in the town, placed pickets along all the roads, and waited to be joined by Grumble Jones. So far, with minor exceptions, the expedition had progressed according to its blueprint, and Imboden could be satisfied with what he had accomplished.

3

Jones's command, composed of four regiments and three battalions of Virginia cavalry and a small complement of infantry and artillery, had started out from Lacey Spring on the morning of April 21.[20] On the first day out the three thousand soldiers left the Valley Pike two miles below Harrisonburg and moved northward toward Brock's Gap, crossing both rolling and rough country and battling the same kind of weather that had slowed Imboden's march in its early phases. On the 22nd, the command splashed across the North Fork of the Shenandoah River at a ford made hazardous by a raging current, and that night bivouacked twenty miles below the city of Moorefield. Rain fell constantly through the night, dampening the spirits as well as the clothing of the raiders. The next day, however, their morale was revived by some welcome sunshine and the beautiful country through which they found themselves marching. Passing White Sulphur Spring, at the eastern base of Branch Mountain, an artilleryman attached to Jones's column stared in awe at the magnificent vista: "It is a beautiful spring, boxed with white marble slabs, and the water is clear as the purest virgin crystal, and very sulphury. The surrounding mountain scenery is wild, grand, and magnificent: spurs of the Branch Mountain and long wooded ridges thickly clad with laurel and ferns rise around the spring and its neighborhood in every direction which bounds the view of the beholder."[21]

As the raiders moved slowly up the mountain, heavy fog began to surround them, and again rain fell in sheets. At some places the mist was so thick that Jones's men could see no farther than fifty yards ahead. Again morale suffered,

★★★★★★★★★★★★★★★★★★★★★★★

20. Summers, *The B & O in the Civil War*, p. 127; Boehm, "The Jones-Imboden Raid," p. 17.

21. George M. Neese, *Three Years in the Confederate Horse Artillery*, pp. 155-56.

for the troopers could not be sure that Yankees did not lay in wait in front of them; for five hours they wandered about with obscured vision. Finally they began to descend the western slope of the mountain and passed below the fog line. At the same time, the rain ceased, and the advance guard of the column could catch a glimpse of the lovely Moorefield Valley below, its wheat fields and pasturelands. The artilleryman with the eye for beauty commented that "Moorefield, almost in the center of the picture, looked in the evening glow like a bright jewel with an emerald setting."

On that evening of the 23rd, Jones guided his command to the shore of the South Branch of the Potomac, where he met his first serious obstacle. The recent rain had raised the water level so high that only at a site some twenty-five miles upriver could the cavalry cross. Artillery and infantry would not be able to continue their journey; with angry reluctance Jones ordered such units to remain at the river for a few days longer and then return to the Shenandoah Valley.[22] He would proceed with only his seven cavalry units and a single company of partisan rangers, less than two thousand five hundred men.

On the 25th, which was chilly in the extreme, Jones crossed his mounted men over the South Branch at the upstream ford and took them northwestward through an icy rain.[23] Then action began. At Greenland Gap, a pass through Knobly Mountain, the raiders were confronted by a force of eighty-five Federals[24] who had evacuated Moorefield upon Jones's approach. The Yankees, armed with an artillery battery, occupied a commanding position, but Grumble drew up his leading regiments and prepared to make a frontal attack.

His soldiers did not respond with overwhelming enthusiasm. As they slowly formed for the charge, one trooper noted that "The men's teeth chattered together, and their knees rattled against the sides of their horses." He explained that this "was the effect of the cold, increased by nervous excitement."[25]

★★★★★★★★★★★★★★★★★★★★★★★

22. Ibid., pp. 157-58.

23. John N. Opie, *A Rebel Cavalryman With Lee, Stuart, and Jackson*, p. 118.

24. Boehm, "The Jones-Imboden Raid," p. 18.

25. Opie, *A Rebel Cavalryman*, pp. 118-19.

About sunset, the 7th Virginia Cavalry swept forward to the call of bugles, scattered a team of enemy pickets, then ran hard against an infantry force that had barricaded itself inside a log church amid the pass. The Federals put up stiff resistance, cutting the 7th Virginia in two, seriously wounding its commander, and preventing its rear ranks from following the forward squadrons in the attack.[26]

General Jones, cursing at the top of his voice, came up to personally re-form the attacking force. He had already been forced to detour twenty-five miles to cross the South Branch and was not amused to find another obstacle blocking his route; he had to reach the Baltimore and Ohio was rapidly as possible if he was to cooperate properly with Imboden's command. With no artillery, he could not shell the little fort into surrendering; hence Jones attempted to bluff his way to victory by sending the enemy commander, under flag of truce, a message notifying him that he was surrounded by many thousands of Confederates armed with cannon. But Captain Martin Wallace of the 23rd Illinois Infantry was not duped. He replied that he would hold on even if a million Rebels confronted him, but doubted that Jones had a single artillery piece, and added: "We will fight to the last crust and cartridge."[27]

The reply enraged Jones further. He had in his command several kegs of gunpowder with which he planned to blow up the Cheat River trestle work; now he decided to send his pioneer corps, composed of details from each of his regiments and battalions, to lodge a cache of powder under the log fort. At the same time, he provided the pioneers with axes to be used to break the fort's windows so that lighted straw could be tossed inside the structure, igniting the powder.

By the time Jones had made his dispositions, evening had come, and in the darkness he sent another message to Captain Wallace, proclaiming that unless the Federals surrendered they would all be blown to hell within five minutes.

Wallace thought the matter over and decided to hold firm.

★★★★★★★★★★★★★★★★★★★★★★

26. Franklin M. Myers, *The Comanches: A History of White's Battalion, Etc.*, p. 162.

27. Boehm, "The Jones-Imboden Raid," p. 18.

He returned a polite reply suggesting that Jones himself go to hell.[28]

At that, Grumble sent his pioneers toward the fort from two directions. They had been told to go directly to the building and with the rifle butts punch out the caulking in the logs, then to fire their muskets and pistols through the cracks and fling the burning hay through the windows. The men advanced, dismounted as ordered, and for a time it appeared that the plan would work to perfection. Then things began to go to pieces. The men with the gunpowder could not move close enough to plant their kegs, for the Yankees kept them back with a well-directed fire at long range. Those with axes and straw managed to get into their assigned positions but, firing their pistols wildly in the darkness, did as much damage to their comrades as to the enemy. Grumble Jones belatedly realized that by placing his attacking forces so closely together he made it inevitable that they would pick off each other by mistake. Then, too, as one Confederate officer noted, "The Yankees fired coolly and rapidly, and almost before the pioneer corps could light the first bundle of straw and throw it into the house, every man of the corps was down, either killed or wounded."[29]

In desperation, the survivors pooled their combustibles and gave them to a private from White's Virginia Battalion, who carried them to the roof and set the fort on fire. The flames forced the defenders to capitulate, whereupon Jones's men collected them as prisoners. Captain Wallace's stubborn resistance had cost the Confederates nearly one hundred casualties, plus four and a half hours of lost time.[30]

At last Jones could again take up his march. His soldiers gained the road that would lead them across the Alleghenies and into Maryland, and all that night rode through freezing weather. Upon entering Maryland, Jones divided his force, personally leading the main column toward an important objective, Rowlesburg, while Colonel A. W. Harman took a mixed force of cavalry and partisans to the village of Oakland, there to cut telegraph cable and burn B & O bridges. A third segment of the command, a single cavalry squadron

★★★★★★★★★★★★★★★★★★★★★★★★

28. Myers, *The Comanches*, pp. 162-63.

29. Ibid., pp. 163-65.

30. Boehm, "The Jones-Imboden Raid," pp. 18-19.

under Captain Edward H. McDonald, had already started for Altamont, twelve miles east of Oakland, for the purpose of burning other rail bridges, after which he would join Harman and follow him via Kingwood and Morgantown to the main force.

After the detachments had ridden off, Jones moved over the Northwestern Turnpike and arrived near Rowlesburg early in the afternoon of Sunday, April 26. He immediately rode to the Cheat River bridge, which was defended by about 250 members of the 6th Virginia (Union) Infantry, who were stationed behind piles of crossties and logs at both ends of the span as well as atop steep hills nearby.[31]

Several previous raids against the Cheat River viaduct had proved unsuccessful, and Jones was determined that his would not fail to destroy that imposing and costly structure. He called on one of his most trusted subordinates, Lieutenant Colonel John Shac Green of the 6th Virginia Cavalry, and told him to drive the nearest enemy contingent from its works. At this juncture, unfortunately, communication between Jones and Colonel Green began to disintegrate. Jones later reported that he ordered his subordinate to charge over the bridge, capturing Rowlesburg without delay and contingent upon no other condition.[32] However, Green was to insist that the general urged great caution, implying that an attack would be successful only if Green proceeded to the works without raising an enemy alarm.[33]

In either case, Green moved toward the bridge, supported by sharpshooters from the 7th and 11th Virginia Cavalry. On the way, however, he discovered that despite his best efforts the Federals had received advance word of his approach and had manned rifle pits that gave them a commanding vantage point from which to menace the attacking column.[34]

Instead of leading the attacking force, as he ought to have done, General Jones was by now far to the rear, and so Green was entirely on his own.[35] Heeding what he thought to

★★★★★★★★★★★★★★★★★★★★★★★★

31. Summers, *The B & O in the Civil War*, p. 128.

32. *Official Records*, series I, vol. 25, pt. 1, p. 117.

33. Ibid., pp. 127-28.

34. Opie, *A Rebel Cavalryman*, pp. 121-22.

35. Boehm, "The Jones-Imboden Raid," p. 19.

be specific orders to move warily, the lieutenant colonel made only a limited assault, then halted his dismounted regiment before the enemy riflemen could decimate its ranks. The Virginians wished to resume the attack, but Green carefully studied the Federal hilltop positions and the makeshift barriers at the ends of the span, and called a full retreat. He pulled out so quickly that some of his supporting units found themselves cut off and captured.

The raiders had failed at a crucial stage of their expedition. Jones was furious with Colonel Green, and later had him court-martialed for failing to obey orders (the lieutenant colonel was subsequently acquitted of the charge). It seems nonetheless clear that Grumble was at least as much to blame for the repulse as his subordinate. And he compounded his error by not making a second attempt to carry the objective. Although several of his colonels suggested that a better-organized attack by about four hundred dismounted carbineers would carry the enemy works, Jones balked. Noting that darkness was coming on, he suspended operations against the enemy: "We will attend to them in the morning."[36]

But dawn found him leading his soldiers away from Rowlesburg toward Morgantown, Fairmont, and points farther west. He had decided to accept failure at Cheat River in the hope of quickly spreading destruction to other sections of the B & O and to neighboring towns.

4

Jones enjoyed greater success during the remainder of his mission. He pushed his tired riders through small towns below and above the railroad, including Evansville, Kingwood, and Morgantown,[37] along the way contending with local militia and bushwhackers who constantly bedeviled his troops but did not seriously threaten their progress. Perhaps in retaliation for the sniping, some of the Confederates began to drop out of formation and cast about for homes and stores to loot. Grumble did not approve of unauthorized foraging, and whenever possible made display of his feelings.

★★★★★★★★★★★★★★★★★★★★★★★★

36. Opie, *A Rebel Cavalryman,* pp. 122-24.

37. Summers, *The B & O in the Civil War,* p. 129.

On one occasion during the march from Rowlesburg he saw
two enlisted men proudly exhibiting their spoils—a hoop
skirt and a parasol. Jones forced the first man to wear the
skirt around his neck and compelled the second to hold the
umbrella over Jones's head during that entire afternoon, in
full view of the column.[38]

At dawn on the 29th, Jones reached the suburbs of Fairmont, yet another Federal-held depot on the B & O, and
found militiamen holding hills above and west of the town.
The Federals, armed with some cannon, were determined to
protect the 615-foot-long suspension bridge over the Monongahela River; Jones was committed to burning it.[39] Grumble
split his column into three units and led them—some afoot,
some on horseback—against the enemy positions. A Rebel officer saw the nearest defenders scatter "like sheep" as portions of the raiding command seized the town and the line of
hills beyond. Most of the Yankees took refuge beside the
bridge and opened with their artillery, until Jones placed
another segment of his force in their rear, persuading them
to surrender.[40] After forcing them to lay down their arms,
Grumble employed his staff officers at writing paroles for all
the captives.

While the documents were being distributed, the raiders
went to work on the span with their gunpowder. In due
course the bridge—the costliest and most imposing structure
on the B & O—went crashing into the Monongahela, kicking
up a gigantic spray of water and giving Jones one of his most
impressive feats of the expedition. Afterward his men trans-
formed nearby trackage into smoldering heaps of metal.

Finally, their work well done, the Rebels returned to the
road and marched southwestward toward Clarksburg. Jones
had finished, at least for now, with the Baltimore & Ohio; he
wished to link up with Imboden and complete the operation
before a strong force of pursuers could head him off.[41]

Jones's men had faith in their leader, but some nevertheless wondered if he might not be pushing his luck by pene-

★★★★★★★★★★★★★★★★★★★★★★★

38. Myers, *The Comanches*, pp. 166-67.

39. Angus James Johnston II, *Virginia Railroads in the Civil War*, p. 152.

40. Myers, *The Comanches*, pp. 168-69.

41. Opie, *A Rebel Cavalryman*, p. 133.

Smoldering railroad trackage. COURTESY LIBRARY OF CONGRESS.

trating enemy territory so deeply with a relatively small force of troopers. Also, morale was again suffering from bad weather, in which the column had to ride intermittently, and from lack of rations and forage (the limited quantities of both issued at the start of the expedition had run low some time ago, and Grumble's strictures against looting made it difficult for the soldiers to augment their supplies).

Still, the Confederates ought to have been bouyed up by their accomplishments, the failure at Cheat River notwithstanding. They had already inflicted a considerable amount of damage to railroad resources, had gathered a large quantity of cattle and horses from the countryside, and had fought off several bands of regular troops, militia, home guardsmen, and bushwhackers—though they had been forced to go most of their way without artillery and infantry support. Moreover, Jones had maneuvered them so quickly over such a circuitous route above and below the railroad that his enemy had been too confused to mount a concerted pursuit effort. Jones's comings and goings had brought panic not only to western Virginia and parts of Maryland, but also to eastern Ohio and lower Pennsylvania. Governor Curtin of the Keystone State, fearing an emergency such as that brought on by Stuart's Chambersburg raid, grew concerned about the safety of Pittsburgh when he heard of the Confederates' presence in the Morgantown area. Not even President Lincoln, who wired him that "I do not think the people of Pennsylvania should be uneasy about an invasion," could fully assuage Curtin's worries.[42]

In addition to these achievements, Jones could take pride in the accomplishments of the two raiding detachments he had sent out after reaching Maryland on the 26th. Colonel Harman's force, which rejoined Jones early on April 28, had cut B & O trackage and telegraph wires at Altamont and Oakland, had demolished rail bridges and culverts at other locations, had captured several small enemy outposts near the tracks, and had run loose through the countryside as far as the Pennsylvania border—indicating that Governor Curtin indeed had cause for worry. The detachment gathered up a goodly number of serviceable animals, created havoc in several pro-Union counties in western Virginia, and successfully contended with numerous snipers, some of whom they captured and executed near Morgantown. Afterward, their mission fully accomplished, Harman's men raced after Jones's fast-moving column and overtook it before it had captured Fairmont.

While Harman's detachment did its job, Captain McDonald's single cavalry squadron, the other raiding detachment, carried out its instructions to the letter, damaging several small bridges at Altamont and on the 28th returning with Harman to the main column.[43]

Marching out of Fairmont with his reunited command, Grumble Jones continued southward in search of Imboden. He moved up the West Fork Branch of the Monongahela, heading directly toward the enemy stronghold of Clarksburg. He did not change course till he reached the Federal picket lines, whereupon he swerved east and farther south, riding rapidly so that the Yankees could not cut his route of detour.

★★★★★★★★★★★★★★★★★★★★★★

42. Boehm, "The Jones-Imboden Raid," p. 19.

43. Summers, *The B & O in the Civil War,* pp. 130-33.

On the last day in April the raiders reached the Northwestern Virginia Railroad at the town of Bridgeport. There, adding to the weighty accomplishments of his raid, Jones captured a company of Federal soldiers, made prisoners of several civilian railroad employees, demolished a locomotive, and burned several bridges and trestles.

On May 1, the Confederates arrived at Philippi, the town toward which Imboden's column had moved six days previously. The Rebels rested there for a spell, for many of them—as well as their mounts—were showing signs of excessive fatigue. From Philippi Grumble dispatched part of Harman's command toward Beverly with the huge herd of cattle and horses that the column had collected along its way. Then, after his men had sufficiently relaxed, Jones pushed on westward, at last nearing a juncture with Imboden, still waiting at Buckhannon.[44]

The two commands joined forces on May 2. Jones and Imboden compared notes, congratulated each other on the results of their work to date, and at once drafted plans calling for further destruction to Unionist regions in western Virginia.[45] Although neither of the generals was the most combative leader in the Confederate ranks, neither was apt to terminate an assignment when vital work might yet be accomplished. Both felt that there was ample time to achieve further success, for a determined Federal pursuit had not yet materialized.

Therefore, they recalled their detachments, including Harman's cattle drovers, shifted their common headquarters to the village of Weston, and projected an attack on the Clarksburg stronghold. While they planned, their soldiers spent a leisurely time in Weston, lolling upon the public grounds, playing baseball, writing letters home, and sleeping—diversions that had long been denied Jones's men.[46]

Reports of Federal reinforcements at Clarksburg reached Jones and Imboden on May 4 and forestalled their advance on the city. Looking to other sectors, the generals decided to again part company for a time and to reunite after Jones's

★★★★★★★★★★★★★★★★★★★★★★★★

44. Ibid., p. 135.

45. Abbot, "General John D. Imboden," p. 101.

46. Summers, *The B & O in the Civil War*, p. 136.

force, all of which was mounted, hurried north and west to renew the campaign against the B & O. While Jones spread further destruction, Imboden's infantry, cavalry, and artillery would move south to the hamlet of Summersville, where they would encamp to await Jones's return. The livestock and supply train would accompany Imboden.[47]

Imboden's role in the final phase of the expedition was a minor one. Because of abominable weather—his nemesis all during the raid—his march south was a slow and cumbersome undertaking. Three days were required to cover the first fourteen miles of the journey, and additional delay was encountered when he stopped to capture and assimilate a twenty-eight-wagon Federal provisions train, pulled by 170 mules. By the time the raiding force reached Summersville, Imboden had gathered an almost unmanageable herd of livestock, badly needed by Lee's army, and had rendered damage to still other Union supply depots and garrisons.[48]

Even so, his achievements on this last leg of the operation could not compare with those of Grumble Jones.

5

On May 6, Jones once again started toward the Baltimore and Ohio and the Northwestern Virginia Railroads. As before, he detached Colonel Harman, with two regiments and a battalion, to mangle the latter road. Then Grumble led the main force westward on the Staunton and Parkersburg Pike, hoping to strike the more important railroad near its western terminus.

Colonel Harman again displayed his mettle by breaking the Northwestern line at West Union, burning two rail bridges and capturing almost one hundred Federal guards. After Harman rejoined his superior, Jones took the main column even farther westward, burning three bridges and damaging a rail tunnel at the village of Cairo.[49] Then, toward evening on May 9, he marched away from the railroad and neared oil fields that fronted the Little Kanawha River, some miles

★★★★★★★★★★★★★★★★★★★★★★

47. *Official Records*, series I, vol. 25, pt. 1, pp. 102-3, 119.

48. Boehm, "The Jones-Imboden Raid," p. 19.

49. *Official Records*, series I, vol. 25, pt. 1, pp. 119-20.

below Cairo. The fields were sometimes referred to simply as Oiltown, but the formal name was Burning Springs, and Jones decided to force the place to live up to that description. Oil was contraband and liable to destruction as a spoil of war. Accordingly, torches were ignited and applied to storage tanks, oil wells, pump houses, wagons, and barges. The tanks exploded immediately, throwing fire and fuel in all directions.[50]

For many of the raiders, the resulting spectacle was the most memorable of the expedition. One soldier observed: "Great pillars of flame, resembling pyramids of fire, rose to a prodigious height in the air from the burning wells, lighting the surrounding country for miles." The flames burned incessantly, turning the evening blackness into a brilliant blaze of light.

As a symbol of the destruction wrought by Jones's raiders throughout the expedition, the flames that engulfed Oiltown and sent the nearby river afire had a vital meaning. The symbolism did not escape one onlooker: "It was, in appearance, the flames of an expiring world, and I believe that the men would have so considered it, but for the fact that it was of their own creation. . . . The current carried the flames over water-falls, producing the most fantastic shapes and figures, resembling fiery demons, dancing upon the surface of the river, ever and anon disappearing in the darkness and again appearing. . . ."[51]

Some one hundred fifty thousand barrels of oil were set ablaze before Jones tired of watching the river burn and resumed his march southeastward toward Summersville. By that time a good many of his troopers had been sobered by the sight of so much devastation and were quite willing to leave Burning Springs behind.[52]

Moving via Glenville, Bulltown, and Sutton, Jones reached Imboden's camp on May 14. He reported the extent of his latest depredations and afterward concurred with Imboden that little more could be accomplished in that area. Therefore the raiding leaders split up for the final time and made their separate ways across the Appalachians, reaching the

★★★★★★★★★★★★★★★★★★★★★★★★

50. Boehm, "The Jones-Imboden Raid," pp. 19-20.

51. Opie, *A Rebel Cavalryman*, pp. 135-36.

52. Writing in 1906, one of Jones's old veterans stated: ". . .the soldiers who were with General Jones, at this day, get excited when that fire is mentioned, so terrific was it in appearance." McNeil, "The Imboden Raid and Its Effects," p. 309.

familiar surroundings of the Shenandoah Valley in the last week of May.

Upon receiving news of the raiders' accomplishments, General Lee was immediately gratified. He thanked Jones and Imboden profusely for the five thousand cattle and one thousand two hundred horses they had confiscated during their travels and ordered the animals turned over to the Confederate Commissary. Although some of Grumble's men had already slaughtered and consumed some of the beef and despite the fact that General Samuel Jones commandeered other cattle for his department, many head went to Lee's legions, who received them with unconcealed delight.

Naturally, Lee also had words of praise for the manner in which the raiders had treated the North's great rail system. Jones had destroyed two B & O trains, two dozen railway bridges, a tunnel, and countless other road resources including depot buildings and telegraph lines. For several days the B & O was destined to rely upon convoyed wagon trains to ship Federal supplies around sections of broken track, as well as upon pontoon spans to carry traffic across now-bridgeless streams.

Other results of the raid included violation of public and private property ranging from the theft of a woman's hoop skirt to the burning of hundreds of thousands of barrels of oil along the Little Kanawha. Some eight hundred of the enemy—regulars, militia, and home guards—had been killed, wounded, or captured; about one thousand small arms and some cannon had been confiscated; and various supply bases had been seized, occupied, and sacked. In contrast, Rebel losses had been relatively light, less than ninety casualties being reported by the raiding leaders. Furthermore, four hundred recruits had been added to the Confederate Army during the expedition, fulfilling another of its objectives.[53] Finally, as one of Jones's officers commented, "the Southern sympathizers of that country for a time [were] relieved from the domineering rule which invariably characterized the homemade Yankee, wherever he had the power to annoy his Southern neighbor. . . ."[54]

Jones and Imboden had not realized all of their hopes. They had not succeeded in overthrowing the Unionist gov-

★★★★★★★★★★★★★★★★★★★★★★★

53. Boehm, "The Jones-Imboden Raid," p. 20; Johnston, *Virginia Railroads*, p. 155.

54. Myers, *The Comanches*, p. 175.

ernment that had been established at Wheeling, although they had compelled a score of its lawmakers and functionaries to flee from towns that lay along their route of march. After the raiders' departure, Union sentiment in portions of western Virginia would swell even higher, to the extent that the region would enter the Federal Union as a separate state, functioning as such to date from June 20, 1863.

Nor was the raid wholly a tactical success, for Jones had failed to accomplish anything of importance at Rowlesburg: the Cheat River viaduct continued to stand long after his troopers left that vicinity. The raid also had a decidedly adverse effect upon subsequent Confederate operations against enemy forces in western Virginia. The freedom with which Jones and Imboden had maneuvered through the region convinced the Federal authorities that stronger internal defenses had to be erected. In future months they increased the size of cavalry forces in West Virginia—crucial in chasing down raiders such as Jones and Imboden had led—as well as bolstered garrisons along the line of the B & O and ousted from command those generals who had been unable to meet the invaders' challenge. Foremost among the latter was Benjamin Roberts, who had fled from his headquarters with such speed as had astounded even his enemy. The changes and improvements adopted by the Yankees ensured that Jones's and Imboden's raid would be the last major threat to Union control of West Virginia.[55]

Perhaps the value of the work accomplished by mounted raiders can best be measured by the number of opponents frustrated in attempting to mount a pursuit. Gauged thusly, the Jones-Imboden raid can be considered effective indeed. Several forces in addition to Roberts's command ought to have offered resistance to the Confederates. Most of General Kelley's ten thousand soldiers, dispersed along the B & O from Harpers Ferry to the Ohio River, had proved themselves to be no match for Jones's fast-moving soldiers; only a few outposts had posed serious problems to Grumble. More than three thousand other Federals—comparable in size to Roberts's command—had been available for defense in the Great Kanawha Valley, but were unable to curtail the raiders' movements. Portions of the Federal army in the Shenandoah

★★★★★★★★★★★★★★★★★★★★★★★★

55. Boehm, "The Jones-Imboden Raid," pp. 20-21.

Valley, shifted westward to confront the raiders as their expedition reached high tide, had likewise been of little value.

Departmental commander Ambrose E. Burnside—who three months hence would try desperately to counter John Hunt Morgan's raid through Indiana and Ohio—had revealed himself to be equally ineffectual in combating Jones's men. From his headquarters in Cincinatti he had dispatched some troops to the western edge of the Baltimore and Ohio, and even sent a gunboat to patrol the lower Ohio toward Parkersburg, but might have entirely ignored the expedition for all the good he accomplished. Finally, when one takes into account the thousands of regular troops available for duty in the so-named Middle Department during the spring of '63, he can see that more than twenty-five thousand Federals were stationed in northwestern Virginia at the time of the Jones-Imboden raid.[56]

Grumble Jones, whose mounted soldiers handled the major share of the work during the mission, had achieved success by employing great speed and effective deception. By cutting telegraph wires and rail lines at many different points, by marching and countermarching over a roundabout route, by fragmenting his force to strike various objectives simultaneously, and by skillfully concealing his projected route of march from the enemy, Grumble had stymied Federal efforts to concentrate forces and pick up his trail. Like Imboden, he had had to march through terrible weather and over rough mountain roads, along which hostile citizens and more than a few snipers lay in wait. But he was a dedicated fighter who kept moving each step of the way, never pausing to rest when rest was not imperative, never allowing himself to be overwhelmed by the dangers that accrued from marching so far into hostile land, never permitting fear of enemy pursuit activity to hamper his ability to think rapidly and incisively.

In the end it was his quick-wittedness and his tireless energy—qualities shared by his tired and hungry but rugged soldiers—that made the expedition such a tactical success. It may have been difficult to accept Grumble Jones as a personal friend, but as a soldier in general and a raiding leader in particular, he ranked high indeed, in everyone's estimation.

★★★★★★★★★★★★★★★★★★★★★★

56. Summers, *The B & O in the Civil War*, p. 138.

6

ANOTHER FAILURE ALREADY

Stoneman's Central Virginia Raid (April 29-May 8, 1863)

1

Major General Joseph Hooker was a handsome man, with a lean face, a ruddy complexion, and dark hair graying at the temples. Profane and passionate, he was fond of liquor and, reportedly, the company of scarlet women; hence his name came down through history as a term denoting a prostitute.[1] None of these qualities was of especial help to him as a field general, but fortunately, when he assumed command of the Army of the Potomac in January, 1863, he displayed other characteristics that hinted that he would become a successful army leader.

In addition to his weaknesses for women and drink, he was obsessed with the idea of establishing an invincible field command. He believed the only way to achieve this was to strengthen each of the service arms. Accordingly and without

★★★★★★★★★★★★★★★★★★★★★★★

1. Warner, *Generals in Blue*, p. 235.

148

delay, he reorganized infantry and artillery units, streamlined the military medical department—and upgraded the quality of the mounted wing. In advocating the emergence of a strong and unified cavalry force he made perhaps his greatest contribution to the well-being of his army.

Previous to Hooker's coming, the horsemen of the Army of the Potomac had been treated as second-class soldiers. Many commanders believed them valuable only as scouts, couriers, pickets, and skirmishers for the infantry. As a result, the several divisions of horsemen were scattered almost randomly throughout the army and often were reduced to regiments and companies when sent out to handle the various duties the infantry generals wished performed.[2] Not permitted to belong to a cohesive force with a true identity of its own, the cavalrymen often felt unwanted as well as unappreciated. Simply because they were kept out of decisive combat, few troopers became casualties, prompting foot soldiers to ask a harsh and cynical question: "Who ever heard of a dead cavalryman?" The comment circulated through the army, angering and humiliating all horse soldiers.

Hooker did a great deal to assuage their pain. On February 12 he formed the first full-scale cavalry corps—twelve thousand strong—and separated it from the jurisdiction of the other corps leaders.[3] At last all horse soldiers were part of a unit comparable in size to the army's largest infantry component. From the outset, Hooker's move immensely increased cavalry's self-respect, for the troopers realized that in future campaigning they would be called on to perform service independent of the rest of the field army and not merely as an auxiliary to the foot soldiers.

Unfortunately, although Hooker had a grab-bag of ideas for raising military efficiency, he was not particularly perceptive in assessing the talents of his subordinates. In selecting a commander for his rejuvenated cavalry, he chose a soldier with a celebrated reputation as a prewar dragoon but whose previous Civil War experience hardly recommended him for such an important post. Hooker's choice was Brigadier General George Stoneman, forty years old, dignified in appear-

★★★★★★★★★★★★★★★★★★★★★★

2. Foote, *The Civil War*, 2: 242-43.

3. Boatner, *The Civil War Dictionary*, p. 201.

George Stoneman. COURTESY LIBRARY OF CONGRESS.

ance and deportment, old-army to the core, a decent human being—and a lackluster field commander.[4]

Stoneman had been associated with the cavalry of the Army of the Potomac since the first days of the war; in that respect his selection came about naturally, if not happily. Two months after General McClellan took over the army, following its disastrous showing at First Bull Run, he had placed Stoneman, an experienced Indian fighter, in command of all the horsemen in the army; his commission as brigadier general of volunteers dated from August 13, 1861, which placed him high on the seniority scale. He had quickly shown himself to be an able organizer, as had General McClellan: perhaps Stoneman's efficiency in handling paperwork had recommended him for the position more than his supposed talents in active campaigning.

★★★★★★★★★★★★★★★★★★★★★★★★

4. Bruce Catton, *Glory Road: The Bloody Route from Fredricksburg to Gettysburg,* p. 174; Edward J. Stackpole, *Chancellorsville: Lee's Greatest Battle,* p. 26.

Certainly Stoneman was no great shakes in the field. He led the cavalry when Little Mac moved up the Virginia peninsula, but except for brief flashes of glory, accomplished little of note during that ill-fated campaign. After the peninsula fighting, in fact, Stoneman left the cavalry service to take over an infantry division and later a full corps. It was as a leader of foot soldiers that he was called upon to interpose troops between J. E. B. Stuart, returning from his Pennsylvania raid in October 1862, and Stuart's destination, the Potomac River. Stoneman failed in this not so much because the Confederate leader outwitted him as because he kept his soldiers so far from Stuart's route as to avoid any encounter.

Hence the old dragoon officer brought few solid talents as a field campaigner to his new corps command. Nevertheless, as though he spied some potentially brilliant quality suggested by Stoneman's past services, Hooker made him a major general in mid-March, antedating the appointment to rank from November 29, 1862 and thereby granting him even greater seniority.[5]

It would seem that "Fighting Joe" had weaknesses for vices other than the more common ones. Even more damaging was his inability to recognize and deal with inadequacy among his generals.

2

By early April, 1863, Hooker had been in chief command for two and a half months, but had not succeeded in drawing Robert E. Lee's Army of Northern Virginia into a showdown fight. Hooker kept maneuvering for the initiative from his winter quarters at Falmouth, but Lee remained within strong defensive lines directly south, near Fredericksburg. While Hooker sought a way to flank Lee out of his positions and force him to fall back upon Richmond, the Army of Northern Virginia bolstered its lines still further.[6]

Whatever Hooker's limitations as a judge of men, he was an enterprising strategist. At first he proposed to cross the Rappahannock River below Fredericksburg and move against

★★★★★★★★★★★★★★★★★★★★★★★

5. Warner, *Generals in Blue*, p. 481.

6. Boatner, *The Civil War Dictionary*, p. 136.

Lee's right and rear, choking off his supply lines to Richmond. Later, for a variety of reasons, he was compelled to adopt new strategy, and came up with an even more promising plan, which President Lincoln approved. This time he proposed to drive his opponents southward via a double envelopment and a hard strike against their rear. He intended to turn Lee's left flank by taking half of his 120,000 infantrymen across the Rappahannock at Kelly's Ford, twenty miles northwest of Fredricksburg, then by moving eastward toward the city. Meanwhile, the rest of his army would launch a diversionary attack on Fredricksburg from its other side, to hold Lee's sixty thousand Confederates in place. Reserve forces would be deployed in positions from which to aid either wing. With so much force directed against Lee, Hooker supposed that in a short time the Army of Northern Virginia would be stumbling back toward Richmond, permitting the Federals to mount a fatal siege.[7]

A key facet of Hooker's plan—the strike to be directed against Lee's rear—would be the responsibility of Stoneman's cavalry. To increase pressure on the enemy and close off their avenues of retreat, the Federal troopers would march south two full weeks in advance of the infantry movement. Below the Rappahannock and Rapidan Rivers, Stoneman was to destroy Lee's lines of communications with Richmond and points westward by damaging the length of the Virginia Central Railroad as well as portions of the Richmond, Fredricksburg & Potomac. These lines crossed at Hanover Junction, approximately midway between Fredricksburg and Richmond, and the depot was believed to be Lee's principal supply base. After striking this station particularly hard, Stoneman was to select strong positions astride roads paralleling the R, F & P, to harass the retreating Rebel troops. If all went as envisioned, Stoneman would place unbearable pressure on Lee's rear at the same time as Hooker's infantry smashed into the Confederates from both east and west.

The plan indicated that Hooker had inordinate faith in the ability of the cavalry force he had recently established. In the Federal troopers' favor was a three-to-one numerical advantage against their opponents, the far-understrength cavalry

★★★★★★★★★★★★★★★★★★★★★★★

7. Stackpole, *Chancellorsville*, pp. 92-94, 108-9; Boatner, *The Civil War Dictionary*, pp. 136-37; Catton, *Glory Road*, p. 174.

command of J. E. B. Stuart, as well as the fact that during the greater part of their expedition they would travel far afield of Lee's main infantry force. Even so, Hooker was placing on his horsemen a burden greater than he realized. In effect, he was betting so heavily that his proposed pincers movement would succeed that he was sending Stoneman to exploit that success two weeks before it materialized—a dangerous as well as an imprudent undertaking. If, on the other hand, Hooker believed that Stoneman's cavalry alone would cause Lee to fall back, he never explained how a ten thousand-man force could frighten an army six times as large into such a headlong retreat.[8] As it happened, Hooker also assumed that his cavalry would operate effectively without benefit of proper equipment. Though his quartermasters furnished Stoneman's headquarters with many types of railroad-wrecking instruments, they neglected to provide such crucially needed tools as claw crowbars.[9] Everything considered, Fighting Joe was asking his cavalry to accomplish a task of such size as to give even an experienced corps of horsemen great difficulty—let alone an untried force that had been in existence for only two months.

Nevertheless, the army leader went ahead with his plans. By the second week in April he was able to give his cavalry chief fairly specific instructions. Stoneman was to collect his corps, less one brigade, plus all twenty-two of the cannon relegated to the cavalry, and take them across the upper river at and near Rappahannock Bridge, thirty miles above Fredricksburg, early in the evening of the 13th. From there they would move southward to smash and burn and give General Lee migraine headaches.

Hooker publicized the purposes of the raid as "turning the enemy's position on his left, throwing the cavalry between him and Richmond, isolating him from his supplies, checking his retreat, and inflicting on him every possible injury which will tend to his discomfiture and defeat." He could not resist appending a series of orders calculated to raise Stoneman's enthusiasm to fever pitch: "If you cannot cut off from his column large slices, the general desires that you will not fail

★★★★★★★★★★★★★★★★★★★★★★

8. Stackpole, *Chancellorsville*, pp. 97-98, 105.

9. Johnston, *Virginia Railroads*, p. 149.

to take small ones. Let your watchword be fight, fight, fight, bearing in mind that time is as valuable to the general as rebel carcasses." So much for motivational psychology.

It is doubtful that this pep talk had the desired effect, but Stoneman did start out in approved fashion, leading ten thousand picked riders and his guns, plus no fewer than 275 supply wagons, to the bridge at the hour specified in his written orders.[10] Then, however, came a mammoth snarl in operations. After Stoneman sent an advance brigade, under Colonel B. F. "Grimes" Davis, across the stream to chase away Rebel pickets, raindrops began to fall.[11] Soon the rain became a raging storm, thoroughly drenching those cavalrymen who stood patiently beside their mounts, awaiting the command to cross the river.[12]

They waited in vain. Noting that the roads were fast disintegrating and that the torrent showed no sign of ceasing, Stoneman wired Hooker, still with the main army at Falmouth, that the river was rising, menacing the rickety bridge, and that mud would not permit his cannon and wagons to move.

Stoneman wished to draw his troopers into camp until the skies cleared, but Hooker would not hear of it. He was anxious to send his infantry after Lee, but, as he saw it, before he could do so his cavalry had to march. Tersely he wired Stoneman to leave the guns and wagons behind and proceed without further delay.

Since Stoneman was an old soldier, presumably he recognized his responsibility to obey orders. Therefore, this telegram should have spurred him into action. It did not. Quick, decisive activity was not George Stoneman's long suit; he did not like the look of the pelting rain and the rising river and so decided to wait it out, ignoring his commander's wishes.

Hooker did not anticipate such disobedience. Believing that Stoneman would cross the Rappahannock at dawn on the 15th, he telegraphed the White House and the War Department that the cavalry would soon be striking heavy blows at Lee's communications.

★★★★★★★★★★★★★★★★★★★★★★★

10. Foote, *The Civil War*, 2: p. 263.

11. Catton, *Glory Road*, pp. 175-76.

12. Willard Glazier, *Three Years in the Federal Cavalry*, p. 167.

President Lincoln quickly wired a reply that revealed his disinclination to share Hooker's confidence. The president was looked upon as only an amateur strategist, but showed some shrewdness in that role and was also a perceptive judge of generalship. He had not been particularly enthusiastic over Hooker's choice of Stoneman as cavalry chief; now, moreover, Washington lacked tangible evidence that Stoneman's soldiers had commenced their expedition. Noting that Hooker had recently lost telegraphic contact with Stoneman and therefore could not be certain that he had moved out on time, Lincoln did not question Hooker's act of faith, but commented: "General S. is not moving rapidly enough to make the expedition come to anything. He has now been out three days, two of which were unusually fair weather, and all three without hindrance from the enemy, and yet he is not twenty-five miles from where he started. To reach his point he still has sixty to go, another river (the Rapidan) to cross, and will be hindered by the enemy. By arithmetic, how many days will it take him to do it? I do not know that any better can be done, but I greatly fear it is another failure already. . . ." In the past, dozens of cavalry expeditions had failed ignominiously; the president had no reason to suspect that Stoneman's would end differently.

On the 16th, General Hooker learned how perceptive Lincoln was. That morning a courier from Stoneman brought the news that the cavalry was still in camp above the Rappahannock. Stoneman's communiqué explained that the river had overflowed, part of the railroad bridge had been swept away by the freshet, "almost every rivulet was swimming, and the roads [were] next to impassable for horses or pack-mules."

Quite naturally, Hooker was pained. A lengthy delay such as Stoneman anticipated might warp his plans beyond repair; the army's timetable had already been thrown into disorder. But now there seemed no way out; for one thing, during the time Stoneman tarried on the north bank, the river had indeed risen too high to be safely crossed. Therefore Hooker told the cavalry chief to remain where he was, to keep his supplies up to par by foraging off the land, and to be reaqy to march as soon as the water level fell.[13]

★★★★★★★★★★★★★★★★★★★★★★

13. Foote, *The Civil War*, 2: 263-64; Catton, *Glory Road*, p. 176.

The river did not recede to Stoneman's satisfaction for two weeks. During the interval, he kept his regiments busy by moving them from one locale to another, handling picket and reconnaissance chores above the river. The work was calculated to occupy the men's idle hours and thus keep them in a good mood. It did not achieve the desired effect, for the passing days—broken only briefly by spells of passable weather—made the Federal troopers restive and surly. One of them later remarked that "like the fabled general who marched his army up the hill and then marched it down again, the cavalry corps was kept moving, breaking camp in the morning, marching a little, and going into camp again."[14] Another cavalryman recalled that "the various evolutions grew so wearisome to the restless spirits of the men, that they found vent for their impatience in some half-bitter jests."[15] Presumably, General Stoneman was the common target of this humor.

While the cavalry remained immobilized above the river, Hooker revised his opinion of the troopers' capabilities. No longer trusting them to carry out a crucial phase of his campaign, he finally adopted a new plan, much akin to the old, with the major exception that now the foot soldiers would initiate the operations and the cavalry would perform in a secondary role. After both infantry wings had gone forward to the attack, Stoneman's horsemen would cross the rivers, as before, to mangle railroad lines above and west of Richmond. Despite what the troopers might accomplish, however, Hooker would not depend on them to close off the Rebels' retreat route. Thousands of infantrymen would perform that job as well, for Hooker now intended to smash Lee's army where it stood rather than merely force its retreat southward.

Now that his feelings toward Stoneman had altered, however, Hooker decided not to inform his cavalry chief of the entire scope of his new strategy. He told him only that he should proceed as before, rendering as much damage as possible to the enemy's supply routes, giving him only a hint as to the larger picture of the campaign. Hooker seemed not to mind that by being so close-mouthed he ensured that Stone-

★★★★★★★★★★★★★★★★★★★★★

14. N. D. Preston, *History of the Tenth Regiment of Cavalry, New York State Volunteers*, p. 68.

15. Henry R. Pyne, *The History of the First New Jersey Cavalry*, p. 140.

man would grope about south of the Rapidan, in complete ignorance of how, if at all, his mission would contribute to the overall fortunes of the main army.[16]

Finally, on the afternoon of April 28, the rains tapered off, and this time the skies seemed to promise a spell of clear weather. The day before, the main army had begun to leave its camps, heading for the Rappahannock fords to launch the double envelopment.

The cavalry was supposed to move out in the rear early on the 29th, but the order caught Stoneman only partially prepared to comply. He had scattered his pickets over a long stretch of river bank and had to collect them, as well as to pack up his wagons, before he could march. Owing to other difficulties—primarily the bad roads, rendered worse by infantry passage, as well as a new meteorological obstacle, a dense fog—the corps was able to cross the river neither at the designated point nor at the specified time.[17] For several hours the horsemen were led back and forth along the bank, looking for a manageable crossing spot on the rain-swollen stream. Captain Charles F. Adams, Jr., of the 1st Massachusetts Cavalry, son of the United States Ambassador to England, wrote that he "felt pretty sick of this running round after a ford and began to doubt whether we ever should get across that miserable little river."[18] Finally, late in the afternoon, the horsemen splashed across at Kelly's Ford, an operation accomplished, as Stoneman reported to Hooker, only "by dint of great exertion."

On the south shore the commander spread his maps, called together his brigade leaders, and gave them a generalized briefing on their objectives—matters that he ought to have attended to beforehand. For Stoneman, delay seemed a way of life.

Pursuant to orders, the general halved his force. A three thousand five hundred-trooper division, under Brigadier General William W. Averell (who had embarrassed himself during the pursuit of Stuart's Chambersburg raiders), plus Grimes Davis's brigade and a battery of horse artillery, was to

★★★★★★★★★★★★★★★★★★★★★★★★

16. Stackpole, *Chancellorsville*, p. 109; Catton, *Glory Road*, pp. 177-79.

17. *Official Records*, series I, vol. 25, pt. 1, p. 1058.

18. Worthington Chauncey Ford, ed., *A Cycle of Adams Letters, 1861-1865*, 1: 286.

move to Brandy Station, on the Orange & Alexandria Railroad, then southward along the right-of-way and over the Rapidan to the village of Gordonsville.[19] Along the way Averell was expected to cross the path of Rebel cavalry known to be in that neighborhood. His primary mission was to keep this force occupied while Stoneman's second column operated on the more important rail lines farther eastward.[20]

This second wing included a division led by Brigadier General David McMurtrie Gregg, a reserve brigade under Brigadier General John Buford, and a horse-drawn battery. It had been ordered to intersect the Virginia Central at Louisa Court House, twelve miles southeast of Gordonsville, then to proceed toward Hanover Junction and the Richmond, Fredericksburg & Potomac.[21] The later movements of both forces would be coordinated as closely as possible and at some point, hopefully, Averell would link with the companion column.

Some of Stoneman's units were commanded by officers of high caliber. Generals Gregg and Buford were especially gifted leaders, either of them capable of directing the entire expedition. Stoneman recognized their worth and decided to personally accompany them on the trip. Among the lower-echelon leaders were a pair of talented field officers, an English-born soldier of fortune with hardy nerves and a mustache of incredible length, Colonel Sir Percy Wyndham; and Lieutenant Colonel Hasbrouck Davis of the 12th Illinois Cavalry, who with Grimes Davis (no relation to him) had fought his way out of Harpers Ferry the previous September when the garrison was surrounded and much of it captured by Confederate legions.[22] A third colonel of some ability was Judson Kilpatrick, a cocky little Celt who was a heller in the field but was much more erratic than many of his fellow brigade commanders. Kilpatrick's penchant for glory seeking would one day prompt him to raid Richmond with a command of his own.

★★★★★★★★★★★★★★★★★★★★★★★

19. *Official Records*, series I, vol. 25, pt. 1, p. 1058.

20. Brackett, *History of the United States Cavalry*, p. 305; Stackpole, *Chancellorsville*, p. 106.

21. Johnston, *Virginia Railroads*, p. 144.

22. Boatner, *The Civil War Dictionary*, p. 227.

His instructions finally imparted, Stoneman dispatched Averell's division, with its attached brigade, and soon afterward went forward with Gregg's and Buford's force of three thousand five hundred. The march began auspiciously. The

Cavalry raiders leaving camp. COURTESY LIBRARY OF CONGRESS.

weather remained sloppy, the roads not yet dry, but the sensation of movement helped revive the spirits of the cavalrymen. At last they had escaped their cheerless camps and no longer were in the saddle simply to ward off inertia. They suspected they were about to wreak merry havoc on enemy communications, and some believed their ultimate objective to be the Confederate capital. To many soldiers, ending the war was merely a matter of capturing Richmond.

Averell's column was first to make contact with the enemy. Not long after the Federals started down the Orange & Alexandria, portions of two small Rebel brigades, led by Robert E. Lee's son and nephew, Brigadier Generals Rooney and Fitzhugh Lee, crossed the Federals' route of march. Averell correctly decided that he must keep these Confederates busy, and made dispositions accordingly. However, the yet-inexperienced raiders allowed Fitz Lee to escape eastward, while Rooney Lee's brigade pounded quickly toward the south. Averell took up the chase in limited fashion, following Rooney Lee through Culpeper Court House as far as Rapidan Station.[23] At this point the Federals were still several miles short of their objective, but when the Rebels slipped across the Rapidan River and burned the bridge after them, Averell was stymied. He stood still, unable or unwilling to throw his troopers over nearby fords to combat Lee's much-outnumbered soldiers.[24]

Meanwhile, Stoneman's second column had progressed rather slowly, though unopposed by Rebel horsemen, and on the evening of April 30 halted in fields just below the Rapidan and a considerable distance northeast of Averell. By now another spring storm had developed, so the troopers prepared for a wet and muddy night on constant alert.[25] The chaplain of the 6th Pennsylvania Cavalry remembered years afterward: "Hungry, wet, and fatigued, we were illy prepared to spend a night in standing to horse, but such were our orders; and without unsaddling, the regiment was drawn up in close column of companies, the men dismounted, and ordered to stand at their horses' heads all night. No fires could be kindled; and . . . it became very cold, and our clothing being wet, we suffered greatly before morning. Many sank exhausted at their horses' heads, and with reins fastened to wrist, slept for hours despite the discomfort. . . ."

That evening Stoneman made clear to every regimental commander the specific nature of the tasks to be performed during the mission. When the field officers gathered inside the general's sodden tent, they were directed to send to the rear all supply wagons and mules, and those horses that could not be expected to cover fifty miles a day. The route ahead would be difficult, but from now on ground had to be covered in quick time; otherwise, Lee's main army might

★★★★★★★★★★★★★★★★★★★★★★

23. Johnston, *Virginia Railroads,* p. 144; Stackpole, *Chancellorsville,* p. 267; "Stoneman's Raid in the Chancellorsville Campaign," *Battles and Leaders of the Civil War,* 3: 153.

24. Abner Doubleday, *Chancellorsville and Gettysburg,* p. 69; Johnston, *Virginia Railroads,* p. 145; William Brooke Rawle, ed., *History of the Third Pennsylvania Cavalry,* pp. 230-31. This last includes a detailed itinerary of Averell's operations.

25. Brackett, *History of the United States Cavalry,* pp. 305-6.

change front and sweep down on them like hawks attacking chickens.[26]

That night unwelcome news came in from Averell. Stoneman learned that instead of pushing on to Gordonsville, the brigadier was marking time in the Rapidan Station vicinity. Averell apparently was in great fear of being surrounded by Stuart's troopers, whose numbers he greatly exaggerated.

Stoneman was far from sympathetic. He could not afford to detach any horsemen as reinforcements, for he must proceed with his own work, which lay in the direction of Richmond.[27] In communicating with Averell, in fact, he managed to confuse his subordinate rather than aid him. Stoneman's dispatches were so vague and ambiguous that Averell received the impression he should remain indefinitely at Rapidan Station, holding Rooney Lee at arm's length. Later Stoneman claimed that he instructed Averell to make short work of the enemy, then form a juncture with the other raiding column.

The upshot of this communication breakdown was that Averell dawdled above the Rapidan for a day and a half. Not until May 2 did General Hooker—then involved in a general engagement near Chancellorsville—learn of his idleness; when he did, he promptly ordered Averell to rejoin the main army. Even this communiqué did not rouse the cavalry general into action; a second directive was necessary to pry Averell loose from his position and send him moving twenty miles eastward toward Hooker's side.[28]

With a battle in progress, Hooker had little time to interrogate Averell about his questionable contribution to the expedition. Instead, he put him to work reconnoitering the army's right flank. In contrast to the orders Averell had recently received from Stoneman, this directive was clear and precise. Still, the division leader could not obey. After spending a brief time in the field, he returned to tell Hooker that the area under discussion was too rugged to admit of cavalry work.[29]

★★★★★★★★★★★★★★★★★★★★★★★

26. S. L. Gracey, *Annals of the Sixth Pennsylvania Cavalry*, pp. 137-39.

27. *Official Records*, series I, vol. 25, pt. 1, p. 1058.

28. Stackpole, *Chancellorsville*, pp. 267-68; "Stoneman's Raid in the Chancellorsville Campaign," p. 153.

29. Doubleday, *Chancellorsville and Gettysburg*, p. 69.

Now, at last, Hooker lost his temper. He gave Averell a dressing-down, relieved him of his command, and replaced him with Brigadier General Alfred Pleasonton. This demonstrated, if nothing else, that Fighting Joe had a finite supply of patience, after all. He was unusually sympathetic with inept subordinates, willing to go far beyond normal limits to accommodate their eccentricities and tolerate their blundering. But Averell was so incompetent that Hooker could accept his excuses no longer.

3

General Stoneman, for all his fumbling and dilatoriness, did possess one quality that Averell, and at times even Hooker, lacked. He had boundless self-confidence; he truly believed in himself as well as in his soldiers. Conversely, he felt that they believed in him.

In his report of the expedition, filed some days after its conclusion, he noted his feelings at the start of this important stage of the raid, after communicating with Averell. The self-commentary is quite revealing: "From that moment I felt sure that we should meet with success if it lay within the reach of human effort; and here I take the occasion to say that from that time out to the completion of the expedition I never, under the most trying circumstances and the most discouraging prospects, saw a look or heard a word from officer or private soldier that indicated doubt or fear, nor during the whole trip did I hear a murmur or a complaint. . . ."[30]

Stoneman may well have shut his ears to avoid hearing what he did not wish to hear. On the night of April 30 a great many of his men, soaked by rain and shivering in camp without benefit of fires to ward off discomfort, murmured and complained quite a bit. Still, he was essentially correct in saying that his soldiers possessed confidence that their expedition would succeed. Thus far they had encountered no concentrated opposition, and the route toward Richmond and its environs seemed to lay clear. If so, they would soon have the chance to work off pent-up frustrations by wrecking railroad trackage, telegraph lines, and wagon trains, without fear of enemy retaliation.

★★★★★★★★★★★★★★★★★★★★★★★★

30. *Official Records*, series I, vol. 25, pt. 1, pp. 1058-59.

The spirits of the men again improved during the night, for the rain diminished, then ceased. But at two A. M., the hour appointed for the resumption of the march, the soldiers found themselves surrounded by a nearly impenetrable fog bank: mist rolled along the river bank like a curtain of steam. Vision was restricted to a distance of a few yards, and Stoneman lacked a native guide to locate the proper roads.

When daylight came on May 1 the column finally could move, fog having dissipated. The troopers lurched forward, stumbling around south of the river until they happened upon the correct route, then rode on, nervously fingering their carbines and watching for the appearance of gray-clad riders. None appeared. Above Verdiersville they crossed a trail of fresh manure and scattered refuse, indicating that Stuart, with Fitz Lee's brigade, had headed toward Fredricksburg to rejoin the main Rebel army. Stoneman appeared much relieved by the discovery. For the rest of that day, the march proceeded without incident.[31]

Turning westward, Gregg's division and Buford's brigade pushed forward the next day to the Virginia Central, striking the tracks at Louisa Court House about three A. M. Gregg took elaborate steps to ensure a successful attack against enemy troops whom he expected to encounter in the depot village. Setting up his artillery and forming Colonel Percy Wyndham's brigade in support, he directed Judson Kilpatrick to split his brigade into three columns to strike above, in, and below the town. Fire-eater Kilpatrick, captivated by the idea, rode at the head of the force that charged through the depot. He was mightily disappointed to find that the morning darkness hid only a few Confederates. Nor were many north or south of Louisa Court House; Gregg's detailed preparations had been unnecessary, for the Rebels were easily rounded up.

The raiders gladly settled down to their work of destruction. Above and below the depot, trackage was ripped up and manhandled out of position—approximately twenty miles worth. Also wrecked were water towers, culverts, depot housing, and some adjacent municipal property.[32] Before grounding the telegraph lines, Federal officers tapped them

★★★★★★★★★★★★★★★★★★★★★★★★

31. Ibid., p. 1060.

32. Ibid., pp. 1060, 1082.

and, by posing as local operators, gathered information from the enemy capital. "For nearly an hour we received rebel intelligence," a trooper commented. "When the discovery was made in Richmond that the 'Yankees' held the line, some very decided remarks of disapprobation came over the wires . . . [whereupon] they ceased to communicate."

A short distance east of the station could be seen small bands of Rebel horsemen, who had come up to keep a watchful eye on the raiders. Sir Percy Wyndham's brigade was sent in that direction to observe in turn.[33] The staring match was a complete standoff; no Rebels entered the town until after Gregg's and Buford's men departed the area late in the day.[34] By that time, various raiding detachments, including a band of Regulars from the 1st U. S. Cavalry, had gone to neighboring depots to mutilate more trackage, as well as to burn bridges over which enemy forces had to cross to combat the raiders.

The reunited command then pushed farther south, reaching Thompson's Cross-Roads, below the South Anna River, early that evening. The cavalrymen bivouacked there for the night, and there Stoneman gave his subordinates still more instructions, covering their duties during the balance of the mission. From stragglers and freed Negroes the raiders had heard reports of the fighting now taking place farther north; General Hooker supposedly had the Confederates reeling in retreat. The reports heightened Stoneman's determination to make the utmost of the remainder of his time by striking Lee from the rear while the main army presumably crushed his flanks.

Stoneman later recalled that, after assembling his division and brigade leaders, "I gave them to understand that we had dropped in that region of country like a shell, and that I intended to burst it in every direction, expecting each piece or fragment would do as much harm and create nearly as much terror as would result from sending the whole shell, and thus magnify our small force into overwhelming numbers. . . ."[35]

In other terms, Stoneman intended to again split his main force. He projected no fewer than five independent move-

★★★★★★★★★★★★★★★★★★★★★★★

33. Gracey, *Sixth Pennsylvania Cavalry*, p. 141.

34. Glazier, *Three Years in the Federal Cavalry*, p. 178.

35. *Official Records*, series I, vol. 25, pt. 1, p. 1060.

ments by subordinate forces, calculated to do as much damage as feasible along the widest possible front.

Two regiments under Colonel Wyndham were to move directly south, to strike the James River at the village of Columbia, there to destroy the large canal aqueduct over the nearby Rivanna River. Afterward the regiments should continue toward Richmond, destroying material at every step of the way. If practicable, Wyndham was also to send a party across the James to destroy the railroad bridge over the Appomattox River.

Meanwhile, Kilpatrick, with his old regiment, the 2nd New York, and supporting troops, was to push southeastward to the Chickahominy River, which meandered down the Virginia peninsula. He was ordered to wreck rail bridges in that area as well as to cut important telegraph lines, continuing his destruction in the direction of Richmond, much like Wyndham.

A third force, Hasbrouck Davis's 12th Illinois, was authorized to continue damaging the Virginia Central near the depot at Atlee's Station and, at Ashland, to initiate the destruction of a line that ran perpendicular to the Central, the Richmond, Fredricksburg & Potomac.

General Gregg was directed to take the 1st Maine and 10th New York Cavalry, plus some artillery, and lay waste to railroad and foot bridges on and near the South Anna River; a third regiment, the 5th Regulars, would follow Gregg to certify that the bridge wreckers did a thorough job. Finally, one of Stoneman's aides-de-camp, Captain Wesley Merritt, was to lead a detachment from the 1st Maryland "to do what he thought he could accomplish in the way of destroying bridges, &c."

It seemed a thorough plan. If Stoneman had his way, future travelers would have a most difficult time navigating the trails through central Virginia. If all of it worked as anticipated, General Lee, too, might have hard days ahead, when trying to supply his army with rations and supplies from depots south of Fredricksburg.

While the raiding detachments did their work, Stoneman would remain behind with a scratch force of five hundred men from Buford's brigade, to cover the several movements. He probably assumed that his role would consist of no more than sitting tight and waiting for his units to return, their vandalism completed.

By three A. M. on May 3, the detachments had ridden off. Stoneman had directed them to reach their assigned targets within twelve hours, so that each would set to work at approximately the same time, thereby confounding Lee and preventing him from using his communications to rush troops to the threatened areas.[36]

Hence the raid had reached its critical stage, with the decisive work now to be done.

4

Colonel Wyndham's regiments did perhaps the most efficient job of all the detachments. Word of his coming raced ahead of his column,[37] but only a pair of Rebel cavalry squadrons crossed his path before he could reach Columbia; these he easily drove toward the town. After destroying a bridge fifteen miles from Thompson's Cross-Roads, he led his troopers shouting and shooting into the village.

In Columbia Wyndham spent much time setting fire to quartermaster's, ordnance, and commissary stores, and also disposed of a large cache of medical supplies badly needed by Lee's army. Meanwhile, he sent some of his men to chop up several canal boats in the James, including some laden with forage, and then turned his attention to the massive aqueduct that spanned the river canal.

Tugging anxiously at his outsize mustache, Wyndham sent an officer to examine the aqueduct for possible flaws in the stonework that supported it. However, the subordinate took a short look at the thick concrete abutments and went back to tell Wyndham that any attempt to damage it severely would be futile. With a shrug, the Englishman remounted his command and rode off in the direction of Jefferson Davis's capital, spreading minor destruction along the canal.

Shortly before the Federal detachment cleared Columbia, nevertheless, the major in command of Wyndham's old regiment, the 1st New Jersey, decided to make one effort to wreck the aqueduct. Employing fifty men and an immense supply of cartridges, he sought to blow a gaping hole in the stonework. But even as he began to work a gap in one of the

★★★★★★★★★★★★★★★★★★★★★★

36. Ibid., pp. 1060-61.

37. Samuel H. Merrill, *The Campaigns of the First Maine and First District of Columbia Cavalry*, p. 98.

Sir Percy Wyndham. COURTESY LIBRARY OF CONGRESS.

buttresses, he chanced upon several barrels of gunpowder and a thousand feet of waterproof fuse, and decided to use the new resources. Unfortunately, before able to sink the powder into the canal and blow out the stone foundations, the major was recalled to his regiment by Wyndham. Rooney Lee's men had been sighted heading toward Columbia, and they outnumbered the 1st New Jersey; a quick escape became imperative.[38]

A strict timetable influenced Wyndham to relinquish his intention to cross the swollen James and strike the rail span over the Appomattox.[39] After damaging the canal for a long distance, he headed back to Thompson's Cross-Roads, easily eluding Rebel pursuers, and reached the starting-point of his detached mission at eight o'clock that evening, having covered fifty miles in sixteen hours.[40]

Kilpatrick's detachment had the most dangerous route to travel, and never did return to Thompson's Cross-Roads. By hard marching—a favorite practice, which had given him the nickname "Kil-cavalry"—Kilpatrick reached the Fredricksburg Railroad at daylight on the 4th and there destroyed several miles of track, telegraph wires, and depot structures. Afterward he boldly advanced in the direction of the Rebel capital via the Brook Turnpike,[41] driving in enemy pickets. His coming caused consternation in Richmond; church bells rang in warning and home guardsmen ran for their muskets and hunting knives.

With an audacity that loomed in pleasant contrast to the timidity characteristic of many Federal cavalry leaders, Kilpatrick charged an artillery battery a few miles above the capital and forced its crew to retire in hot haste. In this sector Kilpatrick's troopers also swept down upon a fifteen-man detachment detailed to Brigadier General John H. Winder, Richmond's Provost Marshal, and made them prisoners.[42] Unable to resist the urge to address a document from

★★★★★★★★★★★★★★★★★★★★★★

38. Pyne, *First New Jersey Cavalry,* pp. 144-45.

39. Johnston, *Virginia Railroads,* p. 147.

40. *Official Records,* series I, vol. 25, pt. 1, p. 1085.

41. Ibid., p. 1084.

42. Glazier, *Three Years in the Federal Cavalry,* p. 181.

"Richmond," Kilpatrick took time to hand the captives parole papers with that heading.

Winder's chief aide, whom the band had been escorting, was astonished by the Yankee leader's devil-may-care attitude. "You're mighty daring sort of fellows," he told the little colonel, "but you will certainly be captured before sundown."

Smiling briefly, Kilpatrick granted that the officer might be correct, "but we intend to do a mighty deal of mischief first!"

Leaving a portion of his force to deal with other enemy contingents, Kilpatrick pushed on to strategic Meadow Bridge over the Chickahominy, and set it ablaze. His enthusiasm steadily increasing, he then happened on a Rebel locomotive, which he ran off the flaming span and into the river.

At length, Confederate columns came into view along the Brook Pike, and Kilpatrick decided that he had overstayed his time. Since local defenders had blocked the roads connecting him with Stoneman, the colonel hauled out his maps, studied the geography of the nearby Virginia peninsula, portions of which were garrisoned by Union troops, and suddenly cried: "To horse, men! We're all right; we're all safe yet!"[43]

Escorted by a Negro guide, Kilpatrick led his men to Hanover Town, on the banks of the Pamunkey River. He crossed the stream aboard flatboats that he then burned to foil a further enemy pursuit. Moving down the peninsula, he continued to pillage. He burned one hundred wagons laden with foodstuffs, which he found along his route, as well as sixty thousand barrels of corn, wheat, and clothing piled at a local supply depot. In all, he laid waste to three enemy wagon trains, surprised and captured various bands of enemy soldiers, eluded other bands including several cavalry regiments reportedly sent from Stuart's headquarters—and reached the Federal lines at Gloucester Point at ten A. M. on May 7, after covering almost two hundred miles in less than five days.[44] By then, Kilpatrick had effectively demonstrated that bold maneuvering could gain dramatic results.

★★★★★★★★★★★★★★★★★★★★★★★

43. James Moore, *Kilpatrick and Our Cavalry,* pp. 49-50.

44. *Official Records,* series I, vol. 25, pt. 1, p. 1084; Comte De Paris, *History of the Civil War in America,* 3: 120.

The other Federal detachments achieved less spectacular feats. Captain Merritt's team of raiders destroyed a bridge on the South Anna; Gregg's two regiments burned others, including Ground Squirrel Bridge, but were prevented by Rebel infantry and artillery from adding still other spans to their list of spoils. Gregg's troopers also ripped up track on the Gordonsville & Richmond Railroad before remounting for the ride back to Stoneman. Unlike Kilpatrick, General Gregg had no trouble in doing so, and reached Thompson's Cross-Roads on the evening of the 4th.[45]

Lieutenant Colonel Davis's command experienced many of the same difficulties that had plagued Kil-cavalry, but surmounted them with no less élan. Riding down the South Anna toward the Richmond, Fredericksburg & Potomac line, Davis burned bridges, scattered enemy guerrillas who sought to surround him, then charged into Ashland, to the surprise of the town's residents. "Words cannot describe," Davis later wrote, "the astonishment of the inhabitants at our appearance." After slicing telegraph wires and warping trackage, the raiders captured a hospital train crammed with convalescents, spirited away several head of horses, wrecked stables, storehouses, and two locomotives, and nabbed an eighteen-wagon supply train outside the town.

At Hanover Station during the evening of May 3, Davis's men again struck the Virginia Central, burning depot buildings and a trestle-work bridge and also scattering rolling stock along the tracks. Afterward the lieutenant colonel guided his soldiers toward Hanover Court House, thence in the direction of Richmond, and bivouacked that night seven miles north of the capital.

Finally, Davis's detachment passed to the Richmond & York River Railroad, near which it was confronted by another train, this carrying able-bodied infantrymen, supported by cannon aboard flatcars. The Federals imprudently charged the train with two squadrons in the van, while the Rebels scrambled from the cars into battle positions behind the steep rail embankment. The defenders roughly handled Davis's men, who retreated after losing two killed and several wounded.[46]

★★★★★★★★★★★★★★★★★★★★★★★

45. *Official Records,* series I, vol. 25, pt. 1, pp. 1082-83.

46. Ibid., pp. 1086-87.

Unable to penetrate the enemy line, Davis broke for the peninsula, as had Kilpatrick. Crossing several deep streams, some of them guarded by enemy pickets, the harried unit joined Kil-cavalry's men near Gloucester Point, where, as Kilpatrick himself noted, it "found safety and rest under our brave old flag."[47]

5

While all of the detached operations were proceeding apace, General Stoneman waited at Thompson's Cross-Roads, nervously scanning the area for bands of Rebel cavalry. His expectations were satisfied when he learned that Rooney Lee's soldiers, able to roam freely now that Averell was gone, had begun to advance on his rear. But Stoneman's five hundred men were far from helpless. When the advance detail of Lee's command appeared, part of the Federal force charged it on horseback with raised sabers. At once the Confederates took to their heels, and thereafter posed few problems.

After Wyndham, Gregg, and Merritt rejoined him, and once he realized that Kilpatrick and Davis must have headed toward Gloucester Point to escape pursuers, Stoneman began to seek reasons for returning to Hooker's army. There were plenty from which he might choose: the fancied proximity of heavy Rebel forces, the absence of recent word from Hooker, new and ugly rumors about the fortunes of the main army, the dwindling state of Stoneman's rations and forage, the used-up condition of his horses, and others.[48] Any would have been sufficient to prompt Stoneman to pull out.

He began his withdrawal by sending General Buford northwestward on a diversionary operation calculated to convince the Rebels that the raid had not yet ended. Meanwhile, on the night of May 5, the main column marched toward a grouping point at Orange Springs, on the North Anna River; and the next day Buford ended his diversion and marched there as well.[49] Rain began to fall once again, spreading mis-

★★★★★★★★★★★★★★★★★★★★★★★★

47. Ibid., p. 1084; Preston, *Tenth New York Cavalry*, p. 75.

48. *Official Records*, series I, vol. 25, pt. 1, pp. 1061-62.

49. Johnston, *Virginia Railroads*, p. 149; George B. Davis, "The Stoneman Raid," *Journal of the U. S. Cavalry Association* 24 (1913-14): 548.

ery among the blue-clothed columns. "The night was very dark," recalled a trooper, "and much of the way led us through dense woods, intensifying the darkness; and for several hours it was utterly impossible for one to see the person riding immediately in advance, or even the head of the animal upon which he was himself mounted. We marched all night, wet, hungry, and tired. . . ."[50]

After a cautious ride, Stoneman's force reached the Rappahannock at Kelly's Ford late on the 7th. There the troopers learned that Hooker's army had been decisively defeated in the Wilderness a few days before, and had returned to its old camps north of the river. The reaction of Charles F. Adams, Jr., may have echoed the sentiments of many of Stoneman's tired, dejected troopers: "I felt sick of the war, of the army, almost of life. . . ."[51]

Swimmimg their animals across the stream, once again high from rains, the soldiers reached the safety and comfort of their lines during the afternoon of May 8. Without wasting time, Stoneman sat down to review the expedition in a written report, praising his men—and himself—for having achieved a strategic success of grand proportions.

He was deluding himself. His raid did not merit such a description because he had failed to employ detachments large enough or working long enough to render more than temporary damage to rail lines, bridges, depots, and canals—all of which fell far short of the decisive destruction Hooker had planned for Lee's communications.[52] Neither important spans on the Virginia Central nor the main supply hub of the Army of Northern Virginia at Guiney's Station on the R, F & P, had been touched by Stoneman's raiders, though loosely guarded by the enemy.[53]

As it had happened, Stoneman traveled an almost entirely clear path through middle Virginia, because Lee deemed his operation a mere nuisance raid, not worth the effort involved in dispatching a large force to quell it. As Lee realized, scars such as Stoneman inflicted could be healed in a relatively

★★★★★★★★★★★★★★★★★★★★★★★★

50. Gracey, *Sixth Pennsylvania Cavalry*, p. 149.

51. Ford, *Cycle of Adams Letters*, 1: 293.

52. Johnston, *Virginia Railroads*, p. 150.

53. Doubleday, *Chancellorsville and Gettysburg*, p. 68; Catton, *Glory Road*, p. 228.

short time. Within a few days burned bridges would be re-built, broken trackage replaced, and grounded telegraph wire restrung. In point of fact, trains were again running down the R, F & P by May 5, two days after the Federals had damaged it, and along the Virginia Central by May 8.[54]

Ironically, the most significant effect of Stoneman's raid was that it had deprived Hooker's army of a major portion of its cavalry support at a critical time.[55] Stoneman's opponents, Stuart's main body, had therefore marched unhindered into the Virginia Wilderness near Chancellorsville, where Fitzhugh Lee spied an exposed Federal flank and notified his uncle. As a result, Stonewall Jackson had smashed that flank, tipping the battle in the Confederates' favor.[56]

Stoneman's casualties—fewer than ninety men killed or wounded, 307 missing—indicated to Hooker that the cavalry had not been seriously engaged. Hooker also noted that thousands of horses had been rendered unserviceable from hard marching during the ten-day trip.[57] Discovering that no long-range benefits accrued from the expedition—and pained by stories in Southern newspapers that Richmond could have been captured had Stoneman possessed nerve enough to try—Hooker relieved the cavalry chief, just as, earlier, he had replaced the inept Averell.

In justice to George Stoneman, it should be stressed that his instructions had been unconscionably vague, not explicitly stating the amount of damage Hooker expected him to inflict on Lee's supply lines. Furthermore, terrible weather had been a significant factor in the raid's disappointing outcome. Even so, subordinates such as Kilpatrick and Hasbrouck Davis had shown promise in field command, and there was at least a grain of truth in one participant's comment that this first sustained maneuver by a Federal mounted corps had a great effect on the morale of the troopers in the Army of the Potomac.[58]

★★★★★★★★★★★★★★★★★★★★★★★

54. Johnston, *Virginia Railroads*, p. 149; Stackpole, *Chancellorsville*, p. 110.

55. Charles D. Rhodes, "Federal Raids and Expeditions in the East,' *The Photographic History of the Civil War*, 4: 122.

56. Boatner, *The Civil War Dictionary*, p. 803.

57. Foote, *The Civil War*, 2: 314.

58. Pyne, *First New Jersey Cavalry*, p. 146; Preston, *Tenth New York Cavalry*, p. 77.

Still, although the raiders had been encumbered by few major difficulties such as a wide-scale enemy pursuit and heavily defended objectives, they had returned after gaining no decisive results.[59] Therefore the raid seemed barren not only to General Hooker but to all in the North, particularly those officials in Washington responsible for directing the Federal war effort. One of the most intelligent of these proved to be Lincoln himself, for the president had occupied firm ground when predicting in the early going that the operation would prove a failure. On the other hand, with General Stoneman in command, backed by General Averell, Lincoln could have anticipated little else.

★★★★★★★★★★★★★★★★★★★★★★

59. Benjamin W. Crowninshield and D. H. L. Gleason, *A History of the First Regiment of Massachusetts Cavalry Volunteers*, p. 120; Moses Harris, "The Union Cavalry," *War Papers: Read Before the Wisconsin M. O. L. L. U. S.* 1 (1891): 362.

7

A MONTH OF HOPES
AND DESPAIRS

Morgan's Indiana and Ohio Raid
(July 1-26, 1863)

1

When Brigadier General John Hunt Morgan set a goal for
himself, he allowed no one to deter him from reaching it. By
late June of 1863 he had conceived a bold notion to take his
Tennessee-based two thousand five hundred-man cavalry division into Kentucky, then across the Cumberland and Ohio
Rivers, to raise merry hell in the Federal-held states of Indiana and Ohio. The plan reflected Morgan's love of daring
and scorn for danger, and seemed to promise a campaign
more dramatic than his three previous large-scale raids
through Tennessee and Kentucky. His subordinate officers,
kindred spirits to him in their preference for adventure,
were more than willing to put the scheme to the trial. And
Morgan's troopers, whom many observers believed the most
reckless in the Confederate service, would have followed
their commander to Siberia had he hankered to take them
there.

The only hitch was that Morgan's superior, General Bragg,

did not want to risk damage to his cavalry on such a chancy, long-range operation. Morgan noted Bragg's disapproval, thought matters over for a short period, then proceeded to make preparations to carry out the plan regardless.[1]

By his determination, he finally won Bragg's approval of a limited campaign. Morgan was authorized to slip over the Cumberland, seize Federal weapons and beef on the hoof, and quickly return to the Confederate lines. Careful to give the impression that he would faithfully adhere to these instructions, the "Beau Sabreur of the South" called together his two brigade commanders, Colonels Basil Duke (his brother-in-law) and Adam R. Johnson, and revealed to them his true intentions. The trio agreed to keep their ultimate objectives a secret from everyone else involved.

The colonels realized that such a strike as Morgan had in mind was needed to distract the attention of Federals above the Cumberland from the movements of Bragg's main army. The Army of Tennessee was in peril, having recently been depleted by the loss of several divisions, which, under General Joseph E. Johnston, had been rushed to the defense of Vicksburg. Recognizing that this had placed his army in a vulnerable position before Rosecrans's Army of the Cumberland, Bragg had recently decided to withdraw to more defensible positions below the Tennessee River. Even he admitted that a cavalry raid in a distant sector would be a means of relieving pressure from his withdrawing forces and might also prevent an attack by the enemy.[2]

The commander of the Confederate forces could not peer into the future, and so Bragg did not know that his reinforcement of Vicksburg would be for naught. Early in July Grant's army would strangle the life out of the fortress after a successful siege. And to add to the disastrous chain of events that threatened the fortunes of the Confederacy, the decisive battle of Gettysburg would end in Union victory during the same period.

Morgan's brigade leaders went ahead with plans for his unauthorized mission, never stopping to question their

★★★★★★★★★★★★★★★★★★★★★★★★

1. Cecil F. Holland, *Morgan and His Raiders*, pp. 223-25.

2. Basil W. Duke, "Morgan's Indiana and Ohio Raid," *The Annals of the War, Written by Leading Participants, North and South*, pp. 241-43.

commander's planned disobedience. Years afterward, Colonel Duke stated:

"This expedition into the Northwestern States had long been a favorite idea with him and was but the practical development of his theory of the proper way to prosecute the war, to-wit: by going deep into the country of the enemy. He had for several weeks foreseen the necessity of some such diversion in General Bragg's behalf, and believed that the period for the accomplishment of his great desire was at hand."[3]

Duke and Johnson, therefore, could see the need for such a bold undertaking even if General Bragg seemed not to; like a goodly number of officers in the Army of Tennessee, Morgan's colonels had a low opinion of the querelous, timid, often inept army leader.

As Duke noted, Morgan had been itching to implement his plan for quite some time. His patience to get under way had been frayed badly two weeks ago, when compelled to shelve his project temporarily in order to lead his division into East Tennessee in an ultimately futile pursuit of some invading Union cavalry. Bad roads and rough weather had played hob with his command, which did little to relieve the brigadier general's frustration.[4] He did not care for limited campaigns of that stripe, for they forced him to wear out mounts and men pursuing a goal that did not particularly interest him. Independent and given to improvisation, he preferred to ride freely, unrestricted by orders calling for him to be in a specific locale at a certain time in order to carry out a specifically designated task. He had imagination, creativity, a flair for the dramatic (as had more than a few Confederate cavalrymen), and long-distance raiding through an enemy's land was the sort of project he found most appealing.

Therefore, when the time came for him at last to be off on his raid beyond the Cumberland, he went about it with a sensation of satisfaction and happy anticipation. On the morning of July 2, at his new headquarters at Burkesville, Kentucky,

★★★★★★★★★★★★★★★★★★★★★★

3. Basil W. Duke, *Morgan's Cavalry,* p. 297.

4. D. Alexander Brown, *The Bold Cavaliers: Morgan's 2nd Kentucky Cavalry Raiders,* p. 178; H. C. Weaver, "Morgan's Raid in Kentucky, Indiana, and Ohio," *Sketches of War History, 1861-1865: Papers Read Before the Ohio M. O. L. L. U. S.* 4 (1896): 280.

he had his troopers saddle up and push westward.[5] Resulting noises—jingling harnesses, the creak of saddle leather, and the heavy tred of horses, wagons, and cannon over the dusty Kentucky roads—were pure music to Morgan. He sensed that his soldiers were eager to be off on a sustained march, even if they did not know their destination. He was correct; as one of his troopers recollected in laconic fashion years later: "We were ready and willing to go." The man had implicit faith in his commander's judgment, though he suspected only that the expedition was in some way intended to help Braxton Bragg "get out of the state."[6]

Riding at the head of his eleven regiments, Morgan at once became the center of attention. Soon after the march got under way, the men in the vanguard of the column struck up a homespun ditty in his honor. In a resounding chorus, they saluted the general and his brother-in-law with an insistent refrain: "Here's the health to Duke and Morgan—Drink it down!"[7]

It is not hard to understand why Morgan, upon sight, drew so much admiration. He was tall and broad-shouldered, with a flowing mustache, an elegant goatee, and an intelligent, kindly face made thin by a receding hairline. One admirer commented: "Easily approached, all men were his friends. I never saw him otherwise than neatly dressed, and he was often elegantly attired, always a gentleman."[8] On this day he wored a plumed felt hat; the affectation seemed to link him in direct relationship with J. E. B. Stuart. There were many people in Kentucky and Tennessee—Federal as well as Confederate—who considered Morgan the military equal, in every sense, to the dashing Virginia cavalier. Quite a few of those who had fought against him in the past swore that Stuart could be no more wily nor pugnacious than he.

Only a few miles north of camp, already deep in territory hotly fought over by both armies, Morgan's two thousand five hundred riders came up to the lower bank of the Cum-

★★★★★★★★★★★★★★★★★★★★★★★★

5. Duke, *Morgan's Cavalry*, p. 300.

6. L. D. Hockersmith, *Morgan's Escape: A True History of the Raid of General Morgan, Etc.*, p. 15.

7. Brown, *The Bold Cavaliers*, p. 179.

8. George Dallas Mosgrove, *Kentucky Cavaliers in Dixie: Reminiscences of a Confederate Cavalryman*, p. 129.

John Hunt Morgan. FROM *Photographic History of the Civil War.*

berland. This day the river was a formidable obstacle, stoked with debris from an unusual summer freshet, water lapping over the shoreline.[9] It would take several hours to ford the river, which at this locale was nearly a half-mile broad.

★★★★★★★★★★★★★★★★★★★★★★★★

9. Howard Swiggett, *The Rebel Raider: A Life of John Hunt Morgan,* p. 129.

Morgan rightly took this as an indication that rough times lay ahead. But he went to work immediately, ferrying Basil Duke's brigade and four dismantled cannon across at a point opposite Burkesville, aboard what Duke later called "two crazy little flats that seemed ready to sink under the weight of a single man, and two or three canoes."[10] Colonel Johnson's troopers, crossing at Turkey Neck Bend, several miles downstream, had even greater difficulties, for fewer boats were available to them. Johnson's men had to fashion rafts to pass weapons and·ammunition across, after which they dived into the deep water beside their mounts and began paddling. Those who could not swim grabbed their horses' tails and were pulled through the stream. In small groups, wet men and animals reached the far shore, where they stopped to dry themselves as best they could. Some soldiers, who had waded naked into the Cumberland, hurriedly donned their uniforms.[11] As he made his way through the water, Morgan congratulated himself on his daring: the Yankees would hardly suspect that a large force of cavalry would try to cross a river so swollen by rain.

Still, Morgan could not have expected such a large fording operation to go undetected. Along the north shore of the Cumberland stretched a formidable line of enemy outposts, filled with many soldiers who had tangled with the Rebel raiders in the past. Those nearest the crossing sites drew their rifles up and showered minié balls upon the first cavalrymen to reach dry ground.

The Confederates responded with quick action. Many of those still naked picked up firearms from the rafts in which they had been kept dry. Without waiting for either their horses or their clothes, they charged the Federal pickets with blazing guns. Other of their comrades reached the north bank and went to their aid, and for several minutes a brisk skirmish swirled along the shore. After suffering many casualties, the enemy fled. Although the weight of Rebel numbers alone had decided the outcome of the contest, Morgan took considerable satisfaction from it, especially since part of the defeated force had been detached from the 1st

★★★★★★★★★★★★★★★★★★★★★★★★

10. Duke, *Morgan's Cavalry*, p. 300.

11. Hockersmith, *Morgan's Escape*, p. 16.

Kentucky (Union) Cavalry, commanded by an old and bitter foe, Colonel Frank Wolford.

The surviving Federals scrambled into the thick woods that fringed the river and headed toward local headquarters, spreading news of Morgan's coming. One wounded man of Wolford's regiment carried the alarm to a nearby farmhouse, where a woman dressed his injury, then mounted a horse and rode twenty miles to the infantry camp of Brigadier General Samuel Carter at Somerset. Mud-spattered and with her hair hanging limply to waist length, the woman gasped out the message which the trooper had given her: "John Morgan, with two brigades, has crossed the Cumberland near Burkesville and is marching on Columbia!"[12]

Soon a manhunt was on.

2

Although the depth of the Cumberland River had made the Rebel crossing difficult, it had also made it possible. As Morgan had foreseen, his enemy had not suspected that even a man as audacious as he would attempt such a hazardous maneuver. Hence they had not been particularly alert on July 2 and had offered no great resistance.

Ironically, the Federal troops in lower Kentucky had been expecting Morgan to break loose on a new raid for quite some time. Alerted to that probability by Bragg's assailable position—which seemed to indicate that his cavalry would attempt a diversionary operation—as well as by Confederate deserters who spread rumors about an upcoming raid, Brigadier General Henry M. Judah, commanding a cordon of Federal outposts in southern Kentucky, had been waiting for Morgan to make his move as early as June 18.[13] Since thousands of Federals, of all arms, patrolled the upper bank of the Cumberland, Morgan's successful crossing had been extraordinary.

Because the major portion of Bragg's army was still intact, still maneuvering for positions below the Tennessee, General Rosecrans felt obliged to remain in its front with his Army of

★★★★★★★★★★★★★★★★★★★★★★★★

12. Allan Keller, *Morgan's Raid,* pp. 19, 26-27.

13. Weaver, "Morgan's Raid," p. 281.

the Cumberland and was unwilling to detach additional troops to run down Morgan's raiders. Principal responsibility for pursuing the invaders rested upon commanders in those areas which the Rebels traversed.

Atop the local chain of command was Major General Ambrose Burnside, who now headed the Army and the Department of the Ohio, with headquarters at Cincinatti. On July 3, as he began mustering field troops to run down the invaders, Burnside wired Secretary of War Stanton: "Morgan broke through our lines at Burkesville yesterday with 4000 or 5000 cavalry and started for the interior of the state." Shortly afterward, General Rosecrans also sent an urgent telegram to Washington, stating that "The Rebel Cavalry has crossed the Cumberland. Morgan is in Kentucky."[14] Rosecrans realized that more words were not necessary to make clear the gravity of the situation. His short message would be sufficient to send a cold sweat down the backs of all those concerned with the safety of Federal communications in the West.

General Judah, one of Burnside's division leaders, had originally been entrusted with the responsibility of coming to grips with Morgan. In fact he had attempted to break up the proposed expedition even before it got under way—with unfortunate results. Judah was a notoriously slow mover, but he had three subordinates who were as much given to decisive action as he to idleness and timidity. One among the trio was Colonel Wolford, a massive, slab-faced, dark-haired guerrilla chief who looked much like an Indian, though rarely maneuvered with Indian-like stealth. The second officer was Brigadier General Edward Hobson, leader of one of Judah's brigades; he was a balding, keen-eyed soldier in his late thirties who usually fought like a bulldog. The third was a gray-haired, distinguished looking brigadier named James M. Shackleford, one of the most widely respected Kentuckians in the Federal ranks.[15]

Judah's hope of destroying the Rebel raid in its incipiency fell apart because he did not unleash these capable officers, who were eager to implement their own plans for defeating Morgan. Then, too, Judah failed to properly cooperate with other local commanders such as General Carter at

★★★★★★★★★★★★★★★★★★★★★★

14. Swiggett, *The Rebel Raider*, p. 130.

15. Brown, *The Bold Cavaliers*, pp. 59-60, 214.

Somerset.[16] And even before Morgan forced his way across the swollen Cumberland, Judah became unable to put his infantry on the enemy's trail straightaway. At a critical moment, the foot soldiers found themselves trapped below the Green River, which, like the Cumberland, had risen to flood stage.

Judah's performance drove General Burnside into a fit of rage, and meant that only mobile regiments could quickly take up the chase. General Hobson, who was the highest-ranking officer in a position to lead a pursuit, had at his disposal almost four thousand blue-coated cavalry and mounted infantry,[17] who were more than slightly eager to clash with the Rebel raiders. When the various mounted units were told of the pursuit plan, an Ohio officer noted that "The information . . . was received with tumultuous cheers."[18]

Colonel Wolford's soldiers mounted for the ride during a driving summer rainstorm, their rubber ponchos protecting them and their weapons from the elements. These were not the most comfortable conditions under which to start a decisive chase; however, the Federal cavalrymen were not accustomed to easy living. They had often battled Morgan's Kentuckians—some of whom were hometown neighbors —and regarded such combat as a grudge fight, whose stakes involved personal pride. Too often in those past battles the Union troopers had come out second best; now they thirsted for lasting revenge. The rough, muddy trail that lay ahead promised difficulties the like of which they had not encountered in two grueling years of war. Yet, one Union cavalryman remarked that his comrades would follow that trail "If it led them even to the State of Maine."[19]

3

Once over the Cumberland, Morgan's men headed for the village of Columbia, their march spearheaded by the 14th

★★★★★★★★★★★★★★★★★★★★★★

16. Weaver, "Morgan's Raid," pp. 281-87.

17. Keller, *Morgan's Raid*, pp. 29, 56, 67; *Official Records*, series I, vol. 23, pt. 1, p. 656.

18. Theodore F. Allen, "Six Hundred Miles of Fried Chicken," *Journal of the U. S. Cavalry Association* 12 (1899): 163-64.

19. Ibid., p. 164.

Kentucky regiment, commanded by the general's brother, Colonel Dick Morgan. Behind that unit rode the balance of Johnson's brigade, consisting of four other Bluegrass regiments; Basil Duke's brigade, comprising four Kentucky units and one from Tennessee, was farther to the rear. The troopers seemed in good spirits. They had bivouacked for the night after crossing the river and now, on this morning of July 3, were cheered to find that the annoying rain had ceased and that bright sunlight was drying the various mud puddles along the Columbia road.[20]

The column loped along at a pleasant pace, with many of the men singing, making music with mouth organs, or chatting casually with one another. After their brief battle with the outpost troops above the river, they had met no strong Federal resistance, and had no reason to suspect that the situation would radically change without sufficient warning. Morgan's scouts and the riders at the point of the column were among the most experienced lookouts in the army; if Yankees headed their way, they would be spotted and their movements quickly evaluated. There then would be time for General Morgan to make defensive dispositions.

As the march proceeded, Morgan rode up and down the line, conversing with officers and men. His soldiers responded amiably, for they genuinely liked him. Morgan treated them more like back-home friends (which many of them were in fact) than as soldiers subject to his authority. However, this familiarity indicated a weakness in Morgan's leadership. As Bragg's inspector generals had noted, Morgan's men seemed to consider themselves members of some gentlemen's club, in which everyone was responsible only unto himself for following rules. Morgan exercised the loosest form of discipline, as though unwilling to injure his men's feelings by ruling with a heavy hand. As a consequence, his troopers were apt to run wild now and then, foreseeing few repurcussions. Looting and straggling seemed favorite diversions, and whenever these could be accomplished without blatant conspicuousness, the men indulged themselves. By being lax in controlling his men, Morgan secured their affection, just as by his heroism he won their re-

★★★★★★★★★★★★★★★★★★★★★★

20. Duke, *Morgan's Cavalry*, p. 304.

spect; but his lack of control gave his command a widespread reputation for rowdyism and insubordination.

This situation reflected another, more serious flaw in Morgan's personality. Unable or unwilling to discipline his men, neither could he discipline himself. His frequent flights of romantic imagination were not often coupled with that essential level-headed awareness of reality that was J. E. B. Stuart's saving grace. Morgan went beyond romanticism; he could be moody, erratic, even unstable. Sometimes his unpredictability of temperament would cancel out his native shrewdness, for his self-aggrandizement could lead him into irrational acts for the sake of winning glory and renown. On such occasions, his personal flaws placed his soldiers' lives in jeapordy.[21] In retrospect, his present expedition would prove a particularly apt case in point.

Morgan did not attempt to curtail his men's merriment on this first full day of the march; today he would play the indulgent father, glorying in his children's innocent amusement. He did not know that had certain momentous events occurring elsewhere in the country been publicized among his column, his men's merriment would have halted with chilling abruptness. July 3 might be a sunlit, pleasant day in southern Kentucky, but in western Mississippi and central Pennsylvania the afternoon was a terrible one for the Confederacy. At Vicksburg, General Pemberton was petitioning Ulysses Grant for surrender terms; and at Gettysburg, Major General George Pickett was bringing upon the field the fifteen thousand infantrymen who would make the doomed charge forever marking the high tide of the Confederate Army. When Pickett's tide receded, the hopes of the Southern forces would crumble into dust.

But at this moment the only dust that attracted Morgan's attention was that stirred into life by the movements of a distant mounted column moving toward the head of the raiding force. He was informed by his scouts that this was a detachment of Wolford's cavalrymen, approaching Columbia from the opposite direction. It was a small band; there was no cause for alarm.

As usual, the scouts were right. The oncoming cavalry

★★★★★★★★★★★★★★★★★★★★★★

21. Stephen Z. Starr, *Colonel Grenfell's Wars: The Life of a Soldier of Fortune*, pp. 46-47.

comprised units from three Ohio regiments—fewer than five hundred men. Morgan's point riders met them on the outskirts of the village, where many on both sides dismounted and took up positions in nearby buildings. When the Confederate vanguard came up, however, the Ohioans hastily remounted and were soon on their way up the road, the Rebel advance guard baying fiercely at their heels.

Morgan took his column through Columbia at an easy gait, an operation that lasted all day. By nightfall, the rear units were sleeping among streets, yards, and orchards at the edge of the village.[22] The townspeople suffered dearly for the cavalry's slowness in marching through; fugitives from the column took the opportunity to loot some homes for items of use to them. Coming as it did at the start of the expedition, the plundering was a clear indication of Morgan's laxness as a disciplinarian.

Realizing that local Federal forces must be preparing defense lines in the interior of Kentucky, Morgan pushed on next day, Johnson's brigade in the lead. Early that morning the advance guard encountered its first concentrated measure of enemy resistance. At Tebb's Bend, near which the cavalry had to cross the Green River, Colonel Orlando H. Moore of the 25th Michigan Infantry had assembled some four hundred bluecoats to halt the Rebel march. Morgan made a costly error by underestimating the strength of Moore's entrenched position. Without even attempting to make a diversionary or flank movement, he ordered Colonel Johnson to strike the Federals head-on with one regiment, the 11th Kentucky. The Kentuckians raced forward, reached the trench line, and were gunned down in droves. Its colonel killed in the charge, the regiment retreated. Re-forming, the 11th attacked again and then a third time—with the same result. Morgan then shelled the enemy position with the four light artillery pieces that accompanied his cavalry—with no different effect. Earlier, Colonel Moore, in answer to a surrender demand by Morgan, had stated that "The Fourth of July is a bad day for surrenders, and I must therefore decline." The reply should have indicated the amount of determination the Yankees possessed; now, finally, Morgan realized what he was up against. Recalling all units, he broke

22. Keller, *Morgan's Raid*, pp. 29-30.

off the fight and pushed northward toward the town of Lebanon, carefully bypassing Moore's works.[23]

After bivouacking on the Lebanon road that night, the command witnessed a murder within its ranks. A captain who had been placed under arrest for filching a pocket watch from a civilian prisoner shot and killed his captor, Morgan's assistant adjutant general, so he might escape. He then vanished into the night—a flesh-and-blood example of the corruption spreading slowly but implacably through the gray ranks.[24]

The next morning the raiders pushed on to Lebanon, which they found guarded by parts of four Federal regiments under Lieutenant Colonel Charles Hanson, 20th Kentucky Infantry. Hanson's force included sons of Bluegrass families, some of them brothers of Morgan's men. Hoping to march through town without launching a fratricidal attack, Morgan made a show of force calculated to convince Hanson that his outnumbered force must capitulate. Drawing his leading regiments into a two-line front, the Beau Sabreur of the South confronted the enemy positions at short range, then lobbed a few cannon balls inside the nearest works. Finally, when Hanson refused to yield his position, Morgan reluctantly ordered a charge, led by the 2nd and 8th Kentucky. After a prolonged battle in ninety-degree heat, Hanson ran up a white flag, and Morgan's main body entered Lebanon without further molestation. But by then the Kentucky cavalry regiments had suffered fifty casualties; one of their dead was nineteen-year-old Lieutenant Tom Morgan, the raiding leader's favorite brother.[25]

The invaders tarried only long enough to gather up needed accoutrements at the local supply depot, afterward resuming their march in the direction of Springfield. As the column maundered on in muggy evening darkness, a whole company of Kentuckians deserted the ranks, and bands of mounted Federals, now sniping at the column's tag end,

★★★★★★★★★★★★★★★★★★★★★★★

23. Brown, *The Bold Cavaliers*, pp. 181-82; *Official Records*, series I, vol. 23, pt. 1, pp. 645-46.

24. Duke, *Morgan's Cavalry*, pp. 308-9.

25. Brown, *The Bold Cavaliers*, pp. 182-84; Holland, *Morgan and His Raiders*, pp. 229-30.

began to close in, gobbling up stragglers.[26] The casual, joy-ride nature of the early stage of the march had disappeared; the farther north Morgan rode, the more dangerous the operation became, and the longer the odds against his division returning in one piece to Tennessee.

At four in the morning on July 6, the command entered Bardstown, within striking distance of the Ohio River. Citizens of the great port cities of Louisville and Cincinatti, farther up the river, grew highly alarmed, and their newspapers ran banner headlines proclaiming Morgan's coming. In Cincinatti, General Burnside rushed thither and yon, still trying to raise a force of infantry and cavalry capable of coping with the emergency.

In Bardstown, Morgan's men corned a unit of home guardsmen and easily forced them to surrender. They then captured three locomotives on the nearby Louisville & Nashville, did some damage to local military stores, and afterward settled down to a six-hour rest—the first long respite Duke's brigade had been privileged to take in two days. Morgan realized that horses as well as men were fast wearing out, but he also knew that he must keep moving.

The next two days were spent in grueling travel toward the Ohio, during which Morgan's men simultaneously fought off their pursuers and the sweltering July heat. Finally, at dawn on the 8th, they reached the river at Brandenburg, Kentucky.[27] Looking across the wide, shimmering expanse of the Ohio, the cavalrymen smiled in self-satisfaction. They knew that by crossing, they could unleash a storm of fear such as the North had only once experienced, during Lee's advance into Pennsylvania. Kentucky was a border state —Confederates had maneuvered freely in parts of it since the earliest days of the war—but across the Ohio was Indiana, and Indiana represented hitherto inviolate Federal soil.

Even before coming up to the river, Morgan had done a great deal to spread alarm across the Northern states. In this he had been assisted by George A. Ellsworth, a Canadian-born trooper whom his comrades called "Lightning," perhaps because he had a fondness for a whiskeylike concoction of

★★★★★★★★★★★★★★★★★★★★★★★★

26. Swiggett, *The Rebel Raider*, p. 131.

27. Keller, *Morgan's Raid*, pp. 45-46, 49.

that name. Ellsworth, a telegrapher extraordinary, had proved his worth all along the way by intercepting Federal messages and sending spurious telegrams of his own. By cutting into a telegraph line, grounding one wire, and attaching his "bug" to another, he tapped out authentic-sounding reports doubling or trebling the size of Morgan's force and spreading rumors about the existence of other Rebel commands operating with it. Federal wires were soon buzzing with the fabrications, adding further to the discomfiture of local commanders.[28]

While Morgan's troopers gathered on the south bank of the river, they were peppered at long range by local inhabitants and home guards on the Indiana side. The Rebel leader countered by unlimbering his guns and shelling the Indianians back to high ground. Then he crossed the crack 2nd Kentucky in a fleet of steamboats, which some of his scouts had captured the day before after riding into Brandenburg in advance of the main body. From the south bank most of the Confederates watched raptly as the single regiment scrambled onto the Indiana shore, preparing to dislodge the citizen-soldiers. Suddenly, however, a tin-clad gunboat steamed around a bend in the river and began to spray the Indiana shore and then the Kentucky side with her concealed guns. It was a chilling moment for Morgan, who realized that he might be trapped on the south bank and left naked to an attack from the rear when pursuers caught up to him. His fear dissipated only after his artillery chief set up two cannon on the lip of the bluff above the town and gave the gunboat a dose of round shot. After an hour's duel, the little ship gave up the contest and steamed upstream. Later in the day she reappeared, but once again was chased off by the Rebel artillery.[29]

The entire day was consumed by ferrying the division over the river aboard the makeshift fleet. The men paddled across cheerfully, aware that at long last the march that had carried them out of lower Kentucky had reached Yankeedom. Again an almost festive air seemed to seize the men, who were further cheered when the crossing came off smoothly. Not a single man was lost during the operation.

★★★★★★★★★★★★★★★★★★★★★★★

28. Ibid., pp. 46-47.

29. Hockersmith, *Morgan's Escape*, pp. 18-19; Duke, "Morgan's Indiana and Ohio Raid," pp. 248-50.

Indiana immediately pleased the troopers. On the far shore were dozens of well-stocked farmhouses and barns, deserted and ripe for the looting. Fresh bread, chickens, fruits and vegetables disappeared; meanwhile, the ferryboats in the river were set afire to prevent their use by pursuers: the flames were at once visible to Federals miles to the rear.

It was midnight before the last of Morgan's soldiers was on Northern soil. Once again the long, winding column stirred into life and rode onward.

The Rebel rear guard remained for a time along the river bank, making certain that the boats burned so thoroughly that Federals could not salvage them. Then, suddenly, the men heard the crack of rifle fire, and peering into the distance saw the shadowy figures of horsemen on the opposite shore. This was the advance eschelon of General Hobson's force: the Yankees had arrived on the scene just an hour or two late.[30]

Realizing that their escape had been a near thing indeed, but grateful that good fortune seemed to be favoring them, the men of the Confederate rear guard remounted and pushed on through Indiana.

4

By now the Federal pursuit column had swollen to huge size. By order of General Burnside, Hobson had taken command of two Kentucky cavalry regiments; plus General Shackleford's force, consisting of an entire Kentucky cavalry regiment, part of another, a section of an Indiana light artillery battery, and various mixed forces. The latter included Colonel Wolford's two regiments of mounted Kentuckians and Tennesseans, and a howitzer battery, as well as Colonel August V. Kautz's 2nd and 7th Ohio cavalry regiments.[31] The total force was better than four thousand men—entirely sufficient to bring John Hunt Morgan to bay, if strength alone indicated a decisive advantage.

On the other hand, Hobson's column had been riding strenuously for more than a week by the time the Rebels crossed the Ohio, and many of its horses—to say nothing of

★★★★★★★★★★★★★★★★★★★★★★★★

30. Keller, *Morgan's Raid*, p. 65.

31. Weaver, "Morgan's Raid," p. 289.

their riders—were badly in need of rest and food.

General Hobson was driven by a burning passion to collar Morgan, but he was not particularly lucky, nor was he a brilliant strategist or tactician. Yet he had foreseen that his adversary was planning to cross into Indiana at or near Brandenburg, and had so advised the Federal commander of the District of Kentucky, at Louisville. Unfortunately, Hobson temporarily halted his pursuit near Bardstown Junction in order to communicate with Louisville in the hope that its commander would send gunboats to oppose the Rebel ferry effort.

Hobson also had to stop for needed rations. The general in charge at Louisville—relieved to hear that his city was not due for a visit by Morgan—quickly dispatched the supplies by rail. Even so, the pursuers lost valuable time waiting for them, and the loss proved fateful. On the 8th, finally heading north again, Hobson lost further hours by halting for part of the evening near Garnettsville, Kentucky, where he compelled a family of Southern sympathizers to serve him and his officers a first-class meal. Later that night, Hobson received his first important piece of intelligence from a group of Federal scouts who had infiltrated the Rebel column: Morgan was ferrying his men across the Ohio. Promptly the Federal march resumed, but most of the pursuers reached the river just as Morgan's rear guard disappeared over the horizon in Indiana.

Hobson was now in a bind. His orders, according to one account, called for him "to assume command of all the cavalry within reach and to pursue Morgan night and day until he either captured him or drove him from the state." Quite obviously Morgan was now out of the state—though not driven out by Hobson. The Confederate invasion of Indiana seemed to remove the raiders from the general's jurisdiction, although Hobson, a lawyer in civilian life, knew that to obey the spirit of the law was an obligation more sacred than to adhere precisely to its word. On a mail boat in the Ohio he met with Shackleford and other subordinates. They thrashed out the matter, and finally decided to share responsibility for following Morgan into Indiana as soon as transports could be rounded up for animals and riders.[32]

★★★★★★★★★★★★★★★★★★★★★★

32. Ibid., pp. 290-94.

It seemed that Hobson's desire to bag the raiders was growing stronger with every obstacle thrust across his path. On the other hand, he himself was at least partially to blame for Morgan's head start.

5

As the sweating, dust-covered Confederates plodded through lower Indiana, heading northeastward, the Hoosier State mobilized to offer resistance. In every city and town along Morgan's route of march citizens grabbed shotguns and rifles, donned home guard uniforms, or went off to fight in work clothes. Farmers left their fields untilled and barns standing open as they banded together, toting squirrelguns, muskets, and even flintlocks. John Hunt Morgan was to them an evil legend; he had to be stopped and killed and his soldiers dispersed as quickly as humanly possible —the homes and fields of Indiana had to be made safe at all costs.

They flocked to rendezvous depots by the thousands; some boarded trains and were shuttled south to close off roads leading from the Ohio. Major General Lew Wallace, the Federal hero who would turn writer and one day pen *Ben Hur*, was recalled from furlough and assigned to command all of the home guards called out to halt the invaders.[33] Wallace was capable of handling a large command, which was fortunate, for he would be leading some sixty thousand soldiers and citizen-soldiers before the crisis ended.

The home guardsmen offered continual but not over-whelming resistance to Morgan's march. Yet, although they failed to assemble in sufficient force to curtail the Rebel advance, they did slow it at several points. Near the town of Corydon about five hundred armed civilians, firing from behind fence-rail barricades, killed many of Colonel Dick Morgan's Kentuckians before Colonel Johnson scattered them with a heavy frontal attack and an artillery barrage. On July 10, the day that Hobson's cavalry at last crossed the Ohio, the raiders encountered one hundred fifty militiamen outside the village of Salem and dispersed them after a short

★★★★★★★★★★★★★★★★★★★★★★★

33. Swiggett, *The Rebel Raider*, pp. 137-38.

struggle.[34] Thus far the home-grown warriors had proved only a nuisance, but Morgan knew that being constantly delayed by roadside barriers and armed civilians would prove a disastrous handicap sooner or later.

From Salem, Morgan dispatched patrols to burn bridges and destroy track on the Louisville & Chicago Railroad. And while in the village the raiders retaliated against the local defenders by looting private and public buildings. Morgan said nothing as he watched his men burn the rail station and sack nearby homes.

That same day the raiders rode north to Vienna, licking their lips in remembered pleasure after drinking whiskey stolen from saloons in Salem. Simultaneously, General Hobson, pushing along with determined speed, was leading his cavalry into Corydon, thirty miles down the trail.

Morgan was aware that Hobson had elected to continue his pursuit, but at first he showed a conspicuous lack of concern for his opponents' whereabouts. He was not alarmed even after Lightning Ellsworth put his bug to work and turned up information that Indianapolis, several miles due north, was jammed with militia and that in several towns below the raiders' route thousands of other defenders were gathering. Then, deciding to be prudent, Morgan veered sharply eastward from the Vienna area, trotting back toward the meandering Ohio River.[35]

In so doing, he skillfully detoured around several militia encampments and managed to keep a day's ride ahead of Hobson. On the surface, things continued to go fairly well for the raiders—the Hoosier commanders had been wholly unable to place a strong force of trained soldiers across their trail. Yet, of course, Morgan did have troubles. His horses were giving out, requiring the Confederates to commandeer every four-footed nag they could gather from the hostile countryside. In large measure the animals' fatigue was owing to the fruitless marching General Bragg had ordered Morgan's men to undergo before the movement over the Cumberland had commenced.

In contrast, the pursuing Federals, traveling through friendly territory, were able to replace tired horses more eas-

****

34. Keller, *Morgan's Raid*, pp. 71-79, 81-82.

35. Ibid., pp. 84-85.

ily. And while Morgan's men had to subsist on any foodstuffs they could pilfer, Hobson's cavalrymen were fed three meals a day in the saddle by a populace who looked upon them as saviors. One of the Federals noted that chicken and black-berry pie were issued to the cavalry almost hourly during the trip across Indiana. Fowl, a commodity in particular abundance, was offered so freely by local farmers that at one point a cavalryman asked an indulgent farm woman for bacon or corn bread instead, as he feared pinfeathers would soon sprout on him.[36] The trooper who recalled this request forgot all the dangers and hardships of the pursuit and when looking back upon it years later described it as "six hundred square miles of fried chicken."[37]

Meanwhile, Morgan continued on his wearisome way, bypassing another contingent of two thousand armed citizens near the Ohio River by a *ruse de guerre*. He attracted wide attention by directing the head of his column toward the river at Madison, where the home guardsmen quickly gathered, then headed abruptly northward once more, leaving his would-be opponents staring at the dust clouds stirred up by his horses' hooves.[38] Once again Indiana communities farther north took alarm, and Governor Oliver P. Morton conferred anxiously with General Wallace to plan statewide strategy. Despite the meeting of their minds they could not predict Morgan's movements far enough in advance to block his path. The Confederates maneuvered too swiftly and too craftily for them, exhibiting every nuance of guerrilla wisdom. Furthermore, Lightning Ellsworth continued to tap the telegraph lines, spreading fallacious reports about Morgan's activities. Federal telegraphers, who kept Morton and Wallace posted on all such intelligence, grew thoroughly confused.

At Sunman, Indiana, on July 13, the weary raiders, having worked their way across the Hoosier State in five days' time, prepared to cross the Ohio line. At this point the great metropolis of Cincinatti lay a relatively brief distance off Morgan's right flank. Some of the younger and more aggressive officers proposed a dash into the city, and

★★★★★★★★★★★★★★★★★★★★★★

36. Allen, "Six Hundred Miles of Fried Chicken," p. 166.

37. Ibid., p. 170.

38. Keller, *Morgan's Raid,* pp. 86-87.

its capture. But Morgan, who had again turned wary, wished to keep moving. He began to fear that at long last strong opposing forces were massing nearby in hopes of crushing him. Colonel Duke later wrote of him: "If we could get past Cincinatti safely the danger of the expedition, he thought, would be more than half over. Here he expected to be confronted by the concentrated forces of Judah and Burnside, and he anticipated great difficulty in eluding or cutting his way through them. Once safely through this peril, his escape would be certain. . . ." Beyond Cincinatti, Duke realized, infantry could not be moved ahead by rail in sufficient force to cut them off, and he felt that the raiders could continue to outdistance any mounted pursuers.[39]

And so, at midday on the 13th, Morgan led his soldiers over the Whitewater River into Ohio, burned the bridge behind him, and passed just north of Cincinatti, where Burnside was frantically trying, as he had been for the past two weeks, to raise defense contingents.[40]

Just before the sun went down that night, Morgan saw two sights that made him realize that even after clearing Cincinatti he would still be in a tight corner. He watched as many of his men, completely exhausted after a grueling ride without sufficient rest, slumbered in their saddles, some of them aboard horses that had gone lame. Morgan grew even more concerned when he looked to his rear and saw dust clouds rising in the near distance. Colonel Wolford, leading Hobson's advance, was now only a couple of hours behind him.

Morgan's men soon demonstrated how lack of discipline can be exacerbated by the rigors of almost constant travel. That evening a wide gap developed between Johnson's and Duke's brigades; and Duke's men, covering the rear, lost contact with their comrades for a time.[41] Stragglers, increasing in number, had become a major threat to Confederate security; if captured they might be forced to reveal such information about Morgan's rate of march and probable destinations as would enable militia to divine his future positions.

★★★★★★★★★★★★★★★★★★★★★★★

39. Duke, *Morgan's Cavalry*, pp. 324-25.

40. John S. Still, "Blitzkrieg, 1863: Morgan's Raid and Rout," *Civil War History* 3 (September 1957): 294.

41. Duke, *Morgan's Cavalry*, pp. 326-27.

Although General Burnside was a fumbler, he did have thousands of recruits at his disposal; thus Morgan breathed much more easily when his men finally cleared Cincinatti at dawn on the 14th. But his ordeal had by no means ended. Later that day, at Camp Dennison, a rendezvous for convalescent soldiers, the raiders stumbled into a skirmish against a small force of ambulatory wounded. During the engagement, a train carrying three hundred Union recruits chugged through the camp grounds, heading for Morgan's line. The train might have menaced the Confederates had Colonel Duke not derailed it by placing a barricade of cross ties upon the track.[42]

After the skirmish, the column—by now reduced to fewer than two thousand effectives—moved on to the town of Williamsburg, reaching it about four o'clock in the afternoon. There they tumbled from their mounts into a meadow, where Morgan allowed them to sleep for the first time since sun-up the day before. During that thirty-five-hour period, the raiders had covered ninety-five miles—farther than any force of comparable size had marched in such a period. Figuring that by burning the bridge over the Whitewater he had at least temporarily stymied Hobson's troopers, Morgan allowed them to slumber in peace all through the night.[43]

After the respite, Morgan's brother, with his regiment and some scouts, turned again southward toward the Ohio River on a diversionary and foraging expedition. The band rode toward Ripley, constantly battling small groups of militia who eagerly staged ambushes. Word of Dick Morgan's coming raced ahead of him, and in the little river towns along his route people lined the boardwalks to gape at the gray-clad invaders. Morgan noted that many of the private and municipal buildings were decorated with patriotic bunting. By this time the colonel—as everyone else in the Confederate column—knew that the North was celebrating the twin Federal victories in Mississippi and Pennsylvania. Disheartened but not yet defeated, he finally turned back north to link up with the main column.[44]

★★★★★★★★★★★★★★★★★★★★★★

42. Brown, *The Bold Cavaliers*, p. 209.

43. Keller, *Morgan's Raid*, pp. 133-34.

44. Swiggett, *The Rebel Raider*, pp. 143-44; Still, "Blitzkrieg, 1863," p. 295.

While the Rebel command rested at Williamsburg, the pursuit forces were slowly drawing a net about it. In addition to the cavalry under Hobson, Wolford, Shackleford, and Kautz, a force under General Judah was now crowding Morgan's rear. The division leader who had been outmaneuvered by Morgan at the outset of the expedition had loaded thousands of cavalrymen and mounted infantrymen aboard steamboats and had ferried them to Cincinatti, thence to Portsmouth, Ohio, to overtake the Rebels. Now Judah, to the right of Hobson's troops, was coming on with as much speed as he could muster. On the other flank of Hobson's force was a two thousand-man militia command under Colonel Benjamin P. Runkle. Runkle's men had been outwitted by Morgan farther down the line but were determined to salvage a second chance. On the Ohio River, Lieutenant Commander LeRoy Fitch, U. S. N., was moving upstream with a small fleet of gunboats, intent on keeping the raiders from crossing into West Virginia. A division of Federals under Brigadier General E. P. Scammon rode aboard Fitch's ships, ready to disembark and fight at a moment's notice. In addition to these organized forces, numerous bands of amateur soldiers were swarming on the fringes of Morgan's column, chopping down trees to obstruct its movements and sniping at the raiders from behind every available piece of cover.[45]

Morgan continued to ride along the column, speaking words of encouragement and advice, attempting to activate his soldiers' last reserve of endurance. But it was a titanic effort and by now Morgan himself, realizing that his enemy was moving closer on all sides, was beginning to lose confidence and hope.

6

On July 18, nearly three weeks after leaving Kentucky, Morgan finalized plans for his return. Aware that amphibious Federals were striving to close off the Ohio River fords, he decided to head for the shallows at Buffington Island, about midway between the towns of Pomeroy and Parkersburg. His men plodded through several nondescript villages,

★★★★★★★★★★★★★★★★★★★★★★★★

45. Keller, *Morgan's Raid*, pp. 140, 144-45; *Official Records*, series I, vol. 23, pt. 1, p. 656.

skirting home guard units, then charged through a ravine a few miles north of Pomeroy, running a gantlet of rifle fire from militiamen gathered there, and finally halted at the hamlet of Chester. In Chester, Morgan searched for a native who might guide him to the nearest crossing site. In the meantime, he permitted his soldiers to rest for almost two hours. When at last they remounted and moved on, they headed directly for the Ohio.

Reaching the river at sundown, Morgan found that defensive works had recently been thrown up nearby to guard the approaches to the crossing. Entrenchments and redoubts there were soon empty, for the militia who had erected them fled in fear for their lives during the night. Unaware of this, the raiding leader called another halt, desiring to wait until morning to attack the works. For some reason, Morgan disdained to send scouting patrols to reconnoiter the strength of the imagined enemy force, preferring to let his men sleep blissfully throughout the night. It proved a fatal mistake.[46]

Next morning, with mist rising in clouds from the river, part of Duke's brigade charged the empty works. Surprised by the outcome, Duke then prepared to cover Johnson's brigade as the latter crossed. But time had run out. Without warning, Duke's advance riders found themselves facing groups of mounted Federals who had appeared to the east, west, and south—General Judah's men. Duke also spied two enemy gunboats anchored in the river, guarding the crossing point. One of the trapped Confederates watched the Union soldiers charge forward on foot: "They came down on us like the grasshoppers used to come down on the farmers of Kansas."[47]

The skirmish that broke out along the triangular bottom between the river and a hilly ridge to the west spelled doom for Morgan. Judah's men had spread themselves across the base of the triangle; the Rebels could retreat only by the Chester road or through a narrow gap at the top of the wedge. Soon only the latter route was open, for General Hobson, finally coming upon the scene of action, was charging down the road from Chester with his four thousand troopers.

★★★★★★★★★★★★★★★★★★★★★★★

46. Holland, *Morgan and His Raiders*, pp. 245-46.

47. Hockersmith, *Morgan's Escape*, p. 20.

Morgan attempted to disengage by sending Johnson's brigade through the narrow upper defile while Duke formed a rear guard to protect the withdrawal. But at that juncture Hobson struck Duke's men, attempting to crush them between his force and Judah's. Outnumbered three-to-one, Duke surrendered after a bitter but short struggle. Captured with him were Dick Morgan and better than seven hundred raiders. Still, Duke had held his ground long enough to permit John Hunt Morgan, Colonel Johnson, and fewer than one thousand others to make an escape.[48]

After Morgan slipped away into the distance, the Federals collected Duke's men, confiscated their arms, and then agreed to a request by the sweaty, grimy Confederates that they be allowed to bathe, under guard, in the Ohio. Soon the prisoners and many of their equally dirty captors were splashing about in the river in a curious frolic, "enjoying," as one Union officer put it, "the most necessary bath they ever had in their lives."[49]

Meanwhile, General Morgan and the escapees stumbled on in a series of arcs that took them north, then south, then north again, in the general direction of Zanesville. Their horses were at the end of their endurance—but in no worse condition than Hobson's now winded animals. Back at the Ohio, General Shackleford, aware that Morgan was wandering almost blindly, like a fox maddened by injury, gathered the best horses he could find and led a new pursuit.

The surviving raiders played the game to the very last. They trotted through the villages of Cheshire, McArthur, Nelsonville, and Eagleport, keeping barely a step ahead of Shackleford's mixed bag of pursuers. They wandered on to Senecaville, past Cambridge, and toward Steubenville and the distant Pennsylvania border. For another week the doomed march continued, while riverboats and locomotives filled with Federals searched the local waterways and land routes for the last fragment of Morgan's once intact command.[50]

★★★★★★★★★★★★★★★★★★★★★★★★

48. Allan Keller, "Morgan's Raid Across the Ohio," *Civil War Times Illustrated* 2 (June 1963): 36; Weaver, "Morgan's Raid," pp. 303-5; *Official Records*, series, I, vol. 23, pt. 1, pp. 640-42.

49. Allen, "Six Hundred Miles of Fried Chicken," p. 174.

50. Still, "Blitzkrieg, 1863," pp. 300-301; Keller, "Morgan's Raid Across the Ohio," pp. 36-37.

The raid came to a quiet end on July 26. By this time Morgan had only seven hundred troopers in his immediate command. Colonel Johnson and three hundred other survivors of the struggle at Buffington Island had managed to work their way across the Ohio shortly after the skirmish, and would eventually return to the Confederate lines in East Tennessee.[51] On a country road near Salineville, in east-central Ohio, Morgan's seven hundred found themselves hopelessly hemmed in by various forces of regular cavalry and militia. Not wishing to surrender to General Shackleford, in his rear, the Rebel leader handed his sword to Captain James Burbick, commanding a company of mounted militiamen.

An hour later the Federal regulars caught up with the vanquished raiders. Although not entitled to the honor in the strictest sense, Shackleford, as ranking officer on the scene, took credit for the capture and dashed off a dispatch to General Burnside. Cherishing brevity, he kept the message to a single sentence. And being a devout church-goer, he stated that he had bagged Morgan singlehandedly, "by the blessings of Almighty God."[52]

7

Morgan's raid made more than its share of positive gains, although it also resulted in the loss of one thousand four hundred veteran cavalrymen to the Confederate Army (most of them were later imprisoned like common criminals in the Ohio State Penitentiary, although General Morgan and a few subordinates tunneled their way out and escaped back into the Confederacy). The expedition shook Southern morale by revealing that its legendary Beau Sabreur was not invincible, despite the propaganda turned out by its newspapers; and it marked the last of Morgan's effective contributions to his army. Still, his raiders had tied up more than five thousand full-time pursuers for almost a month, had captured and paroled six thousand Northern troops, mostly militiamen and home guards, and had destroyed millions of dollars' worth of

★★★★★★★★★★★★★★★★★★★★★★★★

51. Holland, *Morgan and His Raiders*, p. 247.

52. Keller, *Morgan's Raid*, pp. 218-28; *Official Records*, series I, vol. 23, pt. 1, pp. 643-44.

property in Kentucky, Indiana, and Ohio. Additionally, the operation had delayed a projected invasion of East Tennessee by General Burnside, had held up Federal reinforcements that might have made impossible Bragg's victory at Chickamauga that September, and had sent a wave of terror splashing across a huge section of the Northwest.[53]

Nevertheless, even had they been privileged to foresee the great amount of damage that resulted from the campaign, it is doubtful that most of the Confederate raiders would have embarked on such an expedition, given the nightmarish effort that it ultimately required. As it was, few of the surviving participants ever forgot it. One of them spoke for all those who had ridden with Morgan, Duke, and Johnson when in later years he summed up the expedition:

"It was a month without a day's rest, a month of battles and skirmishes, a month of hopes and despairs, such as seldom falls to the lot of human beings."[54]

★★★★★★★★★★★★★★★★★★★★★★★★

53. Keller, "Morgan's Raid Across the Ohio," p. 37.

54. Hockersmith, *Morgan's Escape*, p. 28.

8

WAGONS
IN THE VALLEY
Wheeler's Middle Tennessee Raid
(September 30-October 9, 1863)

1

In February, 1862 Braxton Bragg sent two of his cavalry leaders to harass Union traffic on the Cumberland River. The senior officer, Joseph Wheeler, recently promoted to major general, decided that the best way to carry out his orders was to strike the Federal garrison at Dover, Tennessee, on the left bank of the river. However, Wheeler's immediate subordinate, Nathan Bedford Forrest, did not approve of the plan, and said so in plain terms. Dover's works were well defended and commanded a formidable position, Forrest contended, and even should the Confederates manage to take it, supply shortages would compel them to abandon it after a brief time. The advantages to be gained were not worth the effort required.

But Wheeler did not wish to return to his army without committing himself to battle. Hence he disregarded Forrest's advice and ordered the attack carried out. When Wheeler and Forrest charged with eight mounted regiments, the Yankees inside the town shattered the assault columns, inflicting substantial losses and repulsing the troopers quite handily.

After the debacle, Wheeler retreated to his headquarters, four miles from the battlefield, where he calmly listened to subordinates' combat reports. For a time Bedford Forrest held his anger in check, but at length could bear his superior's imperviousness no longer. The hot-tempered Tennessean jumped out of the camp-chair in which he had been sitting, hovered above the diminutive Wheeler, and thundered: "You know I was against this attack. I said all I could and should against it—and now—say what you like, nothing'll bring back my brave fellows lying dead or wounded and freezing around that fort tonight. You know I mean no disrespect. . . . But you've got to put one thing in that report to Bragg: tell him I'll be in my coffin before I'll fight again under your command!"[1]

Forrest was by no means the only member of the Army of Tennessee who distrusted Wheeler's combat judgment. Many of Wheeler's own men had little faith in his ability, and little love for him personally. They considered him a martinet, a general whose military concepts we so inflexible they could not be revamped to meet fluctuating conditions in battle. And, like Forrest, some of them doubted that he had enough compassion for the soldiers he commanded.

And yet, other soldiers—high-ranking officers as well as enlisted men—thought Wheeler a military genius. He was the youngest major general of cavalry in the Confederacy—he had won his second star and command of Bragg's horsemen at the ripe old age of twenty-six—and, with the exceptions of Forrest and Morgan, was the best-known mounted leader in the western theater of action. He had conducted several important raids and extended reconnaissances in the early years of the conflict and had done an admirable job guarding the Army of Tennessee's flanks on many occasions.[2] In the heat of battle he could be counted on to personally direct his soldiers, no matter the degree of danger involved.

Wheeler's uneven combat record seemed owing to the fact that he rendered effective service only when operating in conjunction with the main army. Under Bragg's influence

★★★★★★★★★★★★★★★★★★★★★★★

1. Lytle, *Bedford Forrest and His Critter Company*, pp. 141-43.

2. Boatner, *The Civil War Dictionary*, p. 910.

and control, Wheeler was a steady performer and contributed significantly to strategic success. But when entrusted
with independent missions, he often went astray. Perhaps the
final weight of the burden of command—such as the weight
he felt at Dover, Tennessee—was something he could not
bear. The pity was that Bragg was so poor a judge of talent
that he could not perceive the truth. Too often he allowed
Wheeler to exercise command during independent operations that he was not qualified to lead, while forcing generals
talented at that work, such as Forrest, to be subject to other
officers' orders.[3]

To look at Joe Wheeler and his military record, one would
think that he possessed few critical shortcomings as a soldier.
His short stature was the only feature that did not conform
to the typical portrait of the successful warrior. He had an
intelligent and sensitive face, accented by a rich, dark beard
and receding hair that effectively disguised his youth. His
body was compact but wiry, indicating litheness of movement. A Georgian, he was a graduate of the West Point Class
of 1859. At the Military Academy, where he spent much of
his time pouring over volumes in the library, he had been
dubbed "Point" by his fellow cadets, since he possessed
neither length, breadth, nor thickness.[4]

The outbreak of war had brought Wheeler a commission
as an artillery officer, then the colonelcy of an Alabama infantry regiment. But his prewar experience as a mounted
rifleman soon gained him a ranking position in the Confederate cavalry service, and by July 1862, Bragg had appointed
him chief of cavalry for the Army of Mississippi. From that
time onward he was associated exclusively with mounted
campaigning, in which he made a name as a fearless and daring fighter. By the close of the conflict, his conspicuous role
in battle would result in sixteen horses shot from under him.
Though occasionally demonstrating some nagging command
failings, he served capably during Bragg's 1862 invasion of
Kentucky and later that year in the bloody Murfreesboro
campaign.[5] By early in 1863 his reputation was far reaching,

★★★★★★★★★★★★★★★★★★★★★★★★

3. John P. Dyer, *"Fightin' Joe" Wheeler*, pp. 123-24.

4. John W. DuBose, *General Joseph Wheeler and The Army of Tennessee*, p. 51.

5. Warner, *Generals in Gray*, pp. 332-33.

Joseph Wheeler. COURTESY LIBRARY OF CONGRESS.

and his soldiers, to a man, referred to him as "Fightin' Joe," a sobriquet they felt he fully deserved.

Thus it was that from an early date Wheeler seemed earmarked for lasting renown. It seemed shameful that in the end his shortcomings as a field commander—critically magnified by the denseness of his superior officer, who failed to make maximum use of Wheeler's talents—combined to tarnish much of the glory he had received early in the war.

A primary example of how General Bragg failed to properly utilize his cavalry chief was the 1863 Sequatchie Valley raid, during which Wheeler almost disastrously squandered away initial success. Perhaps the scheme was ill fated from the hour of its conception, for Bragg made the unhappy mistake of ordering Bedford Forrest to serve under Fightin' Joe during the mission. The fact that Forrest, true to his word, vehemently and unconditionally refused, certainly did not augur well for the expedition.

2

The raid had its origin in the battle of Chickamauga, fought in northern Georgia in mid-September. The bloody two-day struggle marked the only sustained tactical success during Bragg's tenure as commander of the Army of Tennessee. But Bragg allowed decisive victory to elude his grasp by failing to harass and pursue Rosecrans's Army of the Cumberland. Most of the Federal forces fled in disorganized retreat, liable to utter annihilation had Bragg mustered the energy and fortitude to follow up his advantage with a strike against the enemy's flank and rear. Bragg's only effort in that regard was to send Wheeler's cavalry, without infantry support, to strike the retreating columns. On this occasion, Wheeler did not live up to his nickname. He rounded up many Federal stragglers and captured twenty of their supply wagons, but did not ride far enough to seriously challenge those Union cavalrymen desperately trying to cover the withdrawal.[6] Perhaps some of Bragg's timidity had begun to infect his cavalry leader.

The Army of the Cumberland was permitted to seek refuge in the fortified city of Chattanooga, Tennessee, about ten miles northwest of the Chickamauga battlefield. There

★★★★★★★★★★★★★★★★★★★★★★★

6. Dyer, *"Fightin' Joe" Wheeler*, pp. 119-22.

General Rosecrans initially retained control of the forty thousand-man army, although within a month it was destined to pass into the hands of Major General George H. Thomas, who had fought steadfastly at Chickamauga when most of his comrades had been frantic to withdraw. Bragg's army, its men cursing their commander for permitting a gleaming opportunity to slip away, moved slowly northward to besiege Chattanooga from below.

At last recognizing his mistakes, Bragg sought counsel from his infantry commanders regarding his next move. Lieutenant General James Longstreet, on loan from Lee's army in Virginia, replied that the Confederates ought to cross the Tennessee River above the Union-held city and strike Rosecrans's communications network. With his supply routes broken, Rosecrans would have to evacuate Chattanooga or watch his army starve to death. If the Federals withdrew, Bragg could pursue, with a second chance to wipe out his opponents, or could move against General Ambrose Burnside, who was now commanding forces at Knoxville, Tennessee.

At first Bragg seemed to accept Longstreet's advice. But then his old reticence flared up, and he decided to carry out the plan in limited fashion only. To cut the Union communications above the Tennessee, he chose Wheeler's cavalry; the infantry would remain in its present positions.[7]

A few days following the Bragg-Longstreet conference, Wheeler was given instructions to "cross the Tennessee River and press the enemy, intercept and break up all his lines of communication and retreat." By that time, starvation was already beginning to overtake the soldiers in Chattanooga. By hastily retreating into the city, Rosecrans had been forced to rely on an extended and tenuous supply line. Convoyed wagon trains brought provisions from the railroad at Stevenson, Alabama, to the besieged city by lumbering up hillsides and ridges and jouncing over rocky, uneven roads along a roundabout route through the Sequatchie Valley. Railroads that might have run rations and forage into the city more quickly had been cut by Rebel infantry and cavalry. Consequently, the soldiers in the beleaguered stronghold stretched their meager fare to the utmost limits.[8] Their horses and

★★★★★★★★★★★★★★★★★★★★★★★

7. Ibid., p. 122.

8. Grant, *Personal Memoirs*, 2: 21-25; Hancock, *Hancock's Diary*, p. 268.

pack mules died by the thousands, gnawing away at hitching posts, wagon spokes, and the tails of other animals after all grass and shrubbery had been consumed. While this suffering went on, the winds of early winter began to blow through the Tennessee Valley, adding to the discomfort of Rosecrans's men.

The fragile route by which supplies might still be hauled toward the city—the line that stretched sixty miles through the Sequatchie and across Walden's Ridge—was to be Joe Wheeler's target.[9] But he was not as yet permitted to start on his expedition. His original orders were countermanded the same day they were issued, and new directives called for his cavalry first to clear the top of Lookout Mountain, which lay a few miles southwest of the city, so that infantry pickets could be stationed there. Bragg had decided to move his soldiers onto the slopes of that long mountain ridge before settling down to besiege Chattanooga in earnest. Furthermore, he had chosen to reinforce Wheeler's cavalry before dispatching it on the raid against the supply route.

On September 28, after Wheeler's soldiers had driven a small Federal picket force from the mountain top, Bragg instructed General Forrest, whose cavalry division was on outpost service near Athens, Tennessee, to join Wheeler's command.[10] Therefore, for the first time since the attack on Dover, Forrest was faced with the prospect of serving under a general whose judgment he did not trust one iota. Moreover, Forrest, who by now had won deserved personal renown, was loath to subordinate himself to any other cavalry general in that theater, no matter whom. Forrest believed that he was ably suited to lead large bodies of mounted soldiers in independent campaigning—he had demonstrated this capacity time and again—whereas the same could not be said of any other mounted commander of comparable rank and station. The Tennessean felt he had every right to expect that he would be placed in overall command of a consolidated raiding force on such a mission.

In addition to expressing these reservations, Forrest argued against participating in the expedition because his men,

★★★★★★★★★★★★★★★★★★★★★★★★

9. William L. Curry, "Raid of the Confederate Cavalry Through Central Tennessee," *Journal of the U. S. Cavalry Association* 19 (1908-9): 817; Stanley F. Horn, *The Army of Tennessee: A Military History,* pp. 281-82.

10. Dyer, *"Fightin' Joe" Wheeler,* p. 123.

who had performed rigorous service during the Chick-amauga campaign, were in no condition to make a long march, and neither were their mounts. His brigadiers and many of his enlisted men went on record as opposing the mission for the same reasons. But Bragg refused to listen to Forrest's words and went so far as to hint that he would imprison the cavalry leader if he did not carry out his orders at once.

At that, Forrest again lost his temper. He jumped into his saddle and rode to Bragg's field headquarters, where he gave his superior a large piece of his mind. The stormy meeting ended with Forrest balling his fists and telling Bragg: "You have threatened to arrest me for not obeying your orders promptly. I dare you to do it, and I say to you that if you ever again try to interfere with me or cross my path, it will be at the peril of your life!"

Before Bragg had a chance to recover his composure, Forrest remounted and rode off in disgust. Vowing never again to serve under Bragg, the cavalry chief eventually sought out President Jefferson Davis, visiting in Alabama, and from him received an independent command elsewhere in the Confederacy.[11]

Quite possibly, General Bragg was glad to see him go. He had never appreciated Forrest's talents and certainly did not approve of his free-thinking bent. Also, now that Forrest was out of the picture, the expedition aimed at denying the Chattanooga garrison every last crust of bread could proceed without further delay. Turning to Joe Wheeler, a soldier whom he could respect and (as he believed) could understand, Bragg gave specific orders for the expedition: go up the Tennessee to Cottonport, thirty-five miles northeast of Chattanooga, rendezvous there with Forrest's leaderless cavalry, then lead the combined forces westward into the Sequatchie. In the valley Wheeler was to lay waste to enemy wagon trains moving toward the garrison, then sweep westward toward Nashville, wrecking the railroad in that vicinity and damaging supply depots near the tracks.[12]

Wheeler would have to be alert to the movements of

★★★★★★★★★★★★★★★★★★★★★★★

11. Ibid., pp. 123-25; DuBose, *Wheeler and The Army of Tennessee*, p. 207.

12. George B. Guild, *A Brief Narrative of the Fourth Tennessee Cavalry Regiment, Wheeler's Corps, Army of Tennessee*, p. 35.

Union cavalry north of Chattanooga, but Bragg had faith in Fightin' Joe's ability to ward off pursuers, and expected that he would return in full triumph.

3

To give Bragg's main army mobile support, Wheeler left behind a single brigade, under Colonel John H. Kelly. The rest of the command—two divisions under Brigadier Generals John A. Wharton and William T. Martin (officers neither incompetent nor brilliant)—broke camp on the morning of September 30 and moved slowly up the south bank of the Tennessee.[13]

Almost from the first hour of the journey, Federal cavalry on the opposite shore paralleled Wheeler's march, as though daring him to cross the river in their front.[14] Wheeler saw that the blue-clad horsemen were in sufficient strength to cause him trouble, "and I found that any point at which I should attempt to cross could be reached as easily by them as by my command."

While Wheeler's divisions trotted along the shore, the enemy mimicked their movements so closely as to make the Confederate commander irritated and also a bit embarrassed. Finally he determined to cross the river as soon as he linked with Forrest's brigades—regardless of the size of the opposition.

At Cottonport that afternoon, Wheeler found that Forrest had not exaggerated in telling Bragg that his command was in poor condition. As he later reported: "The three brigades from General Forrest were mere skeletons, scarcely averaging 500 effective men each. These were badly armed, had but a small supply of ammunition, and their horses were in horrible condition, having been marched continuously for three days and nights without removing saddles. The men were worn out, and without rations." Forrest's subordinates did their best to convince Wheeler that their soldiers could hardly be counted on to endure another expedition.[15] And it

★★★★★★★★★★★★★★★★★★★★★★★★

13. DuBose, *Wheeler and The Army of Tennessee*, p. 206.

14. Curry, "Raid of the Confederate Cavalry," p. 818.

15. *Official Records*, series I, vol. 30, pt. 2, p. 723.

was noted that a good deal of dissatisfaction was voiced by the rank and file over having to serve again under Wheeler. But all of it was to little avail, for Fightin' Joe was determined to assimilate Forrest's division, minus its chief, into his field force.

After weeding out unfit men and animals, a process that consumed most of that afternoon, Wheeler selected three small brigades from Forrest's command, led by Brigadier General H. B. Davidson and Colonels John S. Scott and George B. Hodge, and formed them into a single unit with Davidson in chief command. Wheeler's force now numbered about four thousand troopers and was armed with six pieces of horse artillery.[16] With Forrest's veterans in advance, the raiding force splashed through the cool water of the Tennessee under cover of evening darkness.

One of Forrest's men looked back upon the crossing several years afterward: "I can never forget the beauty and picturesqueness of the scene that was presented that moonlight night. . . . It happened that the Fourth Tennessee Regiment was in front; and, headed by a single guide. we descended the banks and dropped into the river, and then the line swung down the stream across the silvery surface of the broad waters, like the windings of a huge dark serpent. . . . No creation of art could have been more imposing."[17]

The Federal cavalrymen who had worried Wheeler did not pose much of an obstacle to the fording operation. Most of them retreated precipitously when the advance regiments reached the far shore—no doubt cowed by the artillery pieces that Wheeler had set up along the opposite bank. Only a large picket force offered sharp resistance to the crossing, but though it poured a fusilade into the advance guard from shoreline thickets, the Federal unit did not seriously injure any of the raiders.[18]

Once across the river, Wheeler spent most of October 1 sorting out his mixed command and making preparations for the march. Toward evening the column at last moved forward, but went less than ten miles before a sudden rainfall

★★★★★★★★★★★★★★★★★★★★★★★

16. Dyer, *"Fightin' Joe" Wheeler,* p. 126.

17. Guild, *Fourth Tennessee Cavalry,* pp. 35-36.

18. Ibid., pp. 36-37; *Official Records,* series I, vol. 30, pt. 3, p. 953.

turned the roads into beds of soggy mud. After bivouacking for the night, Wheeler resumed his movement across the now rocky ground toward Walden's Ridge, the boundary of the valley in which they would find the Union wagon train. Late in the day the raiders reached the summit of the ridge one thousand five hundred feet above the surrounding terrain, and halted in preparation for descending into the Sequatchie.[19]

That evening Wheeler called together his division leaders for a conference. His outriders had reported that six miles into the valley the supply train that Bragg had sent them to destroy was in motion toward Chattanooga. Wheeler proposed to personally lead part of his force—about one thousand five hundred men—in capturing and disabling it. He desired the rest of the command to move on to McMinnville, Tennessee, a Federal outpost where large quantities of supplies reportedly had been collected. Most of his officers acquiesced, but General Wharton, the thirty-five-year old Tennessean who led half of Wheeler's force, voiced exception to the plan. Wharton made a practice of fighting by the book, and what his superior had in mind seemed to run contrary to an important military maxim: a commander did not divide a small force when in enemy territory and surrounded by heavy forces.

Wheeler knew that Wharton was referring to the large Federal mounted patrols that ranged north of Chattanooga to cover the garrison and to halt just this sort of raid. Fightin' Joe suspected that such forces were trying to seek him out, but the thought did not harm his confidence: "I have my orders, gentlemen, and I will attempt the work. General Martin will accompany me; General Wharton will go on with the remainder of the command to the vicinity of McMinnville, where I shall join him tomorrow night, if I am alive." With that flourish, the conference ended.[20]

At three o'clock the next morning—six hours before the major portion of the command started northwestward toward the supply outpost—Wheeler moved down the mountainside at the head of his detachment. By his side rode General Mar-

★★★★★★★★★★★★★★★★★★★★★★

19. Dyer, *"Fightin' Joe" Wheeler*, pp. 126-27.

20. DuBose, *Wheeler and The Army of Tennessee*, p. 208.

tin and Colonel John T. Morgan, the latter leading the 51st Alabama Mounted Infantry, the advance regiment.[21]

Reaching the valley floor, the command pressed onward for some miles, cavalrymen carefully scanning the horizon. Finally the point riders sighted and then overtook the nearest section of the immense Federal train—thirty-two wagons, each hauled by six mules.[22] An outcry was immediately raised by the small infantry force guarding this first section of wagons, and rifle fire began to spatter across the broad valley. The vehicles were soon captured, however, the guards along with them.

Leaving a skeleton force to secure the spoils, Wheeler pushed onward with the balance of Martin's command. Another hour of rapid travel brought him up to the flank of the main portion of the supply train. It was quite some sight. "There opened the richest scene that the eye of a cavalryman can behold," a participant observed. "Along the side of the mountain hundreds of large Federal wagons were standing, with their big white covers on them, like so many African elephants, solemn in their stately grandeur. They had been rushed up there by the teamsters and abandoned. This was too rich a bonanza to be left without an escort; and in a few moments the rifles sounded from the mountain sides, indicating that we would have to do some fighting for such booty."[23]

The trooper was correct in supposing that such a column would not be left unguarded. Large contingents of cavalry had accompanied it, riding both in front and rear, and musket-wielding infantrymen had walked alongside the train until parked.[24] Now the soldiers were dug in, ready for fighting, and as the sun spread its morning glow across the valley the Confederate cavalrymen charged the train at full tilt, screaming the Rebel yell.

At first Wheeler's attack was unsuccessful. The parked trains were a difficult obstacle to surmount, and the guards had excellent vantage points from which to direct their fire.

★★★★★★★★★★★★★★★★★★★★★★★

21. Ibid., pp. 208-9.

22. Dyer, *"Fightin' Joe" Wheeler*, p. 128.

23. Guild, *Fourth Tennessee Cavalry*, pp. 37-38.

24. *Official Records*, series I, vol. 30, pt, 2, p. 723.

Parts of two regiments under Colonel Morgan charged the escort troops but were repulsed posthaste and in poor order. Wheeler then rode up to Colonel A. A. Russell, commander of the 4th Alabama Cavalry, and ordered him to charge the train. John Allan Wyeth, a young trooper who in later years would become a distinguished surgeon and a biographer of Nathan Bedford Forrest, took part in the attack: "As soon as our line could be formed, we rode forward at full speed, and receiving a volley at close quarters, were successful in riding over and capturing the entire escort within a few minutes."[25]

But those minutes were frantic with action. The attackers jumped their horses over the Federals' makeshift barriers, grappled in hand-to-hand fighting with the infantry and the dismounted cavalry, and shot, slashed, and punched their way to success. When the overwhelmed enemy threw up their hands in surrender, Wheeler rode in to find that he had captured a force nearly equal to his own in size—almost one thousand two hundred officers and men. More important, he had taken more than eight hundred wagons stocked with provisions and four thousand mules.[26]

After disarming their prisoners and herding them toward the rear, the raiders gave their devoted attention to the spoils. Few of the troopers had ever seen anything approaching the scope of this vast train, and few could restrain themselves from doing some unauthorized foraging. Wheeler had been ordered to destroy the train, not loot it, and he went among the soldiers, reminding them of this. But his men were not famed for their iron discipline, and as soon as the general had moved on they began to rifle the wagons, many of which had been overturned while attempting to flee.

Hundreds of Confederates galloped along the line of vehicles, which stretched ten miles up the valley, to burn and dismantle them. Other detachments were sent to shoot or saber the mules and thereby prevent later attempts at hauling supplies to the Federal garrison. Trooper Wyeth was charged with destroying some of the wagons, but even he could not resist making off with plunder. Spying some overturned barrels that contained cheese and crackers, the hun-

★★★★★★★★★★★★★★★★★★★★★★★

25. John Allan Wyeth, "The Destruction of Rosecrans' Great WagonTrain," *The Photographic History of the Civil War*, 4: 160, 162.

26. Guild, *Fourth Tennessee Cavalry*, p. 38.

gry youngster helped himself, filling his haversack with the delicacy, and was about to remount when a stern-faced Wheeler reined in beside him. "Get out of that wagon!" the general roared. Wyeth obeyed without delay and fell in beside Fightin' Joe. Years later he recalled that he "had the honor of riding side by side with my commander for some distance further among the captured wagons. As he turned back, he ordered the small squadron that was in advance, to go on until the last wagon had been destroyed, which order was fully executed."[27]

For eight hours the Confederates lay waste to the captured train. Numerous bonfires sent flames crackling through the valley, and occasional explosions announced that another cache of ammunition had been torched. Finally all wagons had been destroyed and their mules left dead or dying in their traces.[28]

The perilous situation in Chattanooga would henceforth become worse still. Wheeler's work ensured that in subsequent weeks dozens of Federal soldiers would die of starvation or exposure (the wagons had also contained quantities of badly needed overcoats, boots, and hats). Even if this break in Rosecrans's supply line proved only temporary, the Army of the Cumberland might have no alternative to evacuating the city. Thirty wagons that had eluded Wheeler's grasp by detouring through a little-known mountain trail toward Walden's Ridge would not bring Rosecrans enough provisions to compensate for the shortages.[29]

4

While Wheeler's men occupied themselves burning wagons, General Wharton's two thousand five hundred soldiers were en route to McMinnville. In the lead was the complement from Forrest's command, led by General Davidson. Only thirty-two years old, Davidson was one of several callow mounted commanders in the western theater, but possessed years of experience as a dragoon: his military service dated

★★★★★★★★★★★★★★★★★★★★★★★

27. Wyeth, "Destruction of Rosecrans' Wagon Train," p. 162.

28. Dyer, *"Fightin' Joe" Wheeler*, p. 129.

29. Wyeth, "Destruction of Rosecrans' Wagon Train," p. 164.

from the Mexican War, in which he had fought at age fifteen.[30] He was an action-loving man who liked to ride at the forefront of every march, as he did on this occasion.

Nearing the Federal supply base early that afternoon, Davidson personally led a charge by Colonel Hodge's advance battalion, which drove in the enemy pickets. By the time that the rest of Hodge's brigade reached the village, the general was holding the Federal rifle pits that surrounded the garrison. He then had Hodge emplace his battery of howitzers to add cannon power to his men's rifle and small-arms' fire. Davidson had settled down for a sustained contest at long range when General Wharton and the main column rode up and deployed.

Wharton at once suggested they try a different tactic. He ordered Colonel Hodge to approach the town under a flag of truce and to demand its surrender. He saw no sense in launching a frontal or flank attack if bloodshed could be avoided entirely.

To Wharton's and Davidson's mild surprise, the Federals were responsive to the idea. The garrison commander was Major Michael L. Patterson, son-in-law of Tennessee Provisional Governor Andrew Johnson; he had only six hundred men in his command and suspected that the Confederates who had taken his rifle pits had a great many more than that. At first he was willing to capitulate only if it could be proved to his satisfaction that he was outnumbered. Wharton and Davidson refused to accede to his request to count the Rebel troops—whereupon the major lost his nerve and surrendered unconditionally.[31]

When the Confederates entered the town in triumph, they took the opportunity to perpetrate, according to Patterson, "the most brutal outrages on the part of the rebels ever known to any civilized war in America or elsewhere." The distraught officer no doubt exaggerated the facts, but it was true that the victors helped themselves to the supplies stored in the village. They appropriated boots, overcoats, breeches, and headwear, as well as "watch, pocket-book, money, and even finger-rings, or, in fact, anything that happened to please their fancy." Perhaps they surmised that their com-

★★★★★★★★★★★★★★★★★★★★★★

30. Warner, *Generals in Gray*, p. 67.

31. *Official Records*, series I, vol. 30, pt. 2, pp. 726-27.

rades in the Sequatchie Valley were enjoying similar privileges, and decided that they themselves should not be outdone.

On the morning of the 4th, as the raiders went about the business of destroying McMinnville's quartermaster and commissary stores, General Wheeler appeared with the rest of his command. By now a good many of his soldiers had re-clothed themselves and had procured some food for their empty stomachs. By now, too, Wheeler's antilooting convictions had altered; despite Major Patterson's pleas, he made no attempt to curtail the widespread plundering still going on in the town. No doubt Wheeler did not wish to try to impress his will on the raiders in Davidson's force because he feared them. He realized they were dissatisfied that Bedford Forrest had not personally led them on the expedition and were angrily reluctant to take orders from anyone but him.[32]

The reunited command marched out of McMinnville early on October 5 and moved in the direction of Murfreesboro, scene of fierce fighting the previous December and January. Wheeler made a brief demonstration toward the city, then headed southward and captured a stockade that guarded the railroad bridge over Stone's River, making prisoners of fifty-two Federals. He spent the major portion of that day chopping down the trestle-work span and ripping up trackage for a distance of three miles below the river.

The next day, moving on, the column destroyed railroad stock, a locomotive, and all the trestle bridges between Murfreesboro and Wartrace, as well as captured several contingents of bridge guards. At Shelbyville (General Davidson's hometown), Wheeler's men again captured and burned enemy supplies after frightening garrison troops into flight. Afterward Wheeler bivouacked his three divisions near Shelbyville, along the Duck River; the commands camped close to each other, so that they might support one another in event of a crisis.[33]

The expedition was nearly over. Wheeler had succeeded in wrecking millions of dollars worth of valuable supplies and had avoided being set upon by a large pursuit force. Thus far he had suffered only a handful of casualties, and thanks

★★★★★★★★★★★★★★★★★★★★★★

32. Dyer, *"Fightin' Joe" Wheeler*, p. 131.

33. *Official Records*, series I, vol. 30, pt. 2, p. 724.

to the ingenuity of General Wharton had captured a large enemy depot and garrison without having to fight a pitched battle. Had Wheeler been able to return to Bragg's army without further delay, the expedition would have returned to his name the glitter that had been tarnished by such debacles as the assault on Dover.

But it was not to be. Wheeler would not be permitted to escape with unblemished triumph. Unknown to him, disaster was approaching his command on the evening of October 6, and would overtake it the next morning.

5

Some Union cavalry forces had actually anticipated Wheeler's raid; others had been alerted to it on October 1, the day Fightin' Joe's men struck westward across the Tennessee. Scouts and pickets had circulated the news of the Confederate cavalry's march along the river, and consequently Rosecrans's chief fo staff, Major General James A. Garfield, sent a sharp message to the Federals patrolling near Wheeler's vicinity: "The enemy's cavalry has crossed the river in heavy force a short distance below Washington, and designs making a raid on our communication." Garfield ordered the ranking cavalry commander to leave a couple of his regiments to guard the river, then to move with all other available forces into the Sequatchie Valley in the vicinity of Anderson's Cross Roads; infantry and artillery units would be dispatched, if possible, to support the horse soldiers.[34]

The mounted leaders who were to take major parts in the pursuit were Brigadier General George Crook, commanding the Second Cavalry Division of the Army of the Cumberland, and Brigadier General Edward M. McCook, who led the First Division. After October 4, however the cavalry corps chief, Brigadier General Robert B. Mitchell, would assume command of all pursuit forces, taking direct charge of McCook's force, while General Crook ranged ahead of the main pursuit body with orders to seek out Wheeler and destroy him in battle.

All was activity and excitement at Crook's headquarters, three miles from the Tennessee River, when the news of

★★★★★★★★★★★★★★★★★★★★★★★★

34. Ibid., pt. 4, p. 21.

Wheeler's movement came in. An officer in the 1st Ohio Cavalry recalled: "Crook was giving orders to his brigade commanders, staff officers and orderlies were galloping off on the several roads carrying orders. The artillery was ready for action—companies, battalions and regiments were swinging into line, and horses, as well as officers and troopers, seemed to imbibe of the general feeling that there was fight in the air."[35]

In a drenching storm, Crook started out to catch the Confederates marching westward. From the beginning the rain hampered the pursuit and ensured that Crook would not be able to fulfill Rosecrans's wish that Wheeler be stopped short of entering the Sequatchie. By the time the Second Cavalry Division began to descend the mountains into the valley, on October 3, Crook learned that Wheeler had already divided his command and that both forces had twelve to fourteen hours' head start.

Perceiving that he could not move fast enough to overtake the force personally led by Wheeler, Crook turned in the direction of McMinnville, following Wharton's and Davidson's divisions. Next morning the Federals struck Wharton's rear guard near the supply base but succeeded in rounding up only a few stragglers. Later that afternoon the pursuers again overtook Wharton's rear and this time engaged a Texas cavalry brigade in a fierce skirmish, which raged until darkness fell. By the time the Texans escaped under the cover of night, Crook had suffered almost fifty casualties; however, he could not ascertain the extent of his opponents' losses.

That night Crook's men encamped near McMinnville, painfully aware that they had been too late to protect either the garrison or the wagons in the valley. Still, the cavalrymen hoped eventually to catch both of Wheeler's forces and make the Rebel raider pay for his audacity. Not even the fact that their rations had begun to run perilously low dampened the horsemen's hopes. The commander of one Union company reported that breakfast the following morning consisted of "two little hard sour apples to the man."[36]

Early on October 5 Crook's three thousand five hundred soldiers entered McMinnville and were shocked by signs of

★★★★★★★★★★★★★★★★★★★★★★★

35. Curry, "Raid of the Confederate Cavalry," pp. 818-19.

36. Ibid., pp. 819-20.

the depredations that had occurred the day before. Wheeler had departed, leaving in his wake piles of smoldering debris and an apoplectic Major Patterson, who continued to curse the thieving Rebels. But General Crook was just as amazed to learn that the garrison "had surrendered without making any resistance."[37]

Crook spent a brief time in the village; soon he was pounding onward in hot pursuit of the Confederates. Riding in the direction of Murfreesboro, he again came up to the tag end of the now-reunited enemy command. The Rebels were drawn up in line of battle when Crook arrived with his advance regiments, so he quickly sent the 2nd Kentucky (Union) Cavalry to menace the enemy rear guard with a saber charge led personally by one of his brigade chiefs, Colonel Eli Long. The five-mile-long charge sent many raiders scrambling for cover, after which the contest degenerated into a stand-off in tangled woodlots. When darkness descended, the Rebels were again able to draw off, and the Federals camped for the evening.[38]

By now the First Cavalry Division, under General McCook, had also ridden hard after Wheeler's soldiers. It had entered the Sequatchie Valley some hours after Crook's division, and had chased off the remnants of Wheeler's force, who were putting the last touches to their wagon burning. When General Mitchell arrived on the field and superseded McCook, he led the division crosscountry to McMinnville, arriving there on the morning of the 5th but after both the Confederates and Crook had passed through. He too proceeded quickly to Murfreesboro, and later came upon the scene of Crook's latest skirmish with the Rebels. Early on the 6th Crook's men, in the lead, and McCook's soldiers, some hours' march to the rear, moved through Murfreesboro, drew badly needed rations and forage from the depot there, and started after Wheeler again, in the direction of Shelbyville. About eight miles from that town, McCook's division finally overtook Crook's.[39]

The Federals chose not to remain united for long. The next morning, closing in on the enemy, they discovered that

★★★★★★★★★★★★★★★★★★★★★★★★

37. *Official Records*, series I, vol. 30, pt, 2, pp. 684-85.

38. Ibid., pp. 685-86.

39. John W. Rowell, *Yankee Cavalrymen: Through the Civil War with the Ninth Pennsylvania Cavalry*, pp. 152-53.

Wheeler had divided his force once more. Part of it was now located on Duck River near Warner's Bridge, and a smaller command was moving on the village of Unionville, a short distance to the northeast. As a result, General Mitchell marched toward Unionville with McCook's troopers, while Crook advanced along the southward-running Farmington Road toward the Confederates' riverside bivouac.[40]

For a time Wheeler had suspected that his pursuers were at hand. For that reason he had directed General Davidson, whose command occupied the most vulnerable position, to pull back and join with Martin's division once the enemy came into view. But when Crook's soldiers moved against him, Davidson, inexplicably, disregarded his superior's instructions and moved below Duck River.[41]

Despite Wheeler's foresight, most of the Confederates in Crook's path did not know trouble was near until too late. A trooper recollected: "The first intimation that we had of the presence of the enemy was when cannon balls came crashing through the timber and we could hear the firing of our men and the enemy out on the pike, half a mile off."[42] Quickly Davidson found himself isolated from support and in grave danger. Then Crook charged a mounted infantry brigade against the Rebels, pushing them into a dense cedar thicket.

To press his advantage, Crook sent Colonel Long to deliver a supporting charge similar to that he had led two days before. When the troopers surged forward, part of Davidson's command was pushed back three miles farther before it attempted to make a stand in another thicket near the village of Farmington. Noting that the geography precluded normal cavalry operations, Crook returned to the mounted infantry regiments in his division and had them attack the woods afoot. The tactic yielded prompt results; the Rebels were chased from among the trees in wild haste.[43]

★★★★★★★★★★★★★★★★★★★★★★★

40. George B. Davis, "The Cavalry Operations in Middle Tennessee In October, 1863," *Journal of the U. S. Cavalry Association* 24 (1913-14): 888.

41. *Official Records*, series I, vol. 30, pt. 2, p. 724. Some of the Federals later assumed that Wheeler had deliberately left a portion of his command in a vulnerable position, to lure the Yankees into a fight: see B. F. McGee and William R. Jewell, *History of the Seventy-Second Indiana Volunteer Infantry of the Mounted Lightning Brigade*, p. 201.

42. Guild, *Fourth Tennessee Cavalry*, pp. 43-44.

43. *Official Records*, series I, vol. 30, pt. 2, pp. 686-87.

Confederate Colonel Hodge, sent by Wheeler to reinforce the crumbling line, found a portion of Davidson's command "wild and frantic with panic. . . . they rode over my command like madmen, some of them stopping only, as I am informed, when they reached the Tennessee." The panicky soldiers caused Hodge's horse to stumble and fall; then they scrambled over the colonel as he lay sprawled on the ground. By the sheerest luck Hodge was able to remount and escape capture.[44]

Crook's cavalry and mounted infantry pressed their attack, gunning down the retreating Confederates and sabering their mounts—while their artillery shelled other segments of Davidson's division. The Federals had a pretty fair idea of the extent of damage Wheeler's soldiers had inflicted upon their supply lines, and they were aching to exact every last drop of revenge.

The attack rolled forward with inexorable momentum. One participant later recalled that "there was plenty of hard fighting, but to Crook's men it was one continuous forward movement." Not even a Rebel battery could stem the pursuit. For a time its gunners unleashed what a Union soldier called a "terrific" fire, which sounded "like a great tornado," but soon a Union battery challenged it and knocked the enemy cannon out of action by blowing up a nearby caisson.[45] Afterward, Crook's men came on with even greater speed and force, driving every Rebel cavalryman from their path. Finally they crashed against Martin's division, which Wheeler late that afternoon sent to aid Davidson's rear echelon. At least temporarily, the Federal advance was halted.[46]

Still, only two factors saved Wheeler's men from annihilation. Darkness fell upon the Duck River shoreline before Crook could send Colonel Long to launch an all-out attack against Confederate units making a desperate stand. More critically, a full brigade, under Colonel Robert H. G. Minty, absented itself from the Second Cavalry Division when Crook needed it to stop an enemy flank threat, crucial if Long was to succeed in his attack. For his mistake Minty was relieved of

★★★★★★★★★★★★★★★★★★★★★★★

44. Ibid., p. 727.

45. Curry, "Raid of the Confederate Cavalry," p. 827.

46. *Official Records*, series I, vol. 30, pt. 2, p. 724.

command; in his battle report Crook charged him with being disposed "to frustrate my designs in a covert manner."[47]

After the bitter fighting ended, Wheeler withdrew his troopers, setting up a rear guard to hold back Crook's advance regiments till the vanguard of the raiding column could make its escape.[48] Then the Confederates raced at top speed toward the safety of the Tennessee River, many miles to the south. By this point Wheeler was entirely willing to run from his opponents. His once-triumphant raid had almost become a debacle greater than any the Confederate cavalry in the West had ever experienced, and now his overriding concern was to salvage whatever glory might remain to him.

By sundown on October 9 Wheeler had reached the head of Muscle Shoals, the only fordable point on that stretch of the Tennessee. He put his soldiers across the river with only minor difficulties.[49] Many of his soldiers—perhaps thinking of their three hundred comrades who had become casualties at Farmington (another one hundred were cut off by Crook while trying to reach the river)—expressed deep relief when they saw the Union divisions come up to the far shore of the Tennessee aboard their lathered horses, too late to inflict further damage.[50]

After marching a short distance below the river, Wheeler allowed his men to bivouac and sample some of the food they had confiscated from the Federal wagons and the McMinnville supply houses. Only then could he permit himself a respite from work and the opportunity to ponder the dangers he had faced above the river.

Future events revealed that the damage he had inflicted upon Rosecrans's wagon train and supply bases was nearly fatal to the Army of the Cumberland; later reports estimated that up to one thousand wagons had been burned or dismantled in the Sequatchie Valley. However, the Federal forces in Chattanooga lived with the threat of widespread starvation for only three weeks. Then they were saved, when Grant, fresh from his triumph at Vicksburg, came to their relief

★★★★★★★★★★★★★★★★★★★★★★

47. Ibid., p. 687.

48. Ibid., p. 728.

49. Dyer, *"Fightin' Joe" Wheeler*, pp. 134-35.

50. Boatner, *The Civil War Dictionary*, p. 911.

with thousands of reinforcements and forged new supply routes for the beleaguered garrison. In November Grant decisively defeated Braxton Bragg in battle southeast of Chattanooga and lifted the Confederate siege.[51]

Despite the destruction and pillaging he had caused, Wheeler learned that his raid was a pyrrhic victory, because the rough handling he had received at Farmington disorganized and for a time emasculated his command. Crook's pursuit had also prevented Fightin' Joe from engaging in operations that Bragg had planned for him in conjunction with movements by other cavalry leaders such as Major General Stephen D. Lee and Brigadier General Philip Roddey.[52]

To some degree Wheeler was responsible for permitting the disastrous Farmington battle to take place, by tarrying too long in Middle Tennessee after raiding McMinnville and by allowing Crook's cavalrymen to find him largely unprepared to meet an assault. Once again, Wheeler had barely escaped disgrace while leading an independent mission involving substantial numbers of raiders. Still he would not admit that a subordinate such as the now-departed Forrest would have been more ably suited than he to lead such an expedition.

Nevertheless, the operation had a happy epilogue for Wheeler. After midnight on the 9th he spied a comfortable-looking house and sought out its master to ask permission to encamp his soldiers on the adjoining grounds. After giving his approval, the owner introduced the general to his young, recently widowed daughter. The pretty girl was thrilled to meet the man whose exploits she had heard so much about; in turn, Wheeler was struck by her charm and beauty. Before the cavalry broke camp and moved on, Wheeler began to think himself in love with Mrs. Daniella Jones Sherrod.

Their romance would survive the war, and the couple would be married in February 1866 in the house where they had first met.[53] Thus, despite its unpleasant finale, the Sequatchie Valley expedition would always provide a lasting and happy memory for Fightin' Joe.

★★★★★★★★★★★★★★★★★★★★★★★

51. Grant, *Personal Memoirs,* 2: 31-40, 61-88.

52. Boatner, *The Civil War Dictionary,* p. 911; Rowell, *Yankee Cavalrymen,* p. 150.

53. Dyer, *"Fightin' Joe" Wheeler,* pp. 135-36, 244.

9
TO BURN
THE HATEFUL CITY
The Kilpatrick-Dahlgren Raid
on Richmond
(February 28-March 4, 1864)

1

There were many ambitious men in the ranks of the Union armies, but few lusted after success and glory with the single-mindedness of Judson Kilpatrick. Midway through the Civil War, possessed of a military career that had won him the rank of brigadier general of volunteers at age twenty-seven, Kilpatrick set specific goals for himself and determined to prosecute the remainder of the conflict in a manner that would assure their attainment. He determined, first, to become governor of his native state, New Jersey, and eventually President of the United States.

Kilpatrick's stature and appearance may not have seemed in keeping with his dreams of greatness, for he looked the part of neither warrior nor statesman. Ferret-faced, diminutive, and scrawny, he prompted one officer to comment that few men could look at him without laughing.[1] Yet he was animated by a constant charge of nervous energy that burned in his pale eyes and arrested the attention of a great many with whom he came into contact. A commanding

Judson Kilpatrick. COURTESY LIBRARY OF CONGRESS.

orator, Kilpatrick was rarely at a loss to describe his future plans or to explain why he could hardly fail to fulfill them. His words, compelling in their intensity, had the ring of conviction.

His military career had begun in remarkable style. A May 1861 graduate of West Point (where he often brawled with Southern-born cadets over the secession issue), he had achieved early recognition as the first Regular Army officer to be wounded in action, suffering a grapeshot injury that June in the skirmish of Big Bethel. After a short stint in in-

★★★★★★★★★★★★★★★★★★★★★★★

1. Bruce Catton, *A Stillness at Appomattox*, p. 4.

fantry service, he accepted a commission as lieutenant colonel of a New York volunteer cavalry regiment, and after only a few weeks in the field decided that mounted warfare was to his liking. He soon distinguished himself as one of the most promising young cavalrymen in the Virginia theater, demonstrating a particular aptitude for raiding Confederate communication lines.[2] His reputation soared when, as a full colonel, he commanded a force of horsemen during Stoneman's 1863 raid above Richmond, making the most aggressive showing of all the Union cavalry officers involved. His fame crested a month later at Brandy Station, the largest cavalry battle ever fought in North America. Although the Union forces were defeated in that engagement, Kilpatrick showed so much spunk and resourcefulness that he won promotion to brigadier general three days later.

At that point, he might have fallen back upon his hard-won laurels. Had he not accomplished any greater deeds thereafter, his reputation would nevertheless have remained solid. But his career was fated to take a drastic turn downward.

Kilpatrick was a complex man; some of his personality traits contradicted others. Unlike many members of the Federal officer corps, he neither drank nor gambled; yet certain other vices were dear to his heart, particularly womanizing. Despite marrying in 1861, he was notorious for his licentiousness, often consorting with camp-followers while campaigning. He professed to be a fair-minded man who constantly held the best interests of his soldiers in mind. But he lacked integrity and, it would seem, a fundamental sense of human decency, driving his men and their mounts so roughly and so thoughtlessly that he won the appelation, "Kil-cavalry." As a field general, his aggressiveness brought him a reputation as a hell-for-leather fighter. But though he displayed a marked contempt for fear, he could not always think clearly under pressure, and occasionally he appeared as eager to withdraw from a fight as he had been to enter it. His erratic habits, especially those which seemed to indicate that he was liable to lose his head when beset by self-invited peril, prompted many of Kilpatrick's own soldiers to endorse

★★★★★★★★★★★★★★★★★★★★★★

2. Warner, *Generals in Blue,* p. 266.

one staff officer's opinion that he was "a frothy braggart, without brains."[3]

He definitely used poor judgment during the battle of Gettysburg, which started the downward arc of his career. On the third day of the fighting, while Confederate infantry under Pickett attacked the center of the Federal line, Kilpatrick—by now a division commander—directed one of his brigade leaders to assault a strong position held by another Rebel infantry force. Since the attacking unit would be greatly outnumbered as well as outpositioned, the order was suicidal. But Kilpatrick was worried because he had been kept out of the decisive combat thus far. He realized that only a commander who committed his men to battle would win renown on this field. When the brigade commander protested the order, Kilpatrick unfairly implied that he was a coward—whereupon, to prove his courage, the young subordinate led the charge as ordered, lost much of his force in a futile effort, and was himself killed.[4]

The repercussions of the incident soiled Kilpatrick's reputation ever afterward. Later fighting failed to return his good name, a circumstance that rankled him furiously. By the early months of 1864 his career appeared definitely in eclipse, and almost desperately he sought a means of salvaging his future.

Early that February he perceived what appeared to be a gilt-edged opportunity. In recent months the North had been aroused by the plight of Federals who languished in Virginia prisons. Food and medicine were in scarce supply throughout the Confederacy, causing starvation and disease to sweep the prison camps, many of which had become hell holes where inmates died by the dozens. Early in the month, more than one hundred Union officers—including the intrepid Colonel Abel Streight—had tunneled out of Richmond's notorious Libby Prison to bring word of the sufferings they had endured to officials of Abraham Lincoln's government.[5]

★★★★★★★★★★★★★★★★★★★★★★★

3. Virgil Carrington Jones, *Eight Hours Before Richmond,* pp. 33-34; George R. Agassiz, ed., *Meade's Headquarters, 1863-1865: Letters of Colonel Theodore Lyman, Etc.,* p. 79.

4. Boatner, *The Civil War Dictionary,* p. 275.

5. For detailed information on the outbreak at Libby Prison, see Roach, *The Prisoner of War,* pp. 99-118.

Northern newspapers picked up their story, publicizing to the hilt the privations and indignities that the escapees' comrades still suffered in Libby and the other Virginia lock-ups.

The shrill public outcry placed further stress on the president, who by now was desperately seeking a blueprint for peace. With the conflict moving into its fourth year, no end to the fighting was in sight: the Union war machine had badly faltered since producing the great victory at Gettysburg.

Lincoln's predicament came sweetly to Judson Kilpatrick's ears, for he sensed that fate was opening a door for him. Gradually he formed a plan to march his cavalry division out of its winter camp near Stevensburg and Culpeper and into Richmond, some seventy miles to the southeast, destroying parts of the city and freeing its prisoners.[6] It was true that a scheme to take the Rebel capital had recently fizzled out, when Major General Benjamin F. Butler launched a massive infantry-cavalry expedition from his Fort Monroe headquarters. However, the blame for Butler's failure could be laid on a Federal deserter, who had reached the enemy's line with advance word of the movement, giving Confederates time to gather along the raiders' route and foil their plans.[7] Then, too, Ben Butler was far from being a military genius, and Kilpatrick felt that if he himself could lead such a raid success would be much more likely. "Kil-cavalry" knew that during this season Richmond was thinly guarded—so said the Northern spies who operated throughout the city.[8] Lee's Army of Northern Virginia was encamped near Fredricksburg, several miles above the city, facing General George Gordon Meade's Army of the Potomac. No substantial Confederate force appeared to be in a position to combat a fast-moving raiding team.

Kilpatrick was a very vocal fellow, and being colorful enough to provide good copy had ingratiated himself with the journalists who accompanied the field army. Through a combination of personal lung power and the initiative of his newspaper acquaintances, word of his plan to capture Rich-

★★★★★★★★★★★★★★★★★★★★★★

6. Catton, *A Stillness at Appomattox*, p. 5.

7. *Official Records*, series I, vol. 33, pp. 143-45.

8. Catton, *A Stillness at Appomattox*, p. 6.

mond soon circulated around army headquarters and then throughout Washington. President Lincoln, who despite Butler's failure believed that a cavalry operation against the Rebel capital was a feasible undertaking, heard the news. He sent word that the cavalry general should come to the White House and provide him personally with a detailed outline of his plan.

Kilpatrick needed no persuasion. Leaving the sumptuous mansion in which he had resided in Stevensburg, he rode north to see the president, explained his plan to him, then did the same for officials at the War Department. The government's reaction was to Kilpatrick's liking: he was directed to return to his headquarters and draft a formal outline of the plan, with the understanding that it would win approval if he could pen it as graphically as he had vocalized it.

Returning south, the general must have felt that official approval was only a formality. He had gone out of his way to sell the president on the idea, and believed he had won him over by remarking that the expedition would provide an ideal means to distribute through Virginia copies of Lincoln's amnesty proclamation. The proclamation, which offered a conditional opportunity for Southerners to return to the Union fold, without recriminations, had long been a pet idea of the president.[9]

Approval did indeed come through in a short time, for Kilpatrick's plan sounded just as promising on paper. He proposed to take four thousand troopers and six cannon across the Rapidan River to Spotsylvania Court House, from which village two detachments would ride in different directions to damage portions of the Virginia Central and Richmond, Fredricksburg & Potomac Railroads—lines that Kilpatrick had partially destroyed during Stoneman's raid. Meanwhile, the main force would continue south, crossing the North Anna River before moving on the Rebel capital.

One of the detachments would rejoin the main force along the way, and the command would advance on Richmond from the direction of Hanover Junction, after destroying railroad bridges and supplies at the depot there. Kilpatrick hoped that Butler's army might bring up supporting troops

★★★★★★★★★★★★★★★★★★★★★★★★★★

9. Jones, *Eight Hours Before Richmond*, pp. 25-26.

as his raiders galloped through the city, destroying its military value and freeing the inmates at the Libby and Belle Isle prison camps.

Finally, the second detachment, comprising about five hundred soldiers, would approach the city from the south, along the lower bank of the James River, and would cooperate with the main column in its attack. Following a successful assault, the entire command would retreat either by the route the main column had taken from the north or via the peninsula, to seek relief within Butler's lines. Five days' rations would be carried by the troopers and, since speed of movement would be essential, no wagons would make the journey.[10]

Kilpatrick's plan received quite a bit of critical attention. His immediate superior, Major General Alfred Pleasonton, commanding the Cavalry Corps of the Army of the Potomac, was asked his opinion of the project; his reaction was not in the least favorable—primarily, it would seem, because the plan had not originated with Alfred Pleasonton. Then, too, Pleasonton still shuddered at the memory of Stoneman's raid, which had cost the corps dearly in lost horses and supplies but had reaped no strategic success.

Other cavalry officers also denounced the scheme as too dangerous and risky. Yet the army commander did not voice disapproval of the project. General Meade, a careful, deliberate leader, did not wholly approve of the bold tone that Kilpatrick's idea struck, but he was aware that the president was in favor of it and so said nothing against it. Additionally, Meade was consoled by scouting reports indicating that Richmond was guarded by only three thousand local militia, some field artillery, and a small cavalry force. The only veteran Rebel forces of considerable size between Lee's army and the Rebel capital were one thousand five hundred troopers under Major General Wade Hampton, and if they tried to interfere they would be overwhelmed in a pitched battle by Kilpatrick's larger command. In the end, Meade's decision not to interfere with Kilpatrick's ambitions proved a crucial factor in the plan's acceptance. By the middle of February

★★★★★★★★★★★★★★★★★★★★★★

10. H. P. Moyer, comp., *History of the Seventeenth Regiment, Pennsylvania Volunteer Cavalry*, p. 230.

Kilpatrick was authorized to send an officer to Washington to select for the expedition the best horses available.[11]

With that, excitement and activity swept through the winter camp of the Third Cavalry Division of the Army of the Potomac. Eagerly and confidently, Judson Kilpatrick began to prepare in earnest for the operation that would either secure his future or cripple it beyond repair.

2

On the day Kilpatrick received authority to choose horses for the raid, a mustachioed young cavalry colonel with a wooden leg trotted up to Kil-cavalry's headquarters. With some difficulty, the officer dismounted and, supported by a pair of canes, hobbled inside the mansion to exchange salutes with the commander of the Third Division.

The visitor was Ulric Dahlgren, twenty-one years old, a Philadelphia-born aristocrat, son of Rear Admiral John A. Dahlgren of the Federal Navy, and one of the bravest and most daring officers in mounted service.[12] Once strikingly handsome, his features had been worn from many months of convalescence after his wounding in battle the previous July; now he appeared thin and emaciated. But though his recuperation had been slow and the loss of his right leg had come as a wretched jolt, young Dahlgren was every bit as energetic as he had once been, and was determined that his injury would not keep him out of action. Recently he had returned to Washington after a lengthy vacation aboard one of the ships in his father's blockading squadron off Charleston, South Carolina, and in the capital had heard rumors of an impending cavalry expedition. Speculation identified Judson Kilpatrick as the leader of the operation, and Dahlgren decided to head south and seek him out.[13] Such an expedition would provide an excellent opportunity to prove to the army

★★★★★★★★★★★★★★★★★★★★★★★

11. Jones, *Eight Hours Before Richmond,* pp. 28-29; Catton, *A Stillness at Appomattox,* p. 5.

12. Swiggett, *The Rebel Raider,* p. 206. A prominent Union official who knew young Dahlgren well declared that "A more gallant and brave hearted fellow was not to be found in the service. . . ." Howard K. Beale, ed., *Diary of Gideon Welles* 1, p. 538.

13. J. A. Dahlgren, *Memoir of Ulric Dahlgren,* pp. 209-10.

Ulric Dahlgren. FROM *Photographic History of the Civil War.*

that Ulric Dahlgren was not a helpless cripple who deserved to be shuffled into the discard.

When Kilpatrick received him at his headquarters, it was not their first meeting. On the very day the colonel had been wounded—during the pursuit of Lee's army after Gettysburg—Dahlgren had been temporarily attached to Kilpatrick's division. On that occasion the general watched Dahlgren lead a mounted charge against Confederate infantry retreating through Hagerstown, Maryland.[14] Immediately Kilpatrick sized up the young officer as a kindred spirit, a man he would be pleased to have for a subordinate.

It took but a short time for Dahlgren to convince Kilpat-

★★★★★★★★★★★★★★★★★★★★★★★

14. *History of the Eighteenth Regiment of Cavalry, Pennsylvania Volunteers,* p. 85.

rick that he would be an asset to the upcoming raid. Once the colonel declared his willingness to serve in any capacity, and demonstrated that he still could ride and fight on horseback, Kilpatrick agreed to make him commander of his principal detached force, the five hundred-man unit that would strike Richmond from the south while the main body swept down from the north. The general's decision was not purely owing to his admiration of Dahlgren's courage and skill. Ever with an eye on the main chance, Kilpatrick realized that the colonel's impeccable social credentials would lend the expedition extra prestige.[15]

At once he put the colonel to work at handling the administrative details of the mission. A conscientious desk officer as well as a hard fighter, Dahlgren began to draft the necessary orders as well as copies of land maps on which the routes of march were defined. In the meantime, Kilpatrick conferred with his lower echelon commanders, oversaw the shipping of horses to Stevensburg, and made periodic visits to Washington for further talks with government officials. In other words, while Dahlgren handled the office-clerk chores, Kilpatrick galavanted about doing what he enjoyed most —talking up his great ideas.

As it developed, he talked much too loudly and too freely. His inability to keep his plans secret had already brought Dahlgren into the picture, but instead of keeping quiet from this point on, Kilpatrick seemed to grow more verbose and voluble with each passing day. Soon rumors were so rife in the capital that the city's newspapers began to prepare stories and maps on the expedition, scheduling them for publication as soon as official news of its commencement was received. Spies in the capital relayed the news to their superiors in Virginia, and even the Richmond papers began to openly speculate about a coming raid.

Even without reading these reports, General Robert E. Lee expected such an operation to take place. The Confederate commander had anticipated a mobile strike at Richmond for the past few months. Aided by reports from his scouts, he was able to pinpoint the very ford over the Rapidan River that Kilpatrick would use during his mission. Still, Lee believed that such a raid would fare no better than Stoneman's,

★★★★★★★★★★★★★★★★★★★★★★★

15. Jones, *Eight Hours Before Richmond,* p. 33.

considering the Richmond defenses strong enough to thwart a winter assault.[16]

Seemingly unaware of any breach of secrecy, Judson Kilpatrick worked out the final details of his plan. Primarily, he saw to it that a proper complement of troopers was drawn for the mission. His main force and Dahlgren's detachment would consist of soldiers from the Third Division, plus picked units from the First Cavalry Division.[17] He also supervised the drawing of rations and ammunition and directed that all unfit riders and horses be separated from the ranks before the march began.

The cavalrymen ordered to report to his headquarters —especially those temporarily transferred from the First Division—were puzzled about the nature of the upcoming assignment. But as the bustle of activity swept through the cavalry camps, they began to suspect what was in the offing. A member of the 17th Pennsylvania wrote: "Five days' rations of hard bread, sugar, coffee and salt were issued, but no meat, the command evidently being supposed to furnish meat for itself from some source other than Uncle Sam's commissary. This looked extremely raidish. Commanding officers of detachments were ordered to see that all horses were well shod, inspection of arms and ammunition, everything in the best condition possible." The increased workload was burdensome, but the trooper added: "Everybody was in excellent humor, for nothing so delights the heart of a cavalryman as to go on a scout or a raid. It is easier to get a trooper or even a hundred for a raid than to get one to groom an extra horse."[18]

On February 27 Kilpatrick received his formal orders. He was directed to move the next evening "with the ulmost expedition possible on the shortest route past the enemy's right flank to Richmond, and by this rapid march endeavor to effect an entrance into that city and liberate our prisoners now held there and in that immediate vicinity." Additional orders authorized Dahlgren's participation in the mission. The colonel was expected "to render valuable assistance from his

★★★★★★★★★★★★★★★★★★★★★★★★

16. Ibid., pp. 35-36, 59-60.

17. Hillman A. Hall, W. B. Besley, and Gilbert G. Wood, comps., *History of the Sixth New York Cavalry*, p. 173.

18. Moyer, *Seventeenth Pennsylvania Cavalry*, p. 233.

knowledge of the country and his well-known gallantry, intelligence and energy." Still, no detailed instructions ever reached Kilpatrick's hands; Meade's chief of staff notified him that he had full discretion to carry out, in any way practicable, those plans which he had explained verbally and on paper to President Lincoln: Kilpatrick had won the *carte blanche* he had desired.[19]

On the other hand, the heavy weight of accountability rested squarely on his shoulders. He alone would be to blame if the raid ended in failure, for he alone was responsible for its planning and execution. Dwelling on such a possibility would do him no good, so he concentrated on the steps that would be taken to increase the likelihood of his success. General Meade had prepared three large diversionary maneuvers to arrest the attention of gray-clad signalmen occupying vantage points atop the mountains surrounding the Culpeper-Stevensburg vicinity. Already, two infantry regiments in Major General John Sedgwick's VI Corps had trudged southwestward to the area near Madison Court House, accompanied by cannon, ambulances, and supply wagons, as though heralding a march by the entire army. At the courthouse town, the infantrymen were to join a one thousand five hundred-trooper contingent led by the boyish Brigadier General George Armstrong Custer; the latter would then ride farther south to Charlottesville.[20] And shortly before Custer's men marched, another infantry force, part of Major General David Birney's III Corps, was also to move southward from Brandy Station. The three operations would hardly escape the notice of the Rebel lookouts, who would doubtless inform their superiors that large-scale enemy activity was planned farther toward the west instead of in the direction of Richmond.[21]

As these movements got under way, Kilpatrick, early on the 28th, met for the final time with his subordinates to plan preraid strategy. To them he stressed that his and Dahlgren's columns, after making their divergent ways below the Rapi-

★★★★★★★★★★★★★★★★★★★★★★★

19. *Official Records,* series I, vol. 33, pp. 173, 183.

20. For further information on this little-known phase of the Kilpatrick-Dahlgren campaign, see James O. Moore, "Custer's Raid Into Albermarle County: The Skirmish at Rio Hill, February 29, 1864," *The Virginia Magazine of History and Biography* 79 (July 1971): 338-48.

21. Agassiz, *Meade's Headquarters,* p. 77.

dan, must be in position to simultaneously strike the Confederate capital by ten A. M., March 1.[22] When the conference ended, most of the brigade and regimental leaders returned to their own units, while Kilpatrick downed a nonalcoholic toast to the success of his mission.

While Kilpatrick drank, young Dahlgren sat down in his tent to write some lines to his relatives and friends. Already he had sent a lengthy letter to his father, expressing his feelings about the expedition, including his belief that "If successful it would be the grandest thing on record and if it fails many of us will 'go up.' I may be captured or I may be 'tumbled over,' but it is an undertaking that if I was not in it I should be ashamed to show my face again. . . ."[23] Now he composed a similar letter to his aunt in Washington. Again he mentioned the possibility of his not returning from the mission, although he deemed that highly unlikely. Even so, he enclosed the letter he had written his father, and told his aunt: "If I do not return, then give it to him."[24]

3

By six o'clock that evening, the colonel was back in the saddle, leading his five hundred troopers out of Stevensburg. The riders, who had been culled from five of the most experienced regiments in the Cavalry Corps, headed south toward Ely's Ford on the Rapidan. Kilpatrick's three thousand soldiers would remain in camp for another hour before moving out in Dahlgren's rear.

To the west could be seen low-hanging fog, gleaming white in the winter moonlight. The clouds gave worries to Lieutenant Reuben Bartley, a signal officer accompanying Dahlgren. Bartley was to handle flags by which the detachment hoped to keep in communication with the main force; he realized that fog might prevent Kilpatrick's men from observing any signals he might transmit.[25]

But his concern did not affect the colonel in command,

★★★★★★★★★★★★★★★★★★★★★★★★

22. J. H. Kidd, *Personal Recollections of a Cavalryman with Custer's Michigan Cavalry Brigade in the Civil War*, p. 246.

23. Dahlgren, *Memoir of Ulric Dahlgren*, p. 211.

24. Jones, *Eight Hours Before Richmond*, p. 37.

25. Ibid., pp. 44-45.

nor did the bitter chill of the night air. Ulric Dahlgren was leading his first sizable raiding force, a position he had long wished to hold. He would not have traded places with any man at that hour—with the possible exception of Judson Kilpatrick.

An early moment of success made his spirits soar even higher. Thanks to the adroitness of a nineteen-year-old Irish scout named Martin Hogan, the advance guard of the detachment crossed the Rapidan above the assigned ford and without firing a shot surrounded a seventeen-man Rebel picket post guarding the crossing site.[26] By eleven o'clock, the Confederates, cursing their ill luck, were riding under guard to Kilpatrick's main force, now in motion. Dahlgren meanwhile moved on, crossing all of his men into enemy territory and hurrying toward his next port of call, Spotsylvania Court House, a dozen miles south of the river.

When the captured pickets reached Kilpatrick, he was highly pleased to learn that this first barrier on the road to Richmond had been cleared. Some hours after his command came up to the Rapidan he dispatched a message to General Pleasonton: "Twenty miles nearer Richmond, and all right. Will double my bet of $5,000 that I enter Richmond."

Had he known what was then occurring within Dahlgren's ranks, however, he would not have been so confident. Soon after fording the river, Dahlgren had unwittingly picked up additional riders, a pair of Confederate scouts named Scott and Topping. Clad in blue uniforms stripped from captured stragglers, the scouts slipped into the marching formation, their faces shrouded by the darkness of evening. Carefully noting the size and heading of the raiding force, the pair later rode off to bring word of the movement to their commander, Wade Hampton.[27]

Ignorant of the spies comings and goings, Dahlgren's men rode into and through Spotsylvania, heading south toward Frederick's Hall, a depot on the Virginia Central Railway that had been targeted for destruction. Below the courthouse town Dahlgren and Kilpatrick took separate trails, not expecting to meet again until they smashed through the Rebel

★★★★★★★★★★★★★★★★★★★★★★★★

26. Moore, *Kilpatrick and Our Cavalry,* pp. 144-47.

27. Jones, *Eight Hours Before Richmond,* pp. 46-48.

capital almost forty hours later.[28] The young colonel showed no anxiety about marching off on his own for, as far as he knew, all had gone smoothly thus far. He had no cause to suspect that his luck would soon turn sour.

At eight o'clock on the morning of the 29th, Kilpatrick's soldiers galloped up to the outskirts of Spotsylvania. Feeling as feisty as their commander, the troopers of an advance regiment, the 17th Pennsylvania, swooped down on an old lady trying to herd a flock of geese out of the crowded road. The woman raised her broom to ward off the soldiers, but could not prevent them from taking saber practice at her flock. A participant recalled: "With the men it was 'against geese right cut' or 'against geese left cut,' and most effectively did it curl up the neck of goose or gander. Quite a few were decapitated, their heads tumbling into the dust." Finally the poor woman stood still as the riders thundered past, laughing at her. Then, losing her composure, she cried in a shrill voice: "You'ns are nothing but nasty dirty Yankees after all, so you'ns all are!"

Kilpatrick led his main column a mile farther, then crossed the Po River before allowing his men to rest and eat. However, Kil-cavalry's hallmark was an apparent disregard for the comfort of his cavalrymen, and he embellished his repu-

Drawing of Kilpatrick-Dahlgren raid. COURTESY LIBRARY OF CONGRESS.

★★★★★★★★★★★★★★★★★★★★★★★

28. Boatner, *The Civil War Dictionary*, p. 460.

tation by allowing the troopers a painfully brief period for cooking rations. When the march resumed, a jest began to spread along the column. "This is one of old Abe's jokes," said the troopers, "plenty of rations, but no time to eat them."[29]

While the three thousand five hundred in the main body swung eastward, tearing down telegraph lines to prevent word of their movements from reaching Richmond, Dahlgren's men came up to the line of the Virginia Central just above Frederick's Hall. In that vicinity he added to his haul of prisoners by capturing some Rebel officers conducting court-martial proceedings in the field.[30] Then he turned his attention to the nearby depot, where, according to reports, the artillery of Lee's Second Corps had gone into winter quarters. The heavy and light guns might be ripe for the taking.

Dismounting and hobbling over to his new prisoners, Dahlgren questioned them about what to expect at the station. Their answers did not please him. Large units of cavalry and sharpshooters protected the artillery, said the captives, and a regiment of infantry was encamped not far from the cannon park. Dahlgren refused to accept their stories, believing them fabrications, until an aged Negro who lived on a neighboring plantation corroborated them. After some deliberation, the colonel decided not to risk seeing his command shot to pieces at the depot. He sent his men on a detour to the east of Frederick's Hall, burned a long stretch of track, then pushed southward toward the James River.

Dahlgren's decision was regrettable for two reasons. The Confederate prisoners had indeed been lying, and the old Negro had been ignorant of the true state of affairs at Frederick's Hall. Only a handful of infantrymen—no match for Dahlgren's five hundred veterans—were stationed at the depot. The cavalrymen could have done crucial damage to the guns, thereby depriving the Army of Northern Virginia of much of its artillery strength.

Even more unfortunate was the fact that had Dahlgren pulled up at the depot he would certainly have captured a train moving westward on that stretch of track. Few passengers were aboard but they included an officer who was re-

★★★★★★★★★★★★★★★★★★★★★★★★

29. Moyer, *Seventeenth Pennsylvania Cavalry,* pp. 234-35.

30. Moore, *Kilpatrick and Our Cavalry,* p. 147.

turning from Richmond to his field headquarters at Orange Court House—General Robert E. Lee.[31]

4

By midday on the 29th Wade Hampton was aware that Federals were running loose through his bailiwick. He had received precise information about Dahlgren's route from the spies Scott and Topping; and from a third trooper, Sergeant George Shadbourne, he had learned of the movements of Kilpatrick's main force. Hampton at once passed the news on to his superior, J. E. B. Stuart, but received no reply. Finally he came to see that he himself would have to organize a pursuit. However, at his present position only three hundred members of the 1st and 2nd North Carolina Cavalry regiments, plus a two-gun section of an artillery battery, were within easy reach. Quickly he sent these forces southward along the Richmond, Fredericksburg & Potomac, while notifying his Maryland cavalry brigade, under Colonel Bradley Johnson, to move out of Taylorsville and join in the chase.[32] Even with the addition of Johnson's command, Hampton would be outnumbered by the Yankee raiding forces; he was obliged to fight anyway.

While Hampton mobilized his troops, Judson Kilpatrick was leading his raiders toward Beaver Dam Station, a wood depot on the Virginia Central a few miles east of Frederick's Hall. To this point the general had been nagged by only one problem. Lieutenant Joseph Gloskoski, the signal officer who rode with him, had found the land too flat and wooded to provide lofty observation points; hence he had been unable to communicate with Lieutenant Bartley in Dahlgren's column. Now, however, Kilpatrick grew concerned about another problem. As he neared Beaver Dam, the skies turned steel gray and snow began to fall, menacing the progress of the column. Additionally, the snow would blank out the countryside, ensuring that Gloskoski and Bartley would have no chance whatsoever to earn their pay.[33]

★★★★★★★★★★★★★★★★★★★★★★★

31. Jones, *Eight Hours Before Richmond*, pp. 51-53.

32. *Official Records*, series I, vol. 33, p. 201; Manly Wade Wellman, *Giant in Gray: A Biography of Wade Hampton of South Carolina*, pp. 133-34.

33. *Official Records*, series I, vol. 33, p. 189.

Snow was coming down heavily when the advance guard of the main column clattered into Beaver Dam. The raiders galloped up so quickly and unexpectedly that they captured the local telegrapher before he could tap out an alarm to Richmond. Knowing nothing of Hampton's movements, Kilpatrick assumed that his movement had gone unheralded so far; perhaps his entrance into the capital would be similar to his arrival at Beaver Dam.

Buffeted by snow and cold winds, Kilpatrick's men warmed themselves by setting several fires at the station. They torched the telegraph office, freight house, passenger depot, engine house, water tower, and several miscellaneous outbuildings, in addition to hundreds of cords of wood stacked alongside the track. A sheet of flame rose above the surrounding woods, illuminating a frenetic scene. A cavalryman observed that "The dark forms of our soldiers jumping and dancing around . . . seemed from a distance like demons on some hellish sport."

Marching on, the soldiers were slowed and made uncomfortable by bands of concealed snipers whom they encountered intermittently.[34] And when he reached his next stopover—Ashland, along the Fredricksburg Railroad, about seventeen miles north of Richmond—Kilpatrick suffered further distress. At Ashland he heard a rumor that two thousand enemy infantry and artillerymen had deployed at a nearby railroad bridge.[35] As Dahlgren had been cozened by exaggerated reports of enemy strength at Frederick's Hall, Kilpatrick was taken in by this news, for the strength of the bridge guard was greatly magnified. Unable to ignore the rumors, he dispatched a major from the 6th New York Cavalry, with 450 troopers, to keep the Rebel force occupied and thus cover the movements of the main column.

The detachment did a competent screening job, enabling Kilpatrick to push onward for Richmond. Therefore Kil-cavalry's confidence, though shaken, remained intact.[36]

★★★★★★★★★★★★★★★★★★★★★★★★

34. Moyer, *Seventeenth Pennsylvania Cavalry*, pp. 235-37; Hall, Besley, and Wood, *Sixth New York Cavalry*, p. 174.

35. *Official Records*, series I, vol. 33, p. 184.

36. Hall, Besley, and Wood, *Sixth New York Cavalry*, pp. 174-75; Moore, *Kilpatrick and Our Cavalry*, p. 149.

He felt he still possessed an excellent chance to capture the capital and, incidentally, win unparalleled renown.

By ten A. M., March 1, the hour he had fixed for the joint attack, Kilpatrick was still five miles above Richmond. The weather had thrown off his timetable; by now the snow had ceased, but an icy rain was falling, slowing progress and making his soldiers ever miserable. Despite all this, he felt that the men seemed eager to gallop through the Richmond streets; at any rate, he could tell himself so.

So far Kilpatrick had not received a single message from Dahlgren, but he tried not to worry. Having faith in the colonel's ability, he supposed that Dahlgren's men were now moving into positions to attack the capital from below the James River. He refused to admit to himself that, for all he knew, the five hundred-man column had vanished from the earth.

Kilpatrick moved warily for almost two miles before meeting his first measure of resistance. Suddenly, from behind crude earthworks on both sides of the Richmond road, came rifle and artillery fire.[37] As the shooting intensified, it became apparent that Kilpatrick had been naive in supposing that Richmond would not detect his approach. In truth, the city had been alerted to the raid the previous day, receiving reports from Hampton's scouts as well as from citizens who had observed Dahlgren near Frederick's Hall. Now the local defense battalion had turned out, and its members fought so well that Kilpatrick began to suspect that he had collided with veteran regulars. So thinking, his confidence began to fray at the edges. Still, he pushed ahead, suffering dozens of casualties.

After he had advanced a short distance, the Confederate resistance grew so heavy that the general was forced to dismount and deploy. The fighting that had begun so suddenly in the icy rain soon expanded into a full-scale engagement, with riflemen on both sides falling dead or wounded into the sodden road. When the racket of battle swelled to a steep pitch, Kilpatrick realized that he would not be able to hear the sounds of skirmishing farther south if Dahlgren was now attacking the city.

Prevented from using his artillery by lack of cover, and

★★★★★★★★★★★★★★★★★★★★★★

37. *Official Records*, series I, vol. 33, p. 184.

finding a mounted assault impossible on the muddy ground that led to the breastworks, Kilpatrick was forced to fight his men afoot, using only carbines and pistols. This he did throughout the afternoon, but he could gain no clear-cut advantage over his opponents.[38] After a time, one of his brigade commanders, Brigadier General Henry E. Davies, Jr., suggested a two-pronged attack against a crucial sector of the works, and his superior accepted the plan. But just as one of the two forces, a dismounted detachment numbering five hundred men, moved forward to cover the main assault, Kil-cavalry changed his mind. His old psychological ailment had flared up—he had lost his nerve. Influenced by an idea that the enemy was being reinforced by both infantry and artillery, and still concerned that he might be facing Confederate veterans instead of militia, Kilpatrick ordered his entire command to swing northward. Although some of his officers protested the withdrawal, the maneuver was carried out in brief order. By the time full darkness had come, the raiders had gone into a cold night's bivouac near the hamlet of Mechanicsville. They were rejoined there by the 450-man detachment sent to hold off the bridge guards near Ashland.[39]

During the early part of that evening, Kilpatrick was nagged by second thoughts. He bitterly disliked the idea of giving up his glorious project, and dreaded the consequences. Now, soothed by the warmth of a campfire and no longer surrounded by enemy defenders, he dredged up enough confidence to make another effort. During the weary journey to Mechanicsville, his scouts had insisted that the city defenders, rank amateurs at warfare, had massed north of Richmond to stop him, and that many other sectors lay unguarded.[40] Kilpatrick paid heed to their opinion because if true, he would become the laughing-stock of the Army of the Potomac should he retreat.

Although his soldiers were achingly tired as well as numb with cold, Kilpatrick ordered them to remount. Troopers stumbled sleepily toward their animals, slowly resaddled, and swung aboard. One officer managed to get on his horse and

★★★★★★★★★★★★★★★★★★★★★★★

38. Ibid., p. 192.

39. Ibid., pp. 184-85.

40. Ibid., p. 185.

with half-closed eyes kicked viciously with his spurs. The animal bucked and reared, but did not move forward; so the officer spurred it again, until finally he realized that the horse was still tethered to the nearest tree.[41]

Before midnight Kilpatrick had formed two attack forces, each consisting of five hundred troopers, which he determined to throw against the city's works. With his artillery and the rest of his mounted men the general himself would remain at the Chickahominy River bridge near Mechanicsville, covering the attackers' rear.[42]

Just as the two detachments started off, Federal pickets along the road from Hanover Court House were driven in by mounted Confederates. Within a few minutes, Kilpatrick's camp was a scene of utter confusion, for Wade Hampton's veterans were charging through it from several directions, firing their pistols, flailing about with sabers, and trampling fallen Yankees.[43]

Kilpatrick tried desperately to stem the attack, and succeeded momentarily in forcing some of the Rebels back. But when Confederate artillery opened up, he lost the last vestige of his fortitude. Unable to see the road to Richmond in the darkness, he collected his men as best he could and ordered them to retreat from the bivouac area. A trooper later remembered: "Some one gave the command, 'Stand to horse!' soon followed by 'Mount!' 'Form ranks!' 'By fours, march!' . . . when Kilpatrick's voice was heard above all others, 'Forward!' but just which way was the query, as it was utterly impossible to distinguish roads, points of compass or anything else." The soldier remarked that only by following the noises made by comrades' horses splashing down the muddy road could the blue-clad soldiers find their way to safety. At last Kilpatrick brought his main force clear of the charging Rebels, but by then his scattered command was riding away from Richmond, toward the peninsula. Since Hampton's men were still dogging his rear, he knew that he would have to continue his retreat.[44]

★★★★★★★★★★★★★★★★★★★★★★★★★

41. Kidd, *Personal Recollections of a Cavalryman*, p. 255.

42. *Official Records*, series I, vol. 33, p. 185.

43. Wellman, *Giant in Gray*, pp. 134-35; Asa B. Isham, *An Historical Sketch of the Seventh Regiment Michigan Volunteer Cavalry*, pp. 38-39.

44. Moyer, *Seventeenth Pennsylvania Cavalry*, p. 243.

Irony played a role in Kilpatrick's withdrawal. Not only had he been repulsed outside the capital by bands of civilian defenders and militia, but Hampton's attackers were so few that their general had been forced to wait until darkness fell before striking the Federal bivouac.[45] Only under cover of night, and only when surprising soldiers who had spent almost forty-eight mind-dulling hours in the saddle, could Hampton have hoped to succeed in scaring Kilpatrick's men into retreating.

About eight A. M. on March 2 Kilpatrick was able to form a battle line near Old Church, below the Pamunkey River. His men, revived by morning sunlight, repulsed Hampton's advance guard and chased the Rebel riders back toward Richmond. Then at last they were free to feed their horses, cook rations, and grab some sleep. Counting the gaps in his regiments, Kilpatrick found that during the fighting the previous night he had suffered two officers and fifty men killed or captured, and one hundred horses were missing.

The general remained near Old Church till early in the afternoon, hoping to hear some news from or about Dahlgren. Not a particle of information reached him. Reluctantly and dejectedly, he resumed his march down the peninsula toward the safety of Ben Butler's defenses.[46] His line of march closely paralleled the route he had followed the previous May, when returning from Stoneman's expedition. Then, however, Kilpatrick had been able to take pride in his recent accomplishments, knowing that he would be welcomed back to the army with words of praise. Today all that lay ahead was humiliation and anger; those who greeted him at Fort Monroe would bestow no accolades upon him. They would frown and whisper behind his back and perhaps even guffaw over his total and abject failure.

5

Ulric Dahlgren's fate would be much the same as his superior's, although more tragic. Kilpatrick and the soldiers in the main column would not learn the full story of his

★★★★★★★★★★★★★★★★★★★★★★

45. Jones, *Eight Hours Before Richmond*, p. 68.

46. Moyer, *Seventeenth Pennsylvania Cavalry*, pp. 244-45.

plight until they reached Butler's lines. When the news began to circulate, they would be stunned by the bitter details.

After leaving Frederick's Hall, Dahlgren's column approached the line of the James River at an easy gait. All had gone well for the small detachment, and the colonel remained unaware of the missed opportunities at the depot. His men, as Kilpatrick's, had already distributed hundreds of leaflets proclaiming Lincoln's policies on amnesty, placing them in the hands of dazed citizens, on the counters of country stores, and upon the porches of private homes. And the raiders had struck heavy blows to the Virginia populace not only by destroying public and private property but also by luring droves of slaves away from their masters. Blacks had fallen in with the column on foot or aboard stolen horses, driven by a simple and earnest hope that they would be led out of bondage.

Colonel Dahlgren had even found time to pay a visit on Mrs. James A. Seddon, wife of the Confederate secretary of war, who lived on a charming estate near Goochland Court House. During the brief call, the colonel learned that years ago his father had been one of the old woman's beaux; in honor of the happy memory he toasted Mrs. Seddon's health over goblets filled with blackberry wine. Afterward, Dahlgren put aside his romantic charm and, leaving the house, returned to the grim business of war.[47]

The first truly troublesome moment for Dahlgren occurred when he reached the James River that afternoon. Ironically, a freed Negro named Martin Robinson was blamed for the situation.

Dahlgren had confidently dispatched one hundred men to destroy boats, mills, and grain stores north of the James. He planned to cross the stream with his remaining troopers as quickly as allowable.[48] However, when the column reached Jude's Ferry, where it was to ford, Dahlgren found the rain-swollen water too high to admit a crossing. This seemed to indicate treachery on the part of Robinson, who had willingly guided the detachment to the site, assuring the soldiers that the ford could be crossed under any conditions. An even

★★★★★★★★★★★★★★★★★★★★★★★

47. Catton, *A Stillness at Appomattox*, pp. 13-14.

48. George E. Pond, "Kilpatrick's and Dahlgren's Raid to Richmond," *Battles and Leaders of the Civil War*, 4: 95.

temper was not among Ulric Dahlgren's enduring traits; finding his troops stymied and unable to comply with Kilpatrick's instructions, he flew into a rage and ordered the Negro hanged from the nearest tree. Someone ripped a bridle strap from his horse, other men laid hands on the guide, and within minutes Martin Robinson's lifeless body was dangling from a sturdy branch.[49]

Dahlgren would have to continue toward Richmond along the north bank. Trying to fight down his anger and frustration, he started off, committed now to striking from the westward. Realizing that his difficulties at the river, snow, rain, and rough ground had combined to slow his progress, he sent an officer and five troopers to locate Kilpatrick and tell him that the column would not be able to attack Richmond till dusk. Dahlgren never again saw the couriers, and neither did Kilpatrick, for Confederates captured them soon after they started out.[50]

Later that day, still some miles short of the capital, Dahlgren was sickened to hear distant sounds of battle, which meant that north of the city Kilpatrick was launching his assault. When the noise taped off and ceased, Dahlgren could not say whether Kilpatrick had succeeded, but was nagged by the fearful suspicion that the attack had been repulsed. Throughout the day the colonel led his men onward through mud and falling snow, the stump of his leg burning and chafing against its wooden limb.

Shortly before night settled over the area, Dahlgren at last reached the western outskirts of Richmond. All at once he heard the crack of sniper fire. In gathering darkness, his column began to recoil against rifle blasts that came from amid woodlots along both sides of the trail. Enraged, the colonel ordered his men to gallop ahead and cut down every bushwhacker. For more than two miles the column charged toward the capital, capturing dozens of prisoners in the cold dusk, but losing heavily in return. With his soldiers toppling from their saddles by twos and threes, Dahlgren's fury turned to alarm. Then, when mounted soldiers appeared across his path, the young leader decided that a great many

★★★★★★★★★★★★★★★★★★★★★★

49. Catton, *A Stillness at Appomattox*, p. 14.

50. Virgil Carrington Jones, "The Story of the Kilpatrick-Dahlgren Raid," *Civil War Times Illustrated* 4 (April 1965): 18.

reinforcements had swelled the enemy's ranks. Now certain that Kilpatrick had failed in his attack, Dahlgren decided to clear out. He led his soldiers above the city, bypassing the roadblock, and when he had skirted Richmond marched them northeastward toward the Pamunkey River.

As he retreated from his objective, Dahlgren may have turned prophetically gloomy. Only days ago he had envisioned himself at the center of the greatest cavalry operation of the war. Now, when he returned to the army after his debacle, he might well be removed from field service—the fate he had so desperately wished to avoid. No matter how he tried, he would not be able to escape the veil of failure that would shroud each of Kilpatrick's subordinate commanders.

That night march was utterly miserable. The raiders were pelted by rain and snow as well as occasional rifle fire from concealed positions. The weather made it difficult to keep the column closed up, for the falling snow obscured vision and obliterated horses' hoof prints. As a result the command split into two parts late that night. Some eighty men under Dahlgren kept to the main route, while three hundred others, under Captain John F. Mitchell of the 2nd New York, took a different trail. Crossing the Chickahominy River at Meadow Bridge, the larger force fought off mixed bands of Rebels and rode toward Tunstall's Station on the Richmond & York River Railroad, where Kilpatrick had planned an emergency rendezvous.[51] There Mitchell's tired, muddy, and chilled soldiers caught up with Kilpatrick late on March 2 and brought him the unpleasant story of Dahlgren's travail west of Richmond.[52] Afterward, Mitchell accompanied the rest of the command on the gloomy retreat down the peninsula, leaving Dahlgren—wherever he was—entirely on his own.

6

When he became aware that most of his men had gone their own way, Colonel Dahlgren must have felt naked and

★★★★★★★★★★★★★★★★★★★★★★

51. Jones, *Eight Hours Before Richmond,* pp. 75-76; Catton, *A Stillness at Appomattox,* p. 15.

52. Moyer, *Seventeenth Pennsylvania Cavalry,* p. 245.

vulnerable as well as fearfully lonely. But he led his eighty men through the night, crossing the Chickahominy north of the point where both Kilpatrick and Mitchell had done so, then moving over the Pamunkey near Hanovertown and driving northward and eastward in a wide curve. Word of his coming spread through the areas he traversed, and Confederate regulars and home guardsmen massed in pursuit.[53]

One of the regulars who heard the news was Lieutenant James Pollard of Company H, 9th Virginia Cavalry. When he got word of Dahlgren's movements between the Pamunkey and Mattaponi Rivers, Pollard immediately scoured the vicinity and rounded up twenty-five of his men, all of them serving locally on detached duty.[54]

By the afternoon of the 2nd Pollard had learned that Dahlgren's men seemed to be heading for Gloucester Point on the York River, and he set out to capture them. Late in the day his riders began to close in on the raiding band, which recently had crossed the Mattaponi aboard a single rowboat, with their horses swimming alongside. Along the riverbank, Pollard learned, the Yankees had fought a delaying action against a contingent of bushwhackers, during which the spunky young colonel in command stood on the near shore, a cane tucked under his arm, firing his pistol at his enemy until he thought it proper to climb into the boat.[55]

As evening approached, Pollard decided to move cross-country in an attempt to head the raiders off. His shortcut took him through the village of Stevensville, where he accumulated other followers, including two improbable warriors, Edward Halbach, the local schoolmaster, and one of his pupils, thirteen-year-old Billy Littlepage.[56] In due course Pollard's band struck a road that the raiders would have to take unless they decided to double back. The lieutenant deployed his veteran and amateur soldiers in woods near an area known as Mantapike, and waited.

At the same time, Dahlgren was driving his men through

★★★★★★★★★★★★★★★★★★★★★★★★

53. Jones, *Eight Hours Before Richmond,* pp. 86-87.

54. *Official Records,* series I, vol. 33, p. 219.

55. Swiggett, *The Rebel Raider,* p. 208.

56. J. William Jones, comp., "Kilpatrick-Dahlgren Raid Against Richmond," *Southern Historical Society Papers* 13 (1885): 546-47.

Stevensville and toward Mantapike.[57] The troopers were nearly at the end of their endurance. Some rode two to a horse, since so many mounts had gone lame or had died. By now, all but two of the Confederates Dahlgren captured had managed to escape, disappearing behind the curtain of the storm. Quite a few of the runaway slaves had also departed, although dozens of others remained to the rear of the little column, looking apprehensively about the dark pine trees that stretched alongside the country road.

When he reached Mantapike Hill, Dahlgren halted his command and rode a short distance in front of it. He could hear suspicious noises—hushed voices, the click of triggers.

The colonel rose in his stirrups and pulled out his Navy Colt pistol. He had visions of home guards or bushwhackers scurrying among the trees, and was in no mood to brook further annoyance from them. Thus he pointed his revolver at the nearest neck of woods and shouted: "Surrender, or I'll shoot!" When he received no immediate reply, he pulled the trigger. The percussion cap failed to ignite, and the pistol did not fire.

Seconds later, the darkness exploded into flashing lights and crashing sound as Lieutenant Pollard and his men fired down the length of Dahlgren's column. A New York trooper riding behind the colonel found that "every tree was occupied" and that the bushes glowed in the night as though set afire by the shooting.[58]

Dahlgren fell with the first volley, five buckshot in his body; he was dead before striking the ground. Dozens of his troopers were knocked out of their saddles onto the frosty ground, and horses bucked and reared in the narrow road, some of them slashing at their fallen riders with sharp hooves. The column bunched up as confusion spread down the line; Negroes ran screaming and surviving cavalrymen galloped amid them.

Some of the troopers who had not been hit hurriedly dismounted and joined the Negroes in the flight among the trees. A few huddled in a roadside field and tried to form a

★★★★★★★★★★★★★★★★★★★★★★

57. *Official Records,* series I, vol. 33, pp. 205-8.

58. Louis N. Boudrye, *Historic Records of the Fifth New York Cavalry,* p. 109; R. L. T. Beale, "Part Taken by the Ninth Virginia Cavalry in Repelling the Dahlgren Raid," *Southern Historical Society Papers* 3 (1877): 220.

getaway plan while returning the fire of their concealed enemy. Others remained mounted and galloped through breaks in the fences that lined the road, seeking places of refuge.

Gradually the confusion in the road abated. At last Pollard and his soldiers came out to collect the wounded and round up uninjured survivors. Afterward he told his fighters to stand on their guard to be ready for subsequent action; he planned to lead them in pursuit of the escapees when morning came.[59]

While the veterans took up their posts, the citizen-soldiers began to grope along the dark road for souvenirs—anything of value that the retreating Yankees might have left behind. Young Billy Littlepage joined in this activity. Roaming far from most of the hunters, he soon came upon a number of treasures in the dirt—a pocket watch, a cigar case, and a notebook and some papers. Intrigued but puzzled by the last two items, he took them to his schoolmaster.

When Edward Halbach had a chance to examine the book and papers, he realized that they had been taken from the body of the Yankee commander. Their contents were so startling that at once he showed them to Lieutenant Pollard.[60] In turn, Pollard stared at them in wonderment, for he was shocked by the statements set down in their pages.

One of the handwritten passages read: "... we will cross the James River into Richmond, destroying the bridges after us and exhorting the released prisoners to destroy and burn the hateful city; and do not allow the Rebel leader Davis and his traitorous crew to escape. . . ."

In another place was written: "Jeff. Davis and Cabinet must be killed on the spot."[61]

7

The papers found on Ulric Dahlgren's body unleashed a furious controversy that was fated to sear the country for

★★★★★★★★★★★★★★★★★★★★★★★★

59. *Official Records*, series I, vol. 33, pp. 208-9.

60. Jones, "Kilpatrick-Dahlgren Raid Against Richmond," pp. 547-49.

61. *Official Records*, series I, vol. 33, pp. 219-20; Jones, *Eight Hours Before Richmond*, p. 148.

several months. Pollard forwarded them to Richmond, along with Dahlgren's wooden leg, which he removed from the corpse to authenticate the documents. In the capital (where the body later was put on public display), Jefferson Davis himself read the memorandum book and the orders that had been written on stationery bearing the title of Kilpatrick's headquarters. The documents were then given over to Davis's military secretary, General Braxton Bragg, Secretary of State Judah P. Benjamin, and other Confederate officials. In time, the Richmond newspapers received access to the papers, which they published in full, raising the furor of local citizens to a fever pitch. Meanwhile, Bragg and some of Davis's associates proposed hanging all captured raiders, deeming this fitting retaliation for the barbaric and atrocious style of warfare that Dahlgren and Kilpatrick had sought to use against the Rebel government.

For a time it seemed that some form of vengeance such as Bragg had in mind would be exacted. But when General Lee was sounded out, he replied that although arson and assassination may have been on the Yankees' agenda, no such deeds had been carried out. In any case, if the captives were executed, would not the Federal government reply in similar fashion? Lee asked: "How many and better men have we in the enemy's hands than they have in ours?" Furthermore, the general was skeptical of the validity of the Dahlgren papers.

Other army commanders, particularly in the Federal ranks, entertained like doubts. When Lee sent photographic copies of the papers into the Union lines under flag of truce, General Meade collared Kilpatrick, who had returned to the main army. Kil-cavalry heatedly denied that any such orders had been issued to the raiding force either by himself or by Dahlgren; nor had anyone even conceived of killing Jefferson Davis and his cabinet members or reducing Richmond to charred rubble. Meade forwarded Kilpatrick's reply to Lee, adding that neither he himself nor President Lincoln had given approval to terrorist activities when they had authorized Kilpatrick to launch the expedition.[62]

Bitter about his disastrous defeat, Kilpatrick would not let the matter rest there. After examining the photo copies, he

★★★★★★★★★★★★★★★★★★★★★

62. *Official Records,* series I, vol. 33, pp. 218, 222; Jones, *Eight Hours Before Richmond,* pp. 114, 128, 140.

announced that the papers had been forged by Confederates and planted on Dahlgren's body, so their discovery might strengthen the spirit of secession. He pointed out that the Confederate government was making effective propaganda by widely publicizing the papers at home and abroad, seeking supporters who would denounce Yankee fiendishness.[63] Kilpatrick added that one major fact gave credence to his claim: one of the handwritten papers found on the colonel's body was signed "U. Dahlgren." How, asked Kilpatrick, could Dahlgren have misspelled his own name?[64] This, he contended, proved conclusively that the papers had originated with propaganda-minded Rebels after the colonel's death.

Northern newspapers picked up Kilpatrick's reply and made much of his assertions, as well as his condemnation of the inhumane abuse heaped upon Dahlgren's body by his killers. In this, the general's anger seemed entirely justified, for Lieutenant Pollard's men had deprived the colonel's corpse not only of its wooden leg but also one of its fingers, which someone had cut off to make a prize of the jeweled ring that ornamented it.[65] (Dahlgren's body was originally interred in an unmarked grave in Richmond, but was located by Union sympathizers, who later exhumed it and reinterred it in a secret gravesite outside the city. Finally, at the request of the colonel's father, the remains were brought to their final resting place in North Hill Cemetery, Philadelphia.)[66]

Confederate spokesmen countered Kilpatrick's remarks by theorizing that a military secretary must have prepared the written orders, misspelling the colonel's name. The controversy was revived many years after the war when one of the Rebel officers who had examined the papers reported discovering that the name had not, in fact, been spelled

<hr>

****

63. For examples of propaganda methods, see *Official Records*, series I, vol. 33, p. 218, as well as *Official Records of the Union and Confederate Navies in the War of the Rebellion*, Series II, Volume 3, pp. 1070, 1072, 1113, 1115, 1146. For more information on the forged papers theory, see Swiggett, *The Rebel Raider*, pp. 213-16, 216n. The last-named also exhibits photographs of documents allegedly planted on Dahlgren's body by the Confederates.

64. Swiggett, *The Rebel Raider*, pp. 209, 214.

65. *Official Navy Records*, series I, vol. 9, p. 541.

66. For theory and fact regarding the exhuming of Dahlgren's corpse, see Meriwether Stuart, "Colonel Ulric Dahlgren And Richmond's Union Underground," *The Virginia Magazine of History and Biography* 72 (April 1964): 152-204.

wrong; ink that had leaked through one of the written papers had stained the page containing Dahlgren's signature. Part of the letter "y" in the word "destroying" on the previous page had soaked through at the precise spot to make the "h" in the colonel's name appear to be an "l," and vice versa.[67]

But this bit of detective work seems unnecessary; without it, the Confederates still had ample cause for their outcry. The memo book found beside the papers on Dahlgren's corpse contained many of the same incriminating statements as those in the written orders. No one, not even the colonel's father, ever denied that these were in Ulric Dahlgren's handwriting.[68]

Therefore it seems clear that although the written address was never read to the raiders, it had evolved from ideas propounded either by Kilpatrick or Dahlgren. It is likely that they originated in Kilpatrick's brain, for they reflected a certain type of warfare that the general advocated. For him, war knew no niceties and had to be won by any means possible. Kilpatrick the pragmatist, the antiromantic, would have betrayed no compunction about building a career upon the ruins of Richmond and the dead bodies of the Confederate hierarchy.

Nevertheless, the Confederates did not respond in kind. General Lee's advice about avoiding drastic retaliation prevailed, even after the fire-eaters had grown hoarse from crying vengeance. Perhaps Lee's allusion to prisoners in Federal hands had done the trick, or perhaps the matter was resolved because, as a Confederate War Department clerk phrased it, "Retaliation for such outrages committed on others having been declined, the President and cabinet can hardly be expected to begin with such sanguinary punishments when *their own* lives are threatened. It would be an act liable to grave criticism."[69] In either case, the captured raiders were thrown into prison alongside the very people they had set out to liberate, but none was executed for his alleged crimes.

The most unfortunate result of the bitter *cause célebr* was

★★★★★★★★★★★★★★★★★★★★★★

67. Jones, "Kilpatrick-Dahlgren Raid Against Richmond," pp. 559.

68. Jones, *Eight Hours Before Richmond*, p. 174n.

69. J. B. Jones, *A Rebel War Clerk's Diary,* 2: 166.

the revelation that a tangible shift in the tenor of the conflict had occurred. Heretofore the war had been fought, as it often seemed, in almost gentlemanly, civilized fashion—like some improbable tournament. Kilpatrick's raid indicated that early in 1864 the war was settling into a new pattern, as a grim, win-at-any-cost contest, with fratricidal violence no longer cloaked in a disguise fashioned from literature by Sir Walter Scott.[70]

In such a war, Judson Kilpatrick might have been expected to attain lasting prominence. But his failure outside Richmond ensured that he would not win the fame and public adulation he craved. His grand project had ended as a pitiful flop, 340 raiders having become casualties and almost six hundred horses and an indeterminable amount of equipment having been lost. All but a few captive Confederates and runaway slaves had been returned to their own people. Worse still, two mounted columns had failed to seize Richmond against the defensive efforts of forces only a fraction of the size of the combined raiding command. Kilpatrick's three thousand troopers had been beaten back from the city gates by about five hundred defenders and six cannon. Dahlgren had been defeated by fewer than three hundred members of the local defense battalion. About all the raiders had accomplished was the destruction of miscellaneous railroad and private property, plus the distribution of hundreds of copies of Lincoln's amnesty policy to Virginians who, recalling the barbarity of Kilpatrick's raid, would now think twice about accepting Mr. Lincoln's offer of brotherhood.[71]

Bad weather had played a significant role in the raiders' failure, as had ill fortune, dramatically exemplified by the capture of messengers riding from Dahlgren to Kilpatrick. But flaws in Kilpatrick's character had also spelled disaster for the expedition. He had fallen back with success nearly in his grasp, plagued by self-doubt and indecision on the threshhold of Richmond, while the door to glory stood half open, desperately guarded by a scratch force of amateurs whom he could have pushed aside with a little effort.

★★★★★★★★★★★★★★★★★★★★★★★★

70. Catton, *A Stillness at Appomattox*, pp. 9-10, 18.

71. Ibid., pp. 16-17; Jones, "The Story of the Kilpatrick-Dahlgren Raid," p. 21.

Because of his debacle, Judson Kilpatrick would not attain his most cherished goals. He would not receive an increase in rank during the remainder of the conflict. In fact, his career would never again be considered brilliant, or even promising. He would not become president of the United States. He would even relinquish his dream of becoming governor of New Jersey. He would settle for a modest Congressional bid, and in the 1880 election would be soundly defeated.[72]

★★★★★★★★★★★★★★★★★★★★★★

72. Warner, *Generals in Blue*, p. 267; Jones, *Eight Hours Before Richmond*, p. 142.

10

DEATH OF A LEGEND

Sheridan's Richmond Raid
(May 9-24, 1864)

1

When Lieutenant General Ulysses Grant came to Virginia in the spring of 1864 to make his field headquarters with the Army of the Potomac, he brought several subordinates from the western theater. This was only natural, for Grant wished to have by his side men upon whom he could rely, men whose capabilities he had come to admire and whose military acumen he knew how to utilize. Yet, with the exception of a single man, those who accompanied him were mere staff officers. Only Major General Philip H. Sheridan came to assume a field command in Virginia.

Grant, it developed, had no desire to tamper with the chain of command in the Army of the Potomac. Major General George Meade was still in immediate command of that army—he would make decisions affecting its tactical operations, while Grant proscribed grand strategy—and Meade should have the power to make personnel changes. But while Grant upheld Meade's authority to assign subordinate commanders to duty, he was so impressed with Phil Sheridan's talents that he felt compelled to find him a ranking position with the great Federal army in the East. Grant realized that the Army of the Potomac was waging a campaign crucial to the national cause, and therefore critically needed Sheridan's expertise.[1]

Phil Sheridan had recently turned thirty-three, stood barely five feet, five inches tall, weighed only 115 pounds after a debilitating campaign in Tennessee,[2] and had a rugged but plain face marked by a prominent nose. thick eyebrows, a wispy mustache, and close-cropped dark hair. Despite his size—perhaps because of it—he was intense and scrappy, often allowing an Irish temper to control his tongue. Wherever he went he radiated energy and infected soldiers with a sense of self-confidence that enabled them to serve to the fullest extent of their abilities. In addition to being able to inspire his men, "Little Phil" was adept at leading them on the battlefield, constantly going forth into the whirlpool of combat as though danger was an abstraction. His spunk, plus his inconspicuous stature, the common circumstances of his brith and upbringing, and his modest academic accomplishments (he had graduated from West Point in 1853, ranking in the bottom third of his class), endeared him to the average soldier, who perceived Sheridan to be a kindred spirit.

He had achieved most of his fame as infantry commander, winning recognition as a division leader at Perryville, Murfreesboro, and Chickamauga. During the Chattanooga campaign in November 1863, his foot soldiers had assured their commander's reputation by clawing their way up steep Missionary Ridge, then wresting its summit from Confederate troops—doing all of this without orders, for the high command supposed the feat too difficult to be accomplished in a single movement.

Yet earlier in his Civil War career Sheridan had served as colonel of a Michigan cavalry regiment and was, at heart, a dedicated trooper, with a firm grasp of mounted tactics and a flair for organizing cavalry commands. These traits had attracted Grant's attention early in '64,[3] for Grant was aware

★★★★★★★★★★★★★★★★★★★★★★

1. Grant, *Personal Memoirs*, 2: 117-18, 133-34.

2. Philip H. Sheridan, *Personal Memoirs*, 1: 338.

3. Warner, *Generals in Blue*, pp. 437-38.

Sheridan and subordinate officers (left to right); Generals Wesley Merritt, David McMurtrie Gregg, Philip H. Sheridan, Henry E. Davies, Jr., James Harrison Wilson, and Alfred T. A. Torbert. Picture taken in 1864. COURTESY LIBRARY OF CONGRESS.

that Meade's cavalry, which had never served under a commander who grasped the nuances of mounted campaigning at the corps level, was in need of a thorough revamping under a new leader. Thus Grant had chosen him to succeed Alfred Pleasonton as leader of the Cavalry Corps of the Army of the Potomac.

Sheridan quickly justified Grant's faith. As soon as he assumed his new duties he set about retooling the cavalry by training its men rigorously, thoroughly equipping them with the best weapons and accoutrements available (with the cooperation of the tireless new chief of the U. S. Cavalry Bureau, James H. Wilson), and reshuffling commanders and regiments to ensure maximum fighting capacity.[4] By early May, as the army prepared to march into its first campaign under Grant, the once-disorganized corps had been fully repaired. The horse soldiers, who for so long had been unable to face their opponents on equal terms, were now hopeful of turning the training and discipline given them by Sheridan into battlefield victories, thereby redeeming themselves for past failures great and small.

However, it soon became apparent that Phil Sheridan would require time to settle comfortably into his new position. During the first spring campaign, in the Virginia Wilderness, the Federal horsemen had a difficult time, compelled to combat rough and tangled terrain as well as J. E. B. Stuart's cavalry. Untutored in corps command, Sheridan made some glaring mistakes at reconnaissance and allowed portions of his force to be cut off from their comrades and nearly destroyed by the more experienced Rebel cavalrymen.[5] By battle's end, the Union horse soldiers had been severely handled, and had received new psychological scars affecting their morale, but nevertheless remained intact and hopeful of future success.

Irritated by his mistakes, Sheridan vowed to make amends in his next engagement. But when the armies subsequently maneuvered toward Spotsylvania Court House, some ten miles southeast of the Wilderness, the cavalry leader was again frustrated. In order that his troopers might reach the town ahead of their enemy, thus securing a strategic foothold for the main army, Sheridan sent his men to perform a series of errands in the Spotsylvania vicinity. Unknown to him, however, General Meade happened upon two of the three cavalry division commanders and changed their orders, an act that had a crucial bearing on the later fighting. The third division carried out its orders to seize the town, but found no comrades within supporting distance. As a consequence it was forced from the village by approaching Rebel infantry, preparing the stage for another brutal endurance contest between the main bodies of the opposing forces.[6]

★★★★★★★★★★★★★★★★★★★★★★★★

4. Edward G. Longacre, *From Union Stars to Top Hat: A Biography of the Extraordinary General James Harrison Wilson,* p. 108.

5. Thomason, *Jeb Stuart,* pp. 488-89.

6. Longacre, *From Union Stars to Top Hat,* pp. 118-19.

Both Sheridan and Meade grew intensely disgusted with the situation—Sheridan because Meade had countermanded his orders without advance warning, and Meade because one of the cavalry divisions had trotted down a road filled with infantry, confusing the main army and slowing its advance. On the forenoon of May 8 the generals met at army headquarters and unleashed invective at one another. The shouting match was a stand-off, although the hot-tempered Sheridan had the last word, remarking that if Meade would only refrain from meddling with the cavalry corps the horsemen would show their worth by meeting Stuart's soldiers in battle and annihilating them.

Meade spoke to Grant about Sheridan's impertinence, but the lieutenant general did not feel that Meade should have taken offense. He explained that Sheridan sometimes let his temper get the best of him but that his anger was usually provoked by just cause. He stated his belief that Sheridan could make good his boast about smashing Stuart. After Meade had left his tent in a huff, Grant contacted the little Irishman, held a short conference with him, and gave him full authority to go ahead with what he had told Meade he would accomplish.[7]

Little Phil was ecstatic. Such authority permitted the launching of the first independent campaign by the streamlined cavalry corps.[8] It would give his men's spirits a tremendous boost just to be free from the Wilderness, giving up the onerous burden of scouting for the main army. But the cavalry chief did not consider these the only benefits of such an expedition. He had implicit faith in himself and in his soldiers, and fully expected that they would humiliate their much heralded opponents. He had come east with a marked skepticism about Stuart's supposed invincibility and was determined that he would elevate his career by removing "Beauty" as a threat to Federal military progress.

In a matter of hours Sheridan had sent for the leaders of his divisions—Brigadier Generals Wesley Merritt (temporarily commanding the First Cavalry Division), David McMurtrie Gregg, and James H. Wilson, the latter recently freed from

★★★★★★★★★★★★★★★★★★★★★★★

7. Bruce Catton, *Grant Takes Command*, pp. 215-16.

8. Theodore F. Rodenbough, "Sheridan's Richmond Raid," *Battles and Leaders of the Civil War*, 4: 189

his duties in the Cavalry Bureau. To them he imparted his plan: it called for the corps to detour around the left of Grant's army, still in front of Spotsylvania, head south to cut enemy rail lines, threaten unguarded Richmond, and thereby lure Stuart into a fight. After they had whipped the Confederates, the cavalrymen were to seek refuge with Butler's army, which had a supply base at Haxall's Landing on the James River, about ten miles below the Confederate capital. That done, the troopers would return to Grant's headquarters by the handiest route.[9]

Sheridan of course realized that the plan would be effective only if Stuart was broken, a feat that no other Federal mounted chief (and several had held prior tenure) had been able to achieve. He stressed to the division leaders his opinions about that possibility: "We are going out to fight Stuart's cavalry in consequence of a suggestion from me; we will give him a fair, square fight; we are strong, and I know we can beat him, and in view of my recent representations to General Meade I shall expect nothing but success."[10]

2

The next morning—which was breezeless and bright with sunlight—ten thousand horsemen set out toward Richmond. The column stretched for more than a dozen miles, partially due to artillery batteries, ammunition trains, ambulances, and pack mules that accompanied the regiments.[11] At its head rode Sheridan, as energetic and confident as ever. The corps headed north from Spotsylvania, made a wide curve to the east beyond the Wilderness, angled southward across the line of an unfinished railroad, and then, farther on, over the Ny, Po, and Ta Rivers. From the start, old soldiers in the column were impressed by the unhurried, untroubled atmosphere that pervaded the march. Instead of moving briskly at the trot, as had so many other raiding leaders during past years,

★★★★★★★★★★★★★★★★★★★★★★★★

9. *Official Records*, series I, vol. 36, pt. I, p. 789; Moyer, *Seventeenth Pennsylvania Cavalry*, p. 73.

10. Sheridan, *Personal Memoirs*, 1: 370.

11. Richard O'Connor, *Sheridan, the Inevitable*, p. 164; Rodenbough, "Sheridan's Richmond Raid," p. 189.

Sheridan had elected to proceed at the walk, which seemed to say that he was not so apprehensive about future dangers as to make horseflesh suffer in order to reach some objective in record time.[12]

However, the leisureliness of the pace did not make the march a pure pleasure. In later years, one volunteer officer looked back upon the operation and recalled some of the annoyances and discomforts it had given him and his comrades:

"There is nothing particularly exciting or delightful in thumping along at a trot in a cavalry column. The clouds of dust, sent up by the thousands of hoof-beats, fill eyes, nose, and air passages, give external surfaces a uniform, dirty gray color, and form such an impenetrable veil, that, for many minutes together, you can not see even your hand before you. Apparently, just at the point of impending suffocation, a gentle sigh of wind makes a rift, and a free breath is inspired. Dust and horse-hairs penetrate every-where. Working under the clothing to the skin, and fixed by the sweat, the sensation is as though one was covered by a creeping mass of insects. Accumulations occur in the pockets; the rations come in for their full share, and with the bacon, particularly, so thoroughly do dirt and horse-hairs become incorporated, that no process of cleansing can remove them. . . ."[13]

As the column jounced, rocked, and clattered along the old Telegraph Road, which led directly toward the Rebel capital, the troopers began to speculate about the nature of the movement. Sheridan seemed especially close-mouthed this morning, and his plan had been put into motion too quickly to permit the spread of those rumors which usually attended such an undertaking. One participant recalled that "As the sound of the cannonading between the opposing armies grew more and more to the right and rear, the inspiration suddenly seized the men that they were on a raid."[14] Perceiving an upcoming clash with Stuart, the troopers realized they

★★★★★★★★★★★★★★★★★★★★★★★

12. *Official Records,* series I, vol. 36, pt. 1, p. 789; Louis H. Carpenter, "Sheridan's Expedition Around Richmond, May 9-25, 1864," *Journal of the U. S. Cavalry Association* 1 (1888): 304.

13. Asa B. Isham, "Through the Wilderness to Richmond," *Sketches of War History, 1861-1865: Papers Read Before the Ohio M. O. L. L. U. S.,* 1 (1888): 207-8.

14. Preston, *Tenth New York Cavalry,* p. 175.

would soon see if Sheridan had fully recovered his aplomb after his beating in the Wilderness.

As Little Phil had anticipated, Stuart quickly learned of his movement and sent forces in pursuit. At his immediate disposal the Rebel chieftain had two brigades from Major General Fitzhugh Lee's division and a separate brigade under Brigadier General James B. Gordon, an aggregate of four thousand five hundred sabers.[15] The entire force rode out from below Spotsylvania Court House only a few hours after the raiders had begun marching, and spurred onward to gain the Telegraph Road. By now Stuart had divined his enemy's intentions, supposing that Sheridan proposed to enter and seize Richmond—as Kilpatrick had endeavored only two months ago—from the few thousand militia and regulars who guarded it.[16] Accordingly, he chased the raiders with as much speed as possible, not fearing to engage a force that boasted more than twice the soldiers he had on hand. In truth, Stuart could have brought thousands of additional troopers with him, but felt obligated to leave two brigades under Wade Hampton with Lee's main army, to prevent Grant from turning its flank. So Stuart, too, was extremely confident of his ability to best his enemy in open combat—to the point of pursuing with only about two-thirds of his command.

The Confederate cavalry chief made such dispositions as he believed would harass Sheridan and halt him short of his goal. In advance of his main force, he sent one of Fitz Lee's brigades, under Brigadier General Williams C. Wickham, to gain the Yankees' rear, following Wickham with Gordon's men plus the other brigade in Lee's command, Brigadier General Lunsford Lomax's.[17]

Though ignorant of Stuart's strategy, Sheridan realized that Rebel pursuers must be maneuvering in his rear. He was not worried, for the expedition had been launched for the prime purpose of attracting Stuart and forcing him to accept battle. The single-column march, Merritt's division in the lead, continued at a methodical pace, the troopers admiring

★★★★★★★★★★★★★★★★★★★★★★★

15. Boatner, *The Civil War Dictionary*, p. 749.

16. Davis, *The Last Cavalier*, pp. 385-86.

17. William W. Hassler, "The Battle of Yellow Tavern," *Civil War Times Illustrated*, 5 (November 1966): 7.

the glorious May morning and rejoicing at having escaped the dark and clotted nightmare of the Wilderness.[18]

The first spell of fighting occurred late that afternoon, when Wickham's Confederates, their horses foam flecked from rough travel, overtook Sheridan's rear guard. Part of Brigadier General Henry Davies's brigade of Gregg's division turned about and drew line of battle. Despite riding so long and hard, the Confederates launched a furious attack and succeeded in drawing off with a number of prisoners.[19] Finally a combined effort by Davies's 6th Ohio, 1st New Jersey, and 1st Massachusetts drove Wickham away, and the march was able to proceed.[20] The immense column turned off the Telegraph Road and struck westward toward one of its subsidiary objectives, Beaver Dam Station on the Virginia Central Railway, an advance supply depot for Lee's army that had been a Federal target in several earlier raids.[21] As he rode on, Sheridan must have wondered how long it would take for Stuart to thrust his main force across the raiders' path and initiate the decisive combat.

At Mitchell's Shop, above Beaver Dam, Wickham's reformed brigade came up and sparred again with Davies's rear regiments. This time the Yankees lured a charging Confederate squadron into their ranks, then surrounded the contingent and crushed it into human fragments in front of General Wickham's eyes.

After the brutal skirmish, while Sheridan moved forward to the upper bank of the North Anna River, General Stuart, with the major portion of the pursuit command, joined Wickham's remnants. After a short talk with his brigade leaders, Stuart decided to push westward with Gordon's brigade and head Sheridan off, while Wickham and Lomax, again united under Fitz Lee, nipped at the raiders' heels. Stuart rode down the length of his command, receiving the

★★★★★★★★★★★★★★★★★★★★★★★★

18. James Harrison Wilson, *Under the Old Flag*, 1: 406; Isham, "Through the Wilderness to Richmond," p. 206.

19. Alphonso D. Rockwell, "With Sheridan's Cavalry," *Personal Recollections of the War of the Rebellion: Addresses Delivered Before the New York M. O. L. L. U. S.*, Third Series (1907), pp. 230-31.

20. Crowninshield and Gleason, *First Massachusetts Cavalry*, p. 206.

21. Carpenter, "Sheridan's Expedition Around Richmond," p. 305.

cheers of his men, and then pounded off with Gordon's troopers for the set-to.[22]

Sheridan reached the North Anna after dusk. Pleased by his progress, the cavalry commander sent Merritt's division over the river at Anderson's Ford, while Gregg's and Wilson's soldiers encamped for the night above the stream.[23] Soon afterward, the Rebels again sparred with the Federal rear echelon, compelling Wilson's men, now covering the shank of the column, to turn about and enlarge the scope of the engagement.[24]

While the skirmishing on the north shore raged on, Sheridan attended to some of his wrecking duties. He directed Merritt to send a single brigade—four Michigan regiments under the young brigadier George Custer—to capture the nearby Beaver Dam depot. While some of Gregg's regiments operated north of the station,[25] Custer's Wolverines, led by the 1st Michigan, charged into the depot, scattered the few defenders on hand, and frightened the local quartermasters into burning warehouses, in order that their contents, a million rations of meat and a half million of bread, would not fall into enemy hands. Custer's people also captured a train and liberated its cargo, several hundred Federals who had been captured in the Wilderness days before and were enroute to Richmond prisons. After destroying those supplies not burned by the Rebels, plus two locomotives and one hundred cars, the Michigan troopers laid waste to ten miles of trackage and reserve medical stores.[26] Finally, their job meticulously done, the raiders evacuated the station and returned to Sheridan, joining Gregg's detachments along the way. Once Beaver Dam was empty, Stuart's forces regrouped amid its smoldering wreckage, where the Confederate leader plotted revenge for Sheridan's devastation.[27]

★★★★★★★★★★★★★★★★★★★★★★★★

22. Davis, *The Last Cavalier*, p. 388.

23. *Official Records*, series I, vol. 36, pt. 1, pp. 789-90.

24. Sheridan, *Personal Memoirs*, 1: 375.

25. Hall, Besley, and Wood, *Sixth New York Cavalry*, p. 185.

26. Moses Harris, "The Union Cavalry," *War Papers: Read Before the Wisconsin M. O. L. L. U. S.*, 1 (1891): 365; Isham, "Through the Wilderness to Richmond," p. 208.

27. Samuel H. Miller, "Yellow Tavern," *Civil War History*, 2 (March 1956); 64.

Bridge ruined by Sheridan's raiders. COURTESY LIBRARY OF
CONGRESS.

"The next morning," a Massachusetts officer recollected,
"reveille was sounded by the enemy with artillery and carbines, instead of the friendly trumpet or bugle. . . ."[28] Shortly
before, Stuart had unlimbered his batteries of horse artillery
and directed them to shell Gregg's division as it prepared to
ford the North Anna and join Merritt's command. Wilson's
division remained on the north bank till Gregg got safely a-
cross, protecting the rear against dismounted Rebel skirmishers and standing firm despite the cannonade. On the

★★★★★★★★★★★★★★★★★★★★★★★

28. Crowninshield and Gleason, *First Massachusetts Cavalry,* p. 206.

south shore, Sheridan decided to keep marching, waiting for Stuart to strike him from the front, in which case the Federals could maneuver more easily. Therefore, his column trotted calmly toward the South Anna River. The troopers rode unmolested during the balance of the day, for Stuart's main force did not follow in their wake.[29] The Federals again had the opportunity to admire the weather and the lovely roadside foliage as well as to consider the coolness displayed by Sheridan thus far.

Some memorable incidents occurred during the day's march, however, when the raiders came into contact with citizens who lived above the South Anna. The commander of the 10th New York Cavalry, while on a detached mission, stopped at a large and lavish home to ask some directions of the inhabitants. Two pretty girls appeared. When they learned the identity of their visitor they immediately turned hostile, and began to berate the officer in terms that a great many Virginia citizens had used on similar occasions in the past. The officer weathered their tirade in respectful silence until one of his hostesses became needlessly vituperative: "You Yankees mistake the character of the people you are trying to subjugate. Why, sir, we never knew what it was to work until the exhausted condition of our country by reason of this war made it necessary for us to do so!" She added that the dress she wore had been made from raw material by her own hands, and proclaimed that by such resourceful efforts would the women of the South aid their menfolk in driving the hated invaders from their soil.

The regimental leader appeared to be amused. "Well," he replied drily, "if the war has been the means of teaching your people to work and to take a pride in it, as you appear to, it has been productive of some good."[30]

Saying nothing more, he doffed his cap in parting and rode off, leaving the girls abashed as well as angry.

3

Although May 10 was largely an uneventful day for the

★★★★★★★★★★★★★★★★★★★★★★★

29. *Official Records*, series I, vol. 36, pt. 1. p. 790; Carpenter, "Sheridan's Expedition Around Richmond," p. 306.

30. Preston, *Tenth New York Cavalry*, pp. 176-77.

Federals, it was a busy one for their adversaries. Deciding to split his force yet again, Stuart prepared to ride out of Beaver Dam Station at the forefront of Lee's division, hoping to shield the Virginia Central from further harm by racing parallel to its tracks. Now Gordon's men would again take up the task of harassing Sheridan's rear.[31]

But before Stuart resumed his pursuit, he attended to personal business. His lovely wife, Flora, and their two young children were visiting at a plantation a short distance from Beaver Dam, and being a devoted husband and father, Stuart did not wish to miss an opportunity to see them, if only briefly. He galloped to the plantation, where he kissed his wife, hugged his children, and chatted for a few minutes. Then he returned to the depot, from which he led Fitz Lee's troopers eastward toward Hanover Junction.[32]

Meanwhile, late that afternoon, Sheridan reached the South Anna River and decided to bivouac there. Before his corps bedded down, nevertheless, he sent Davies's brigade on a raiding mission east to Ashland, on the Richmond, Fredricksburg & Potomac. The detached troopers, principally those of the 1st Massachusetts, wrecked a train, several warehouses, and a half-dozen miles of track. The Massachusetts soldiers afterward held off the 2nd Virginia Cavalry, which Stuart had dispatched to halt them, until the rest of Davies's men could start back to the main column.[33]

The detachment rejoined Sheridan next morning at Allen's Station, another depot on the R, F & P, to which the main column had advanced after breaking camp near the South Anna. By now Sheridan was aware that Stuart and most of his command had skirted the Federals' flanks, although General Gordon's brigade was still operating rearward.[34] Sheridan had no inkling where the shining knight of the Confederacy might be massing to stop him, but he retained his confidence and high spirits. After two full days of marching he had encountered only limited resistance, and his two detached missions against the rail lines had been most success-

★★★★★★★★★★★★★★★★★★★★★★

31. Hassler, "The Battle of Yellow Tavern," p. 8.

32. Thomason, *Jeb Stuart*, p. 492.

33. Crowninshield and Gleason, *First Massachusetts Cavalry*, pp. 206-7.

34. *Official Records*, series I, vol. 36, pt. 1, p. 790.

ful. Apparently, as he had supposed, J. E. B. Stuart's prowess had been legend but not reality.

Late in the morning of the 11th, Sheridan's advance guard and scouts bumped into dismounted Confederates, who sniped at the column and then ran to their horses and galloped off before the Federals could stage a pursuit.[35] It seemed obvious that by hard marching Stuart had at last succeeded in placing his main force across the raiders' path. For the first time during the expedition, the Federals moved ahead warily.

About eleven o'clock they sighted the Rebels in force, most of them dismounted near the intersection of the Telegraph Road and Mountain Road, about six miles above Richmond. North of an old hostelry known as Yellow Tavern, Stuart had deployed for a stand, determined to keep Sheridan's men from reaching the capital city.[36]

Although a division of cavalry barred his way and another brigade continued to prod his rear, Sheridan did not hesitate before thrusting forward into the fight. Noting that Stuart's main force was positioned above the Brook Turnpike, which led straight to Richmond, Little Phil ordered one of Merritt's brigades to drop down below the enemy position, menacing its left flank. The Rebels resisted fiercely, firing from behind trees and rocks and laying down an artillery barrage. But the Union brigade, by sheer determination, flanked Stuart's force, and one of its regiments—the 17th Pennsylvania Cavalry—went far enough south to gain possession of the turnpike. Finding his position untenable, Stuart carefully shifted his men a few hundred yards east of the pike.[37]

In the meantime, Gordon's brigade had again attacked Sheridan's rear with a great deal of energy. The dismounted soldiers at the tag end of the Federal column found themselves confronting hundreds of charging, hollering, sword-swinging horsemen. Some of the troopers in Colonel J. Irvin Gregg's brigade broke and fled, spreading chaos all along the rear of the column. A regimental historian described it as

★★★★★★★★★★★★★★★★★★★★★★★

35. Isham, "Through the Wilderness to Richmond," p. 209.

36. Carpenter, "Sheridan's Expedition Around Richmond," p. 307.

37. Davis, *The Last Cavalier*, pp. 400-401; Hassler, "The Battle of Yellow Tavern," p. 11.

"one of those unaccountable panics which sometimes seize bodies of men without cause. These were all excellent men, needing but a show of resistance to bring them to their senses and duty."[38]

That show of resistance was organized by Captain Charles Treichel, a division staff officer, who rode up to steady the men. His conspicuous presence did the trick. Heeding his orders, the rear guard mounted, rushed up to Gordon's soldiers, and engaged them in a wild melee at close quarters. The men of the 10th New York were caught in the thick of the action, one of them run through by a huge Rebel sword, another pressing his carbine against a Confederate's back and shooting him dead at that range. A third New Yorker had just dodged an enemy saber when he was horrified to see one of his comrades take deliberate aim and shoot at him with his pistol. The bullet missed him by inches and struck its true target, a Confederate who had been about to saber him from behind. A fourth member of the regiment was knocked from his horse but dragged to safety when he grabbed the tail of a passing horse.[39] The strange battle ended when Federal reinforcements forced Gordon's men to beat a temporary retreat.

Unable to focus full attention on the events taking place in his rear, Sheridan moved to exploit the gains made by the regiment that had taken possession of the Brook Pike. He spent much time bringing up Wilson's division and part of Gregg's and placing them behind cover just above Merritt's position. This work proved highly dangerous, for Stuart's 5th Virginia and his horse artillery constantly blasted the open ground over which Wilson and Gregg maneuvered.

Sheridan's dispositions consumed half of the afternoon, but finally, despite the enfilading fire, he was in position to again threaten Stuart's left flank. He also increased the pressure against the Rebel right. However, the additional menace was neutralized when Stuart charged Wickham's dismounted brigade, which drove the Federals in that sector back to the cover of woodlots and ravines.

The crucial stage of the battle came in midafternoon, by which time both Lomax's and Wickham's brigades had regrouped and strengthened their lines. Once again Stuart

38. Preston, *Tenth New York Cavalry*, p. 178.

39. Ibid., pp. 178-79.

seemed in a fairly secure position, the Federals astride the Brook Turnpike notwithstanding. Sheridan had diminished the scope of the fighting by taking time to ponder where Stuart's most vulnerable point lay.[40]

In this he was aided by Custer, who had personally reconnoitered the ground between his Michigan brigade and Lomax's position on the Rebel left. In that area a strategically positioned battery was menacing the Federal column, and Custer thought it the key to Stuart's resistance. He proposed seizing the guns by a mounted saber charge.[41]

Little Phil approved of Custer's combative instincts and allowed him to go forward. Accordingly, the brigadier advanced two dismounted regiments to hold Lomax's attention,[42] while his trusted 1st Michigan—which had done such a thorough job of sacking Beaver Dam Station—rode forward to flank the battery.

After clearing fences and moving slowly over rocky ground, the men of the 1st Michigan increased their pace, charging ahead toward the guns. The Rebel cannoneers were startled to see them close the distance so rapidly. Before the guns could be turned upon the attacking regiment, the Wolverines were among them, slicing downward from the saddle with their sabers, knocking gunners into the dust of the road, shooting others down with pistols, and ducking swipes by a few Rebels who wielded rammer-staffs like swords.[43] Reinforced by advancing troopers from various portions of Merritt's and Wilson's divisions, who dislodged several sections of the Confederate line,[44] the 1st Michigan captured two cannon, a great quantity of ammunition, and dozens of prisoners. Within minutes, both Wickham's and Lomax's men were reeling backward in retreat, and suddenly the road to Richmond lay tantalizingly open.[45]

While Sheridan rode to the head of his attacking troops to

★★★★★★★★★★★★★★★★★★★★★★★

40. Hassler, "The Battle of Yellow Tavern," 11, 46; Carpenter, "Sheridan's Expedition Around Richmond," p. 307.

41. Moyer, *Seventeenth Pennsylvania Cavalry,* p. 74.

42. Isham, *Seventh Michigan Cavalry,* p. 44.

43. Carpenter, "Sheridan's Expedition Around Richmond," p. 308; Miller, "Yellow Tavern," pp. 76-77.

44. Wilson, *Under the Old Flag,* 1: 407.

45. Hassler, "The Battle of Yellow Tavern," p. 46.

lend them encouragement, the Confederate leader, in desperation, did the same to his troopers. But the Rebel center, where Stuart and his aides gathered, was quickly overrun by one of the dismounted regiments in Custer's brigade that had supported the charge of the 1st Michigan. Keeping a grip on his composure, Stuart rallied some of his men for a counterattack. Then, as his 1st Virginia rushed up to beat back Custer's regiments, Stuart sat his horse along a fence-line, calmly emptying his pistol at the now-retreating Federal troopers.

Wearing his plumed hat, astride his big gray charger, the Confederate commander became a conspicuous target. He caught the eye of Private John Huff, of Company E, 5th Michigan Cavalry, one of those fleeing on foot from the 1st Virginia's counter-charge. As he ran past Stuart, Huff raised his pistol and fired a single .44 bullet, which struck his victim in the abdomen. Stuart reeled in his saddle with a mortal wound.[46] Taken up by solicitous staff officers, he cried out to his soldiers: "Go back, go back and do your duty, as I have done mine! I would rather die than be whipped!" By nine o'clock the following evening he would be dead, three hours before his wife could reach his side.[47]

While Stuart's life's blood seeped away, his troopers were put to rout. Their flanks crushed, they could not sustain their counterattack, and Lomax and Wickham recalled their detachments, some of which fled north, others in the direction of Richmond, leaving Sheridan with possession of most of the field. Little Phil attended to the final business of the day by ordering General Gregg to turn part of his division around and meet another attack by Gordon's men against the Federal rear. By the time the Rebel charge came, Gregg had placed his men behind fallen-log and fence-rail breastworks, from which they poured a galling fire into the gray ranks. Afterward the Federals mounted and raced after the now-withdrawing enemy. At last Sheridan had undisputed title to the field.[48]

Little Phil had already done what Grant had asked of him.

★★★★★★★★★★★★★★★★★★★★★★★

46. Davis, *The Last Cavalier,* pp. 405-6.

47. Hassler, "The Battle of Yellow Tavern," pp. 47-48.

48. *Official Records,* series I, vol. 36, pt. 1, p. 791.

He had destroyed a legend by administering to Stuart's cavalry a beating it had never before received (at Gettysburg, where for the first time the Federal horsemen had stood firm against their opponents in full-scale fighting, Stuart had not been pushed from the battlefield). Now, however, Sheridan stopped short of wiping out his adversary. He pressed only a brief pursuit, allowing the Confederates to make their escape. No doubt he acted thus because his victory had been costly; numerous Federals lay dead or wounded on the crossroads terrain. The several attacks the Federals launched and repulsed had disorganized their lines, and Sheridan wished to sort things out before continuing his march through hostile country.

But he was not so cooly businesslike as to refrain from exulting in his victory. The battle at Yellow Tavern, his first full dose of cavalry combat in Virginia, had provided him with his first success. Because of that success, fame would surely come his way. Being a man who cherished favorable publicity, Sheridan recognized that May 11, 1864, would prove to be one of the most precious days of his life.

4

After tending to the dead and injured as well as to their prisoners, the Federal troopers rested for some hours on the battlefield. At three o'clock the following morning, the march toward the Rebel capital resumed, an exuberant Sheridan riding again in the vanguard. Behind him in the darkness rode equally jubilant soldiers, still congratulating each other on their outsize triumph. Had they known of Stuart's wounding, they would have had further cause for rejoicing.

During the trek from Yellow Tavern, rain began to shower the column. One lyrical cavalryman later remembered: "Vivid flashes of lightning lit up the gloom, while peals of thunder rolled away in the distance, to be lost in fresh reverberations near by, each one seeming to increase the fall of rain. Mingled with all this was the continued crack of the carbine, for we were too near the rebel capital to permit its defenders to remain passive."[49]

★★★★★★★★★★★★★★★★★★★★★★★

49. Preston, *Tenth New York Cavalry*, p. 181.

Passive the Confederates certainly were not. During those hours Sheridan's men had spent on the captured field, soldiers defending Richmond had prepared unique obstacles for them. Approaching the city outskirts, General Wilson's troopers, now leading the march, fell prey to torpedos —loaded artillery shells that had been planted along the roadside, rigged to explode when horses tripped trigger wires. Loud blasts shattered the night stillness; several animals and at least one cavalryman were killed.

Enraged by the casualties, Wilson ordered several Rebel captives riding with the column to dismount, probe for the shells in the darkness, and disarm them before more injuries could occur. The prisoners obeyed most reluctantly, fumbling nervously about for the infernal weapons. When located, the shells were ordered placed inside the nearby home of a wealthy planter who reportedly had helped Confederate engineers plant them. Wilson expected that the heavy tred of his horses' feet would activate the sensitive weapons, thus repaying the aristocrat for his treachery.[50]

As they carried out their commander's orders, the troopers again encountered angry Virginia citizenry. A New Jersey soldier noted that the planter's wife "took pains to inform us that she was a cousin of *the Ritchies*, [and] bewailed bitterly our barbarity in placing the torpedoes in her cellar instead of leaving them to blow us up in the road; but her expostulations had no effect upon our hardened natures."[51] As it turned out, no shells exploded, and the couple's house remained standing.

As the march went on, Sheridan began to grow uneasy. The more thought he gave to the work ahead, the more he was troubled by doubts about the advisability of trying to penetrate Richmond. He did not feel that it would be an impossible task—the four thousand soldiers who defended it, predominantly militia and civilians, would provide small opposition to his ten thousand veterans—but entering the city, he finally decided, would be a stunt of little military value. The war would not end once the Confederate capital fell into enemy hands; only by overwhelming the Southern land forces could the Union be preserved. Furthermore, should

★★★★★★★★★★★★★★★★★★★★★★

50. O'Connor, *Sheridan, the Inevitable*, p. 170.

51. Pyne, *First New Jersey Cavalry*, p. 242.

Sheridan seize the capital, thousands of reinforcements would be dispatched from Lee's army to ensure his inability to hold it for long. No, Richmond was not a proper objective—to cap the expedition, the raiders should circumvent the city and seek the shelter of Butler's supply base.[52]

Even so, Sheridan nearly rode into Richmond against his will. The pitch-black cover of darkness obscured geographical guideposts; consequently his column lurched forward spasmodically, groping for the proper roads. An artilleryman serving with the horse soldiers observed that "The halts were frequent and exasperating. It was so dark that we could only follow the cavalry by putting a bugler on a white horse directly in rear of the regiment in front of us, with orders to move on as soon as they did. . . ."

In the rainy gloom, Wilson's division became separated from the forces in its rear, and forged ahead of Sheridan's main body. Since Little Phil was now riding farther back, he did not at once realize what had happened. Finally young Wilson halted his troopers at a crossroads where several unidentified roads converged. Unfamiliar with the region, he could not determine which path would lead him above and east of the city, in the direction of Mechanicsville.

At the critical moment, a mounted man in a blue uniform appeared out of the night and told Wilson that Sheridan had sent him to guide the column eastward. Some instinct made Wilson suspicious of the man, but he desired to grasp any opportunity to reach safety. He ordered his soldiers to resume the march in the direction the stranger indicated.

After several minutes' travel, the Third Division found itself facing what appeared to be city outskirts. Soon afterward, a barrage of rifle shots ripped into the column, killing several horses in its forefront and wounding their riders. The unidentified guide had led Wilson's men up to the outer line of Richmond defenses, which was manned by militiamen, supported by artillery. Just as distressing was the news, quickly received, that the rest of Sheridan's corps had located the proper road and was now moving eastward, leaving Wilson's men without supports. The only grain of satisfaction Wilson could sift from the situation was the knowledge that

★★★★★★★★★★★★★★★★★★★★★★

52. Sheridan, *Personal Memoirs,* 1: 386.

one of his brigade leaders had blown out the brains of the Rebel spy who had led them astray.[53]

While Wilson deployed his soldiers for a fight, Sheridan and the main column met heavy resistance from Confederate veterans and civilians who had thrown up breastworks along the road to Mechanicsville. Here the opposition was not so concentrated as that which Wilson had encountered, but was sufficient to force Sheridan to alter his plans once more. He had intended to move below Richmond once he marched far enough eastward to avoid its defenses. But now, with dawn still an hour away, darkness prevented him from launching a coordinated attack against the Rebels and thus march on as planned. Therefore he decided to head north across the Chickahominy River,[54] then move much farther east than he had planned, making certain he was far from the city's outer works before recrossing the river and striking for the James. By now Sheridan had been apprised of Wilson's marching error and the tight corner in which he had been placed. He sent the Third Division's leader word of his intention to cross the Chickahominy over Meadow Bridge, then ordered a courier: "Go back to General Wilson, and tell him to hold his position. He *can* hold it, and he *must* hold it!"[55]

Wilson was entirely capable of doing so. By the time the message reached him, he had decided that he was not in such a frightening situation as he had supposed. The riflemen manning the outer defenses were shooting too high to do much damage to the Third Division and were not using their artillery effectively. By now Wilson's troopers had dismounted behind trees and amid underbrush and were sparring with the militia, directing their fire at the powder flashes visible in the dark.[56]

Soon the rainy sky began to brighten as the light of dawn made its feeble appearance, and Sheridan led Merritt's division to the bridge. Gregg's division, still bringing up the rear, meanwhile engaged in still another skirmish initiated by

★★★★★★★★★★★★★★★★★★★★★★★

53. Rodenbough, "Sheridan's Richmond Raid," p. 191; Charles C. MacConnell, "Service With Sheridan," *War Papers: Read Before the Wisconsin M. O. L. L. U. S.,* 1 (1891): 289.

54. *Official Records,* series I, vol. 36, pt. 1, p. 791.

55. Pyne, *First New Jersey Cavalry,* p. 244.

56. Longacre, *From Union Stars to Top Hat,* p. 125.

Gordon's tireless cavalrymen, who had refused to give up after Yellow Tavern. During this fighting, the Confederate brigade leader suffered a mortal wound.[57]

Sheridan's nerves were tested when Merritt's advance guard discovered that the precious foot bridge over the Chickahominy had been partially unplanked by the enemy, to prevent a crossing. With two of his divisions involved in sharp fighting, and his entire corps perhaps trapped in hostile territory, Sheridan might have allowed the situation to harm his judgment. Some of his officers certainly grew frightened. One of them later wrote in his diary: "It was to me a day of the greatest anxiety I ever experienced. There we were . . . the fortifications of the city behind us . . . and the Cavalry of Stewart [sic] holding the strong and easily defended position at Meadow Bridge before us—this and the pelting rain and howling thunder all conspired to make things look gloomy."[58]

But Sheridan shrugged off the gloom. He directed several of Merritt's men to strip timber from abandoned houses along the river and repair the bridge floor. While they obeyed, he ordered Custer's troopers to charge across a railroad span that paralleled Meadow bridge and drive back the Confederates who had gathered on the north bank of the stream. Some members of Colonel Alfred Gibbs's brigade even used the ruined bridge, swarming across "on the bare trestles," according to one participant, "creeping, crawling —any way to get across."[59] After a determined fight, Custer and Gibbs put the defenders to flight. They then helped their comrades repair the wider span so that all of Sheridan's soldiers could cross in quick time.[60]

As dawn broke, Sheridan watched the progress of the repair work from a small hilltop. Unknown to him, an observer atop a hill inside the Richmond defenses was also commenting about the progress of the battle. President Jefferson

★★★★★★★★★★★★★★★★★★★★★★★

57. Rodenbough, "Sheridan's Richmond Raid," p. 191; Boatner, *The Civil War Dictionary*, p. 348.

58. Robert G. Athearn, ed., "The Civil War Diary of John Wilson Phillips," *The Virginia Magazine of History and Biography*, 62 (January 1954): 102.

59. E. R. Hagemann, ed., *Fighting Rebels and Redskins: Experiences in Army Life of Colonel George B. Sanford, 1861-1892*, p. 236.

60. Rodenbough, "Sheridan's Richmond Raid," p. 191.

Davis had come out to stand beside his military adviser, Braxton Bragg—who had overall command of the city defenders—and to watch the impudent Yankees turned back from the city.[61] He did not realize that Sheridan had come up to the municipal outskirts inadvertently.

When the bridge had been rebuilt, Merritt's regiments crossed in the rain. That done, Sheridan sent word for Gregg and Wilson to disengage and follow. Once again, Gregg's division rose up and battered the Rebels in its rear, compelling them to hasten away in confusion. Afterward Gregg helped Wilson's men out of a precarious position. When the Third Division turned north from the Richmond defenses the militiamen came forward with blazing rifles, disordering the Federal rear echelon. Gregg's troopers took up positions as reinforcements in a wooded ravine. When the opportunity arose, they unleashed a deadly long-range volley that stopped the defenders cold. Recovering their poise, Wilson's rear units changed front and cracked the Rebels' flank, chasing them back to their works.[62]

Finally Gregg and then Wilson crossed the Chickahominy. Both followed Merritt's division southeastward along the upper shore of the stream. The final skirmish of the expedition occurred when Wilson's men fended off an eleventh-hour attack by pesky survivors of Stuart's corps, who came charging across the bridge after them. The 18th Pennsylvania Cavalry spearheaded a counterattack, which dispersed the Rebels for good and allowed the column to move onward unmolested.[63] At last Phil Sheridan and his soldiers were beyond immediate danger, and the officer who had written in his diary of the troubles that had beset the column at the dismantled bridge now added a happy entry: "But it came out all right."[64]

5

After a short march, Sheridan halted his cavalry on the

★★★★★★★★★★★★★★★★★★★★★★

61. Joseph Hergesheimer, *Sheridan: A Military Narrative*, p. 186.

62. Sheridan, *Personal Memoirs*, 1: 383.

63. *Eighteenth Pennsylvania Cavalry*, pp. 127-28.

64. Athearn, "The Civil War Diary of John Wilson Phillips," p. 102.

north side of the river to aid his wounded and feed his able-bodied troopers. It was also a gesture of defiance, calculated to bolster morale. Though still within range of any pursuing Confederates, "I wished to demonstrate to the Cavalry Corps the impossibility of the enemy's destroying or capturing so large a body of mounted troops."[65]

Later in the day he resumed the march, finally moving over the river at Bottom's Bridge and heading for the James. By now the rain had ceased and the march progressed in relative comfort. Having fought their way out of Richmond with such skill, the cavalrymen could adopt an idyllic frame of mind. As one New York trooper wrote: "The morning of Thursday, the 12th of May, was all that Nature in her most generous mood could bestow. The rain had opened the curling leaves, the fields were resplendent with luxuriant grass,

Return of Sheridan's raiders. COURTESY LIBRARY OF CONGRESS.

★★★★★★★★★★★★★★★★★★★★★★

65. Sheridan, *Personal Memoirs*, 1: 384.

and beautiful gardens by the roadside gave forth a fragrance that was refreshing to the tired and exhausted men. . . ."[66]

Two days later, after crossing White Oak Swamp, the cavalrymen encamped beside the James River in sight of Union gunboats, and drew rations and forage from the Haxall's Landing base. They rested and refit for three days, meanwhile carrying out various minor operations, such as wrecking local bridges, enemy supply caches, and railroad track.[67] On the 17th the troopers started on their week-long return journey to Grant's army, having come almost 140 miles in eight days, suffering about six hundred in killed and wounded.[68] In the process they had inflicted even heavier casualties among the Confederate cavalry, including Stuart's death, which as a morale factor was perhaps of greater weight than all their other losses combined. Despite the many hardships and dangers they had endured, the Federals had done a great deal to increase their self-confidence by defeating the Rebel cavaliers as never before and by gaining a deep faith in the abilities of their new commander. Through eleven subsequent months of war, that faith would never crumble.

Therefore, even though he did not capture Richmond, Sheridan accomplished a great deal in this, his first independent campaign in Virginia. In truth, he satisfied the requirements of his mission even before reaching the enemy capital.

★★★★★★★★★★★★★★★★★★★★★★★★

66. Preston, *Tenth New York Cavalry*, p. 181.

67. Carpenter, "Sheridan's Expedition Around Richmond," pp. 314-17.

68. Rodenbough, "Sheridan's Richmond Raid," p. 192; Hagemann, *Fighting Rebels and Redskins*, p. 237; O'Connor, *Sheridan, the Inevitable*, p. 172.

11

THE DEVIL'S NAVY

Forrest's Johnsonville Raid
(October 16-November 10, 1864)

1

Admiring associates referred to Nathan Bedford Forrest as "The Wizard of the Saddle." His opponents had various other names for him, many of them unprintable. Perhaps the best known of those not obscene was one that William T. Sherman gave him in June, 1864. On the tenth day of that month Forrest administered a humiliating beating to a large infantry-cavalry force that Sherman's subordinates had sent to break up Forrest's command. Five days later Sherman angrily wired Secretary of War Stanton that the Confederate leader had to be followed "to the death, if it cost 10,000 lives and breaks the Treasury. There never will be peace in Tennessee till Forrest is dead." In the same dispatch, Sherman coined the appelation that thereafter was used in times of stress by many Federal commanders in the West: "Forrest is the very devil."[1]

The "Devil" achieved his awesome reputation by fighting

★★★★★★★★★★★★★★★★★★★★★★

1. *Official Records*, series I, vol. 39, pt. 2, p. 121.

General Nathan Bedford Forrest. COURTESY LIBRARY OF CONGRESS.

in a style far removed from the romantic bent that seemed to characterize most Southern cavalrymen. He possessed neither the chivalric charm of J. E. B. Stuart nor Stuart's affection for gaudy uniforms and banjo music. To Forrest, war was not a glorious idyll; it was a bloody contest of grit and endurance. He dressed for it in plain, functional clothing unadorned by scarlet capes or plumed hats, and preferred the rattle of musketry and the rasp of saber upon saber to any other music.

Forrest was the sort of fellow one did not wish to trifle with. He appeared shrewd, perhaps even sinister. He stood an erect six feet, two inches tall, and his physique was robust, featuring especially muscular arms and legs. His voice was a heavy growl, the kind of sound soldiers responded to promptly and with compliance.

Forrest was backwoods born, possessed of only six months' formal schooling. But he had overcome his educational handicap to become a prestigious figure in Bedford County, Tennessee, in which he had been born in 1821. His wealth, plus his position in the community, made it inevitable that he should become a prominent soldier when civil war broke out. He raised and equipped at his own expense a battalion of mounted troops, of which, late in 1861, he was elected lieutenant colonel; and he promptly made a name for himself as a most resourceful cavalryman. As the war revealed, he was a born soldier, with an intuitive knowledge of military tactics. He could deflate high-blown maxims, reducing them to the essentials: when, midway through the war, he remarked about getting there "first with the most men," he indicated that logical, practical soldiering would defeat textbook-bound acumen on any battlefield.[2]

His rise as an officer in the Confederate ranks was commensurate with his skill. A full colonelcy came his way early in 1862; he was appointed a brigadier general that July, and by December of '63 he had won his second star. By that time he had distinguished himself in numerous battles and campaigns, including Shiloh, Murfreesboro, and Chattanooga, and had acquired a reputation as a leader of independent commands second to none among Confederate cavalry generals in the western theater.[3]

★★★★★★★★★★★★★★★★★★★★★★★

2. Boatner, *The Civil War Dictionary*, pp. 288-89.

3. Warner, *Generals in Gray*, p. 92.

A few campaigns particularly illustrated the characteristics that made him a great soldier. During the Federal investment of Fort Donelson in February of 1862 he refused to abide by his superior's decision to surrender to General Grant's army. The night before the garrison formally capitulated, Forrest led his cavalry battalion out of the fort under cover of darkness, crossed ice-cold backwaters, slipped through the Federal picket lines, and returned his command intact to the Confederate lines.[4] During the Streight expedition, he demonstrated superior determination and endurance by tracking down Yankee raiders who far outnumbered his pursuit force, bringing them to bay short of their objectives, though the raiders had gotten a huge head start.

In 1864 Forrest added to his laurels, and to his controversial reputation as well. That summer he gave a vicious pounding to Brigadier General S. D. Sturgis at the battle of Brice's Cross Roads, near Guntown, Mississippi—one of the most lopsided cavalry engagements in the West. In September he moved against General Sherman's communication lines in Alabama and Tennessee, attacking numerous outposts, capturing one thousand two hundred men and eight hundred horses, and causing Sherman to make many fruitless attempts to halt him. In that year he also ranged into West Tennessee, where his cavalry assaulted Fort Pillow, killing 230 of its garrison, the majority being Negro troops, whom the Confederates despised. Northerners' charges that Forrest had massacred the black soldiers would follow him to the end of his days.[5]

Therefore, by the closing months of '64, Forrest had amply demonstrated his ferocity, resourcefulness, determination, and stamina in fighting. By this time he had also gained especial renown as a raiding leader, for he was adept at hit-and-run tactics, could move his men with swiftness and agility to outwit large bodies of pursuers, could make the maximum use of time to destroy objectives marked for ruination, and knew how to maneuver out of a tight spot whenever he found himself so located.

Breaking enemy communications was one of Forrest's favorite chores. He enjoyed the cat-and-mouse game that it

★★★★★★★★★★★★★★★★★★★★★★★★

4. Anders, *Fighting Confederates*, pp. 119-20.

5. Boatner, *The Civil War Dictionary*, pp. 85, 289-91.

usually entailed, and feared matching wits against no Yankee leader, especially when he could move through territory that was familiar to him and to which his opponents were, by and large, strangers.

He took particular pleasure in striking General Sherman's supply lines after the latter embarked on his campaign against Atlanta. By mid-October 1864, Forrest had already laid a heavy hand on Sherman's bases in two states, but was not satisfied. He reported to his departmental commander, Lieutenant General Richard Taylor, that he had done "something toward accomplishing" Sherman's ruin, but nevertheless was "anxious to renew the effort."[6]

In planning to resume this campaign, Forrest studied the attenuated line of supply that connected Sherman's army in Georgia with its depot in far-away Louisville, Kentucky. Running through Middle Tennessee and Kentucky, the network included other important supply bases such as those at Chattanooga and Nashville as well as a new depot on the Tennessee River at Johnsonville. Rail lines in those vicinities had been the target of several Confederate raids, but no decisive damage had ever been inflicted, for the enemy had become experienced at repairing breaks in the track. Consequently, Forrest considered blocking Federal access to the Tennessee and Cumberland Rivers near the point at which they entered the Confederacy. He concentrated on those supply bases which facilitated enemy shipping, especially the one at Johnsonville.[7]

Forrest's command, now resting in Mississippi, was not in the best possible condition to undertake such an operation. In fact, most of his men were still suffering the effects of overexertion during the raids that had occupied their time in recent weeks, and their horses were recovering from the long forced marches they had endured. In speaking of his plans for the coming campaign, Forrest emphasized to General Taylor that his men and mounts "need more rest than I am able to give them at present." Yet he recognized the value in again striking at Sherman's lines; thus it became his intention "to take possession of Fort Heiman on the west bank of the

★★★★★★★★★★★★★★★★★★★★★★

6. Henry, *"First With the Most" Forrest*, p. 368.

7. Campbell H. Brown, "Forrest's Johnsonville Raid," *Civil War Times Illustrated*, 4 (June 1965): 49.

Tennessee River below Johnsonville, and thus prevent all communication with Johnsonville by transports."[8]

So it happened that on October 16 Forrest collected his weary men and set them in motion for Tennessee on yet another expedition. He marched northward out of Corinth, Mississippi with Brigadier General Abraham Buford's division of horsemen, followed by Colonel E. W. Rucker's brigade and two batteries of horse-drawn artillery.[9] By the 21st Forrest had been joined by other portions of Brigadier General James Ronald Chalmers's division, and headquarters had been set up at Jackson, Tennessee. Meanwhile Buford, in advance, had moved almost thirty miles farther eastward. By now Forrest's force on hand numbered perhaps three thousand officers and enlisted men—the total amount then available, but hardly an overwhelming sum with which to do battle with the strong Federal garrisons along the Tennessee.[10]

Unavoidably, the expedition had got off to an inauspicious start. Supplies in West Tennessee were less bountiful than Forrest had anticipated; if the raid developed into a lengthy campaign many of his men would have to ride and fight on empty stomachs. More significantly, Forrest had discovered that his animals were in even worse condition than he had feared. Many horses had already given out, some of them falling to the ground during the march and dying, and others were so badly shod that they had begun to limp noticeably. Concerned that his command might fall to pieces before it reached its target, Forrest extended his layover at Jackson until he could send detachments to local villages to confiscate blacksmith supplies needed to reshoe the animals.[11]

By the 21st Forrest's advance had been detected by Federal commanders in that portion of the state, many of whom had flown into panic. Reports of his movements indicated that the Confederate raider might strike at any or all of the area garrisons such as Memphis and Columbus, Tennessee or

★★★★★★★★★★★★★★★★★★★★★★★

8. Henry, *"First With the Most" Forrest,* p. 369.

9. Lytle, *Bedford Forrest and His Critter Company,* p. 345.

10. Henry, *"First With the Most" Forrest,* p. 370; Jordan and Pryor, *Campaigns of Forrest,* pp. 589-90.

11. Lytle, *Bedford Forrest and His Critter Company,* p. 345.

Paducah, Kentucky. Commanders pulled their advance troops inside their lines, strengthened their defenses to repel an attack, and buffeted superior officers with requests for reinforcements. Such was the renown of the Wizard of the Saddle that mere rumors of his approach—rumors unsubstantiated by fact or even probability—made enemy leaders feel helpless, no matter how secure their position was in truth.[12]

In turn, Forrest grew somewhat apprehensive that he himself might be the vulnerable one. He began to think that his enemies might move against him before he could strike, threatening his flanks and rear. Certainly his opponents in the forts held the aggregate numerical advantage; should they muster the nerve to cross the Tennessee at or near the town of Clifton, for instance, the threat thus posed to his rear would prevent him from moving farther.

But no Federals made such a threat. All were much too concerned with firming up their defenses to try to take the initiative against Forrest and his troopers. By the 24th Forrest was satisfied that no operation would be launched against him from either Memphis on the west or Clifton to the east; therefore his expedition could go forward. By this time he had refit his command, had reorganized it by recruiting in West Tennessee and by shifting about subordinate commanders, and had mustered his utmost possible strength.

On that day he led Chalmers's soldiers from Jackson northeastward toward Fort Heiman, close to the Tennessee-Kentucky line, ready to resume his harassment of Sherman's arm of supply.[13] Had his opponents capitalized upon either the delays he had suffered to date or the relatively small size of his force, he might not have progressed even this far. Because of the self-absorption of the Federal commanders along the river, the Devil would be permitted to strike again.

2

Buford's veteran division, consisting of Brigadier General H. B. Lyon's Kentucky brigade and Colonel Tyree Bell's

★★★★★★★★★★★★★★★★★★★★★★★★

12. Brown, "Forrest's Johnsonville Raid," p. 49.

13. Henry, *"First With the Most" Forrest*, p. 371.

brigade of Tennesseans, marched on ahead toward the river. Amid the cavalrymen rumbled several artillery pieces, including two huge twenty-pounder Parrott rifles that had been sent up from Alabama to give Forrest long-range fire power. More than a day's ride to the rear came Forrest himself, accompanying Chalmers's command, comprising Colonel Rucker's brigade as well as parts of two other understrength brigades: Chalmers's division had been reduced, by the hardships of recent campaigning and the loss of detached troops on temporary duty elsewhere, to a shadow of its former size.[14]

On October 28 Buford's men reached the once-active but now-neglected neighborhood around Fort Heiman, an abandoned Confederate garrison on the left bank of the Tennessee, directly across the river from the larger and more famous Fort Henry. Buford placed Lyon's brigade inside the abandoned works, along with the two Parrott rifles, manned by cannoneers from Lieutenant E. S. Walton's battery. Farther upstream (south) of the works, Buford deployed Bell's Tennesseans at Paris Landing, near the mouth of the Big Sandy River. Next to Bell he emplaced two of the cannon from Captain John Morton's battery, to sweep the river from concealed positions.[15]

Since there were no garrison troops on this stretch of the west bank, it was obvious to Forrest's soldiers—who had been kept in ignorance of their commander's objectives—that he was not aiming to engage land forces. With passing time the troopers realized that he was gunning for river traffic, intent on stopping transports from running the Tennessee and carrying supplies to and from the Johnsonville depot, more than thirty miles to the south.

When specific orders were finally issued, the men learned just how diligently General Buford intended to carry out Forrest's plan. He had thoroughly mapped his strategy: his men were to keep themselves hidden from view, so that they might not discourage approaching vessels from coming into

★★★★★★★★★★★★★★★★★★★★★★★

14. *Official Records,* series I, vol. 39, pt. 1, p. 970; Jordan and Pryor, *Campaigns of Forrest,* p. 591.

15. John W. Morton, "Raid of Forrest's Cavalry on the Tennessee River in 1864," *Southern Historical Society Papers,* 10 (1882): 261-62; Hancock, *Hancock's Diary,* pp. 494-95.

cannon range. Only transports heading south on the river were to be fired on, and only after they had passed Fort Heiman; this to ensure accuracy of fire. Initially the cannoneers would not make targets of ships returning empty from Johnsonville; Buford was not one to squander ammunition. He was not one to place complete reliance on his cannon, either. He dismounted his troopers and deployed them to support the guns with rifle fire, in case any of the ships they encountered boasted armaments that could challenge the artillery. The sharpshooters were directed to snipe at officers and crewmen atop the decks of the passing vessels.[16]

By the evening of the 28th, Forrest, with Chalmers's division, had not yet arrived at the river, but Buford had dug in and was ready to fight. Though eager for action, he managed to hold his men in check when four steamers sailed north (downriver) from Johnsonville, riding high and light. The ships made tempting targets, and the Rebels must have yearned to pull the lanyards of their heavy guns.[17]

About nine o'clock the next morning the transport *Mazeppa* rewarded the soldiers' patience by steaming into sight on her run up the river to the supply base. The Confederates allowed her to pass a two-gun section that Buford had recently emplaced just north of Fort Heiman. Then, when she came abeam of the middle section of guns, the division commander gave the signal to commence firing. The heavy Parrotts soon joined the light artillery, dotting the riverbank with clouds of cannon smoke. After three accurate rounds from the batteries, *Mazeppa* became unmanageable and drifted ashore on the opposite bank, where her crew abandoned ship.

To reach the disabled vessel, one of Buford's most enterprising (and least bashful) troopers stripped to the buff, tied a pistol about his neck, and paddled across the river on a pank to take possession of the prize. When he reached the ship, her captain, who had remained aboard, helped him courteously onto the deck. The soldier recrossed the river in the ship's yawl, which Buford then used to ferry a work detail to the *Mazeppa*. They attached a hawser to her and soon

★★★★★★★★★★★★★★★★★★★★★★

16. Brown, "Forrest's Johnsonville Raid," p. 50.

17. Lytle, *Bedford Forrest and His Critter Company,* p. 346.

the badly damaged steamer was resting at anchor on the west bank.[18]

Forrest would have been pleased to know that his men had seized a vessel that carried large supplies of flour, footwear, blankets, hardtack, and other goods of as much use to its captors as to the Federals for whom they had been intended. Buford doled out such supplies as his soldiers would find useful, then helped himself to a demijohn of French brandy also found aboard the ship. The enlisted men were not pleased by his appropriation of the liquor: "Hold on, General," one of them cried, "save some of the whiskey for us!" But the tall, ruddy Kentuckian replied in a loud, good-natured tone: "Plenty of shoes and blankets for the boys, but just whiskey enough for the General!"[19]

After removing *Mazeppa's* supplies and storing them on the shore, Buford's men sighted three Federal gunboats approaching from the direction of Johnsonville. They scrambled back to their guns and in a matter of minutes were firing so rapidly and accurately that the ships decided not to venture farther. As night fell, Buford busied himself by rounding up all local wagons and teams, to cart the *Mazeppa's* cargo out of range of any subsequent Federal naval attack. When finally finished with the vessel, he saw to it that she was put to the torch, along with a pair of barges that she had in tow.[20]

The next morning brought a flotilla's worth of unsuspecting ships into the Rebels' clutches. The first was the *Anna*, another Federal transport, which came downriver from the depot, blithely unaware that *Mazeppa* had met an untimely fate the day before. Buford decided to rescind his order of the previous day and signalled his men that ships leaving Johnsonville, too, were fair game.

Passing Fort Heiman, *Anna* was blasted by salvos from the Parrott guns as well as from the light cannon above the garrison. Then, upon reflection, Buford determined to salvage the vessel. Riding to the riverbank, he halted the cannonade and shouted to the Federal captain to "come to" against the

★★★★★★★★★★★★★★★★★★★★★★

18. Henry, *"First With the Most" Forrest*, p. 372.

19. Morton, "Raid of Forrest's Cavalry," p. 263.

20. Hancock, *Hancock's Diary*, p. 496.

shore. The ship's skipper replied that he would do so at the lower landing and rang his signal bell to indicate his desire to fully comply with Buford's orders. But instead of cutting speed, *Anna* suddenly raised steam and raced past the landing, making a desperate run for safety. Buford ordered his gunners to resume firing, but by then the ship was so near the shore that the cannoneers could not sufficiently depress their pieces to do her fatal damage. Shells ripped into her pilot house and chopped down her masthead, but the *Anna* managed to float down the river until within the protective embrace of Federal gunboats far above Buford's positions.[21]

A few hours afterward, the Union gunboat *Undine*, which had convoyed the *Anna* from Johnsonville almost to the point at which she had come under fire, appeared on the scene. Having learned of *Anna's* plight, she had returned to offer help, not knowing that in the meantime her companion had steamed to safety. Followed closely by another transport, *Venus*, and two barges, the tinclad gunboat passed the lowermost Rebel gun emplacement before the Confederates began firing. As the cannon unleashed its barrage, General Bell's brigade at Paris Landing drew bead on the ship's portholes, forcing her crew to keep low.[22]

While the unusual battle raged, one of Buford's regiments, Colonel Clark Barteau's 2nd Tennessee Cavalry (which had endured a variety of frustrations chasing Grierson's raiders a year and half before), was sent to a point some eight hundred yards below Paris Landing. There the regiment's executive officer faced his soldiers and improvised an order that he could not have found in any book on cavalry tactics: "Dismount, and prepare, on foot, to fight—a gunboat!"[23]

Undine sought to bring as many as possible of her eight howitzers to bear on the enemy's positions. But within an hour the rifled Parrotts at Fort Heiman had sent four shells through her gun casemates, and another round had exploded in the fireroom, leaving four crewmen dead and three wounded. Still the captain refused to abandon ship and finally maneuvered her into a position too far downriver to be

★★★★★★★★★★★★★★★★★★★★★★★★

21. Morton, "Raid of Forrest's Cavalry," pp. 263-64.

22. Lytle, *Bedford Forrest and His Critter Company*, p. 347.

23. Hancock, *Hancock's Diary*, p. 498.

reached by the guns at Paris Landing and too far upstream to be harmed by those at Fort Heiman.

Despite Buford's effective firepower, the Federal ships kept coming. While the *Undine* floundered about, the transport *Venus* steamed north from Johnsonville, ignorant of the trouble ahead. The damaged gunboat tried to signal her to keep out of danger, but the transport did not pay heed. Consequently she soon came abeam of the Rebels' upper battery. This time the cannoneers' shooting was not so accurate, and the *Venus* escaped material damage; however, her captain was killed by a shell fragment or musket cartridge, and in desperation the ship anchored alongside the *Undine,* huddling there for safety.[24]

Several minutes later, yet another transport sailed into view. She, too, ignored *Undine's* danger signals, and paid for it by coming under heavy fire. After being blasted almost to pieces, the *J. W. Cheeseman* limped over to the west bank, where some of Buford's men boarded her and captured her crew.

On the morning of the 31st, Bedford Forrest arrived on the scene with Chalmers's one thousand-man division.[25] The Confederate commander was mildly surprised by the scope of General Buford's spoils. After directing that the two light artillery batteries accompanying Chalmers should be added to the river emplacements, the general sought out Buford and congratulated him on his achievements. A strict teetotaler, Forrest might even have forgiven Buford for his intemperance, had the demijohn incident been reported to him.

Forrest was a versatile cavalryman. He was vastly experienced in fighting afoot, frequently using his troopers as though mounted infantry. As indicated by Buford's cannonade, he also knew how to organize artillery support. But at no time in his career had he ever felt the need to study naval warfare. Now he would have to learn by trial and error, if he was to complete his campaign to tie up Federal shipping along the Tennessee.

At once he set out to take full command of his little navy.

★★★★★★★★★★★★★★★★★★★★★

24. Henry, *"First With the Most" Forrest,* p. 373.

25. Morton, "Raid of Forrest's Cavalry," p. 267.

Examining his prizes, he found that the *Cheeseman* had been too heavily damaged to permit further service, but both *Undine* and *Venus,* which by now had surrendered to Rebel boarding parties, were still seaworthy. The *Undine,* with her eight twenty-four-pounder guns, would be of particular help to the command, should other gunboats come downriver to challenge the raiders to a renewed contest. (As a point of fact, this had already happened. Shortly after Chalmers's advance forces had arrived at the river, the gunboat *Tawah* had steamed out of Johnsonville, dropping anchor a mile and a half from the nearest Confederate guns. At once she singled out the upper battery as a target, but got off only a few salvos before one of Chalmers's gunners got her range. Once the cannon started firing in reply, *Tawah* steamed upriver to join some of her companions.)[26]

Forrest's fleet took shape rapidly. He selected teams of cavalrymen to do duty on the ships, and as soon as he again had the river to himself he gave them a crash course in seamanship by allowing them a few hours to practice maneuvering the *Undine* and the *Venus* between the artillery positions. It did not take the troopers long to become adequate at navigation, thanks to the guidance they received from Captain Frank Gracey of the 3rd Kentucky, who had once been a steamboat pilot on the Cumberland River. Forrest made Gracey the *Undine's* skipper, and appointed Lieutenant Colonel William A. Dawson of the 15th Tennessee captain of the *Venus.* The latter accepted the post only after Forrest assured him, with a grin, that he would not cashier the landlubber colonel in the event he somehow lost his ship through mishandling.[27]

In truth, Forrest suspected that the plans he had formulated would place both his ships in more than a little danger. If the inexperienced crewmen encountered resistance from Federal vessels, they could easily be outmaneuvered and seized. And Forrest was aware that both upriver and down, enemy gunboats were available to oppose him. At Johnsonville, in addition to the *Tawah,* were the tinclads *Key West* and *Elfin,* boasting an aggregate of twenty-five guns. To the

★★★★★★★★★★★★★★★★★★★★★★★★

26. *Official Records,* series I, vol. 39, pt. 1, p. 873.

27. Lytle, *Bedford Forrest and His Critter Company,* pp. 347-48; Jordan and Pryor, *Campaigns of Forrest,* p. 597.

north, near Paducah, was a Union flotilla composed of the flagship *Moose* and the gunboats *Brilliant, Victory, Paw Paw, Curlew,* and *Fairy,* mounting seventy-nine guns all told. To face these potential challengers, Forrest could count on only twenty-six cannon, including the pair of Parrotts that he had mounted aboard the *Venus.*

However, Forrest's specialty was making maximum use of minimum resources. Though he realized that in a full-dress sea battle his fleet would be no match for the Yankees, he hoped to lure more Federal gunboats and transports into range of his shore batteries by making his own ships appear vulnerable to recapture. To this end he set his shore-based cavalrymen to cleaning their rifles and stockpiling ammunition, and counseled his gunners about the methods of delivering an accurate fire.

But the desired situation failed to materialize; no more ships came into range, either from Johnsonville or Paducah. Realizing that the Federals were allowing him the next move, Forrest decided not to keep them waiting, even though to take the offensive with such an untried force as his was not safe military procedure.

On the rainy morning of November 1 he moved his fleet upriver toward the supply depot,[28] determined to blast it to ruins with broadsides from his ship howitzers as well as salvos from his land-based artillery. On land, Chalmers's mounted troops and some of the horse artillerymen kept pace with the ships, to protect them from the gunboats they would encounter at Johnsonville. In the meantime, Buford's division, with Morton's battery, followed in the wake of the column, to offer similar protection against the six gunboats near Paducah.[29]

This was by far the strangest raiding force the Wizard of the Saddle had ever commanded. Yet his hopes were as high as they had been on past occasions, when leading winding columns of dust-covered troopers against the Yankee invaders of Kentucky, Mississippi, Alabama, and Tennessee. And the novel atmosphere of this expedition gave it an exhilarating flavor. The cavalrymen on the captured ships seemed to

★★★★★★★★★★★★★★★★★★★★★★

28. Brown, "Forrest's Johnsonville Raid," pp. 52-53.

29. Jordan and Pryor, *Campaigns of Forrest,* p. 597.

enjoy service afloat; they laughed and jibed with their land-bound cohorts, rang signal bells and hoisted pennants as though preparing to battle men-of-war on the high seas.

The rather light-hearted nature of the march began to infect Forrest himself. Riding alongside the ships, he must have considered the sound of his new title, and probably decided that he liked it. After all, "Commodore Forrest" had a prestigious ring to it.

3

On the first leg of their trip upriver, the landlubber crews of *Undine* and *Venus* had a fine time; the ships cut through the water so speedily and effortlessly that the converted cavalrymen grew pleased that they had gone to sea. But their comrades on land found the going rough, for the roads along the riverbank were knee-deep in mud and the surrounding foliage was thick and thorny. The artillerymen experienced the greatest difficulties, pushing their guns forward from position to position, often being forced to haul cannons and caissons out of slimy bogs. After a time the land troops, no longer able to tolerate the jibes of the lucky men aboard the ships, lost their temper. They responded with warnings of what would happen to the crewmen as soon as enemy gunboats came into view.[30]

On the night of the 1st the entire command bivouacked at Danville, near the ruins of a railroad bridge across the Tennessee. The land-sea advance resumed next dawn, and continued without mishap until late in the afternoon, when the ships came within sight of Green Bottom Bar, six miles north of Johnsonville. Because her crew had grown overconfident from the ease with which they had navigated the river thus far, the *Venus* steamed ahead of the *Undine* and her supporting troops. Suddenly she rounded a bend and found herself facing the Federal ships *Tawah* and *Key West*. The gunboats attacked at once and Forrest, watching on shore, sensed disaster.

Soon after the enemy opened fire, *Venus's* crew abandoned ship in great haste. Driving her ashore, they fled into the woods along the west bank of the river. The Federals then

★★★★★★★★★★★★★★★★★★★★★★

30. Wyeth, *Life of Forrest*, p. 524.

boarded *Venus,* rejoicing in her recovery. Any triumph over Bedford Forrest, however minor, was fondly cherished.

When *Undine* steamed upriver to aid her sister ship, the Yankees almost bagged her as well. But seeing *Venus* abandoned and the Federal ships maneuvering to offer resistance, Captain Gracey changed his mind about putting up a fight. As soon as the gunboats discharged broadsides at close quarters, *Undine* changed course and raced back down the stream till beyond reach of their guns. Forrest was relieved that the enemy did not pursue the retreating vessel.

The ill fortune that had befallen *Venus* did not temper Gracey's boldness for long. At noon the next day *Undine,* supported by Forrest's land forces, made an appearance alongside Reynoldsburg Island, less than four miles from Johnsonville, and tried to coax three other Federal gunboats into range of the batteries. Three times *Undine* sailed temptingly into view, but the lieutenant in charge of the small enemy flotilla near the supply base refused to accept the challenge.

Seeing that his opponents would not be lured, Forrest took his land forces to a point directly across from Johnsonville. He spent the rest of that day and the morning of the next deploying his troops for the attack. Rain came down heavily, complicating the tasks of positioning troopers in line of battle and emplacing cannon in the muddy bottom across from the depot. Although most of the guns bore on Johnsonville, others went into battery far to the north, to discourage any interference from ships running upriver from Paducah. Forrest and his chief artillerist, Captain Morton, did their work so covertly—much of it by night—that the garrison troops across the river had no idea that Confederate cannon were facing them.

By morning of the 4th, four units of artillery had been wheeled into position. Two of the batteries, under Morton and Captain T. W. Rice, were ready to lob shells amid Johnsonville's rail yards, storage houses, and loading docks. Farther north, in a position to halt downriver shipping, was a two-gun section under Lieutenant Walton; it had been unlimbered not far from the head of Reynoldsburg Island, near which *Undine* had hove to. And the lowermost battery, commanded by Captain J. C. Thrall, protected Forrest against any attacks from upriver.[31]

★★★★★★★★★★★★★★★★★★★★★★

31. Brown, "Forrest's Johnsonville Raid," p. 54.

However, before Forrest could unleash his cannonade, new trouble appeared on the horizon. Spurred by reports of river fighting near Johnsonville, Federal leaders farther north had dispatched the Paducah-based gunboats, under Lieutenant Commander Le Roy Fitch, to quell the trouble. At eight A. M. the enemy fleet appeared off Reynoldsburg Island. Shortly afterward, Lieutenant Edward M. King sallied forth from the Johnsonville vicinity with three other tinclads, including two that had already provided dangers for Forrest, *Tawah* and *Key West*. The converging flotillas pinned the Confederate-manned *Undine* in their middle and left her ripe for recapture.

Undine made a determined fight of it. Aided by fire from the lowermost batteries, Rice's and Walton's, her inexperienced crew stood off the nine attacking ships—mounting a total of one hundred guns—until she began to run low on coal. Captain Gracey instructed his men to abandon ship, but not before he had taken steps to scuttle her. Tearing open mattresses in the crew's quarters, Gracey soaked them in oil and placed them in the powder magazine and the main cabin. After every crew member had waded ashore, the erstwhile commodore set the materials on fire. Shortly after he leaped into the water and swam to safety, the last of Forrest's fleet exploded into a fiery cloud.[32]

Beyond forcing the *Undine's* destruction, the Federal fleet accomplished nothing. Lieutenant King's gunboats were badly battered by the two Rebel batteries and had to steam back to Johnsonville. Commander Fitch, near Reynoldsburg Island, kept up his firing till noon but did not dare venture through the Island chute. Thus, several enemy men-of-war only a few miles downriver from Forrest's main force elected not to interfere with the assault on Johnsonville.

A few minutes before two P. M. Forrest was ready to proceed with the most important item on his agenda. With Generals Buford and Bell he took position behind one of John Morton's cannon, intending to observe the firing of the first shot.

Across the river, all seemed tranquil at the depot. A few gunboats were getting up steam, preparing to reconnoiter the area downriver. Obviously, Forrest's cannonade would come as a rude surprise. As it turned out, Colonel Charles R. Thompson, commanding at Johnsonville, had taken no spe-

★★★★★★★★★★★★★★★★★★★★★★★★

32. Henry, *"First With the Most" Forrest*, pp. 375-76.

cial precations to meet any form of attack. The Rebel raiders were out of Thompson's sight and therefore his mind.

Promptly at two o'clock, one of Morton's men yanked a lanyard. After explosion and recoil, a cannon ball landed within the depot, spreading destruction. The other guns quickly joined in, and soon shells were smashing Federal transports and gunboats at the landing. For forty minutes the guns made targets of the steamboats. Several craft went up in flames; others drifted out of control, ramming their sister ships and spreading the fire. Lieutenant King panicked at the heavy barrage, and, unable to pinpoint its source, or-

Ruins at Johnsonville, Tennessee. COURTESY LIBRARY OF CONGRESS.

dered his crews to put all undamaged ships to the torch so that, if captured, they could not be used by the enemy. With Colonel Thompson's compliance, all ships at the landing eventually went up in smoke and flames.[33]

While the vessels blazed, Forrest decided to concentrate his firepower elsewhere. His gunners elevated their pieces and soon were striking the depot's warehouses and rail shops. They were opposed by about fourteen cannon on the hills above Johnsonville, but since the east side of the river was banked much higher than the shore the Rebels occupied, the Union guns could not be depressed enough to bear upon many of Forrest's artillery emplacements.

Many buildings caught fire from the burning ships, making the Confederates' job a thorough one. One storehouse atop a hill held hundreds of barrels of liquor; when it went up in flames the barrels burst and blazing alcohol sent a stream of blue fire down the hillside. Other burning warehouses added the ripe odors of bacon, ham, and coffee to the reek of alcohol. Within two hours, Johnsonville was an almost solid sheet of flame; for a mile along the river, buildings and ships blazed out of control. One of Colonel Thompson's officers later described the scene as "awfully sublime."[34]

Across the water, the Rebels were in lofty spirits. The troopers supporting the guns cheered wildly whenever an accurate shot pounded the depot grounds. Celebrating was indeed in order, for Forrest's plan had worked almost flawlessly. By using his miniscule fleet and his shore artillery with such imagination, he had thoroughly disrupted Federal shipping and had disposed of supplies with an aggregate value of more than two million dollars. The destruction ensured that the supply base at Johnsonville would never again be put into commission. Additionally, Forrest had held off a fleet of warships that could have prevented all of his other accomplishments.

Late in the afternoon, by which time the Confederate cannon had also silenced a counter-battery fire from across the river,[35] Forrest ordered his artillerymen to cease shelling. He

★★★★★★★★★★★★★★★★★★★★★★★★

33. Brown, "Forrest's Johnsonville Raid," pp. 56-57.

34. Henry, *"First With the Most" Forrest,* pp. 377-78.

35. *Official Records,* series I, vol. 39, pt. 1, p. 875.

collected his enthusiastic troopers, put them into marching formation, and withdrew from the riverbank.

At Johnsonville, his opponents were vastly relieved to see him go. For a time Colonel Thompson feared that Forrest would ship his troopers across the river to put last touches to his work of devastation—though the colonel ought to have seen that the burning fleet along the riverbank made this an impossibility. Still, Thompson's worry was not uncommon; similar fears often occupied the minds of Forrest's adversaries. In fact, panic at the idea of Forrest's crossing spread so wildly through the base that the civilian railroad agent at Johnsonville ran off with a train of cars loaded with refugees, so that Forrest might not get his hands on them. The agent did not halt till the train had carried him sixty miles from the depot.[36]

With Colonel Rucker's brigade remaining temporarily behind to cover the withdrawal, most of Forrest's men marched several miles southward, the glare of flaming ships and buildings lighting their way through the gathering darkness. The next morning, after a short and successful skirmish with Federals manning Fort Johnson, south of the supply base, Rucker's troopers followed their comrades. By November 10 the entire force was back in Mississippi, during the last two weeks having captured and destroyed four gunboats, fourteen transports, twenty barges, twenty-six artillery pieces, and having taken about 150 prisoners, comprising the crews that had surrendered *Venus, Undine, J. W. Cheeseman,* and *Mazeppa.* The greatest spoils were those burned at Johnsonville, including quartermaster's stores estimated at from 75,000 to 120,000 tons. In the process, the Rebels had suffered eleven casualties, a relatively small total.[37]

Despite the colossal amount of destruction heaped upon Johnsonville, Forrest's raid had few lasting long-range effects, for General Sherman, who had already started on his march to the sea, had built up a large reserve supply of rations and matériel. Even so, Forrest's campaign ensured that Federal communication lines in the West would never again be whole, and again made Sherman a worried and uneasy

★★★★★★★★★★★★★★★★★★★★★★★

36. Ibid., p. 862.

37. Ibid., pp. 868, 871. Forrest later claimed that he had caused $6,700,000 worth of damage at Johnsonville; Federals estimated the loss at $2,200,000.

man.[38] Moreover, the operation was important for displaying Forrest's tactical genius, particularly his aptitude for improvising an attacking force to meet unforeseen circumstances. Very vew commanders, Federal or Confederate, could have turned naval officer for the length of time Forrest found necessary to outmaneuver and outwit his opponents; and perhaps no other could have achieved such remarkable results.

★★★★★★★★★★★★★★★★★★★★★★

38. Brown, "Forrest's Johnsonville Raid," p. 57.

12

THE LAST LONG RIDE

Wilson's Selma Campaign
(March 22-April 29, 1865)

1

On February 23, 1865, seventeen thousand Federal cavalrymen paraded in review before Major General George H.
Thomas at Gravelly Springs, Alabama. The horsemen looked
ready and eager to resume campaigning after almost two
months of inactivity; they were trim and hard muscled, showing none of the flabbiness that usually beset soldiers while in
winter quarters. Their horses were sleek and powerful, although in supply sufficient to mount only a little more than
half the command. The soldiers carried sabers that had been
sharpened almost to a razor's edge and carbines and pistols
so polished as to catch the reflection of the sunlight. Behind
the long columns rolled hundreds of well-stocked supply
wagons and three batteries of horse artillery, whose cannoneers rode proudly upon the limbers and caissons that
trailed the guns. Bugles blared up and down the lines and
short-tailed guidons rippled in the frosty breeze.

Watching the vast spectacle, General Thomas was highly
impressed. He had never before reviewed such a large force
of rugged, well-equipped horse soldiers. As a veteran of
frontier dragoon service, the general undoubtedly wished
that he might ride at the head of the command instead of his

twenty-seven-year-old subordinate, Brevet Major General James Harrison Wilson.

Young General Wilson was proud to display his corps, and grew mightily gratified when he learned of the strong impression it had made upon his guest. His gratification was enhanced by the fact that Thomas provided his only hope for winning approval of an expedition into the Deep South, where Wilson hoped to crush the last working parts of Jefferson Davis's war machine.[1]

Already Wilson had enjoyed a remarkable career. He had graduated from West Point a year before war broke out; when fighting began served as a staff officer to Ulysses Grant in the West; and had received his first star late in 1863, shortly after he turned twenty-six. After a brief but effective stint as administrative head of the U. S. Cavalry Bureau, he entered field service as a mounted division leader under Grant and Sheridan in Virginia. He won a glittering reputation of Spotsylvania, during Sheridan's Richmond Raid, and in the Shenandoah Valley campaign. Afterward he was breveted a two-star general and was dispatched to Alabama and Tennessee to reorganize William T. Sherman's sprawling and disorganized cavalry corps.

Evolving order from chaos in an almost unbelievably short time, he went on to attain new fame during the battle of Franklin, becoming the first Federal cavalryman to defeat Bedford Forrest in an even fight. Then, in December of 1864, he achieved spectacular success under General Thomas during the battle of Nashville. There Wilson's rejuvenated corps tipped the balance of battle by dismounting and snaking around the left flank of General John Bell Hood's Army of Tennessee, forcing the well-entrenched Confederates to flee. Thereafter Wilson led his troopers on a relentless pursuit of Hood's shattered army, driving it out of Tennessee and eventually into Mississippi, where it posed no threat to vital Union positions.[2]

By anyone's standards, Wilson, in this early season of 1865, stood in the front rank of Federal cavalry commanders. At so callow an age he commanded more mounted regiments than

★★★★★★★★★★★★★★★★★★★★★★★

1. Francis F. McKinney, *Education in Violence: The Life of George H. Thomas and the History of the Army of the Cumberland,* pp. 433-34.

2. Warner, *Generals in Blue,* pp. 566-67.

had served under any other Union leader, not excluding Sheridan, and few such leaders could boast a string of victories as impressive as Wilson's. A campaign into the depths of the faltering Confederacy—to be launched concurrently with Grant's final drive against Lee's army in Virginia —would seem a fitting way to climax his exceptional career.

Unfortunately, such thinking was not in the mind of General Grant, who formulated the strategy for all Federal land forces. With Hood's army out of the fighting, the general-in-chief had already elected to fragment Thomas's Army of the Cumberland, transferring various infantry corps to more active theaters. Now Grant was concentrating his attention on Sherman's campaign in the Carolinas and upon his own effort against Lee; thus he spent relatively little time considering how Wilson's cavalrymen might best be used in the coming, final campaign. He had authorized Thomas to detach a portion of Wilson's corps, "say five thousand men," to make a demonstration against enemy cities such as Selma and Tuscaloosa, Alabama. The operation was supposed to draw the enemy's attention from more important Federal thrusts, such as Major General E. R. S. Canby's overland drive against Mobile. It appeared that Grant could perceive no more effective way of utilizing Wilson's great fund of manpower.[3]

Though young, Wilson was as ambitious as any old-line Regular. He was driven by a compulsion to succeed and to win renown that could only be described as massive; hence such a plan was a huge disappointment to him. He had enough horses to mount twice as many soldiers as Grant wished to push south, and was pained by the thought of campaigning with a fraction of his force on hand.

Thus, in fact, this grand review had come about for General Thomas's benefit. Wilson realized that Thomas was sympathetic toward his plan for a grand campaign against all enemy citadels in Alabama and Georgia. Wilson had been serving directly under him for the past three months and the pair, despite the twenty-year discrepancy in their ages, had formed an intimate working relationship. "Pap" Thomas had come to consider Wilson the peer of any cavalry commander he had ever known, and shared with him a great many ideas about how such a large body of horse soldiers ought to be

★★★★★★★★★★★★★★★★★★★★★★

3. Wilson, *Under the Old Flag*, 2: 180.

employed in combat.[4] Wilson desperately hoped that the sight of these seventeen thousand well-appointed troopers would make Thomas visualize the effect of the blow they could deal the Deep South, if permitted to campaign as a cohesive force.

After the final horseman had passed by, General Thomas met in private with his cavalry chief and discussed with him a number of topics. Finally, to his subordinate's relief and joy, Thomas indicated that Wilson's efforts had not been in vain. After eliciting Wilson's detailed opinions about a large-scale cavalry strike, Thomas announced that he would petition Grant for permission to authorize Wilson's hoped-for mission. This was tantamount to assuring him that he would be able to move ahead with plans to take as many troopers as available against not only Selma and Tuscaloosa but also Montgomery, Alabama, Columbus, Georgia, and other important manufacturing centers in the interior of the Confederacy. In the process, however, Wilson's so-called Cavalry Corps of the Military Division of the Mississippi would be obliged to again confront Forrest's troopers, who by now had been reinforced and, still dangerous, lurked in and near middle Alabama.[5]

After thanking Thomas whole-heartedly, Wilson quickly went about revamping his plans and briefing his subordinates about the new latitude they would be given. A great enthusiasm—akin to that he had felt almost a year before, when assuming his first field command—took hold of him, and he communicated it to the leaders of the three divisions he would take southward. His lieutenants, Brigadier Generals Edward M. McCook, Eli Long, and Emory Upton, were motivated by many of the same combative instincts as influenced their commander, and each heartily approved of the new plan.

When Wilson sat down with them to project the scope of the force they would command, he already knew that litttle more than twelve thousand soldiers would be available for service. By this time he had lost the services of four full divisions, originally under his authority. One had accompanied

★★★★★★★★★★★★★★★★★★★★★★

4. Longacre, *From Union Stars to Top Hat*, pp. 165, 179.

5. *Official Records*, series I, vol. 49, pt. 1, p. 342; McKinney, *Education in Violence*, p. 434.

Sherman's infantry on its march; another had been ordered to join Canby's expedition against Mobile; a third had been returned to Middle Tennessee to combat enemy irregulars who harassed Loyalist residents; and only recently Wilson had reluctantly decided to leave behind his Fifth Cavalry Division, under an old veteran, Brigadier General Edward Hatch, when new campaigning commenced.[6] Hatch's command, which had rendered outstanding service at Nashville and during the pursuit of Hood, had lost so many of its horses during the rigorous service in Tennessee that only a small percentage of its personnel could have participated in duties come spring. Wilson had stripped it of its few remaining animals—as well as its precious seven-shot Spencer repeating carbines—and given them to one of General McCook's brigades that lacked sufficient quantities of both items.[7]

Even so, Wilson realized that he would move south with more cavalrymen than had ever embarked upon such an operation. And to all indications, the last bastions of the Cotton States lay open to him, protected only by Forrest's veterans and contingents of militiamen. Forrest's troopers and their attached infantry and artillery would of course provide stiff opposition, but having defeated them previously, Wilson was not paralyzed with fear at the thought of again meeting them in battle.

Nevertheless, he correctly assumed that he should do all he could to gather intelligence regarding Forrest's plans and dispositions. To facilitate this, he sent scouts and spies along his proposed route, and they brought back valuable information about the Confederates' strength and positions. Wilson learned that his force would far outnumber Forrest's and that the Rebel chief had spread his forces across a wide area stretching from eastern Mississippi to central Alabama; he would have to regroup them before he could effectively lead them in opposition to the raiding force. Wilson had no illusions about being able to move south unmolested, but his scouts' opinions strengthened his conviction that he could make the journey intact and victoriously.

★★★★★★★★★★★★★★★★★★★★★★

6. Wilson, *Under the Old Flag*, 2: 175-77.

7. Pierce, *Second Iowa Cavalry*, pp. 162-63; Edward A. Davenport, ed., *History of the Ninth Regiment Illinois Cavalry Volunteers*, p. 174.

As General Thomas had predicted, Grant subsequently approved the revised campaign plan and gave Wilson "the latitude of an independent commander." The lieutenant general nevertheless stipulated that the raid should get under way as quickly as possible, so that it might still benefit General Canby.[8]

Wilson wished to comply, but found himself unable to do so. Little in the way of eleventh-hour training was required, for he had drilled his cavalrymen throughout the winter, envisioning some sort of campaigning in the spring. However, heavy rains in early March made the Alabama roads impassable and postponed the starting date of the expedition. Fretting about the delay, Wilson wrote his friend Adam Badeau, who was serving in Virginia as Grant's military secretary, and asked him to inform his employer that "I shall not lose a moment I can possibly avoid in getting away." As soon as the roads dried, he told Badeau on March 7, his men would march south in fine fettle and "if things turn out right in the new venture upon which we are about to start they . . . will win their recognition. I have no fear but when my new report is received General Grant will do all for us we are entitled to. You may begin to look for it about the 1st of May—." He appended his hope that the operation would lead him directly across Georgia, in Sherman's wake, thence up the Carolina coast to join in the campaign to annihilate Lee in Virginia.

However, two weeks later he and his troopers were still at Gravelly Springs, where the weather had only recently begun to turn fair. Another last-minute delay—trouble securing sufficient supply wagons and forage stock—"greatly provoked" Wilson, but as he wrote Badeau, he was "powerless to help it." Yet he dwelled on the thought that, as soon as conditions permitted, he would take the field with a command "well armed, splendidly mounted, perfectly clad and equipped."[9]

The long-awaited day proved to be March 22. That morning—almost three months after they had gone into winter quarters—Wilson's divisions broke camp and poised before southward-leading roads. A few more soldiers than he had anticipated had become available for duty—his command

★★★★★★★★★★★★★★★★★★★★★★★

8. Wilson, *Under the Old Flag*, 2: 181, 183-86.

9. Longacre, *From Union Stars to Top Hat*, pp. 200-201.

consisted of approximately thirteen thousand five hundred cavalrymen, about one thousand five hundred of them still without mounts and serving on foot as wagon guards. The men were, in the main, young, husky, confident, and willing to do battle against Forrest.[10]

Wilson rode alongside the column on his dapple-gray gelding, "Sheridan." The young commander made an imposing picture in his trim blue uniform, topped by a heavy cavalry greatcoat, an ornate forage cap, and long black jackboots. He

General James Harrison Wilson and staff. Wilson in center of picture, in unbuttoned jacket with saber resting upon his leg and with right profile to camera. Picture taken in 1864. COURTESY LIBRARY OF CONGRESS.

was of medium height, but looked tall and robust in the saddle. His face—dark, probing eyes, slightly pinched jaws, and a tight, thin mouth, fringed by an imperial mustache—was

★★★★★★★★★★★★★★★★★★★★★★★

10. Elbridge Colby, "Wilson's Cavalry Campaign of 1865," *Journal of the American Military History Foundation*, 2 (Winter 1938): 208-9.

stern and businesslike, but neither cold nor harsh. He looked enormously proud as he took his position in the vanguard, calling to mind a description one of his staff members had bestowed upon him: "our cavalry Mural—Wilson."[11]

Bugles began to call, and the immense blue line started forward on what would prove to be a full-scale campaign rather than a typical cavalry raid. Wilson had no intention of launching a limited strike against objectives such as communication lines, avoiding battle as much as possible so he might quickly return to his starting point. He was aiming to destroy the military potential of whole states by surmounting all manner of defensive works and overpowering every defender who crossed his path. He would continue his journey so long as any objective of strategic importance remained before him.

As he rode off on this chill March morning, several other Federal forces on distant fronts were moving against their enemy. In Virginia, Grant had begun maneuvering anew to pry the Confederates out of the besieged city of Petersburg and toward final defeat; in the Carolinas, Sherman was rolling northward with unlimited energy; in the Deep South, General Canby was driving toward the Gulf Coast; and in Florida, Tennessee, and other theaters of action Union forces were backing their weary opponents into their final corner.

2

A Federal officer always remembered that morning of March 22: "Never can I forget the brilliant scene, as regiment after regiment filed gayly out of camp, decked in all the paraphernalia of war, with gleaming arms, and guidons given to the wanton breeze. Stirring bugle songs woke the slumbering echoes of the woods; cheer upon cheer went up from joyful lips. . . ." He added that his comrades, like Cortez's conquistadores, "burned their ships behind them when they left . . . staking all upon success."[12]

The expedition commenced in a manner that seemed to indicate that success would follow in due course. The corps

★★★★★★★★★★★★★★★★★★★★★★★

11. Lytle, *Bedford Forrest and His Critter Company*, p. 373.

12. Lewis M. Hosea, "The Campaign of Selma," *Sketches of War History, 1861-1865: Papers Read Before the Ohio M. O. L. L. U. S.*, 1 (1888): 85-86.

moved out in three divergent columns, for Wilson believed this would confuse enemy observers. His foresight proved keen, for when they discovered his movements, many of his opponents in northern Alabama supposed that Wilson's ultimate destination was Tuscaloosa; thus they kept well to the west of the Federal columns during the early stage of the raid. In reality, the Union commander considered Tuscaloosa a minor objective, planning to devote most of his energy to attacking cities farther to the east.[13]

Early progress was satisfactory; the invaders covered sixty miles during the first three days of their journey.[14] On the march, Upton's division took the most easterly route, via Russellville and Jasper to Saunders's Ferry, on the west fork of the Black Warrior River. At the same time, Long's division, for a time followed by McCook's, traveled via Cherokee Station and Frankfort to Russellville, and from there south to Bear Creek, at which point the two divisions parted company, meeting later at Jasper.[15]

While the Yankees surged forward, Bedford Forrest, now a lieutenant general charged with the defense of parts of three states, tried to fathom their intentions and block their routes of travel. He detected their coming on or about March 25 (though he had anticipated an invasion for several weeks), and decided to keep them busy in front while striking them hard in flank and rear. Thus, he began by doing what Wilson had predicted he would do: he sought to group together his scattered forces, including two divisions under Brigadier Generals Chalmers and William H. Jackson, a pair of brigades led by General Roddey and Colonel Edward Crossland, and various militia and guerrilla forces that were subject to his authority. In trying to mass his troops, Forrest rode eastward from his headquarters near the Mississippi border to alert Roddey, who was at Montevallo, about forty-five miles above Selma. At the same time, Chalmers's and Jackson's commands headed across country from parts east

★★★★★★★★★★★★★★★★★★★★★★★

13. Henry H. Belfield, "The Wilson Raid," *Military Essays and Recollections: Papers Read Before the Illinois M. O. L. L. U. S.*, 4 (1907): 509; "Wilson's Raid Through Alabama and Georgia," *Battles and Leaders of the Civil War*, 4: 759.

14. *New York Tribune*, May 5, 1865, p. 1.

15. *Official Records*, series I, vol. 49, pt. 1, p. 350; Thomas B. Van Horne, *History of the Army of the Cumberland: Its Organization, Campaigns, and Battles*, 2: 348.

to cover both Tuscaloosa and Selma. Hence a crucial race for the latter city had already developed; whichever force got there first might control the entire campaign.[16]

Wilson did not immediately learn of his opponents' pursuit, though he realized that Forrest would not be slow to organize one as soon as he heard the Yankees were on their way. Therefore Wilson pushed his men swiftly through the swamplands and forests of upper Alabama, over quagmires and around quicksand pits and across so many rivers and creeks that he later termed his march "the most remarkable naval expedition ever undertaken by cavalry."[17] In this, he undervalued Forrest's exploits against Johnsonville.

The Black Warrior River provided especial dangers for his command. Swollen by rain and made fast by a raging current, it became a grave for many soldiers in Long's and Upton's divisions, whose horses foundered in the stream, throwing them into the deep water. However, once Wilson's men crossed both forks of the river, they sensed they had passed a turning point. South of the stream, the land was not so rugged or so heavily timbered, and the roads were of greater consistency. So long as Forrest did not strike with unexpected force, the path to Selma lay clear.[18]

By March 29 the raiders had come almost 150 miles.[19] On that day they arrived in Elyton, a nondescript hamlet that one day would expand into the great iron and steel city of Birmingham. There Wilson determined to launch a detached mission calculated both to divert Forrest's attention and to lay waste to an important Confederate rail and manufacturing center. He selected a brigade from McCook's division, commanded by a skilled young Kentuckian, Brigadier General John T. Croxton, and sent it southwestward toward Tuscaloosa. Croxton was ordered to lead astray any Rebels who

★★★★★★★★★★★★★★★★★★★★★★★

16. Belfield, "The Wilson Raid," p. 511; Hosea, "The Campaign of Selma," pp. 87-88, 92.

17. Belfield, "The Wilson Raid," p. 509. At the start of the campaign, one of Wilson's troopers noted that "the whole country was covered with water, the banks of the streams were overflowing, and the conditions could not have been more unfavorable for undertaking such an expedition. . . ." W. L. Curry, comp., *Four Years in the Saddle: History of the First Regiment Ohio Volunteer Cavalry, Etc.*, p. 274.

18. Thomas Crofts, comp., *History of the Service of the Third Ohio Veteran Volunteer Cavalry, Etc.*, p. 188; Hosea, "The Campaign of Selma," p. 87.

19. *New York Tribune*, May 5, 1865, p. 1.

pursued him, to destroy public and military property in the city, plus portions of a railroad farther north, and to rejoin the main body of the command in or near Selma.

Shortly after the one thousand eight hundred troopers had ridden off, Wilson forged ahead to the Cahaba River. Next morning, nearing that stream, he received his first specific information about his enemy's whereabouts: his scouts reported that a portion of Chalmers's division was perhaps fifty miles to the south, moving eastward toward Selma. The Union commander reacted by stripping his command to the lightest marching order, abandoning his wagon train, and crossing the river in haste, hoping to unite his divisions at the town of Montevallo, "where I was sure we should have what all good cavalrymen want—an open country and a clear road to the front."[20]

Early on the afternoon of the 31st, the vanguard of the invasion force reached Montevallo and found Forrest, with Crossland's brigade and a small detachment from Roddey's, waiting just beyond the village. But Wilson was not worried, now that his first combat encounter was at hand, for the Rebel force numbered barely one thousand five hundred and the leading Federal division, Upton's, alone comprised twice as many soldiers.

Despite the odds, Forrest came forward along the Selma Road, inviting the Yankees to battle. Wilson and Upton watched the mounted Rebels advance until they had reached the town limits; then Upton's men, in columns of four, trotted out to meet them. The 5th Iowa led the attack, which split Roddey's force and shoved it steadily rearward. After a brief but vicious fight, the Confederates gave up an attempt to make a stand and retreated hastily in the direction of Selma. The Federals pursued them for a considerable distance, then bivouacked far below Montevallo, amazed by the ease with which they had won their first victory of the campaign.[21]

In high spirits, Wilson pushed on next morning, moving

★★★★★★★★★★★★★★★★★★★★★★

20. Wilson, *Under the Old Flag*, 2: 203-7.

21. *Official Records*, series I, vol. 49, pt. 1, pp. 350, 357-58. Wrote a Federal cavalryman about Selma: "Everybody saw that its capture was a great undertaking, but nobody thought of it as of a thing that *could not* be done. Every man seemed to feel that it *would* be done. A spirit of great cheerfulness and confidence was established throughout the army. . . ." William Forse Scott, *The Story of a ·Cavalry Regiment: The Career of the Fourth Iowa Veteran Volunteers*, p. 440.

directly southward toward the great manufacturing hub on the Alabama River. He knew that Selma was strongly fortified and supposed that he would have to contend with Forrest once again before reaching it, but the success at Montevallo had given him momentum, and his soldiers had begun to believe themselves unstoppable.

An incredibly fortunate event gave Wilson further confidence. Shortly before dawn on April 1 some of General Upton's outriders nabbed a Rebel courier carrying messages from General Jackson to Forrest. The dispatches revealed the positions and intended routes of each of Forrest's units, including those which had not yet caught up with Wilson's column. Apparently Forrest had concluded to link with Chalmers as soon as the latter came upon the scene, making a united effort at assaulting the Federals' front. In the meantime, Jackson's division was moving southeastward from the Tuscaloosa area toward the village of Centerville, aiming to strike Wilson from the rear. Of special importance, the papers also revealed that a small Rebel force held the Centerville bridge over the Cahaba River, across which both Chalmers and Jackson would have to ride to join their commander.[22]

Wilson had barely digested this remarkable intelligence when a courier on a foam-flecked horse rode up to present a dispatch from General Croxton, which had a bearing on the present situation. The leader of the detached brigade reported that he had struck the rear of Jackson's division north of Tuscaloosa the night before. Instead of moving at once against the city, Croxton had elected to follow Jackson's much larger command, intending to compel it to accept battle, thereby preventing it from menacing Wilson's main column.[23]

To seize the golden opportunity thus offered him, Wilson sent the rest of McCook's division twelve miles eastward to Centerville. There the detachment captured the vital bridge, then crossed it to look for Croxton's men and Jackson's Confederates. Finding neither in the immediate vicinity, the raiders recrossed the span and fulfilled their most important orders by setting it ablaze. Henceforth neither Jackson's nor

★★★★★★★★★★★★★★★★★★★★★★★★

22. Belfield, "The Wilson Raid," pp. 510-12; Wyeth, *Life of Forrest*, pp. 593, 595.

23. *Official Records*, series I, vol. 49, pt. 1, pp. 420, 425-26.

Chalmers's division would be able to join Forrest, and Wilson no longer had to fear for the safety of his flank or rear.[24]

That afternoon the main column reached Ebenezer Church, twenty-five miles north of Selma, and again met Roddey's and Crossland's men, plus militia under Brigadier General Daniel Adams. Without the aid of his two largest units, Forrest stood little chance of overpowering his opponents—on this day, finally, he found himself unable to surmount lopsided odds. When General Long launched a heavy dismounted attack, sparked by the 17th and 72nd Indiana Mounted Infantry regiments, Forrest's two thousand defenders reeled in retreat, then formed for a last-ditch stand. One of Forrest's biographers termed the fight "a test between the saber in the hands of as brave a lot of men as ever rode horses, and the six-shooter in the hands of experts that were just as desperately brave."

The Federals, brandishing the swords, nearly succeeded in trapping the Rebel leader. Alongside a creek, Forrest found himself hemmed in among several enemy horsemen, who inflicted saber wounds on him. By an almost superhuman effort, he fought his way to safety. Nevertheless, his men were put to full flight when a dismounted charge by Upton's division smashed a Confederate flank beyond repair. A wounded Forrest led his soldiers all the way to Selma before halting the retreat.[25]

The Federals did not pursue in force till the morning of the 2nd, when they resumed their trek toward their most important objective. As Wilson had noted, his troopers had begun to consider themselves invincible, capable of breaking through any roadblock their enemy could thrust into their path. Now they actually hungered to meet Forrest again.

As if Wilson had not already enjoyed good fortune aplenty, that afternoon he came upon an English civil engineer who had helped lay out the Selma defenses. Having fallen into the hands of evil-looking bluecoats, he was easily persuaded to sketch a map of the works Wilson was to encounter. Thus, by the time the column had reached the city, Wilson had formed a notion about where weak points lay

★★★★★★★★★★★★★★★★★★★★★★★★

24. Wyeth, *Life of Forrest,* pp. 595-96; Hosea, "The Campaign of Selma," p. 92.

25. *Official Records,* series I, vol. 49, pt. 1, pp. 351, 359, 473; Wyeth, *Life of Forrest,* pp. 599-602.

and had considered the best way in which to conduct an assault.

Selma was protected by a formidable conglomeration of abatis, palisades, sharpshooters' platforms, star-shaped forts, water-filled ditches, and gun emplacements stocked by a wide assortment of artillery, heavy and light. Its outer works extended in a half circle above the city for a distance of three miles, and where no defenses existed, the river and an almost impassable swampland protected the garrison. Within these barriers were some seven thousand Confederates, led by Forrest and a half-dozen other generals.

Once he arrived at the city limits, Wilson made a short reconnaissance and found that the Englishman's sketch was "surprisingly accurate," but acted not at all concerned by the array of fortifications. He then directed Long's division to assault the city to the right of the so-called Summerfield Road, while Upton's command was divided to strike in two areas—Upton himself, with a three hundred-man detachment, would penetrate the thick swamp on the extreme left, while the rest of the division charged the city down the Plantersville Road.[26]

Wilson wished to initiate the assault with a dismounted charge by 1,160 of Long's soldiers, reinforced by other portions of the division. The idea seemed suicidal to some of his men. An officer in the 7th Pennsylvania Cavalry, addicted to understatement, later remembered: "It was scarcely presumed, by officers or men, that General Wilson would order dismounted dragoons to make an assault upon such formidable earthworks."[27] Yet Wilson was certain of one fact: his cavalrymen could accomplish that task, if any soldiers could. He ordered Long and Upton to strike as soon as darkness fell.

But Long's men went forward before the designated time. Shortly after five P. M., Chalmers's long-delayed Confederates, making a futile attempt to fight their way inside the city, struck Long's rear, threatening to disorganize the attack. To extinguish the confusion, the division commander ordered an early assault, and his dismounted troopers rushed for-

★★★★★★★★★★★★★★★★★★★★★★

26. Wilson, *Under the Old Flag,* 2: 221-27; Crofts, *Third Ohio Cavalry,* pp. 190-91.

27. William B. Sipes, *The Seventh Pennsylvania Veteran Volunteer Cavalry; Its Record, Reminiscences and Roster,* p. 156.

ward, peppering the works in their front with their Spencer repeaters.[28] With incredible speed they surmounted every obstacle ahead of them, scurrying through the ditches, scaling the parapets, and scrambling inside the works to battle the defenders hand to hand. Aided by Upton's swampland attack against the Rebel right, Long's men pushed the Confederates steadily backward, and, as Wilson later reported, "in less than fifteen minutes, without ever stopping, wavering, or faltering, [they] had swept over the works and driven the rebels in confusion. . . ."[29]

During the height of the attack, General Long suffered a paralyzing head wound, both of his brigade leaders were severely injured, and three hundred other officers and men became casualties. But the survivors secured their sector of the line, then aided the 4th United States Cavalry in capturing Selma's inner works by a mounted charge. Finally the attackers moved inside the city, clearing all defenders from their path. By the time full darkness had settled, General Wilson—who had charged beside Long's column—rode inside the city, congratulating his troopers on their decisive victory. In taking an apparently impregnable city, they had killed, wounded, or captured two thousand seven hundred enemy soldiers, and had forced Bedford Forrest and other survivors to flee for their lives.[30]

Wilson underscored his pride in his soldiers' success in a grandiose address that he circulated among the corps a few days later: ". . . like an avalanche the intrepid soldiers of the Second Division swept over the defenses on the Summerfield road, while the Fourth Division carried those on the Plantersville road. The enemy, astonished and disheartened, broke from their strong works, and Selma was fairly won. . . . Soldiers, you have been called upon to perform long marches and endure privations, but your general relied upon and believed in your capacity and courage to undergo every task imposed upon you. . . . You have fully justified his opinions, and may justly regard yourselves invincible."[31]

★★★★★★★★★★★★★★★★★★★★★★★

28. *Official Records*, series I, vol. 49, pt. 1, p. 438.

29. Ibid., p. 360.

30. Wilson, *Under the Old Flag*, 2: 227-31; Belfield, "The Wilson Raid," pp. 514-15; Hosea, "The Campaign of Selma," pp. 98-101.

31. *Official Records*, series I, vol. 49, pt. 1, p. 393.

In closing his message, he added a statement that later military historians would fully endorse: "Your achievements will always be considered among the most remarkable in the annals of cavalry."

3

A fantastic cache of booty fell into the raiders' hands. Numerous goods—including thousands of horses, cavalry equipment, and rations—they instantly appropriated. The larger and more strategically valuable spoils they destroyed by fire. A few days after the city fell, the occupation troops burned the city arsenal, iron works, C. S. A. Naval Foundry, powder mill and magazine, nitre works, a huge machine shop, and other factories and warehouses covering an area of fifty acres.[32] The Federals did their job almost too well, for the fires threatened to spread to an unforeseen extent. One cavalryman watched as nearby buildings burned and exploded, "making the whole city a perfect pandemonium. Had it not been for the constant and heavy rain nothing could have prevented the whole city from burning up. This frightened the citizens nearly to death. . . ."[33]

The raiders remained in the captured city for eight days, rounding up enemy stragglers and seeking out Forrest's escapees, as well as resting and refitting. During that time Wilson scoured the vicinity for information that would indicate the progress made by Federal troops in other theaters of combat. But local communication lines had been damaged; he remained ignorant of Grant's recent breakthrough at Petersburg. By now Lee's Army of Northern Virginia was on its final, brief retreat, and the surrender at Appomattox was near. With the end of the war close at hand, Wilson could have remained in Selma, his work done.

However, without orders to cease campaigning, he made plans to leave the city and resume his destructive efforts. Having convinced himself that General Canby did not require his assistance to take Mobile, he dismissed Grant's earlier suggestion that he move in that direction, and decided to

★★★★★★★★★★★★★★★★★★★★★

32. Wilson, *Under the Old Flag* 2, pp. 235-36.

33. McGee and Jewell, *Seventy-Second Indiana Infantry*, p. 565.

push eastward toward the Carolinas via Montgomery and Columbus, two of the few manufacturing citadels remaining to the Confederacy. There he hoped to extend the run of success that had accompanied his every effort thus far.

After a brief but informative flag-of-truce conference with Bedford Forrest—during which the latter remarked, "Well, general, you have beaten me badly"—Wilson surveyed the construction of an enormous pontoon bridge upon which he planned to cross the Alabama. The Federal leader, who had survived some of the fiercest combat in both the eastern and western theaters, barely escaped being crushed between floating debris when the partially completed bridge suddenly collapsed as he stood upon it. The span was quickly repaired, however, and on April 10 the entire command trotted across to the south shore.[34]

The march toward Montgomery, first capital of the Confederacy, posed few difficulties, for the raiders met only token opposition from some of Forrest's cavalrymen, who appeared, at intervals, in advance of the column. Forrest himself, nursing the wounds he had received at Ebenezer Church and aware that he could no longer curtail Wilson's progress, had remained behind with the main portion of his command.

On the morning of the 12th the Federals trotted into Montgomery, stirring up little fuss. Local officials quickly surrendered the city to the advance guard, McCook's division (which, less Croxton's brigade, had rejoined Wilson's main force in Selma following the great battle). Residents turned out in great number to stare at the invaders, but none sought to create trouble. Wilson supposed that they sensed the approach of war's end and were resigned to defeat.

In Montgomery, Wilson heard rumors that Petersburg and Richmond had fallen and that the Confederate States' Government had disintegrated. But since no details were available, he felt obliged to continue east. After destroying warehouses, factories, large quantities of miscellaneous supplies, and a fleet of steamboats on the Coosa River, he marched his men out of the city on the 14th.[35] Two days later, after an uneventful crosscountry jaunt, his column ap-

★★★★★★★★★★★★★★★★★★★★★★★★

34. Wilson, *Under the Old Flag*, 2: 237-46.

35. Ibid., pp. 249-55.

proached the west bank of the Chattahoochee River, directly across from the city of Columbus, Georgia, whose factories and shops furnished all manner of matériel to the Confederate armies.

On this Easter Sunday morning, April 16, Upton's division, led by the 1st Ohio Cavalry, trotted toward three bridges that gave access to Columbus. To get that far the Federals had to brave rifle fire from sharpshooters atop hills near the hamlet of Girard, on the near bank. Finally the Ohioans reached the lowermost bridge, only to find it unplanked and about to be set afire by the enemy. The raiders watched in frustration as the bridge went up in flames, then re-formed when Upton gave his attention to a long foot bridge which stood farther upriver.[36]

It took most of the day for Wilson to form Upton's people for further work. After an artillery bombardment had softened the extensive Confederate lines guarding the bridge, Upton's men deployed for an attack in accumulating darkness. The division commander turned skeptical about success during a night assault, until Wilson reminded him of the evening victory at Selma. Upton then nodded: "By jingo, I'll do it; and I'll sweep everything before me!"[37]

His 3rd Iowa led the attack, its men yelling and blazing away with their carbines as they charged afoot against the foremost Rebel redoubt. Capturing the works after a short struggle, the Iowans charged farther along the road toward the bridge, splitting up to simultaneously strike forts and entrenchments on both sides of the trail. In the midst of the fighting, a small portion of the mounted 10th Missouri galloped down the road under the stars, rode through a small gap in the enemy lines, and managed to seize the vital bridge, capturing its guard force. Only when larger Confederate forces began to close in did the small detachment race back to its starting point.

Back at the main Rebel line, other Federal contingents had rushed up to exploit the gains made by the 3rd Iowa. Smashing ahead with implacable verve, the raiders forced their opponents to throw down their weapons. With no time to gather prisoners, the captors raced past the stunned Confed-

★★★★★★★★★★★★★★★★★★★★★★★

36. Colby, "Wilson's Cavalry Campaign of 1865," pp. 214-16.

37. Wilson, *Under the Old Flag*, 2: 259-60.

erates and took a bridge redoubt defended by 250 men and ten cannon. At that point, many of the attackers shouted to their comrades: "Go for the bridge! Waste no time with prisoners!" Accelerating their pace, they rushed across the span so closely on the heels of the defenders that the Confederates had no time to set fire to the structure. Units from the 4th Iowa, first mounted regiment to cross, clattered through the city streets, bringing down fugitives by firing from the saddle at powder flashes from Rebel rifles. Darkness alone prevented the inflicting of many casualties on both sides.

By ten P. M. Columbus, with thirty-odd guns and about one thousand five hundred prisoners, had fallen to Wilson's soldiers. Most of the defenders who had escaped the city fled eastward in the direction of Macon. They included Major General Howell Cobb, who in antebellum years had been one of Georgia's most vocal secessionists.

As in Selma and Montgomery, Wilson thoroughly destroyed the city's military value. Under his direction, the troopers wrecked the naval yard, the arsenal, foundry, armory, a sword and pistol factory, accoutrement shops, a paper mill, four cotton warehouses, the remaining river bridges, fifteen locomotives, two hundred railway cars, and a recently outfitted iron-clad ram.[38]

While Upton maneuvered about Columbus, a detachment from the raiding column—Colonel Oscar H. La Grange's brigade of McCook's division—had been attacking another important objective, about twenty-five miles to the north. During the afternoon, La Grange's men charged against three sides of Fort Tyler, a square earthwork on the east bank of the Chattahoochee which guarded the adjacent city of West Point, Georgia. After fierce fighting the brigade captured the 250-man garrison, leaving dozens of other Confederates dead and wounded. Afterward the attackers charged into West Point, secured the city, dispersed some Confederate horsemen who dared offer resistance, and put still more factories and supply houses to the torch.[39]

From that point, the road leading eastward to Macon seemed free of major obstacles. On the morning of the 17th

★★★★★★★★★★★★★★★★★★★★★★

38. *Official Records*, series I, vol. 49, pt. 1, pp. 474-75; Colby, "Wilson's Cavalry Campaign of 1865," pp. 218-21.

39. *Official Records*, series I, vol. 49, pt. 1, pp. 428-29.

Wilson's triumphant soldiers crossed the Chattahoochee near both Columbus and West Point, and resumed their march toward the Atlantic coast. Success had begun to snowball for them, and it came as no surprise to Wilson when he learned that the advance guard of the lower column had captured and secured the important Double Bridges over the Flint River, about fifty miles beyond Columbus. To do so, troopers from Colonel Robert Minty's brigade made a long forced march to the span, then covered the length of the bridge in a furious, saber-slashing charge, chasing Confederate guards into nearby woods.[40]

The enemy made another futile effort to halt the invaders on the afternoon of April 20. When the advance regiment in the lower column, the 17th Indiana Mounted Infantry, reached Tobesofkee Creek, fifteen miles from Macon, it found three hundred Rebels in position behind barricades along the stream. Even before the Federals could reach the bridge over the creek, defenders on the far shore began to set it afire with torches. Stymied for only a minute, the regimental commander dismounted his men and led them in a dash, through the flames, upon the stringpieces of the bridge. Once they had reached the other shore, the Federals attacked the entrenchments, gouging the flabbergasted Rebels from their cover and sending them into headlong flight. Wilson noted that "this was the final stand of the Confederates and, as though they realized its futility, they threw down their arms and blanket rolls and fled, mounted and on foot, as rapidly as possible. . . ."[41]

Wilson's men, despite their bountiful supply of self-confidence, stared in awe at their own accomplishment. If even burning bridges and strategically positioned sharpshooters could not stop them, they enjoyed absolute freedom to range as widely through Georgia as they pleased, wreaking devastation wherever they chose. It is conceivable that not even Sherman, on his famous march, enjoyed such liberty of movement or made his presence felt with such dramatic power.

The 17th Indiana continued onward with unchecked progress, leading the column. The regiment met no other Con-

★★★★★★★★★★★★★★★★★★★★★★★

40. Ibid., p. 442.

41. Ibid., pp. 443, 457-58; Wilson, *Under the Old Flag*, 2: 276.

federates till it drew up a few miles from Macon, where it was met by a flag-of-truce party headed by Confederate Brigadier General Fleix H. Robertson. Robertson was carrying a message from Howell Cobb, now in chief command in Macon, and asked that it be sent down the column to the Federal leader.

It took some time for Wilson to receive the communiqué. When at six P. M. it was finally in his hands, he discovered that it contained a telegram informing General Cobb that Sherman and his Rebel opponents had entered into a truce pending the surrender of Confederate forces in North Carolina. Obviously, Cobb expected Wilson to respond by forbidding his soldiers to enter Macon.

By now, however, this could not be prevented, for the Federal advance guard, suspecting trickery on the part of Robertson's truce party, had already charged into the city. By doing so they foiled Rebel plans to destroy bridges that commanded the approaches to Macon. All Wilson could do was to follow with his main force; he rode inside the captured city shortly after full darkness had come, and found that his men had thoroughly secured it, having locked the garrison troops in the local stockade.

Soon the brevet major general met an angry Howell Cobb, who accused him of violating orders to obey an armistice. When the Confederate leader had calmed down Wilson heard that not only Sherman's adversaries but also Lee's Army of Northern Virginia had laid down its arms.[42]

Although the news quickly spread, sending his soldiers into great glee, Wilson was not entirely certain that the war was at an end. In a sense, he probably did not want to believe the report, for, if true, it meant that his soldiers had been stopped short of their ultimate goal—Virginia.

Finding that some local communication lines extended into areas where Sherman's army had recently been stationed, Wilson dashed off telegrams seeking confirmation or denial of the truce report. In the meantime he kept his troopers in and about Macon, much to the displeasure of the citizenry. Early the following evening, however, orders came through from Sherman that the raiders should "desist from further acts of war and devastation."[43]

★★★★★★★★★★★★★★★★★★★★★★

42. Wilson, *Under the Old Flag*, 2: 276-81.

43. Ibid., pp. 283-84.

And so, almost two weeks after Lee had met Grant at Appomattox Court House, the last ride was finally over for James Harrison Wilson.

4

On April 29, General Croxton's prodigal command arrived in Macon, its commander brimming over with eagerness to tell the story of his adventures during his month-long mission. Wilson was amazed to learn that the detached brigade had covered 653 miles, marching and countermarching over rugged terrain, capturing enemy cities, destroying railroad track and factories, defeating small Confederate forces and eluding larger ones. In addition to spreading destruction across a wide strip of western Alabama and eastern Georgia and capturing three hundred prisoners,[44] Croxton had made a crucial contribution to the success of the entire expedition by engaging Jackson's cavalry division long enough to permit the destruction of the Centerville bridge, a feat that made Forrest's defeat inevitable.

Adding Croxton's achievements to the accomplishments of the main body of his raiding command, Wilson totaled up the extent of his damage to the Deep South. The statistics were staggering. In a bit more than a month's time, the raiders had marched an average of 525 miles, capturing five fortified cities, almost seven thousand prisoners (another sixty thousand being paroled and released), thirty-odd stands of colors, 320 cannon, and one hundred thousand stands of small arms. Items that had fallen prey to torch, blasting powder, or crowbar included seven iron works, seven foundries, seven machine shops, five colleries, two rolling-mills, twelve massive factories, four nitre works, one military academy, three C. S. A. arsenals, one powder magazine, one naval armory, five steamboats, two gunboats, thirty-five locomotives, 565 cars, three railroad spans and numerous footbridges, plus 235,000 bales of cotton, and immense quantities of quartermaster's, commissary, and medical stores. In return, Wilson's command had lost approximately sixty offi-

★★★★★★★★★★★★★★★★★★★★★★★

44. *Official Records*, series, I, vol. 49, pt. 1, p. 424.

cers and seven hundred enlisted men killed, wounded, or missing.[45]

Wilson's expedition was destined for a place in history as the most tactically successful of the war. But since it had come long after the close of the conflict's pivotal fighting, it made few strategic contributions to the Federal war effort. Rather, the campaign constituted a vast and tragic wastage of Southern resources, which might have been spared had Wilson been able to open communication with his superior officers even a few days sooner.

Even so, no other mounted invasion force even came close to amassing such a record of success. Grierson's troopers staged the war's most strategically effective expedition, but triumphed primarily because they managed to avoid encounters with large enemy forces. By contrast, Wilson's soldiers not only surmounted heavy opposition from infantry, artillery, and cavalry but also conquered cities and towns defended by almost every conceivable form of protection. By fighting his twenty-three regiments dismounted as often as mounted, making the most of each method's advantages, the young cavalry leader had rewritten the books that set standards for cavalry deployment. In effect, he had led the first and only self-sustained mounted campaign of the Civil War.

★★★★★★★★★★★★★★★★★★★★★★

45. Ibid., p. 369.

BIBLIOGRAPHY

I. Newspapers and Periodicals
Daily Richmond Enquirer
Daily Richmond Examiner
Frank Leslie's Illustrated Magazine
Harper's Weekly
New York Times
New York Tribune
Philadelphia Daily Evening Bulletin

II. Articles
Abbot, Haviland H. "General John D. Imboden." *West Virginia History*, vol. 21, no. 2 (January 1960), pp. 88-122.

Allen, Theodore F. "Six Hundred Miles of Fried Chicken." *Journal of the U. S. Cavalry Association* 12 (1899): 162-75.

Athearn, Robert G., ed. "The Civil War Diary of John Wilson Phillips." *The Virginia Magazine of History and Biography*, vol. 62, no. 1 (January 1954), pp. 95-123.

Beale, R. L. T. "Part Taken by the Ninth Virginia Cavalry in Repelling the Dahlgren Raid." *Southern Historical Society Papers* (hereafter cited as *S. H. S. P.*) 3 (1877): 219-21.

Belfield, Henry H. "The Wilson Raid." *Military Essays and Recollections: Papers Read Before the Illinois Commandery, Military Order of the Loyal Legion of the United States* (hereafter cited as *M. O. L. L. U. S.*), vol. 4. Chicago: Cozzens & Beaton Co., 1907, pp. 503-21.

Bell, Harry, trans. "Cavalry Raids and the Lessons They Teach Us." *Journal of the U. S. Cavalry Association* 19 (1908-9): 142-52.

Boehm, Robert B. "The Jones-Imboden Raid Through West Virginia." *Civil War Times Illustrated*, vol. 3, no. 2 (May 1964), pp. 14-21.

Brown, A. F. "Van Dorn's Operations in Northern Mississippi —Recollections of a Cavalryman." *S. H. S. P.* 6 (1878): 151-61.

Brown, Campbell H. "Forrest's Johnsonville Raid." *Civil War Times Illustrated*, vol. 4, no. 3 (June 1965), pp. 48-57.

Brown, D. Alexander. "Grierson's Raid." *Civil War Times Illustrated*, vol. 3, no. 9 (January 1965), pp. 4-11, 30-32.

Burt, Jesse C. "Fighting With 'Little Joe' Wheeler." *Civil War Times*, vol. 2, no. 2 (May 1960), pp. 18-19.

Carpenter, Louis H. "Sheridan's Expedition Around Richmond, May 9-25, 1864." *Journal of the U. S. Cavalry Association* 1 (1888): 300-24.

Castel, Albert. "Earl Van Dorn—A Personality Profile." *Civil War Times Illustrated*, vol. 6, no. 1 (April 1967), pp. 38-42.

Chaffee, Adna R. "James Harrison Wilson, Cavalryman." *Cavalry Journal* 34 (1925): 271-89.

Colby, Elbridge. "Wilson's Cavalry Campaign of 1865." *Journal of the American Military History Foundation*, vol. 2, no. 4 (Winter 1938), pp. 204-21.

"Colonel Streight's Expedition: Journal of H. Breidenthal, Sergeant Co. A, Third Ohio Vol. Infantry." *The Rebellion Record: A Diary of American Events*, ed. by Frank Moore. New York: G. P. Putnam & Henry Holt, 1864 (Supplementary Volume no. 1—pp. 337-50).

Cook, James F. "The 1863 Raid of Abel D. Streight: Why It Failed." *The Alabama Review*, vol. 22, no. 4 (October 1969), pp. 254-69.

Crouch, Richard G. "The Dahlgren Raid." *S. H. S. P.* 34 (1906): 179-90.

Curry, William L. "Raid of the Confederate Cavalry Through Central Tennessee." *Journal of the U. S. Cavalry Association* 19 (1908-9): 815-35.

Davis, George B. "The Cavalry Operations in Middle Tennessee In October, 1863." *Journal of the U. S. Cavalry Association* 24 (1913-14): 879-91.

———. "The Richmond Raid of 1864." *Journal of the U. S. Cavalry Association* 24 (1913-14): 707-22.

———. "The Stoneman Raid." *Journal of the U. S. Cavalry Association* 24 (1913-14): 533-52.

Day, C. R. "Cavalry Raids—Their Value and How Made." *Journal of the U. S. Cavalry Association* 23 (1912-13): 227-38.

Deupree, J. G. "The Capture of Holly Springs, Mississippi, Dec. 20, 1862." *Publications of the Mississippi Historical Society* 4 (1901): 49-61.

Duke, Basil W. "Morgan's Indiana and Ohio Raid." *The Annals of the War, Written by Leading Participants, North and South* (hereafter cited as *Annals of the War*). Philadelphia: The Times Publishing Co., 1879, pp. 241-56.

Gilpin, E. N. "The Last Campaign—A Cavalryman's Journal." *Journal of the U. S. Cavalry Association* 18 (1908): 617-75.

Harris, Moses. "The Union Cavalry." *War Papers: Read Before the Wisconsin M. O. L. L. U. S.,* vol. 1. Milwaukee: Burdick, Armitage & Allen, 1891, pp. 340-73.

Hassler, William W. "The Battle of Yellow Tavern." *Civil War Times Illustrated,* vol. 5, no. 7 (November 1966), pp. 5-11, 46-48.

Hay, W. H. "Cavalry Raids." *Journal of the U. S. Cavalry Association* 4 (1891): 362-76.

Hosea, Lewis M. "The Campaign of Selma." *Sketches of War History, 1861-1865: Papers Read Before the Ohio M. O. L. L. U. S.,* vol. 1. Cincinatti: Robert Clarke & Co., 1888, pp. 77-106.

Isham, Asa B. "Through the Wilderness to Richmond." *Sketches of War History, 1861-1865: Papers Read Before the Ohio M. O. L. L. U. S.,* 1. 198-217.

James, G. Watson. "Dahlgren's Raid." *S. H. S. P.* 39 (1914): 63-72.

Jones, J. William, comp. "Kilpatrick-Dahlgren Raid Against Richmond." *S. H. S. P.* 13 (1885): 515-60.

Jones, Virgil Carrington. "The Story of the Kilpatrick-Dahlgren Raid." *Civil War Times Illustrated,* vol. 4, no. 1 (April 1965), pp. 12-21.

Keenan, Jerry. "Wilson's Selma Raid." *Civil War Times Illustrated,* vol. 1, no. 9 (January 1963), pp. 37-44.

Keller, Allan. "Morgan's Raid Across the Ohio." *Civil War Times Illustrated,* vol. 2, no. 3 (June 1963), pp. 6-9, 34-37.

King, G. Wayne. "General Judson Kilpatrick." *New Jersey History,* vol. 91, no. 1 (Spring 1973), pp. 35-52.

Longacre, Edward G. "Judson Kilpatrick." *Civil War Times Illustrated,* vol. 10, no. 1 (April 1971), pp. 24-33.

———. "Streight's Raid: 'All Is Fair in Love and War.' " *Civil War Times Illustrated,* vol. 8, no. 3 (June 1969), pp. 32-40.

MacConnell, Charles C. "Service With Sheridan." *War Papers: Read Before the Wisconsin M. O. L. L. U. S.,* 1. 285-93.

M'Gowan, J. E. "Morgan's Indiana and Ohio Raid." *Annals of the War.* Pp. 750-69.

McNeil, John A. "The Imboden Raid and Its Effects." *S. H. S. P.* 34 (1906): 294-312.

Maury, Dabney H. "Recollections of General Earl Van Dorn." *S. H. S. P.* 19 (1891): 191-98.

Miller, Samuel H. "Yellow Tavern." *Civil War History,* vol. 2, no. 1 (March 1956), pp. 57-81.

Moore, James O. "Custer's Raid Into Albermarle County: The Skirmish at Rio Hill, February 29, 1864." *The Virginia Magazine of History and Biography,* vol. 79, no. 3 (July 1971), pp. 338-48.

"Morgan's Ohio Raid." *Battles And Leaders of the Civil War,* vol. 3, ed. by Robert U. Johnson and C. C. Buel (hereafter cited as *B & L*). New York: The Century Co., 1884-88, pp. 634-35.

Morton, John W. "Raid of Forrest's Cavalry on the Tennessee River in 1864." *S. H. S. P.* 10 (1882): 261-68.

Nye, Wilbur S. "How Stuart Recrossed the Potomac." *Civil War Times Illustrated,* vol. 4, no. 9 (January 1966), pp. 45-48.

Pond, George E. "Kilpatrick's and Dahlgren's Raid to Richmond." *B & L* 4: 95-96.

Price, Channing. "Stuart's Chambersburg Raid: An Eyewitness Account." *Civil War Times Illustrated,* vol. 4, no. 9 (January 1966), pp. 8-15, 42-44.

Quisenberry, A. C. "Morgan's Men In Ohio." *S. H. S. P.* 39 (1914): 91-99.

Ray, Frederic. "Chambersburg, Pa.—War Came Three Times to This Northern Town." *Civil War Times,* vol. 2, no. 2 (May 1960), pp. 12-14.

Rhodes, Charles D. "Federal Raids and Expeditions in the East." *The Photographic History of the Civil War,* vol. 4, ed. by Francis Trevelyan Miller. New York: The Review of Reviews Co., 1911, pp. 120-28.

————. "Federal Raids and Expeditions in the West." *The Photographic History of the Civil War* 4: 132-40.

Rockwell, Alphonso D. "With Sheridan's Cavalry." *Personal Recollections of the War of the Rebellion: Addresses Delivered Before the New York M. O. L. L. U. S.* Third Series. New York: G. P. Putnam's Sons, 1907, pp. 228-39.

Rodenbough, Theodore F. "Sheridan's Richmond Raid." *B & L* 4: 188-93.

Speed, Thomas. "Cavalry Operations in the West Under Rosecrans and Sherman." *B & L* 4: 413-16.

Still, John S. "Blitzkrieg, 1863: Morgan's Raid and Rout." *Civil War History* vol. 3, no. 3 (September 1957), pp. 291–306.

"Stoneman's Raid in the Chancellorsville Campaign." *B & L* 3: 152-53.

Stuart, Meriwether. "Colonel Ulric Dahlgren And Richmond's Union Underground." *The Virginia Magazine of History and Biography,* vol. 72, no. 2 (April 1964), pp. 152-204.

Summers, Festus P. "The Baltimore and Ohio—First in War." *Civil War History,* vol. 7, no. 3 (September 1961), pp. 239-54.

Turner, Charles W. "The Richmond, Fredricksburg and Potomac, 1861-1865." *Civil War History,* vol. 7, no. 3 (September 1961), pp. 255-63.

Weaver, H. C. "Morgan's Raid in Kentucky, Indiana, and Ohio." *Sketches of War History, 1861-1865: Papers Read Before the Ohio M. O. L. L. U. S.* 4: 278-314.

Weller, Jac. "The Logistics of Nathan Bedford Forrest." *Military Af-*

fairs, vol. 17, no. 4 (Winter 1953), pp. 161-69.

"Wilson's Raid Through Alabama and Georgia." *B & L* 4: 759-61.

Woodward, S. L. "Grierson's Raid, April 17th to May 2d, 1863." *Journal of the U. S. Cavalry Association* 14 (1903-4): 685-710, and 15 (1904-5): 94-123.

Wyeth, John Allan. "The Destruction of Rosecrans' Great Wagon-Train." *The Photographic History of the Civil War* 4: 158-64.

III. Books

Agassiz, George R., ed. *Meade's Headquarters, 1863-1865: Letters of Colonel Theodore Lyman from The Wilderness to Appomattox.* Boston: The Atlantic Monthly Press, 1922.

Agee, Rucker. "Forrest-Streight Campaign of 1863." Prepared for the 100th Meeting of the Civil War Round Table of Milwaukee, Wisconsin, June 1958.

Anders, Curt. *Fighting Confederates.* New York: G. P. Putnam's Sons, 1968.

Beale, George W. *A Lieutenant of Cavalry in Lee's Army.* Boston: Gorham Press, 1918.

Beale, Howard K., ed. *Diary of Gideon Welles.* Vol. 1. New York: W. W. Norton & Co., Inc., 1960.

Beale, R. L. T. *History of the Ninth Virginia Cavalry, in the War Between the States.* Richmond: B. F. Johnson Publishing Co., 1899.

Bearss, Edwin C. *Decision in Mississippi: Mississippi's Important Role in the War Between the States.* Jackson: Mississippi Commission on the War Between the States, 1962.

Bigelow, John, Jr. *The Campaign of Chancellorsville: A Strategic and Tactical Study.* New Haven: Yale University Press, 1910.

Black, Robert C., III. *The Railroads of the Confederacy.* Chapel Hill: The University of North Carolina Press, 1952.

Blackford, W. W. *War Years with Jeb Stuart.* New York: Charles Scribner's Sons, 1945.

Boatner, Mark M., III. *The Civil War Dictionary.* New York: David McKay Co., Inc., 1959.

Boudrye, Louis N. *Historic Records of the Fifth New York Cavalry.* Albany: S. R. Gray, 1865.

Brackett, Albert G. *History of the United States Cavalry, From the Formation of the Federal Government to the 1st of June, 1863.* New York: Harper & Brothers, 1865.

Brooke Rawle, William, ed. *History of the Third Pennsylvania Cavalry.* Philadelphia: Franklin Printing Co., 1905.

Brooks, U. R. *Butler and His Cavalry in the War of Secession, 1861-1865.* Columbia, South Carolina: The State Co., 1909.

Brown, D. Alexander. *The Bold Cavaliers: Morgan's 2nd Kentucky Cavalry Raiders.* Philadelphia: J. B. Lippincott Co., 1959.

———. *Grierson's Raid: A Cavalry Adventure of the Civil War.* Urbana,

Illinois: University of Illinois Press, 1954.

Castleman, John B. *Active Service*. Louisville, Kentucky: Courier-Journal Job Printing Co., 1917.

Catton, Bruce. *Glory Road: The Bloody Route from Fredricksburg to Gettysburg*. Garden City, New York: Doubleday & Co., Inc., 1952.

———. *Grant Takes Command*. Boston: Little, Brown & Co., 1969.

———. *A Stillness at Appomattox*. Garden City, New York: Doubleday & Co., Inc., 1953.

Cavalry Tactics. Philadelphia: J. B. Lippincott & Co., 1862.

Cheney, Newel. *History of the Ninth Regiment, New York Volunteer Cavalry, War of 1861 to 1865*. Jamestown and Poland Center, New York: Martin Merz & Son, 1901.

Cist, Henry M. *The Army of the Cumberland*. New York: Charles Scribner's Sons, 1882.

Connelly, Thomas L. *Autumn of Glory: The Army of Tennessee, 1862-1865*. Baton Rouge: Louisiana State University Press, 1971.

Cooke, John Esten. *Wearing of the Gray*. Edited by Philip Van Doren Stern. Bloomington: Indiana University Press, 1959.

Cooke, Philip St. George. *Cavalry Tactics or Regulations for the Instruction, Formations, and Movements of the Cavalry of the Army and Volunteers of the United States*. Washington, D. C.: Government Printing Office, 1862.

Crofts, Thomas, comp. *History of the Service of the Third Ohio Veteran Volunteer Cavalry in the War for the Preservation of the Union from 1861-1865*. Toledo and Columbus: The Stoneman Press, 1910.

Crowninshield, Benjamin W., and Gleason, D. H. L. *A History of the First Regiment of Massachusetts Cavalry Volunteers*. Boston: Houghton, Mifflin & Co., 1891.

Curry, W. L., comp. *Four Years in the Saddle: History of the First Regiment Ohio Volunteer Cavalry, War of the Rebellion—1861-1865*. Columbus: Champlin Printing Co., 1898.

Dahlgren, J. A. *Memoir of Ulric Dahlgren*. Philadelphia: J. B. Lippincott & Co., 1872.

Davenport, Edward A., ed. *History of the Ninth Regiment Illinois Cavalry Volunteers*. Chicago: Donohue & Henneberry, 1888.

Davies, Henry E. *General Sheridan*. New York: D. Appleton & Co., 1899.

Davis, Burke. *Jeb Stuart, The Last Cavalier*. New York: Rinehart & Co., Inc., 1957.

Denison, Frederic. *Sabres and Spurs: The First Regiment Rhode Island Cavalry in the Civil War, 1861-1865*. Central Falls, Rhode Island: E. L. Freeman & Co., 1876.

Dodson, William Carey, ed. *Campaigns of Wheeler and His Cavalry, 1862-1865*. Atlanta: Hudgins Publishing Co., 1899.

Doubleday, Abner. *Chancellorsville and Gettysburg*. New York:

Charles Scribner's Sons, 1882.

Downey, Fairfax. *Storming of the Gateway: Chattanooga, 1863.* New York: David McKay Co., Inc., 1960.

DuBose, John W. *General Joseph Wheeler and The Army of Tennessee.* New York: The Neale Publishing Co., 1912.

Duke, Basil W. *A History of Morgan's Cavalry.* Edited by Cecil F. Holland. Bloomington: Indiana University Press, 1960.

————. *Morgan's Cavalry.* New York: The Neale Publishing Co., 1906.

————. *Reminiscences of General Basil W. Duke, C. S. A.* Garden City, New York: Doubleday, Page & Co., 1911.

Dyer, John P. *"Fightin' Joe" Wheeler.* University, Louisiana: Louisiana State University Press, 1941.

Eggleston, George Cary. *A Rebel's Recollections.* New York: G. P. Putnam's Sons, 1887.

Farrar, Samuel Clarke, comp. *The Twenty-Second Pennsylvania Cavalry and the Ringgold Battalion, 1861-1865.* Pittsburgh: The New Werner Co., 1911.

Foote, Shelby. *The Civil War: A Narrative.* Vol. 2. New York: Random House, 1963.

Ford, Worthington Chauncey, ed. *A Cycle of Adams Letters, 1861-1865.* Vol. 1. Boston: Houghton Mifflin Co., 1920.

Freeman, Douglas Southall. *Lee's Lieutenants: A Study in Command.* Vol. 2. New York: Charles Scribner's Sons, 1943.

Glazier, Willard. *Three Years in the Federal Cavalry.* New York: R. H. Ferguson & Co., 1873.

Gracey, S. L. *Annals of the Sixth Pennsylvania Cavalry.* Philadelphia: E. H. Butler & Co., 1868.

Grant, Ulysses S. *Personal Memoirs.* Vols. 1 and 2. New York: Charles L. Webster & Co., 1885-86.

Guild, George B. *A Brief Narrative of the Fourth Tennessee Cavalry Regiment, Wheeler's Corps, Army of Tennessee.* Nashville: pvt. pub., 1913.

Hagemann, E. R., ed. *Fighting Rebels and Redskins: Experiences in Army Life of Colonel George B. Sanford, 1861-1892.* Norman: University of Oklahoma Press, 1969.

Hall, Hillman A., Besley, W. B., and Wood, Gilbert G., comps. *History of the Sixth New York Cavalry.* Worcester, Massachusetts: The Blanchard Press, 1908.

Hancock, R. R. *Hancock's Diary, or a History of the Second Tennessee Confederate Cavalry.* Nashville: Brandon Printing Co., 1887.

Hard, Abner. *History of the Eighth Cavalry Regiment Illinois Volunteers.* Aurora, Illinois: pvt. pub., 1868.

Hartje, Robert G. *Van Dorn: The Life and Times of a Confederate General.* Nashville: Vanderbilt University Press, 1967.

Hartpence, William R. *History of the Fifty-First Indiana Veteran Volunteer Infantry.* Cincinatti: The Robert Clarke Co., 1894.

Henry, Robert Selph, ed. *As They Saw Forrest.* Jackson, Tennessee:

McCowat-Mercer Press, 1956.

―――. *"First With the Most" Forrest.* Indianapolis: The Bobbs-Merrill Co., 1944.

Hergesheimer, Joseph. *Sheridan: A Military Narrative.* Boston: Houghton, Mifflin Co., 1931.

―――. *Swords and Roses.* New York: Alfred A. Knopf, 1929.

History of the Eighteenth Regiment of Cavalry, Pennsylvania Volunteers. New York: Wynknoop-Hallenbeck-Crawford Co., 1909.

Hockersmith, L. D. *Morgan's Escape: A True History of the Raid of General Morgan and His Men Through Kentucky, Indiana and Ohio.* Madisonville, Kentucky: Glenn's Graphic Printing Co., 1903.

Holland, Cecil F. *Morgan and His Raiders.* New York: The Macmillan Co., 1943.

Hopkins, Luther W. *From Bull Run to Appomattox: A Boy's View.* Baltimore: Press of Fleet-McGinley Co., 1908.

Horn, Stanley F. *The Army of Tennessee: A Military History.* Indianapolis: The Bobbs-Merrill Co., 1941.

Humphreys, Andrew A. *The Virginia Campaign of '64 and '65: The Army of the Potomac and the Army of the James.* New York: Charles Scribner's Sons, 1883.

Isham, Asa B. *An Historical Sketch of the Seventh Regiment Michigan Volunteer Cavalry.* New York: Town Topics Publishing Co., 1893.

Johnston, Angus James, II. *Virginia Railroads in the Civil War.* Chapel Hill: University of North Carolina Press, 1961.

Jones, J. B. *A Rebel War Clerk's Diary.* Vol. 2. Philadelphia: J. B. Lippincott & Co., 1866.

Jones, Virgil Carrington. *Eight Hours Before Richmond.* New York: Henry Holt & Co., 1957.

Jordan, Thomas, and Pryor, J. P. *The Campaigns of Lieut.-Gen. N. B. Forrest and of Forrest's Cavalry.* New Orleans, Memphis, and New York: Blelock & Co., 1868.

Keller, Allan. *Morgan's Raid.* Indianapolis: The Bobbs-Merrill Co., 1961.

Kidd, J. H. *Personal Recollections of a Cavalryman with Custer's Michigan Cavalry Brigade in the Civil War.* Grand Rapids, Michigan: The Black Letter Press, 1969.

Kirk, Charles H., ed. *History of the Fifteenth Pennsylvania Volunteer Cavalry.* Philadelphia: pvt. pub., 1906.

Lee, William O., comp. *Personal and Historical Sketches . . . of the Seventh Regiment Michigan Volunteer Cavalry, 1861-1865.* Detroit: Ralston-Stroup Printing Co., 1904.

Lloyd, William P., comp. *History of the First Reg't Pennsylvania Reserve Cavalry.* Philadelphia: King & Baird, 1864.

Longacre, Edward G. *From Union Stars to Top Hat: A Biography of the Extraordinary General James Harrison Wilson.* Harrisburg, Pennsylvania: Stackpole Books, 1972.

Lytle, Andrew N. *Bedford Forrest and His Critter Company.* New York: G. P. Putnam's Sons, 1931.

McClellan, H. B. *I Rode with Jeb Stuart: The Life and Campaigns of Major General J. E. B. Stuart.* Edited by Burke Davis. Bloomington: Indiana University Press, 1958.

McGee, B. F., and Jewell, William R. *History of the Seventy-Second Indiana Volunteer Infantry of the Mounted Lightning Brigade.* LaFayette, Indiana: S. Vater & Co., 1882.

McKinney, Francis F. *Education in Violence: The Life of George H. Thomas and the History of the Army of the Cumberland.* Detroit: Wayne State University Press, 1961.

Mathes, J. Harvey. *General Forrest.* New York: D. Appleton & Co., 1902.

Merrill, James M. *Spurs to Glory: The Story of the United States Cavalry.* Chicago: Rand McNally & Co., 1966.

Merrill, Samuel H. *The Campaigns of the First Maine and First District of Columbia Cavalry.* Portland, Maine: Bailey & Noyes, 1866.

Miers, Earl Schenck. *The Web of Victory: Grant at Vicksburg.* New York: Alfred A. Knopf, 1955.

Milham, Charles G. *Gallant Pelham: American Extraordinary.* Washington, D. C.: Public Affairs Press, 1959.

Moore, Edward A. *The Story of a Cannoneer Under Stonewall Jackson.* Freeport, New York: Books for Libraries Press, 1971.

Moore, James. *Kilpatrick and Our Cavalry.* New York: W. J. Widdleton, 1865.

Mosgrove, George Dallas. *Kentucky Cavaliers in Dixie: Reminiscences of a Confederate Cavalryman.* Edited by Bell I. Wiley. Jackson, Tennessee: McCowat-Mercer Press, 1957.

Moyer, H. P., comp. *History of the Seventeenth Regiment, Pennsylvania Volunteer Cavalry.* Lebanon, Pennsylvania: Sowers Printing Co., 1911.

Myers, Franklin M. *The Comanches: A History of White's Battalion, Virginia Cavalry, Laurel Brigade, Hampton's Division, A. N. V., C. S. A.* Baltimore: Kelly, Piet & Co., 1871.

Neese, George M. *Three Years in the Confederate Horse Artillery.* New York: The Neale Publishing Co., 1911.

Newcomer, Christopher A. *Cole's Cavalry, or Three Years in the Saddle in the Shenandoah Valley.* Baltimore: Cushing & Co., 1895.

Norton, Henry. *Deeds of Daring, or History of the Eighth N. Y. Volunteer Cavalry.* Norwich, New York: Chenango Telegraph Printing House, 1889.

O'Connor, Richard. *Sheridan, the Inevitable.* Indianapolis: The Bobbs-Merrill Co., 1953.

Official Records of the Union and Confederate Navies in the War of the Rebellion. Series I, Vols. 9 and 26; Series II, Vol. 3. Washington, D. C.: Government Printing Office, 1894-1922.

Opie, John N. *A Rebel Cavalryman With Lee, Stuart, and Jackson.* Chicago: W. B. Conkey Co., 1899.

Paris, Comte De. *History of the Civil War in America.* Vol. 3. Philadelphia: Porter & Coates, 1883.

Pemberton, John C. *Pemberton: Defender of Vicksburg.* Chapel Hill: University of North Carolina Press, 1942.

Pickerill, W. N. *History of the Third Indiana Cavalry.* Indianapolis: Aetna Printing Co., 1906.

Pierce, Lyman B. *History of the Second Iowa Cavalry.* Burlington, Iowa: Hawk-Eye Steam Book & Job Print., 1865.

Preston, N. D. *History of the Tenth Regiment of Cavalry, New York State Volunteers.* New York: D. Appleton & Co., 1892.

Pyne, Henry R. *The History of the First New Jersey Cavalry.* Trenton: J. A. Beecher, 1871.

Rhodes, Charles D. *History of the Cavalry of the Army of the Potomac.* Kansas City, Missouri: Hudson-Kimberly Publishing Co., 1900.

Roach, Alva C. *The Prisoner of War, and How Treated: Containing A History of Colonel Streight's Expedition to the Rear of Bragg's Army, in the Spring of 1863.* Indianapolis: The Railroad City Publishing House, 1865.

Rowell, John W. *Yankee Cavalrymen: Through the Civil War with the Ninth Pennsylvania Cavalry.* Knoxville: University of Tennessee Press, 1971.

Scott, William Forse. *The Story of a Cavalry Regiment: The Career of the Fourth Iowa Veteran Volunteers.* New York: G. P. Putnam's Sons, 1893.

Sheridan, Philip H. *Personal Memoirs.* Vol. 1. New York: Charles L. Webster & Co., 1888.

Sipes, William B. *The Seventh Pennsylvania Veteran Volunteer Cavalry: Its Record, Reminiscences and Roster.* Pottsville, Pennsylvania: Miners' Journal Printing Co., 1905.

Sparks, David S., ed. *Inside Lincoln's Army: The Diary of Marsena Rudolph Patrick, Provost Marshal General, Army of the Potomac.* New York: Thomas Yoseloff, 1964.

Stackpole, Edward J. *Chancellorsville: Lee's Greatest Battle.* Harrisburg, Pennsylvania: The Stackpole Co., 1958.

Starr, Stephen Z. *Colonel Grenfell's Wars: The Life of a Soldier of Fortune.* Baton Rouge: Louisiana State University Press, 1971.

Stine, J. H. *History of the Army of the Potomac.* Washington, D. C.: Gibson Brothers, 1903.

Summers, Festus P. *The Baltimore And Ohio in the Civil War.* New York: G. P. Putnam's Sons, 1939.

Sunderland, Glenn W. *Lightning at Hoover's Gap: The Story of Wilder's Brigade.* New York: Thomas Yoseloff, 1969.

Surby, R. A. *Grierson Raids . . . Also the Life and Adventures of Chickasaw, the Scout.* Chicago: Rounds & James, 1865.

Swiggett, Howard. *The Rebel Raider: A Life of John Hunt Morgan.* Indianapolis: The Bobbs-Merrill Co., 1934.

Swinton, William. *Campaigns of the Army of the Potomac.* New York: C. B. Richardson, 1866.

Thomason, John W., Jr. *Jeb Stuart.* New York: Charles Scribner's Sons, 1930.

Tobie, Edward P. *History of the First Maine Cavalry, 1861–1865.* Boston: Emery & Hughes, 1887.

Turner, George E. *Victory Rode the Rails: The Strategic Place of the Railroads in the Civil War.* Indianapolis: The Bobbs-Merrill Co., Inc., 1953.

Van Horne, Thomas B. *History of the Army of the Cumberland: Its Organization, Campaigns, and Battles.* Vol. 2. Cincinatti: The Robert Clarke Co., 1875.

Von Borcke, Heros. *Memoirs of the Confederate War for Independence.* Vol. 1. New York: Peter Smith, 1938.

Warner, Ezra J. *Generals in Blue: Lives of the Union Commanders.* Baton Rouge: Louisiana State University Press, 1964.

———. *Generals in Gray: Lives of the Confederate Commanders.* Baton Rouge: Louisiana State University Press, 1959.

War of the Rebellion: A Compilation of the Official Records of the Union and Confederate Armies. Series I, Vols. 15, 17, 18, 21, 23, 24, 25, 30, 31, 33, 36, 39, 51, 52; Series II, Vols. 6, 7, 8; Series III, Vols. 3, 4; Series IV, Vol. 3. Washington, D. C.: Government Printing Office, 1880-1901.

Washington, Bushrod C., ed. *A History of the Laurel Brigade.* Baltimore: pvt. pub., 1907.

Weber, Thomas. *The Northern Railroads in the Civil War, 1861-1865.* Westport, Connecticut: Greenwood Press, 1970.

Wellman, Manly Wade. *Giant in Gray: A Biography of Wade Hampton of South Carolina.* New York: Charles Scribner's Sons, 1949.

Williams, T. Harry. *Hayes of the Twenty-Third: The Civil War Volunteer Officer.* New York: Alfred A. Knopf, 1965.

Wills, Charles W. *Army Life of an Illinois Soldier.* Washington, D. C.: Globe Printing Co., 1906.

Wilson, James Harrison. *Under the Old Flag.* Vols. 1 and 2. New York: D. Appleton & Co., 1912.

Wolcott, E. L., comp. *Record of Services Rendered the Government by Gen. B. H. Grierson During the War.* Fort Concho, Texas: pvt. pub., 1882.

Wyeth, John Allan. *Life of General Nathan Bedford Forrest.* New York: Harper & Brothers, 1899.

———. *With Sabre and Scalpal: The Autobiography of a Soldier and Surgeon.* New York: Harper & Brothers, 1914.

INDEX

339